Beijing!

UN
Fourth World Conference on Women

Beijing!

UN Fourth World Conference on Women

© Women's Feature Service, New Delhi, India 1998

Extracts may be freely reproduced by the press or non-profit organisations with acknowledgement. WFS would appreciate clippings of published materials.

Views judgement expressed in Beijing! do not necessarily represent the views of Women's Feature Service or any of its funding agencies.

WFS is a Print & electronic media organisation specialising in development issues. It operates the only syndicated all-women news feature service of views and analyses of women in their societies and their perception of local, national and international development.

Illustrations :
Manjula Padmanabhan

Published in India by :
Women's Feature Service,
1, Nizamuddin East, New Delhi - 110 013
wfsdelhi@giasdl01.vsnl.net.in

Printed in India by :
Systems Vision
A-199 Okhla Ind. Area-I, New Delhi - 110 020
systemsvision@poboxes.com

ISBN 81-90 1005-0-5

Contents

ACKNOWLEDGEMENTS

A MESSAGE FROM HELVI SIPILA

PREFACE BY ANGELA E.V. KING

INTRODUCTION BY ANITA ANAND

SECTION I — Half a Century of Women's Advancement
1. Chronology of Events : 1945-1995 1
2. Beijing Declaration 17

SECTION II — En Route to Beijing
1. Introduction *by Anita Anand* 23
2. Platform for Action 27
3. WFS Articles on Critical Areas of Concern 35

   • **Poverty**
   We're Hungry, Cold and Underpaid *by Grace Franklin* 35
   Living Paycheck to Paycheck *by Debby Tomecek* 37

   • **Education and Training**
   Teen Mothers Back to School *by Rebecca Katumba* 39
   Tribals Turn Away From Sex Trade *by Sharmila Banerjee* 40
   Stay in the Kitchen and Out of the Lab *by Valeria Belloro* 42

   • **Health**
   Toning Up Health Care *by Jill Vardy* 45
   Mothers Battle "Nuclear Monster" *by Oksana Kuts* 46

- **Violence**

  Horrific Home Violence Prompts Controversial Law
  by Isabel Sanchez 49

- **Armed Conflict**

  War Brings Increased Tension to Sri Lanka's East
  by Melissa Butcher 51

  The War Must Stop *by Neimat Bilal* 53

- **Economy**

  Coastal Women Find Their Worth *by Yolanda Sotelo-Fuertes* 55

  Rural Women Build a Bank *by Vijita Fernando* 56

- **Decision-making**

  Running Away From Politics *by Rachel Sarah* 59

  From Torture Victim to Minister *by Hadera Tesfay* 60

  One Woman's Campaign for Democracy *by Gretchen Peters* 62

- **Human Rights**

  Awarded for Fighting Rape *by Neena Bhandari* 65

  A Writer Forbidden to Read *by Preeti Singh* 67

  Fundamentalism's War on Women *by Marsha Talcin* 68

- **Media**

  Men on Women *by Isabella Matambanadzo* 71

  Changing The Media's Maxim *by Grace Virtue* 72

- **Environment**

  Women Take Over Wastelands *by Buchy Rao* 75

  Future Cities Need to be Gender-Aware
  by Patralekha Chatterjee 77

- **The Girl-Child**

  Children Face Crisis *by Zoraida Portillo* 80

  A Plan to Stop Child Labour *by Nitin Jugran Bahuguna* 81

4. Preparing for Beijing *by Mallica Vajrathon* 85

   Five Regional PrepComs 92

5. From Mexico to Beijing – 1975-1995 *by Anne S. Walker* 97

6. The Ying and the Yang of a Political Process
   by Soon-Young Yoon 107

   From Nairobi to Beijing
   by Anita Anand and Olivia H. Tripon 112

SECTION III — At Beijing

1. Introduction *by Anita Anand* 117

2. BEIJING WATCH Observes 123
   The Icing, Not The Cake 123
   Working Woman, Working Man 123
   Money, Money and Money 124
   Content Discontent 125
   Keen Youth and Anxious Adults 125
   All in the Family 126
   Inheritance, for a Start 127
   Men on Men 128
   Its made a Difference 128
   Three Weeks in China 129

3. The Experience of Youth 131
   Youth Say Our Future is Now 131
   Children's Express 132
   Girl Feminists Surf the Net 134
   Give Us a Bright Future 135

4. From the Regions 137

   • **Latin America**
   A Diversity of Dynamics *by Virginia Vargas* 137
   Recognising Cultural Diversity *by Thais Aguilar* 140

   • **Europe & North America**
   A Confused Experiment that Worked *by Georgina Ashworth* 142
   History of the Facilitation Initiative 144
   A Woman's Place is in the Economy
   by Natacha Henry and Samme Chittum 146

- **Africa**

A Mission Accomplished *by Njoki Wainaina* 148

The Beijing Game *by Sara Hlupekile Longwe* 151

Delegates Fight to Preserve Regional Gains
  by Colleen Lowe Morna 152

- **West Asia**

Building a Common Agenda *by Fatima Kassem* 156

Muslim Women Stand by Their Differences
  by Leila Deeb 158

The Outcome and Beyond *by Haifa Abu Ghazaleh* 160

Equality Should Include Religion
  by Mona Eltahawy and Leila Deeb 161

Basma Urges More Political Integration of Arab Women
  by Leila Deeb 163

- **South Asia**

India: It's a Long Haul, But We'll Make It *by S.K. Guha* 164

The Coordination Unit *by Suneeta Dhar* 166

Strengthening the Beijing Process *by Asha Ramesh* 168

- **Asia-Pacific**

Real Regions Value Women *by Olivia H. Tripon* 170

A Positive Experiecne *by Riet Turksma* 172

An Amazing Feat *by Jane Rosser* 173

- **Pacific**

Springing to Life With Activity
  by Bernadette Rounds-Ganilau 174

- **Southeast Asia**

Hong Kong: Sharing the Fate of the State
  by Cecilia Young Dong-Ling 177

Thailand: The Grassroots Surface
  by Shashi Ranjan Pandey and Darunee Tantiwiramanond 179

5 Women's Human Rights: A Global Referendum
  by Charlotte Bunch, Mallika Dutt, and Susan Fried 185

Keep the Church in Church, Not In Politics
  by Avian Joseph 188

      Guys and (Inflatable Plastic) Dolls *by Jennifer Griffin* 191

      Muslim Women Say No to Religious Extremism 193

  6. UN Secretariat: The Gatekeepers of Ideas *by John Mathiason* 195

SECTION IV — What the Media Said and Didn't

  1. Introduction *by Anita Anand* 205

  2. Which was the Real Beijing Conference?
      by Margaret Gallagher 209

      Communication Without Limits *by Oksana Kuts* 210

      Pushing Mickey Mouse Media to Make Way for Women
      by Margaret Gallagher 213

  3. Backlash in the US Media *by Lauren Danner and Susan Walsh* 215

      Setting the Airwaves on Fire *by Linda Neuman* 216

      Light, Camera, Conference *by Pat Made* 220

      Media Focuses on the Wrong Issues *by Jennifer Griffin* 224

  4. Tackling Media Bias *by Huang Qing* 227

      On the Air and Making Waves *by Julie Beun-Chown* 228

SECTION V — Into the Millennium

  1. Introduction *by Anita Anand* 233

  2. Contract With the World's Women *by Bella Abzug* 237

  3. More Than Just a Wonderful Abstraction *by Charlotte Bunch* 243

  4. Seizing the Opportunity *by Noeleen Heyzer* 247

AUTHOR PROFILES

INDEX

Acknowledgements

A bit like Beijing itself, this book is the result of many, many kind individuals and institutions who gave time, money and energy to making it happen.

Support to the Women's Feature Service (WFS) for the preparatory phase of the Fourth World Conference on Women (FWCW) in the years 1993-95, for coverage of regional events (in print, radio and video) and production of six daily tabloids, came from core and project funds. The donors were Katholische Frauenbewegung Osterreichs (KFO); Swiss Development Cooperation Office (SDC); UNIFEM; UNICEF; NOVIB, Netherlands; The John D & Catherine T MacArthur Foundation; INSTRAW; EMW and the Ford Foundation, New York and New Delhi.

Additional support for the WFS presence at the FWCW in Beijing was principally provided by the Ford Foundation, USA and India; the population section of the John D and Catherine T MacArthur Foundation, USA; Ministry of Foreign Affairs, Norway; NOVIB, Netherlands; Gender in Development programme of UNDP, New York; UNDP (Regional Bureau for Asia), UNDP Costa Rica; Tides Foundation, USA; UNFPA, New York; Women in Development Europe; (WIDE); Shaler Adams Foundation; Ms. Foundation for Education and Communication, USA; The Sister Fund; and the Samuel Rubin Foundation.

The WFS team of writers, editors, translators, technicians, administrators and photographers could not have got to Beijing without the energy and contributions of some 22 governments, dozens of NGOs and the staff of UN agencies in UNFPA, UNICEF, UNIFEM and UNDP. Our special thanks to Mr Chen Wei, Press Attache, Embassy of the People's Republic of China, in New Delhi, without whose cooperation in getting visa stamps on passports, the WFS team would get only near an airport.

The UN regional commissions, Economic and Social Commission for Asia and Pacific (ESCAP), Economic and Social Commission for West Asia (ESCWA), Economic Commission for Africa (ECA), Economic Commission for Europe (ECE) and Economic Commission for Latin America (ECLA) all assisted in information and providing facilities at each of the regional preparatory conferences. As funds all around were tight, their contributions came in kind – space, paper, duplication facilities and use of equipment.

Each region had an NGO facilitating and coordination committee that helped the WFS with names, addresses, telephone numbers, facts and figures. People, no matter how busy they were made time for interviews, quotes and profiles. Special thanks to Shireen Huq, Bangladesh; Noeleen Heyzer, then Malaysia now New York; Supatra Masdit, Thailand; Irene Santiago, New York; Thanphuying Sumalee Chartikavanij, Thailand; Ramani Guruswamy, Malaysia; Salamo Fulival, the Pacific; Georgina Ashworth, UK; Caroline

Winchurch, Brusells; Gina Vargas; Fatima Kassem, ESCWA.

In China special thanks to Therese Gestaut, Spokersperson of the Conference and Hazel Burnett, the UN-DPI (Department of Public Information) Focal Point for answering our endless questions on logistics of getting clearances from the Ministry of Information. Sarah Burd-Sharpes, UNIFEM's special adviser to the FWCW and Lisa Stearns consultant, Ford Foundation, in assisting with advice on how to get things done.

At the Secretariat in New York where the Conference was put together, Gertrude Mongella the Secretary General of the Conference, Kristen Timothy, Assistant Director and Coordinator of the Conference always welcomed us with open arms, no matter how busy they were. And later, advisers Mallica Vajrathon and Patsy Roberts; and John Mathiason of the Department for the Advancement of Women.

The UN-DPI was of great assistance in many ways. Special thanks to Tina Jorgensen and Hasan Ferdous of DPI. Sonia Lecca, Chief Media Accreditation and Liasion Unit in New York. In NGLS (Non-Government Liasion Service), New York, Barbara Adams.

In UNDP, Joyce Lin-Yueh Yu of the Regional Bureau of Asia who helped put the WFS Beijing project in business; in the Division of Public Affairs, Djibril Diallo; and in gender and development programme, Rosina Wiltshire. In UNFPA, Alex Marshall and Hugh O'Haire who assisted us with information on issues and kept us in the know.

To Mehr Khan and Morten Giersing of UNICEF, New York, a special thanks for providing start up funds for compiling this book. All writers wrote for love. Others we approached, agreed but could not keep their commitment. Maybe they knew that we could only make them famous, not rich. It wasn't for lack of interest. After Beijing, just about everyone was a little burnt out.

There are gaps in the book. Geographical, topical, thematic and analytical. It is not for lack of trying. For two years we cajoled, flattered, blackmailed, and begged people to contribute. Then, in November 1997, we decided to stop and go with what we had. If we put if off any longer, it may have been time for the next world conference on women!

To Manjula Padmanabhan, cartoonist and illustrator, a lot of gratitude. Her illustrations appeared in the NGO Forum daily. She very kindly agreed that they be used for BEIJING!

In the WFS, special thanks are due to Sunanda Bhattacharjea for doggedly chasing writers for their contributions, profiles and photographs and to Taposhi Roychoudhary for her technical assistance in saving the Beijing related material for four years. And of course, to Gouri Salvi for assisting in the "outside view", having once been a WFS insider.

Anita Anand
February 1998
New Delhi

A Message from Helvi Sipila

The advancement of women is a long process. Beijing was one of its milestones.

The Beijing Conference was called a World Conference of Women, just because of an erroneous translation of what it was to be called in its original language, i.e. on women. It was not a Conference of women in any language but on women in every language.

Every conference at the international level concerning the advancement of women was a conference of women prior to the year 1928, when the first inter-governmental Commission on Women took place in the Western hemisphere. It was the Organisation of American States (OAS), which formed an inter-governmental Commission on Women, called 'The Inter-American Commission on the Status of Women'. The name indicates that the government assumed the responsibility for the process concerning the status of women in their regional organisation.

The first effort became known at the League of Nations and some preparatory work started for an organisation of similar activities with its jurisdiction. These efforts did not bring much result, the League of Nations was abandoned, and the Second World War began.

The work of the Inter-American Commission on the Status of Women, however, continued and is still going on, and some of its active members brought the idea to the United Nations right from its beginning.

If we were to trace the history of inter-governmental action at the inter-national level, it is important to know who said what, where.

The list of the delegations participating at the International Conference held in San Francisco for the purpose of establishing an inter-governmental organisation, now called the United Nations, was an uneven, geographically Western-oriented group of 51 states, represented predominantly by men. There were ten women altogether, from all delegations.

History also tells us that it was the knowledgeable women in this group who made the most important contribution to the text of the UN Charter – to provide equality for human beings and to create an organisational system for the promotion of this equality in every way. As a result of this, a special expert Commission on the Status of Women (CSW) was established, first as a sub-commission of the Commission on Human Rights, but almost immediately promoted to the same level with it.

The CSW should get credit for the really effective inter-governmental activity for the advancement of women. It started with 15 members from different parts of the world, and grew along the increasing membership of the United Nations up to its present level.

All parts of the world had to be represented and that was guaranteed by the special distribution on geographical basis. When the number was 32 for a long period in 1960-80s, there had to be 8 from the African states, 6 from Asia and the Pacific, 6 from Latin America and the Caribbean, 4 from the East European Socialist States and 8 from the rest of the world. i.e. the rest of Europe, Canada and the USA, Australia and New Zealand. A special unit at the UN Secretariat was serving this Commission, similar to the Commission on Human Rights.

As a result, improvements were provided by international legislation and other means, first separately in different fields and later by all – including Declarations, Conventions and their supporting system – to guarantee that all States were fulfilling their responsibilities.

The turning point of the activities for the advancement of women, was the declaration of the year 1975 as International Women's Year, recommended by the CSW. In addition to the special theme year, a UN World Conference was requested to be organised within it.

The first UN World Conference was attended by almost all States which were able to do so, i.e. 133 from among the 151 which were invited. At the inter-governmental conference the governments present adopted a World Plan of Action and the UN General Assembly declared the UN Decade for the Advancement of Women 1976-85. It also adopted a reporting system and two additional UN World Conferences in 1980 and 1985, held in Copenhagen and Nairobi. Beijing was the fourth UN World Conference on Women, decided upon at the beginning of the 1990s.

Decisions were made at all of these four World Conferences by governmental delegations, NGOs in consultative status with the Economic and Social Council (ECOSOC) of the United Nations. NGOs were invited to attend the inter-governmental conference, and had the opportunity to speak there, but never to participate in the decision making.

Who were then the 40,000 women in Beijing and the possibly half of this number in Nairobi, the 8,000 in Copenhagen and the about 6,000 in Mexico, who participated in NGO fora named the Tribune or Forum? As the name 'non-governmental' indicates, they were representatives of non-governmental organisations, groups of people or individuals. There was a special organisational system responsible for all the arrangements in each of these gatherings and a great deal of programme available.

I have not even tried to give my comments about the contents of this book. The writers are experts in their own areas and I am interested to read what they have to say.

I have written about things which are rather self-explanatory for those who know the process. But this group gets smaller and smaller every year. We, who are approaching the end of our life and have had the privilege to go through these developments may not have many opportunities in our lifetime to tell these real stories again.

At the opening of the Forum in Beijing I said that we all know the three main goals of the International Women's Year and the World Plan of Action with all their follow-up: EQUALITY, DEVELOPMENT, PEACE.

At that time I felt that we had done most for equality between men and women, with some advances in the field of development. But I felt that in the field of peace, we were still more victims and objects than subjects.

Today I can admit that women have made a great deal of headway by having been accepted and by having been elected or appointed to posts, where they can play an active role in national and international politics. This is felt almost daily especially when women – as Ministers of Foreign Affairs, Ministers of Defence, or Heads of UN agencies – have opportunities to deal with questions of peace and war and the consequences of both.

It is to a great extent women themselves, who have to accept even greater responsibilities and give their total contribution to the subjects for which they have assumed to work. We are proud of the increasing number of women who are doing so. They are important in what they do but also as examples for other women.

It is necessary to bring women to worldwide gatherings in any capacity but the work at home is most crucial for the materialisation of decisions and putting into practise what they have learnt.

The invitation to attend the 50th Anniversary Session of the Commission on the Status of Women in New York last year in my capacity as a former chairperson on the Status of Women in New York, was most inspiring.

The person who was older than I in this group of invited guests, was one of those few women who belonged to the signatories of the UN Charter.

She, and the UN programme of the celebration, prompted me to start a project in my native country to organise an exhibition on my own participation in UN activities – over the last 50 years.

And here I am writing from the middle of the exhibition, where people from many walks of life are interested in seeing what someone from Finland can tell about her own experience in the service of Equality, Development and Peace.

Helvi Sipila
February, 1998
Finland

Preface

United Nations conferences are usually events of great pomp and formality, where complex subjects of multilateral diplomacy are discussed in meticulous detail not easily accessible to the average citizen. Conferences on women never quite fit that mould. First and foremost, the composition of delegations differed. Contrary to other conferences, there was always, even as early as the Mexico City Conference in 1975, a substantial number of women participants, both in the official Government delegations and in the non-governmental community.

Unprecedented numbers of non-governmental organisations and representatives of civil society participated in the preparations and conduct of the United Nations conferences of the 1990s. This holds true for the 1992 Earth Summit in Rio de Janeiro, the 1993 World Conference on Human Rights in Vienna, the 1994 International Conference on Population and Development in Cairo, the 1995 World Summit for Social Development in Copenhagen, and the 1995 Fourth World Conference on Women in Beijing.

More than other conferences, however, United Nations' women's conferences have had the global women's movement and its many national and regional components as essential driving forces behind them. Their commitment turned these conferences into events for which real people, women and men, and not only Governments, took ownership.

Beijing was no exception. Beijing stands for participation in the broadest sense of the term. Women from all walks of life used this event to bring into sharp relief the issues they care about most. For some, it was the question of equal pay for work of equal value. For others, it was access to family planning services and reproductive and sexual health. For others still it was the right to be free from violence in the home, the community and the work place. For all it was about a better, healthier, more productive and safer life for themselves, their families and societies.

Beijing was also about accountability and commitment. Three previous United Nations women's conferences - Mexico City 1975, Copenhagen 1980 and Nairobi 1985 - had laid the groundwork for an emerging global consensus on women's equality, development and peace. Women formed alliances across borders and across issues. They learned from each other, realizing that their concerns differed in degree and scope, but were similar in terms of causes and consequences.

Around the world, women face discrimination in access to rights and opportunities. More often than not, they hold down two fulltime jobs, one unpaid job inside the home, and one poorly paid job in the formal or informal labour market. They, nevertheless, continue to make up a disproportionate share of the world's poorest people, and of the world's illiterate. While women's share in the formal labour market is growing fast, they continue to see their experiences, hopes and expectations pushed aside when it comes to the larger picture of macroeconomics, globalization, and market liberalisation.

Women are the primary caregivers in all societies. They are responsible for ensuring survival for families ravaged by disease or conflict. Yet when social development policies are drawn up, women are usually perceived merely as a vulnerable group in need of a special project. They have the right to vote almost everywhere but on average, make up not more than 11% of decision-makers in legislative and 7% in executive bodies around the world. Despite these low figures, discussions on governance are still largely oblivious to the democratic deficit perpetuated by women's under-representation in decision-making.

Beijing is about accountability for change. The Platform for Action has moved us forward a tremendous step from previous conferences. It identifies clear and practical sets of actions, and assigns responsibility for implementation to various groups of actors to make sure that there is accountability to the women of the world that we are moving in the right direction - the direction of equality for women. Women everywhere are taking up the challenge, and the opportunity, to share the power and to share the responsibility for decisions large and small.

Beijing has changed the way we look at women's realities. These realities can no longer be considered simply as concerns to be addressed by Governments through social welfare and support interventions which are primarily of a corrective nature, designed to alleviate discrimination and disadvantage.

Rather, in the Platform for Action, 189 Governments committed themselves to achieving gender equality and the empowerment and advancement of women. This requires Governments to take a pro-active approach in all its actions, whether in economic or trade issues, in employment, education or health policies, in criminal, family and marriage laws, to account for the differential impact of such measures on women and men. A pro-active approach requires assessing whether a law, a policy or a programme promotes the goal of gender equality, or perpetuates women's inequality.

Implementing the Platform is a multilayered, multifaceted task. It involves Governments, non-governmental organisations and civil society. It also involves the United Nations system and its funds, programmes and specialised agencies. Taken together, all actors are accountable for achieving clear, measurable outcomes for women.

The United Nations' role in this common endeavour has received a new urgency and a clearer focus. Much of this work is emphasising linkages between the Platform for Action and the results of other recent United Nations conferences. This approach underlines that women's issues are an integral part of any societal agenda, whether national or international, and that women's concerns are not their concern alone but the responsibility of society as a whole.

For example, the 50th Anniversary of the Universal Declaration of Human Rights will be observed this year, together with a review of the results of the 1993 World Conference on Human Rights. The Commission on the Status of Women will contribute to this review through its consideration of the sections of the Platform for Action that make up its human rights theme, with the intention of influencing the work of the mainstream human rights activities from a gender perspective. In 1999, there will be a five-year review of the results of the International Conference on Population and Development. Again, the Commission will contribute with a review of the topic of women and health from the Platform so that the gains made at Beijing and in its wake can be fully brought to bear on that parallel process as well.

In the year 2000, a special high-level review will be conducted by Governments to assess progress achieved in implementing the Platform for Action and to consider further actions and initiatives. Non-governmental organisations and organisations of civil society have a major stake in ensuring a productive and forward-looking approach to this review.

The entities of the United Nations system have taken the Platform for Action as a basis for refocusing their programming and project activities. Many of these activities are reflected in a system-wide plan prepared by all the entities of the United Nations family immediately after the conference, to guide collaborative actions over the next several years. The International Labour Organisation, for example, is implementing a programme entitled "more and better jobs for women". UNICEF is placing priority on girls' and women's education and health, and on girls' and women's rights. UNDP has increased the overall share of its resources that are specifically directed at women. The three core women's entities of the United Nations system mentioned in the Platform — that is the Division for the Advancement of Women, INSTRAW and UNIFEM — are providing leadership in policy development, in training and in innovative project funding, respectively. The Secretary-General of the United Nations is accountable to Member States for the work of the Secretariat and, in this task, is assisted by his Special Adviser on Gender Issues and Advancement of Women.

This book provides inspiration to all those who work for the achievement of gender equality. The insights of women and men who, in one way or another, were intimately linked with the preparatory process and with the Conference itself give us a vivid picture of the many struggles, victories and occasional setbacks on the road to Beijing. It is a wonderful account of commitment, hope and ultimately, of success. Their views and analyses confirm that women's equality is a shared societal responsibility, involving Governments and civil society alike.

The critical role of the media in making the conference a part of so many people's lives and in building and sustaining the momentum for women's concerns everywhere, offers important lessons for the future. While it is clear that much work remains to be done, the book compiled so expertly by Women's Feature Service leaves us with a proud sense of accomplishment. The global women's movement, and women everywhere, play a powerful and indispensable role in shaping decisions, policies and action - nationally and internationally.

Angela E.V. King
Assistant-Secretary-General
Special Adviser on Gender Issues and
Advancement of Women
United Nations
February, 1998

Introduction

The Fourth World Conference on Women (FWCW) held in Beijing, People's Republic of China in 1995 was no ordinary event. Neither was it just another conference. It was a momentous occasion witnessed by thousands around the world.

There are no clear numbers of how many people attended the conference in Beijing. The figures range from 30,000 to 50,000. But for those who were in Beijing, it was a show of strength — of the women's movement, the Chinese government and the United Nations.

Since 1975, when the first world conference on women was held in Mexico City, Mexico, there have been many changes. Most important has been the evolution and shift in thinking on the causes of women's low status in society, and the measures required to correct this. The United Nations, as the international organisation of governments with a mandate on development issues, has taken the cue from many players — women's movements, professional women in development, researchers, scholars and activists — in recommending changes to itself as well as governments, organisations and individuals.

Beijing in 1995 saw the culmination of the last 20 years of this shift in thinking, refining of analysis, and coming together of concerns and constituencies from all parts of the world.

To the person on the street, the question could well be — what was the fuss about? Why did so many women clamour to go to Beijing? What did they do there? What did they gain from it?

Those questioning, want to know the meaning of equity, dignity, freedom from violence in their homes, workplaces and streets, the choice to raise families or not, and all the other things women want. After all, they have made inroads into businesses, offices, educational institutions. What more can they want?

Plenty, say women. Beijing, more than any other conference, made it possible to fine tune the analysis and methods by which women could get what they want and need. While solutions were proposed and put into practice along the way, there is new learning, and the 12 critical areas of concern adopted as conference working areas, are a testimony to this.

Since 1975 there have been three other conferences (1980 in Copenhagen, Denmark, 1985 in Nairobi, Kenya), and all have displayed an evolution of thinking — from the issue of integrating women into development to highlighting the issue of gender — an outcome from the realisation that gender (the socialisation of how women and men are raised) is more important than biological differences. This socialisation influences attitudes, ability to change, and to recognise where gender bias lies, in all relationships.

Beijing affirmed that governments in formulating strategies, must ensure that policies are gender sensitive across the board. And, existing policies need to be gender audited —

to check if they are biased towards men and against women — and if so, to change them.

Gender sensitisation means that women and men can learn to look at attitudes and practices to check if they are gender biased and correct them.

A turning point in Beijing was the recognition for women's empowerment — creating an environment or conditions for women to have choices — about education, careers, families. And, to be able to exercise these choices, women need a certain self-esteem and confidence, which can only be acquired in a milieu of love, support and affirmation.

Women's stories from around the world speak of discrimination against them from birth (and some even before that) to death. This is evident in abortion of female foetuses (known as foeticide), infanticide (killing a live infant), abandonment, malnutrition, neglect, incest, rape, lack of education, genital mutilation, work in and outside the home, prostitution, abuse, widowhood, death.

In parts of countries, all over the world, this treatment of girls and women is the norm. On the other hand, there are girls and women who grow up in dignity, loved, nurtured and wanted. They are the exception. Yet, this does not shield them from rape, sexual harassment or discrimination from a wider milieu.

There are laws in countries that discriminate against women — inheritance, guardianship and custody of children, citizenship, marriage, divorce, and pay for the same work as men. Beijing affirmed that these laws need to be examined, revised and changed.

How will all this come about? Delegates at the Beijing Conference — representatives of governments — adopted by consensus, the Platform for Action, the document spelling out action required at all levels, not a legally binding agreement but a contract that governments made with each other, and with the world's women.

Each country, government, institution and individual women and men will have to work strategically, at and across levels to make the change come about.

When this book was conceived, one yardstick was to make it readable for the "person on the street". Besides issues, it was designed to give the reader a flavour of the hard work that went on behind the scenes, in preparation for Beijing. For this, we asked women and men who had played a major role in and outside the UN, in their countries, regions, and on issues, to make a contribution to the book. This task was made easier by the fact that as an organisation whose mandate is to cover development issues from a gender perspective, the WFS was in the know about issues and players in the field.

The WFS was a child of the 1975 first world conference on women in Mexico City, where participants agreed that one of the major reasons behind the low status of women in their societies was their negative portrayal and low position in mainstream media. This critique came at a time when women's movements in the North and South were linking their oppression to colonialism, racism, sexism, and the dominance of the North against the South. The UN Education, Scientific and Cultural Organisation (UNESCO) had been debating on the New International Information and Communication Order (NIICO), which stressed that flows of news and information were predominantly North-South, and male, and was looking for ways to change this.

In 1978, UNESCO proposed the creation of the Women's Feature Service, a project which would highlight "women's issues". The project would consist of features or stories written by women journalists on issues of importance to them. They would be edited by women and carried on the teleprinter wires of national and international news agencies. Twenty years later, of the five WFSs created by

UNESCO, this organisation (originally placed in Inter Press Service) is the only functioning one.

Since 1980 and the Mid-Decade Conference on Women, the WFS team attended the UN women's conferences, covered the proceedings which were sent on the IPS teleprinter wires to clients worldwide. The WFS became independent in 1991, and moved its headquarters to New Delhi, India.

In 1992 the Secretary-General of the UN, Boutros Boutros-Ghali announced the name of Gertrude Mongella to head the Beijing conference. Mongella was in New Delhi as the Head of the Tanzanian Mission. A colleague in UNIFEM, New York, gave me this information and I went to see Gertrude Mongella.

From this meeting started the WFS planning for coverage of the Beijing conference. With bureaux in Latin and North America, the Philippines, Africa and India, and a network of almost 150 women journalists in 60 countries, the WFS commissioned stories on the issues and preparations of the Conference.

It made a plan to cover each of the preparatory regional conferences — in the Philippines, Indonesia, Argentina, Jordan, Austria and Senegal — producing a daily paper at each of the meetings and transmitting its coverage to its media clients. Some of this coverage features in this book. Most of it does not. In addition to features, WFS produced radio and video programmes on the preparatory meetings and the Beijing Conference.

Covering conferences is not easy — especially Beijing. In the section on media review, Margaret Gallagher, Lauren Danner, Susan Walsh and Huang Qing write that mainstream media, especially the Western press, does major injustice to the concerns of women.

Danner and Walsh say, "US reporters are trained to report news that is timely, impacts people, has human interest elements, is unusual or different, happens close to home and shows drama or conflict." Furthermore, they say that news exhibits four biases: it focuses on people instead of problems; emphasises crises over continuity; is fragmented and hard to understand as "a big picture"; and relies on officials as information sources. These biases, they say, extend to covering international affairs as well.

And this further gets reflected in conference coverage, which is what most persons on the street have access to. To counter this and get a more accurate picture, three people were asked to give a jump-start to the book by describing how the Conference was organised, and what the Decade of Women was about. This was done from two perspectives — the official UN, and the NGO — both equally important. The UN conferences were the pivot around which the women's conferences were organised, and the NGO fora brought together thousands of women who came as individuals, as members of women's organisations and women's movements, covering a wide spectrum of networks — children, health, technology, older women, indigenous women, youth, handicapped and disabled, lesbians, single parents, and many more.

Mallica Vajrathon, Anne Walker and Soon-Young Yoon are all veterans of development in their own areas. They have been and are part of UN and NGO processes. Between them, they have at least 55 years of experience on women and development.

Vajrathon describes the preparation of the UN process and how agreements were reached towards the draft Platform for Action. She depicts procedures that so many outside the UN find difficult to comprehend. Her description is an eye-opener to the hard and strategic work of the Conference. She highlights in brief, the workings of the five regional meetings held in preparation to Beijing. This was the first time such meetings were organised — to build consensus from the regions on the issues to be taken to the draft Platform for Action, and an indication of the participatory nature of the process.

In 1975, Anne Walker was part of the IWY (International Women's Year) Tribune in Mexico City. After the Conference she went on to pioneer the International Women's Tribune Centre which became the organising point of the NGO Fora in Copenhagen and Nairobi. Walker's contribution gives a sense of the growth and development of the NGO movement at the UN conferences.

Besides the UN conferences on women, Walker was also present at the NGO gatherings of other conferences — environment, human rights, population and development and describes the organising strategies of NGOs and women's caucuses especially set up to lobby on women's perspectives, with their country delegates, UN staff and their relevant committees.

At the final PrepCom (Preparatory Committee meetings) for the Beijing Conference, Walker says, "The Women's Linkage Caucus was formed.... as an outcome of the women's caucus which had met at each world conference ..... and its statement in March 1995 was probably the most comprehensive of all caucus statements, containing new issues as well as commitments and decisions made at previous conferences. It was a wake up call to governments and the UN that women were not going to let them forget the commitments they had promised to take action on."

Walker also points to the very important communications revolutions — fax, internet — which enabled women who could not be at the conferences as well as those who were, to be in touch with each other, exchange news and views and strategise.

For the Beijing Conference, an important group was the newly formed NGO Secretariat in New York, which was coordinated by Irene Santiago, assisted by an international facilitating committee. A 200-organisation Planning Committee raised funds, organised the regional NGO fora, helped coordinate the women's caucuses, and provided technical support to the regions.

In New York there were 15 people in the Secretariat, with volunteers. Soon Young-Yoon, a member of the Secretariat writes engagingly on the trials and tribulations of conference organising.

She highlights the gains of the Conference, among them the facilitation team that ran the lobbying process representing regional and issue causes and an international committee — Equipo (Spanish for team). It was a new model of mobilising representative groups at an NGO Forum, says Yoon.

All preparations for Beijing cost money. NGOs and women's organisations and movements not exactly being wealthy, spent a great deal of time fund raising. In this, among others, they were assisted by one rather unique process, which deserves special mention — the OECD/DAC-WID — in which one development cooperation agency was designated to coordinate the funding of activities related to Beijing. In each region this designated agency then invited other multi and bi-lateral donor groups to join in and form an IFCB (Inter-Agency Facilitating Committee for Beijing). This group, in turn, facilitated the process with coordination points set up in the countries, regions and internationally.

How well did this work? The fact that each country, region and internationally the NGO community got together and planned what they wanted from Beijing and to take to Beijing, was important. It enabled a pool of resources for organising meetings, travel, publications, inter-actions with the governments, etc. Many women who would have never got to Beijing, were selected to participate in country delegations by a fair process, based on their role in the community and commitment to carry on this work. And for the donors of the IFCB, as Jane Rosser, Assistant Representative of the Ford Foundation in New Delhi and Reit Turksma, the then WID specialist in the Royal Netherlands Embassy in New Delhi, admit, it was an enormous learning experience.

Clearly this initiative worked better in some places than others. What happened to this process after Beijing? As we went to press OECD-DAC WID spokerspersons in Paris said in a communication that a study had been commissioned after Beijing, but was not due in till May 1998.

Other equally creative efforts were used to raise funds. "Send a Sister to Beijing" was coordinated by the NGO Forum Secretariat in New York for women to make contributions for the less fortunate women who wanted to go to Beijing but could not afford to.

And what happened in Beijing? The WFS daily newspaper covered the UN sessions and NGO happenings. With a team of almost 35 people, working out of the Hotel Cactic Plaza, adjoining the Beijing Conference Centre, the paper was put together. Every night it was taken over to the *Earth Times* (the other English daily), which carried it to the printers. The BEIJING WATCH appeared inside the *Earth Times* — a rare happening for both publications.

Despite the fact that the editors and managers of the organisations had applied for permission along the correct channels, when we got to Beijing, we were told the paper could not be published. In a scenario resembling a science fiction movie, permission to publish was given twelve hours before the Conference started. There was to be only one English language newspaper between the two publications. BEIJING WATCH was to appear inside the *Earth Times*, which would deal with the appointed printer. We agreed.

Speculation was rife as to why the newspapers were not being allowed to publish. Nothing anti-national or negative about the Head of State would be allowed, we were told. We understood that. The situation could have been due to a great conspiracy or a big muddle. A Chinese government information official said to me, "We've never done this before." This was probably true for all the arrangements of the Conference.

How does a daily paper cover a conference as large as Beijing? By doing its homework and having a clear criteria. We wanted a balance — UN and NGO coverage, geographical regions, issues, language (English and Spanish), and style (serious and some light). We had a good team, regionally representative, skilled technical assistants and able administrators.

For *At Beijing*, the section in the book in which contributors share their experiences and views of the Conference, we deliberately invited people who had been active, for a long time, in the conference process and issues. As Georgina Ashworth writes, no two people experienced Beijing in the same way. Probably the most delicate issue of the Beijing Conference was it's venue — the People's Republic of China. Many protested the location because of its human rights records. Gertrude Mongella, during preparations for the Conference, often said, "If we were forced to have the Conference in a country in which women's rights are respected, then we may never be able to have the Conference at all."

The same China caused anticipation — for those who had never been there and those who had. The Chinese government itself had never handled an international conference, but were fast learning how to do so. They sent the China Organising Committee (COC) representatives to each of the preparatory regional meetings to get a first hand experience of how the official and NGO proceedings worked.

In the section *At Beijing* individuals share experiences from Latin America, Europe, Africa, Arab States, India, Thailand and Hong

Kong. These tell the story of the preparation for Beijing and their activities at Beijing. Almost all write about the interaction between governments and NGOs and how consensus was reached and where differences exist.

For the Arab States the Conference was an opportunity to come together, something they had not done before — at least in the context of deciding what was needed from the perspective of women — from their states and region. Europe oddly, was a first too. As Georgina Ashworth points out, it had been assumed in preparations for previous conferences, that only developing regions needed to get together. And this time the preparatory meeting in Vienna included North America (USA and Canada) as well.

For Hong Kong it was a first as well. Normally not given a separate status and part of the UK delegations, their preparations were different this time. As Cecilia Young Dong-Ling says "our fate is the same as our state" — unsure, unclear — at the eve of their reverting to China.

For the Pacific too, it was a first. Normally they also came in a category with Australia and New Zealand, and felt that their concerns were subsumed. Or with Asia, which would dominate the preparations. Not so this time. While many meetings were held with Australia, New Zealand and Asia, the Pacific women took the opportunity to build networks, hold workshops and channel their findings in the media.

The Thai experience is somewhat similar to that of many countries in Southeast Asia, especially the emerging economies, which were once Socialist states. Pandey and Tantiwiramanond write about the organising experiences in Thailand and what was gained from these.

A country like India which has a long history of women's organisations and movements, also needed a lot of hard work to pull together. Because while the NGOs had been active, they had also little history of working with the government — satisfactorily that is. For the first time, the efforts of the Coordination Unit, put together with donor support, and the government were in tandem, making for a richer and more productive alliance. S.K. Guha, Asha Ramesh and Suneeta Dhar write about this, from their perspective.

There are successful stories from South Asia — Bangladesh, Pakistan and Nepal, not included in this book.

Yet, trying to meet 40,000 expectations a day is a difficult proposition. All contributors write about this experience, but stress that much was gained. Some, like Sara Longwe, are not quite convinced that women's movements should follow the "Beijing Game". She calls for women to 'elbow for space', and not seek to occupy the one cleared for them. It is a view worth considering.

But what happens to space that is created for women and their concerns? That's mainstreaming. Many women's movements for the last three decades have shunned this space, afraid of co-optation. But as their movements have become rooted, strong and more confident, some of them have begun to participate in the planning and policy levels in their countries, regions and internationally. This is an extremely important contribution, and not an easy one.

Bureaucrats and women's movements have a different vocabulary, style of functioning, and ideologies. Sara Longwe says that the feminist agenda should be formulated by NGOs and presented to the government to put into action. This is what the governments have done all along, and the women's movements have called them up on this. Is it possible that governments and women's movements can work together? Beijing partly answered this. For the first time, negotiating and process building requiring at least two sides was attempted, with some modicum of success. Soon Young Yoon talks about how NGOs in Beijing moved from being outside the UN process to being in the halls, influencing and shaping the agenda.

Bunch, Dutt and Fried argue that some major controversies illustrate what was gained and the limitations of the Platform of Action. For example, many thought that the area of sexual rights could not be won, so the phrase was per se rejected. But these boundaries were extended in the health section of the document which stated that "human rights of women include their right to have control over and decide freely and responsibly on matters related to their sexuality, including sexual and reproductive health, free of coercion, discrimination and violence."

Another major debate they cite centred on the term "universal" and the issue of religion and culture to limit women's human rights. Women sought to maintain the 1993 Vienna World Conference on Human Rights' language that women's human rights are universal, inalienable, indivisible and interdependent. The Vatican, its supporter States, and some Islamic governments, attempted to limit the extent of universal application of women's human rights. They used this debate to claim that there is a feminist imperialism which reflects disrespect for religion and culture, an over-zealous individualism, and an effort to impose Western values which destroy the family and local communities.

True or not, this argument — the authors say — requires thinking about how universality of rights should be argued, without implying homogenisation, especially around religion and culture which can also be positive for some women.

Another area which caused unhappiness was the implementation and resources, and the promises of the Platform of Action that were not backed by adequate commitments from governments or the UN. While the document has strong language on gender integration and coordination within the UN, it is not clear who will carry this task out. Soon Young Yoon points this out as well. While the development community lauds the successes and importance of NGOs to the process, this is not evident in the financial support to these organisations. At least not in the scale of the work expected of them.

John Mathiason, served in the UN Department for the Advancement of Women (DAW), the ex-officio Secretariat of the Conference. DAW traces its origins to the earliest days of the UN when in 1946, the first chairperson of the new Commission on the Status of Women asked that "a United Nations Office on the Status of Women's Affairs in the framework of a Secretariat, run by a highly competent woman be established to be the planning centre for the work, and a clearing house for information about women's activities. It would give women all over the world a feeling of satisfaction to have a special office at the headquarters of the UN."

While women may not appreciate that they have people who speak on their behalf at the UN, very often little is known about the kind of work DAW had done, behind the scenes.

Mathaison points out that in Beijing, for women to participate in power and decision-making, they would have to be involved in sufficient numbers to make a difference. The Platform for Action in paragraph 192 calls for action by governments, national bodies, the private sector, political parties, trade unions, employers organisations, research and academic institutions, sub-regional and regional bodies, NGOs and international organisations to take positive action to build a critical mass of women leaders, executives and managers in strategic decision-making positions.

In terms of targets this critical mass was set by the Economic and Social Council at 30 percent. The introduction of the concept of critical mass and the setting of the target level was a result of work done by DAW.

Another issue, says Mathiason, was the impact of structural adjustment on women. The relationship between structural adjustment policies (in which developing countries had to adjust their polices, thus slowing economic growth and reducing social programmes) of the 1980s and 1990s had been a highly contentious North-South issue.

By looking at the research and its findings, DAW questioned whether the focus on women as victims of structural adjustment was the most appropriate, either normatively or in terms of facts. DAW had begun to see women in the economy as assets, rather than as liabilities. The expert group meeting organised by DAW concluded that while structural adjustment had impacted women (more in the short than long run), attention to gender factors could help mitigate the overall negative effects. It began to see that the most important adjustment strategies should involve investment in women, particularly in terms of growth areas of the economy.

And how will all this come about?

The section *Post-Beijing* gives a picture of what three women see as happening in this period. As Bella Abzug says, the Platform for Action is a contract with the world's women. The major gains in understanding, analyses and articulation of issues and processes of the last two decades is evident in the Platform for Action. This is manifested in, among other things, the mandate of organisations such as UNIFEM, as Noeleen Heyzer points out in her contribution. Beijing made it easier for the world's women to spell out and agree on terms and meanings of notions such as gender, empowerment, and the very strong consensus that women must participate in decision making — at all levels.

In the lead up to, during, and from Beijing the NGO Fora of all regions stressed that despite progress made in the lives of women, governments were continuing to adopt models of development that harmed and hurt women. This referred to economic policies in the form of globalisation and liberalisation, without adequate safety nets for women who were becoming increasingly impoverished. While this is true there is a recognition that maybe the processes and forces of globalisation cannot be stopped. The women's movement has to understand and strategically intervene to uphold women's interests.

Some of this acknowledgement has resulted in national, regional and international efforts of be part of deliberations on trade, aid and other policies.

Campaigns such as *Women's Eyes on the Bank,* focusing on the World Bank's lending policies and practices and the Women and Development in Europe (WIDE) activities around the European Union's (EU) policies — are an indication that women are becoming more sophisticated about the nature of negotiations required.

The efforts of UNIFEM to focus on economic and political empowerment of women — how they can become part of governance structures is also a case in point. By deliberately working with infrastructural bodies such as Planning Commissions, Ministries of governments, Election Commissions, and Census Bureaus to en-gender their agenda — UNIFEM's work, in collaboration with national and regional level NGOs and government bodies to understand and emulate the successes of experiments such as women's credit, cooperatives and self-help programmes is an example. Efforts of agencies such as UNFPA, UNICEF, UNHCR to bring a gender approach to their work and focus on the life cycle approach to issues and challenges is a welcome one.

The 1997 international conference on microcredit sponsored by women's movements, the World Bank and other financial institutions illustrates that people need to talk face to face to share experiences, successes and failures, and sensitise each other about their concerns.

Regional efforts by UN agencies such as UNDP to draw up gender strategies for their work, in consultation with NGOs and other institutions, by appointing gender consultants, doing research and endeavouring to engender the existing institutions — finance, research, training — is an encouraging effort.

The further realisation that governments, UN agencies, development organisations and women's movements need to work together is an extremely important one.

The largest international UN conference ever, achieved many things, which hopefully the reader will find reflected in the contributions. The success of Beijing is reflected in women's stories and anecdotes about their personal transformation, which is not disconnected to their family and community roles. For governments and the UN, Beijing was an opportunity to think together about the practical ways required to improve the status of women, to analyse emerging global and local trends, to design policy and programmes, and to bring the women's movements, organisations closer to participating in these.

Not everything that should or could have been in this book, is here. But the attempt has been to present the issues, history, processes and roles that various participants played in this most significant and path-breaking Conference.

Anita Anand
February, 1998

SECTION ONE

Half a Century of Women's Advancement

1
United Nations and the Advancement of Women

Chronology of Events

26 June 1945

The Charter of the United Nations is signed in San Francisco, setting out three objectives for the new organisation: to foster international peace and security, to promote social and economic progress and to define and protect the rights and freedom of every individual regardless of race, sex, language or religion.

12 February 1946

During the inaugural session of the United Nations General Assembly in London, Eleanor Roosevelt, wife of the former President of the United States of America and United Nations delegate, reads an "open letter to the women of the world" calling for their increased involvement in national and international affairs.

16-18 February 1946

The Economic and Social Council (ECOSOC) establishes the Commission on Human Rights, chaired by Mrs. Roosevelt, with a Subcommission on the Status of Women. A Section on the Status of Women is established within the Human Rights Division of the United Nations Secretariat's Department of Social Affairs. Early chiefs of the Section include Mary Tenison-Woods (Australia) and Sophie Ginsberg-Vinaver (France).

29 April-25 May 1946

The Subcommission on the Status of Women, with Bodil Begtrup (Denmark) as Chair, holds its first meeting at the Bronx campus of Hunter College in New York.

21 June 1946

In its resolution 2/11, ECOSOC states that the Subcommission on the Status of Women shall henceforth be known as the Commission on the Status of Women (CSW) — an elevation in the body's status, making it a counterpart of the Commission on Human Rights.

The **Division for the Advancement of Women,** part of the Center for Social Development and Humanitarian Affairs located in Vienna, Austria, is the United Nations system's focal point for all activities relating to women. Its programmes relate particularly to monitoring and appraising implementation of the Nairobi Foward-Looking Strategies adopted by consensus at the 1985 Nairobi World Conference which concluded the United Nations Decade for Women: Equality, Development and Peace. The Division acts as a secretariat both for the Commission on the Status of Women and for the Committee on the Elimination of Discrimination against Women.

The Division also undertakes research studies and coordinates research, expert group meetings and advisory seminars, particularly on priority themes selected for each year by the Commission

11 December 1946

The General Assembly unanimously adopts resolution 56 (I), recommending that all Member States which have not already done so grant women political rights equal to those granted to men and that, in this connection, States adopt measures necessary to fulfill the purposes and aims of the Charter.

10-24 February 1947

The CSW holds its first session at Lake Success in New York State.

29 March 1947

On the basis of recommendations made by the CSW at its February session, ECOSOC, in its resolution 48 (IV), formalises arrangements for the Commission to be represented in the deliberations of other United Nations bodies and to meet annually.

2 May 1948

The Inter-American Commission of Women adopts the Inter-American Convention on the Granting of Political Rights to Women. The Convention subsequently serves as the model for the 1952 United Nations-sponsored Convention on the Political Rights of Women.

10 December 1948

The General Assembly adopts, in resolution 217 A (III), the Universal Declaration of Human Rights, which sets forth the civil, political, economic, social and cultural rights to which every individual is entitled. The declaration is the first of the three components of an International Bill of Human Rights and includes the proclamation that all human rights and freedoms are to be enjoyed equally by women and men without distinction of any kind.

2 December 1949

The General Assembly adopts the Convention for the Suppression of the Traffic in Persons and of the Exploitation of the Prostitution of Others, calling for the punishment of those who would procure others, with or without their consent, for the purpose of prostitution.

29 June 1951

The International Labour Organization (ILO) adopts the Convention of Equal Remuneration, incorporating the principle of equal pay for men and women workers for work of equal value and calling for rates of remuneration to be established without discrimination based on sex.

28 June 1952

The ILO adopts the Maternity Protection Convention, entitling all women workers to maternity leave with cash and medical benefits.

20 December 1952

The Convention on the Political Rights of Women, one of the first legally binding rights

---

on the Status of Women. It also publishes periodicals, such as Women 2000 and the Data highlights series on women. A complete list of publications is available from the Division.

The Division maintains a major data bank on women. The Women's Information System is a computerised bibliographic data bank comprising some 2,000 United Nations documents which represent much of which the United Nations has produced on paper on women's issues since January 1985. This data is readily available to all users, from Government to individuals by contacting the Reference Room of the Division with specific requests. Users in Vienna enjoy immediate visual access to documents described in the data bank. For users from afar, a mailing list of publishers is provided along with the printout.

agreements negotiated under the auspices of the United Nations, is adopted by the General Assembly, The Convention, under which Member States commit themselves to allowing women to vote, stand for election and hold public office on equal terms with men and without discrimination, comes into force on 7 July 1954.

8 April 1954

Secretary-General Dag Hammarskjold addresses the Commission on the Status of Women. This is the first occasion a Secretary-General has done so.

29 January 1957

The General Assembly adopts the Convention on the Nationality of Married Women, aimed at protecting the right of a married woman to retain her nationality and at eliminating conflicts of law involving the nationality of women who are married, divorced or whose husbands have changed their nationality. The Convention comes into force on 11 August 1958.

25 January 1958

The ILO adopts the Discrimination (Employment and Occupation) Convention, whereby member States would adopt national policies to eliminate discrimination in employment on the basis of race, colour, sex, religion, political opinion, national extraction or social origin.

10 July 1958

ECOSOC, by its resolution 680 B II (XXVI), invites the World Health Organization to undertake a study of the persistence of customs which subject girls to ritual operations and of the measures adopted or planned for putting a stop to such practices.

16 July 1962

ECOSOC, by its resolution 884 E (XXXIV), recommends that Governments of Member States make full use of the United Nations technical assistance programme in human rights and advisory services programme in social welfare services for the purpose of promoting and advancing the status of women in developing countries.

7 November 1962

The General Assembly adopts the Convention on Consent to Marriage, Minimum Age for Marriage and Registration of Marriages, decreeing that no marriage may occur without the consent of both parties. The Convention comes into force on 9 December 1964.

7 December 1962

By its resolution 1777 (XVII), the General Assembly requests the Secretary-General to study means of providing and developing new resources aimed especially at the initiation and implementation of a unified long term United Nations programme for the advancement of women and of expanding assistance

---

Commission on the Status of Women

The 45-member Commission on the Status of Women was set up in 1946 to promote women's rights in political, economic, social and educational fields and to make recommendations on problems requiring immediate attention. To this end, it collects and analyses data to monitor the status of women around the world and prepares recommendations and reports on issues which affect women, including their role in development.

Committee on the Elimination of Discrimination against Women (CEDAW)

The United Nations Committee on the Elimination of Discrimination against Women is composed

for the advancement of women in developing countries.

5 December 1963

By its resolution 1921 (XVIII), the General Assembly asks the Commission on the Status of Women to begin work on a draft declaration on the elimination of discrimination against women.

12 December 1963

The General Assembly designates 1968 as the International Year for Human Rights and the occasion for an International Conference on Human Rights to be held in Teheran. The assembly urges Member States to use the Year — the twentieth anniversary of the adoption of the Universal Declaration of Human Rights — as a deadline for ratifying pending human rights accords, including the 1952 Convention on the Political Rights of Women.

1 November 1965

The General Assembly adopts the Recommendation on Consent to Marriage, Minimum Age for Marriage and Registration of Marriages, which, though non-binding adds a specific minimum age of 15 years to the 1962 Convention on Consent to Marriage.

16 December 1966

The General Assembly adopts the International Covenant on Civil and Political Rights and the International Covenant on Economic, Social and Cultural Rights, which, together with the 1948 Universal Declaration of Human Rights, form the International Bill of Human Rights. Both Covenants contain provisions specifying that all the rights therein apply equally to men and women.

7 November 1967

The General Assembly unanimously approves the Declaration on the Elimination of Discrimination against Women. The Declaration, consisting of 11 articles, proclaims that discrimination against women is fundamentally unjust and incompatible with the welfare of the family and society, calls for new laws to end discrimination against women and resolves that all women must have full protection under the law.

22 April-13 May 1968

The International Conference on Human Rights in Teheran adopts 29 resolutions, including one concerning the promotion for women's rights that elaborates the need for a unified long-term programme for the

---

of 23 experts (jurists, lawyers, teachers, diplomats and experts on women's affairs), acting in their individual capacities rather than as representatives of government. Elected by States that have ratified the Convention, it is their job to monitor implementation of the 1979 Convention on the Elimination of All Forms of Discrimination against Women.

General Assembly resolution adopting the Declaration on the Elimination of Discrimination against Women:

Considering that the people of the United Nations have in their Charter, reaffirmed their faith in fundamental human rights, in the dignity and worth of the human person and in the equal rights of men and women;

Considering that the Universal Declaration on Human Rights assert the principle of non-discrimination and proclaims that all human beings are born free and equal in dignity and rights and that everyone is entitled to all the rights and freedom set forth therein, without distinction of any kind, including any distinction as to sex;

advancement of women. The resolution stresses, among other things, that advancement in the status of women depends upon changes in those traditional attitudes, customs and laws which are based on the idea of the inferiority of women, that education is vital to eliminating discrimination and that technical assistance to women in developing countries should be expanded.

20 October 1970

The General Assembly, in its resolution 2626 (XXV), adopts the International Development Strategy for the Second United Nations Development Decade (1970-1979), which calls for the full integration of women in the total development effort.

6 April 1971

The Ad Hoc group on Equal Rights for Women in the United Nations holds its first formal meeting. Headed by staff member Patricia K. Tsien, the Group aims to improve the status of women employed in the Organisation.

18 December 1972

The General Assembly designates 1975 as International Women's Year, with a three-part theme: equality, development and peace.

19-30 August 1974

The United Nations World Population Conference is held in Bucharest; its Plan of Action affirms the central importance of women in population policies.

5-16 November 1974

The World Food Conference, held in Rome, adopts the Universal Declaration on the Eradication of Hunger and Malnutrition, which calls for the recognition by all States of the key role of women in agricultural production and the rural economy and for the availability of appropriate education, extension programmes and financial assistance to women on equal terms with men.

10 December 1974

The General Assembly endorses the ECOSOC decision to convene during International Women's Year a world conference to examine the extent to which United Nations organisations have implemented recommendations for the elimination of discrimination against women made by the CSW since its establishment and to launch an international action programme aimed at achieving the integration of women as full and equal partners with men in the total development effort.

Taking into account the resolutions, declarations of the United Nations and the specialised agencies designed to eliminate all forms of discrimination and to promote equal rights for men and women;

Concerned that, despite the Charter of the United Nations, the Universal Declaration of Human Rights and other instruments of the United Nations and the specialised agencies and despite the progress made in the matter of equality of rights, there continues to exist considerable discrimination against women;

Considering that discrimination against women is incompatible with human dignity and with the welfare of the family and of society, prevents their participation on equal terms with men, in the political, social, economic and cultural life of their countries and is an obstacle to the full development of the potentialities of women in the service of their country and of humanity;

Bearing in mind the great contribution made by women to social, political, economic and cultural life and the part they play in the family and particularly in the rearing of children;

14 December 1974

The General Assembly adopts the Declaration on the Protection of Women and Children in Emergency and Armed Conflict, affirming that all forms of repression and cruel and inhuman treatment of women and children are criminal acts and that Governments should do everything to spare women and children from the ravages of war.

1975

International Women's Year, with a three-part theme: equality, development and peace, as established by General Assembly resolution 3010 of 1972.

7 March 1975

The United Nations first observes International Women's Day (8 March).

19 June-2 July 1975

The World Conference of the International Women's Year in Mexico City is the first global conference to be held on women's issues, with 133 Governments represented. The Conference adopts a World Plan of Action for the Advancement of Women for the coming decade. Helvi Sipila (Finland), the first woman Assistant Secretary-General of the United Nations (appointed in 1972 to head the Center for Social Development and Humanitarian Affairs), is the Secretary-General of the Conference. Some 6,000 representatives of non-governmental organisations (NGOs) attend the related International Women's Year Tribune.

15 December 1975

The General Assembly, by its resolution 3520 (XXX), proclaim 1976-1985 the United Nation Decade for Women: Equality, Development and Peace, to be devoted to effective and sustained national and international action to implement the World Plan of Action of the 1975 Conference. By the same Resolution, the Assembly calls for the establishment of an International Research and Training Institute for the Advancement of Women (INSTRAW).

1976-1985

United Nation Decade for Women: Equality, Development and Peace, as established by general Assembly resolution 3520 of 15 December 1975.

12 May 1976

ECOSOC decides to establish INSTRAW as

Convinced that the full and complete development of a country, the welfare of the world and the cause of peace require the maximum participation of women as well as men in all fields;

Considering that it is necessary to ensure the universal recognition in law and in fact of the principle of equality of men and women.

Article 1

Discrimination against women, denying or limiting as it does their equality of rights with men, is fundamentally unjust and constitutes an offence against human dignity.

Article 2

All appropriate measures shall be taken to abolish existing laws, customs, regulations, and practices which are discriminatory against women, and to establish adequate legal protection for equal rights of men and women, in particular:

(a) The principle of equality of rights shall be embodied in the constitution or otherwise guaranteed by law;

an autonomous body under the auspices of the United Nations, funded through voluntary contributions. The institute is directed to focus its activities on the needs of women in developing countries. INSTRAW begins operation in January 1980.

8 November 1977

At the first Pledging Conference for the United Nations Decade for Women, pledges of more than $3 million are received for the Voluntary Fund for the United Nations decade for Women, and more than $500,000 for INSTRAW.

18 December 1979

The General Assembly adopts the Convention on the Elimination of all forms of Discrimination against Women, first drafted and approved by the Commission on the Status of women in 1976. The 30-article women's bill of rights is the first international legal instrument to stipulate what constitutes discrimination against women. The Convention comes into force on 3 September 1981.

14-30 July 1980

The World Conference of the United Nations Decade for Women takes place in Copenhagen with delegations from 145 Member States. Sixty-four Member States sign the Convention on the Elimination of all forms of Discrimination against Women. The programme of Action for the Second Half of the united Nations Decade for Women, adopted by the conference, calls for special emphasis on improving women's employment and education. Lucille Mair (Jamaica), the first woman under-Secretary-General of the united Nations is Secretary General of the Conference. About 7,000 NGO representatives attend the NGO forum.

11 December 1980

The General Assembly, by its resolution 35/136, decides to convene in 1985 a World Conference to Review and Appraise the Achievements of the United Nations Decade for Women.

23 June 1981

The ILO adopts the Workers with Family Responsibilities Convention calling for equal opportunities and equal treatment for men and women workers with family responsibilities and for action by States to eliminate discrimination in employment for those with family responsibilities.

(b) The international instruments of the United Nations and the specialised agencies relating to the elimination of discrimination shall be ratified or acceded to and fully implemented as soon as practicable.

Article 3

All appropriate measures shall be taken to educate public opinion and to direct national aspirations towards the eradication of prejudice and the abolition of customary and all other practices which are based on the idea of the inferiority of women.

Article 4

All appropriate measures shall be taken to ensure to women on equal terms with men, without any discrimination:

(a) The right to vote in all elections and be eligible for election to all publicly elected bodies;

(b) The right to vote in all public referenda;

14 December 1971

The General Assembly, by its resolution 36/129, extends the activities of the voluntary Fund for the united Nations Decade for Women, which includes funding for 68 new development projects, beyond the end of the Decade.

16 April 1982

At the first meeting of the States parties to the Convention on the Elimination of all forms of Discrimination against Women, the Committee on the Elimination of all forms of Discrimination against Women (CEDAW), an expert panel to monitor compliance with the 1979 Convention, is established. The Committee holds its inaugural session from 18 to 22 October 1982 in Vienna.

3 December 1982

The General Assembly adopts the Declaration on the Participation of Women in Promoting International Peace and Cooperation, which states that since women and men have an equal interest in contributing to international peace and cooperation, women must be enabled to participate equally with men and in economic, social cultural, civil and political affairs.

1-12 August 1983

The Declaration and Programme of Action adopted by the Second World Conference to Combat Racism and Racial Discrimination, held in Geneva, states that whenever there is Racial discrimination, women are subjected to second layer of discrimination, and calls for detailed legislative and educational measures to combat all forms of discrimination.

11 August 1983

INSTRAW inaugurates its permanent headquarters in Santo Domingo, Dominican Republic.

11 December 1984

The first World Survey on the Role of Women in Development is issued. Updated every five years, the World Survey is a major source of statistical and analytical data on women in global economy.

14 December 1984

The Voluntary Fund for the United Nations Decade for Women is renamed the United Nations Development Fund for Women (UNIFEM) and is made a separate entity in association with the United Nations Development Programme. In 1984, the Fund provides

---

(c) The right to hold public office and to exercise all public functions.

Such rights shall be guaranteed by legislation.

Article 5

Women shall have the same rights as men to acquire, change or retain their nationality. Marriage to an alien shall not automatically affect the nationality of the wife either by rendering her stateless or by forcing upon her the nationality of her husband.

Article 6

1. Without prejudice to the safeguarding of the unity and harmony of the family, which remains the basic unit of any society, all appropriate measures, particularly legislative measures, shall be taken to ensure to women, married or unmarried, equal rights with men in the field of civil law, and in particular:

assistance totalling $24 million to almost 400 projects.

26 February 1985

The Secretary-General appoints a Coordinator for the improvement of the Status of Women in the Secretariat, Mercedez Pulido de Briceno (Venezuela), at the Assistant Secretary-General level. The Secretary-General also establishes a Committee for the improvement of the Status of Women in the Secretariat.

15-26 July 1985

The third global women's conference, the World Conference to Review and Appraise the Achievements of the United Nations Decade for Women: Equality, Development and Peace, takes place in Nairobi, with delegations from 157 Member States present. The final document, the Nairobi Forward-Looking Strategies for the Advancement of Women, is a blueprint for measures to improve the status of women by the end of the century. Leticia Shahani (Philippines), United Nations Assistant Secretary-General, is Secretary General of the Conference. Some 15,000 NGO representatives attended the related NGO forum.

20 April 1987

Nafis Sadik (Pakistan) is appointed Director of the United Nations Population Fund — the first woman to head a major United Nations programme.

26 May 1987

ECOSOC adopts the long-term work programme proposed by the CSW, prioritising implementation of the Nairobi Forward-Looking Strategies.

May 1988

The Section on the Status of Women in the United Nations Secretariat, which in 1972 was renamed and upgraded to the Branch for the Promotion of Equality between Men and Women (headed by Margaret Bruce of the United Kingdom), and in 1979 renamed as the Branch for the Advancement of Women (headed by Manae Kubota of Japan), is further upgraded to become the Division for the Advancement of Women (headed by Chafika Meslem of Algeria). In 1993 the Division moves from Vienna to New York to become part of the newly created Department for Policy Coordination and Sustainable Development.

25 February-5 March 1990

The CSW completes the first review and appraisal of the implementation of the Nairobi Forward-looking Strategies and adopts 21 recommendations for implementing obsta-

---

(a) The right to acquire, administer, enjoy, dispose of and inherit property acquired during marriage;

(b) The right to equality in legal capacity and the exercise thereof;

(c) The same rights as men with regard to law in the movement of persons.

2. All appropriate measures shall be taken to ensure the principle of equality of status of the husband and the wife, and in particular:

(a) Women shall have the same right as men to free choice of a spouse and to enter into marriage only with their free and full consent;

(b) Women shall have equal rights with men during marriage and at its dissolution. In all cases the interest of the children shall be paramount;

(c) Parents shall have equal rights and duties in matters relating to their children. In all cases the interest of the children shall be paramount.

3. Child marriage and the betrothal of young girls before puberty shall be prohibited, and

cles to their implementation. The Commission recommends the convening of a world conference of women in 1995.

5-9 March 1990

The World Conference for Education for All: Meeting Basic Needs, held in Jomtien, Thailand, calls for a universal reduction of the disparities which exist in the education of girls and boys.

29-30 September 1990

The World Summit for Children, held at United Nations Headquarters in New York, discusses the global status of children and emphasises the disadvantages faced by girls as compared to boys. The World Declaration on the Survival, Protection and Development of Children states that improving the status of children depends greatly upon ensuring the equal rights of women.

14 December 1990

The General Assembly, by its resolution 45/129, decides to hold a fourth world conference of women in 1995.

21 December 1990

The General Assembly adopts resolution 45/239 establishing targets for the employment of women in the Secretariat of 35 percent women in professional posts subjects to geographical distribution by 1995 and 25 percent in senior posts.

18 June 1991

The United Nations publishes the World Women 1970 —1990: Trends and Statistics

22 July 1991

The United Nations High Commissioner for Refugees issues. Guidelines on the Protection of Refugee Women which call for special protection for refugee women and girls. In March 1995, the High Commissioner issues Guidelines on prevention and response to Sexual Violence against Refugees.

31 January 1992

CEDAW adopts General Recommendation 19 on Violence against women is covered by most of the articles of the Convention on the Elimination of All Forms of Discrimination against Women.

7 February 1992

The Secretary-General appoints Margaret Joan Anstee (United Kingdom) as his Special representative for Angola (UNAVEM II), the

---

effective action including legislation, shall be taken to specify a minimum age for marriages in an official registry compulsory.

Article 7

All provisions of penal codes which constitute discrimination against women shall be repealed.

Article 8

All appropriate measures, including legislation, shall be taken to combat all forms of traffic in women and exploitation of prostitution of women.

Article 9

All appropriate measures shall be taken to ensure to girls and women, married or unmarried, equal rights with men in education at all levels, and in particular;
    (a) Equal conditions of access to, and study in, educational institutions of all types, including universities and vocational, technical and professional schools;

first woman to be in charge of a United Nations peace keeping mission and the first woman to be appointed as a Special Representative of a Secretary-General.

25-26 February 1992

The Summit on the Economic Advancement of Rural woman is held in Geneva under the auspices of the International Fund for the Agricultural Development. The summit participants - the wives of heads of State or Government - adopt the Geneva Declaration for Rural Women in which they express solidarity with rural women of the world and proclaim their determination to raise awareness of conditions affecting rural women whose decision makers at the national, regional and international levels.

8 March 1992

On the occasion of the seventeenth annual United Nations observance of International Women's day, the Secretary-General announces a Strategic Plan of Action for the Improvement of the Status of Women in the Secretariat from 1995 until the year 2000.

18 March 1992

The CSW accepts the invitation of the Government of China to hold the Fourth World Conference on Women in Beijing.

3-14 June 1992

The United Nations Conference on Environment and Development in Rio do Janeiro adopts the Rio Declaration On Environment and Development, which provides that women have a vital role to play in environment management and development and that their full participation is essential to the achievement of sustainable development. The Conference also adopts Agenda 21, a far-reaching blueprint for sustainable development into the twenty-first century, which calls for the full representation of women and their interests needs and perspective in sustainable development.

14 -25 June 1993

The World Conference on Human Rights in Vienna adopts the Vienna declaration and Programme of Action, which urges Government and the United Nations to ensure equal rights for women and stresses the importance of working towards the elimination of violence against women.

27 July 1993

ECOSOC, in its resolution E/1993/235, agree

(b) The same choice of curricula, the same examinations, teaching staff with qualifications of the same standard, and school premises and equipment of the same quality, whether the institutions are co-educational or not;

(c) Equal opportunities to benefit from scholarships and other study grants;

(d) Equal opportunities for access to programmes of continuing education, including adult literacy programmes;

(e) Access to educational information to help in ensuring the health and well-being of families.

Article 10

1. All appropriate measures shall be taken to ensure to women, married or unmarried, equal rights with men in the field of economic and social life, and in particular:

(a) The right, without discrimination on grounds of martial status or any other grounds to receive vocational training, to free choice of profession and vocational advancement;

to the recommendation of a United Nations task force that INSTRAW and UNIFEM be merged into a unified programme.

20 December 1993

The general Assembly, in its resolution 48/104 adopts the Declaration on the Elimination of Violence against Women, which condemns any act causing physical, sexual or psychological harm or suffering to women in the family or community or the State and urges the state not to invoke custom, tradition or religious consideration to avoid their obligations with respect to the elimination of violence against women.

4 February 1994

CEDAW adopts General Recommendation 21 on equality in marriage and family relations which indicates that the Convention on the Elimination of All Forms of Discrimination in family law.

11 March 1994

The United Nations Commission on Human Rights appoints a Special Rapporteur to collect information on acts of gender based violence and to recommend measures at the national, regional and international levels for its elimination

5-13 September 1994

The International Conference on Population and Development in Cairo affirms that there are four requirements for any programme of population and development: gender equality; empowerment of women; the ability of women to control their own fertility; and the elimination of violence against women.

6-12 March 1995

The World Summit for Social Development in Copenhagen, the largest gathering in history of heads of State or Government, proclaims the central role of women in fighting poverty, creating productive employment and strengthening the social fabric. The Copenhagen Declaration includes a commitment by world leaders to make equality and equity of women and men a priority.

8 March 1995

On the occasion of International Women's Day, the Secretary-General calls on Member States to consider putting the Declaration on the Elimination of Violence against Women into legally binding form.

15 March- 7 April 1995

The CSW undertakes a second review and appraisal of the Nairobi Forward-Looking

---

(b) The right to equal remuneration with men and to equality of treatment in respect of work of equal value;

(c) The right to leave with pay, retirement privileges and provision for security in respect of unemployment, sickness, old age or other incapacity to work;

(d) The right to receive family allowances on equal terms with men.

2. In order to prevent discrimination against women on account of marriage or maternity and to ensure their effective right to work, measures shall be taken to prevent their dismissal in the event of marriage or maternity and to provide paid maternity leave, with the guarantee of returning to former employment, and to provide the necessary social services, including child-care facilities.

3. Measures shall be taken to protect women in certain types of work, for reasons inherent in their physical nature, shall not be regarded as discriminatory.

Article 11

1. The principle of equality of rights of men and women demands implementation in all States

Strategies and holds the first preparatory meeting for the Fourth World Conference on Women

11 April 1995

The Secretary- General appoints Carol Bellamy (United States of America) as the Executive Director of UNICEF, one of the five women to head United Nations programmes. The others are the High Commissioner for Refugees, Sadako Ogata (Japan); the Executive Director of the United Nations Environment programme, Elizabeth Dowdeswell (Canada); the Executive Director of the World Food Programme, Catherine Bertini (USA) and the Executive Director of the United Nations Population Fund, Nafis Sadik (Pakistan).

12 July 1995

The Security Council and the General Assembly elect Rosalyn Higgins (United Kingdom) to the International Court of Justice, the first woman to sit on the Court.

2 August 1995

The United Nations publishes the World's Women 1995: Trends and Statistics.

4-15 September 1995

The Fourth World Conference on Women is held in Beijing. Gertrude Mongella (United Republic of Tanzania), United Nations Assistant Secretary-General, is Secretary-General of the Conference.

(UN, Department of Public Information, New York)

---

in accordance with the principles of the Charter of the United Nations and of the Universal Declaration of Human Rights.

2. Governments, non governmental organisations and individuals are urged, therefore, to do all in their power to promote the implementation of the principles contained in this declaration.

Department of Public Information (DPI)

The Department of Public Information produces printed information products, films and videos, as well as radio and television programmes on women,, organises special events, conducts briefings, responds to requests for information, and maintains active liaison with the media and organisations dealing with topics related to women.

2 Beijing Declaration and Platform for Action

adopted by the Fourth World Conference on Women: Action for Equality, Development and Peace, Beijing, 15 September 1995

BEIJING DECLARATION

1. We, the Governments, participating in the Fourth World Conference on Women,
2. Gathered here in Beijing, in September 1995, the year of the fiftieth anniversary of the founding of the United Nations,
3. Determined to advance the goals of equality, development and peace for all women everywhere in the interest of all humanity,
4. Acknowledging the voices of all women everywhere and taking note of the diversity of women and their roles and circumstances, honouring the women who paved the way and inspired by the hope present in the world's youth,
5. Recognize that the status of women has advanced in some important respects in the past decade but that progress has been uneven, inequalities between women and men have persisted and major obstacles remain, with serious consequences for the well-being of all people,
6. Also recognize that this situation is exacerbated by the increasing poverty that is affecting the lives of the majority of the world's people, in particular women and children, with origins in both the national and international domains,
7. Dedicate ourselves unreservedly to addressing these constraints and obstacles and thus enhancing further the advancement and empowerment of women all over the world, and agree that this requires urgent action in the spirit of determination, hope, cooperation and solidarity, now and to carry us forward into the next century.

We reaffirm our commitment to:

8. The equal rights and inherent human dignity of women and men and other purposes and principles enshrined in the Charter of the United Nations, to the Universal Declaration of Human Rights and other international human rights instruments, in particular the Convention on the Elimination of All Forms of Discrimination against Women and the Convention on the Rights of the Child, as well as the Declaration on the Elimination of Violence against Women and the Declaration on the Right to Development;
9. Ensure the full implementation of the human rights of women and of the girl child as an inalienable, integral and indivisible part of all human rights and fundamental freedoms;
10. Build on consensus and progress made at previous United Nations conferences and summits - on women in Nairobi in 1985, on children in New York in 1990, on environment and development in Rio de

Janeiro in 1992, on human rights in Vienna in 1993, on population and development in Cairo in 1994 and on social development in Copenhagen in 1995 with the objectives of achieving equality, development and peace;

11. Achieve the full and effective implementation of the Nairobi Forward-looking Strategies for the Advancement of Women;

12. The empowerment and advancement of women, including the right to freedom of thought, conscience, religion and belief, thus contributing to the moral, ethical, spiritual and intellectual needs of women and men, individually or in community with others and thereby guaranteeing them the possibility of realizing their full potential in society and shaping their lives in accordance with their own aspirations.

We are convinced that:

13. Women's empowerment and their full participation on the basis of equality in all spheres of society, including participation in the decision-making process and access to power, are fundamental for the achievement of equality, development and peace;

14. Women's rights are human rights;

15. Equal rights, opportunities and access to resources, equal sharing of responsibilities for the family by men and women, and a harmonious partnership between them are critical to their well-being and that of their families as well as to the consolidation of democracy;

16. Eradication of poverty based on sustained economic growth, social development, environmental protection and social justice requires the involvement of women in economic and social development and equal opportunities and the full and equal participation of women and men as agents and beneficiaries of people-centred sustainable development;

17. The explicit recognition and reaffirmation of the right of all women to control all aspects of their health, in particular their own fertility, is basic to their empowerment;

18. Local, national, regional and global peace is attainable and is inextricably linked with the advancement of women, who are a fundamental force for leadership, conflict resolution and the promotion of lasting peace at all levels;

19. It is essential to design, implement and monitor, with the full participation of women, effective, efficient and mutually reinforcing gender-sensitive policies and programmes, including development policies and programmes, at all levels that will foster the empowerment and advancement of women;

20. The participation and contribution of all actors of civil society, particularly women's groups and networks and other non-governmental organizations and community-based organizations, with full respect for their autonomy, in cooperation with Governments, are important to the effective implementation and follow-up of the Platform for Action;

21. The implementation of the Platform for Action requires commitment from Governments and the international community. By making national and international commitments for action, including those made at the Conference, Governments and the international community recognize the need to take priority action for the empowerment and advancement of women.

We are determined to:

22. Intensify efforts and actions to achieve the goals of the Nairobi Forward-Looking

Strategies for the Advancement of Women by the end of this century;

23. Ensure the full enjoyment by women and the girl child of all human rights and fundamental freedoms, and take effective action against violations of these rights and freedoms;

24. Take all necessary measures to eliminate all forms of discrimination against women and the girl child and remove all obstacles to gender equality and the advancement and empowerment of women;

25. Encourage men to participate fully in all actions towards equality;

26. Promote women's economic independence, including employment, and eradicate the persistent and increasing burden of poverty on women by addressing the structural causes of poverty through changes in economic structures, ensuring equal access for all women, including those in rural areas, as vital development agents, to productive resources, opportunities and public services;

27. Promote people-centred sustainable development, including sustained economic growth through the provision of basic education, life-long education, literacy and training, and primary health care for girls and women;

28. Take positive steps to ensure peace for the advancement of women and, recognizing the leading role that women have played in the peace movement, work actively towards general and complete disarmament under strict and effective international control, and support negotiations on the conclusion, without delay, of a universal and multilaterally and effectively verifiable comprehensive nuclear-test-ban treaty which contributes to nuclear disarmament and the prevention of the proliferation of nuclear weapons in all its aspects;

29. Prevent and eliminate all forms of violence against women and girls;

30. Ensure equal access to and equal treatment of women and men in education and health care and enhance women's sexual and reproductive health as well as education;

31. Promote and protect all human rights of women and girls;

32. Intensify efforts to ensure equal enjoyment of all human rights and fundamental freedoms for all women and girls who face multiple barriers to their empowerment and advancement because of such factors as their race, age, language, ethnicity, culture, religion, or disability, or because they are indigenous people;

33. Ensure respect for international law, including humanitarian law, in order to protect women and girls in particular;

34. Develop the fullest potential of girls and women of all ages, ensure their full and equal participation in building a better world for all and enhance their role in the development process.

We are determined to:

35. Ensure women's equal access to economic resources including land, credit, science and technology, vocational training, information, communication and markets, as a means to further the advancement and empowerment of women and girls, including through the enhancement of their capacities to enjoy the benefits of equal access to these resources, *inter alia,* by means of international cooperation;

36. Ensure the success of the Platform for Action which will require a strong commitment on the part of Governments, international organizations and institutions at all levels. We are deeply convinced that economic development,

social development and environmental protection are interdependent and mutually reinforcing components of sustainable development, which is the framework for our efforts to achieve a higher quality of life for all people. Equitable social development that recognizes empowering the poor, particularly women living in poverty, to utilize environmental resources sustainably is a necessary foundation for sustainable development. We also recognize that broad-based and sustained economic growth in the context of sustainable development is necessary to sustain social development and social justice. The success of the Platform for Action will also require adequate mobilization of resources at the national and international levels as well as new and additional resources to the developing countries from all available funding mechanisms, including multilateral, bilateral and private sources for the advancement of women; financial resources to strengthen the capacity of national, subregional, regional and international institutions; a commitment to equal rights, equal responsibilities and equal opportunities and to the equal participation of women and men in all national, regional and international bodies and policy-making processes; the establishment or strengthening of mechanisms at all levels for accountability to the world's women;

37. Ensure also the success of the Platform for Action in countries with economies in transition, which will require continued international cooperation and assistance;

38. We hereby adopt and commit ourselves as Governments to implement the following Platform for Action, ensuring that a gender perspective is reflected in all our policies and programmes. We urge the United Nations system, regional and international financial institutions, other relevant regional and international institutions and all women and men, as well as non-governmental organizations, with full respect for their autonomy, and all sectors of civil society, in cooperation with Governments, to fully commit themselves and contribute to the implementation of this Platform for Action.

SECTION TWO

En Route to Beijing

1
Introduction

Anita Anand

The Beijing Declaration is a preface to the Platform for Action which when adopted became known as the Beijing Plan of Action. A 38-point declaration, it lays the basis for the Plan of Action and serves as an executive summary of the Plan.

The Declaration summarises the various international agreements, under United Nations auspices – children, human rights, environment, population, social development and their relevance to women.

But there are some firsts. The empowerment of women and their participation in the decision making process and access to power, as fundamental for their achievement of equality, development and peace, is mentioned for the first time.

Another first is the importance of designing, implementing and monitoring, with the participation of women, effective and mutually re-enforcing gender-sensitive policies and programmes to foster empowerment of women, also narrowing down the numerous areas where interventions can be made. It addresses the learning (since 1975, 1980 and 1985) that much of what ails women is because of their missing presence in decision making positions.

The twelve areas of concern elaborated in this section give a gist of why the area of concern was chosen, and what action can be taken to change it.

Mallica Vajrathon in her contribution *At the End of a Long Road – Consensus and Commitment* writes eloquently about how the areas of concern were proposed, negotiated and finally agreed to.

She points out that at the preparatory meeting of the CSW and member states, many felt that the critical areas of concern section should be diagonistic, supported by objective, concise and quantitative data, and that the importance of the life-cycle approach in all the areas of concern be stressed.

During this time, the WFS commissioned its contributors to focus on the 12 areas of concern, to serve as a base for the dialogue and discussion in mainstream media, but also appear in the regional conference daily newspapers it was planning to produce.

This section includes two features from each of the twelve areas of concern, written by WFS contributors and offered to mainstream media clients in all regions of the world.

In 1994, from the Ukraine, Oksana Kuts wrote about the group, Mama-86, whose main goal is to raise awareness of environmental issues and children's health in the post Chernobyl era.

In Jamaica, the active group Women Media Watch (WMW) with its visible national profile, featured prominently in the National Report on the Status of Women in Jamaica, being prepared for the Beijing Conference. Grace Virtue profiled the group, their successes, challenges and strategies.

Isabel Sanchez in Costa Rica reported that Congress was to vote on a bill that would address domestic violence against women in the Central American country.

Poverty is probaby the most important disabling factor in the empowerment of women – both North and South. From Scotland and the Czech Republic, among other countries, came stories that brought home the reality of poverty.

Grace Franklin wrote from Glasgow, Scotland about women's groups coming together to write their own plan for the Beijing Conference. Half of the full-time working women are in low paid jobs and only 13 percent of Scottish mothers with a child under 10 work full-time – a half of the average of the European Community. Yet, at a meeting in the official preparatory process for Beijing, a high ranking British official denied that poverty was a relevant topic of discussion in the UK.

In the Czech Republic, Debby Tomecek describes how in 1995, three years after it's split from Slovakia, one in every four women lives alone – widow or divorcee. They raise children on their own and live from paycheck to paycheck.

These and others stories in this section highlight the challenges women face as they raise families, make a living, and strive to participate as citizens in their countries.

This chapter, in more detail than others, provides some distinct views – from the UN and NGO perspective – and how they worked together and separately, at the same time. Learning from each other, strengthening each others' position, and challenging each other to do better, for a common goal: to have a strong, effective and diverse Plan of Action that could be implemented.

If anything, the Beijing process was about negotiation. As Vajrathon says, "The negotiation process seems endless, carrying on not only though the day, but late into the night..."

This took place at the UN conference and at the NGO Forum, starting in 1993, all through the preparatory period, and at Beijing as well.

Vajrathon traces the UN process to get a Platform for Action that would be acceptable to all nations participating in Beijing. This includes rounds of expert group meetings, conferences, regional preparatory gatherings. She describes the outcome of the five regional PrepComs (preparatory committee meetings) as they are called, and their priorities. In other sections, there are more reviews of the work that went into the meetings.

Preparations for the Beijing Conference, says Vajrathon, need to be seen as a continuum of previous UN conferences. Even if each of them had its unique characteristics, there were common facets. For instance, UN rules and procedures for negotiations had to be followed in accordance with adopted guidelines; the ways of conducting the Plenary or working group sessions had to be agreed to in advance during one of the PrepComs, by a bureau or a Steering Committee, in accordance with General Assembly Resolutions.

Vajrathon describes the roles of the various sections of the UN, the process by which language and ideas were incorporated into the Beijing Platform for Action, and gives a clear picture of the hard work negotiation is.

Anne Walker who has participated in the UN-NGO process at very close quarters in New York, traces the transformation of how women organised around UN international conferences and summits, from the late 1960s to the present time.

The 1975 World Conference on Women was a result of the lobbying of women activists since the late 1960s. Parallel to this was the gathering for NGOs or the International Women's Year (IWY) Tribune.

Around 6000 women packed the Centro Medico in Mexico City at the largest consciousness-raising session for women, says Walker.

They wanted to talk and hear about each others' experiences. And despite the fact that media coverage concentrated almost exclusively on North-South differences and conflicts, women found a way to communicate with each other on issues they were involved in and were dear to them.

Women at the Tribune felt that they had little input into the UN process. At the end of the 10-day gathering, the NGO participants at the Tribune marched to the UN meeting with their recommendations.

Back at the UN, at the end of the conference, there was pressure to announce a Decade for Women, the time needed to tackle the issues raised in Mexico City. The IWY Tribune Committee, across the road from the UN in New York, began to receive mountains of mail writes Walker, regarding follow-up to the Mexico City event. Women wanted to know what was next. The UN announced a Decade for Women (1975-85) and the IWY Tribune Project was born.

Five years later in 1980, the Mid-Decade conference was held in Copenhagen, Denmark. Here the International Women's Tribune Centre (IWTC) as it was now known, took on the task of organising a space for NGOs – and 10,000 women came.

At the end of the decade in 1985, Nairobi, Kenya was the site of the conference. Almost 15,000 women attended, and Walker estimates that there were another 5000 local women who were not officially registered as participants. In Nairobi, several important women's networks including the Development Alternatives for Women in a New Era (DAWN) and the Women's Institute for Women, Law and Development (WILDAF) were born. Women were more confident and skilled at organising, mobilising, raising funds, and developing loosely structured networks –– national, regional and international.

Walker points out an important realisation of the three conferences was the recognition that women wanted more of a say in what their governments were planning on their behalf.

At Nairobi the document adopted by the governments present – the Forward-Looking Strategies (FLS) — became the international women's movement treatise, says Walker. Women used it for lobbying their governments and launching new projects.

The next major stage of organising for NGOs was in the early 1990s, when the Women, Environment and Development Organisation (WEDO) based in New York and headed by Bella Abzug, called a meeting to influence the document that would come out of the UN Conference on Environment and Development (UNCED), also known as the Earth Summit.

The Women for a Healthy Planet took place in Miami, Florida in December 1991 with 1,800 women from 80 countries participating. Walker says that the experience of this meeting influenced the development of women's caucuses and revolutionised the way NGOs organised to advocate their issues and concerns at preparatory meetings. She traces the NGO presence in the following UN conferences in the 1990s – human rights (1993), population and development (1994), social development and women (1995) – and their success, in getting women's agenda into the official documents.

The telecommunication revolution also assisted women in getting their message out to thousands more. The Internet – through networks such as Greennet, Econet, Peacenet and especially the Association for Progressive Communications (APC) says Walker, changed the way in which women and groups came together.

In preparations of the Beijing Conference, Walker says that the fax technology really came into its own. When the Chinese

Organising Committee (COC) announced that the location of the NGO Forum had been moved 40 miles away to Huairou, IWTC with the Forum Committee began a campaign to protest this move. Thousands of faxes reached the COC as well as the Secretary-General of the UN.

Soon-Young Yoon in her contribution of the NGO activities throws caution to the winds, bringing in her "immodest" approach. She says that if the 50,000 women gathered in Huairou jumped all at once at the same spot, they could have knocked the earth off its orbit!

At the NGO Forum in Huairou, almost 4000 workshops and panels were offered over a 10-day period. More than 60,000 electronic mail messages were sent and received, and around 100,0000 visits recorded to the NGO Forum World Wide Website. In virtual and real space this was a global conference like no other, says Yoon.

She points out how the international women's movement in Beijing was much more – stronger, diverse and committed – to influencing the UN than ever before. There was an evolution of the NGO Forum from being a rebel camp outside the UN grounds, to a legitimate partner, inside the UN halls.

Political modalities also changed – from confrontation to lobbying, to get points of view across, says Yoon. And along with this the structural change in the relationship of a social movement (the women's movement) to the inter governmental process.

Yoon subscribes much of the success of the NGO Forum to the role of the facilitating committee, which worked with the NGO Forum secretariat. Regional focal points, based by representatives of CONGO, and the NGO Committees on the Status of Women, worked with the New York secretariat. She vividly describes the process of organising the NGO Forum and the numerous challenges along the way.

Both Vajrathon and Yoon point out the national and regional preparations which were largely responsible for the accomplishment of Beijing. At these preparatory meetings there was representation from all interested groups, especially the official delegates.

A major achievement of the Conference, is that gender – as a social construct of the relationships between men and women – was debated and appears in the Plan of Action. This affirms that "biology is not destiny", points out Yoon.

Another first, was a facilitating team which ran the lobbying process representing regional and issue causes and international committees. "Equipo" (Spanish for team) as the team was called was a new model of how to mobilise representative groups at an NGO Forum.

The euphoria over the success of Beijing is accompanied with caution – fundamentalist movements which want to control women's bodies and the family, competition between groups for scarce resources, and diversity as a code of this in the women's movement could be put aside as more mainstream leadership takes over. But these are surmountable threats that can be faced by strengthened NGOs and resources.

This section emphasises the high degree of partnership between the various layers of structures of the Conference – the UN and the NGO Forum – at national, regional and international levels. The visible result is agreement over the 12 critical areas of concern that shaped the organising of the Conference and the Platform of Action adopted by member nations by consensus, and with reservations.

2 Platform for Action

Summary

United Nations, Fourth World Conference on Women. Beijing, China, 4-15 September 1995. Obstacles, Strategies, Action

Since the United Nations held the first world conference on women 20 years ago (Mexico City, 1975), important progress has been made towards achieving equality between women and men. Women's access to education and proper health care has increased, their participation in the paid labour force has grown and legislation that promises equal opportunities for women and respect for their human rights has been adopted in more countries. As a result, important changes have occurred in the relationship between women and men.

Yet discrimination against women is still widespread. Violence against women remains a global phenomenon. Women's equal access to resources is still restricted and their opportunities for higher education and training are concentrated in limited fields. A "glass ceiling" continues to bar women's advancement in business, government and politics. Women are an overwhelming majority of the 1 billion people living in abject poverty and among illiterates. Decisions that affect women continue to be made largely by men.

The Beijing Declaration and Platform for Action, adopted unanimously at the Fourth World Conference on Women (4-15 September 1995) by representatives from 189 countries, reflect a new international commitment to the goals of equality, development and peace for all women everywhere.

The Platform, divided into six chapters, identifies 12 "critical areas of concern" considered to represent the main obstacles to women's advancement. It defines strategic objectives and spells out actions to be taken over the next five years by Governments, the international community, non-governmental organisations and the private sector for the removal of the existing obstacles.

The Platform was further reinforced in the Beijing Declaration. It reaffirmed the commitment of Governments to eliminate discrimination against women and to remove all obstacles to equality. Governments also recognised the need to ensure a gender perspective in their policies and programmes.

Mission Statement and Global Framework

Since the 1985 Nairobi Conference on Women, the world has experienced profound changes, with both positive and negative effects on women. A worldwide movement towards democratisation has opened up the political process in many nations. The growing strength of women's organisations and feminist groups has become a driving force for change.

At the same time, widespread economic recession, political instability, heavy military spending, poorly designed structural adjustment programmes, the servicing of the external debt burden and continuing environmental degradation have had a disproportionately negative inpact on women.

The Platform for Action, an agenda for women's empowerment, seeks to reverse this trend. It seeks to promote and protect the full enjoyment of all human rights and the fundamental freedoms of all women throughout their life cycle. It also calls for establishing the principle of shared power and responsibility between women and men at home, in the workplace and in the wider national and international communities.

The success of the Platform for Action will require a strong commitment on the part of Governments, international organisations and institutions at all levels. It will also require adequate mobilisation of resources at all levels as well as new and additional resources for the developing countries.

Areas of Concern

■ Poverty

Today, more than 1 billion people live in extreme poverty; the overwhelming majority of them are women. In the past decade the number of women living in poverty has increased disproportionately to the number of men, and the risk for falling into poverty is higher for women than for men. Poverty is particularly acute among women living in rural households.

Women are poorer because they have fewer economic opportunities and less autonomy than men. Their access to economic resources, education and training, and support services is limited. They also have very little participation in the way decisions are made. The rigidity of socially prescribed roles for women and the tendency to scale back social services have increased the burden of poverty on women.

The Platform recommends action to:

- Revise, adopt and maintain macroecomomic policies and development strategies that address the needs and efforts of women in poverty;
- Revise laws and administrative practices in order to ensure women's equal rights and access to economic resources;
- Provide women with access to savings and credit mechanisms and institutions;
- Develop gender-based methodologies and conduct research to address the feminisation of poverty.

■ Education and Training

Education is a human right and an essential tool for achieving equality, development and peace. Though overall progress has been achieved in girls' enrolment at primary and secondary levels, girls in many countries still face discrimination due to customary attitudes, early marriages and pregnancies, lack of accessible schools, and inadequate and gender-biased teaching and educational materials. Girls continue to be denied quality education, especially at higher levels and in science and technology.

Investing in formal and non-formal education and training for girls and women has proved to be one of the best means of achieving sustainable development and economic growth.

The Platform recommends action to:

- Ensure equal access to education. Governments are to commit themselves, by the year 2000, to universal access to basic education and completion of primary education by at least 80 per cent of primary-schoolage children. They also agree to close the gender gap in primary and secondary-school education by the year 2000, and to achieve universal education in all countries before the year 2015;
- Eradicate illiteracy among women. Governments are to reduce the female illiteracy rate at least to half its 1990 level;
- Improve women's access to vocational training, science and technology, and continuing education;
- Develop non-discriminatory education and training;
- Allocate sufficient resources for and monitor the implementation of educational reforms;
- Promote lifelong education and training for girls and women.

■ Health

Women's health involves their emotional, social and physical well-being. It is determined by the social, political and economic context of their lives, as well as by biology. The enjoyment of the highest attainable standard of physical and mental health is vital for the life and well-being of women. It is also crucial to their ability to participate in all areas of public and private life. This right must be secured throughout their whole life cycle in equality with men.

The Platform defines reproductive health as a state of complete physical, mental and social well-being and sexual health whose purpose is the enhancement of life and personal relations. Equal relationships between men and women in matters of sexual relations and reproduction require mutual respect, consent and shared responsibility. The Platform recognises of the basic human rights of all couples and individuals to decide freely and responsibly how many children they want to have, and when. They also have the right to obtain information and make decisions on reproduction free of discrimination, coercion and violence.

The Platform recommends actions to:

- Increase women's access throughout the life cycle to appropriate, affordable and quality health care, information and related services;
- Reduce maternal mortality by at least 50 per cent of the 1990 levels by the year 2000 and a further one half by the year 2015;
- Encourage both women and men to take responsibility for their sexual and reproductive behaviour;
- Undertake gender-sensitive initiatives that address sexually transmitted diseases, HIV/AIDS and sexual and reproductive health issues;
- Increase resources and monitor follow-up for women's health.

■ Violence

In all societies, to a greater or lesser degree, women and girls are subject to physical, sexual and psychological abuse that cuts across lines of income, class and culture, in both public and private life. They often face rape, sexual abuse, sexual harassment and intimidation in the workplace. They are particulary vulnerable to systematic violence during war. Sexual slavery, forced pregnancy, sterilisation and forced abortion, prenatal sex selection and female infanticide are also acts of violence. All such acts of violence violate and impair or nullify women's enjoyment of human rights and fundamental freedoms. Such groups of women as migrant workers require special attention because they are particularly vulnerable to violence.

Lack of preventive and protective laws, and lack of access or ineffective enforcement by public authorities of such laws where they exist, only perpetuate and increase violence against women.

The Platform recommends actions to:

- Adopt and implement legislation to end violence against women;
- Work actively to ratify and implement all international agreements related to violence against women, including the UN Convention on the Elimination of all Forms of Discrimination against Women;
- Adopt new laws and enforce existing ones to punish members of security forces and police or any other State agents for acts of violence against women;
- Set up shelters, provide legal aid and other services for girls and women at risk, and provide counselling and rehabilitation for perpetrators of violence against women;
- Step up national and internationl cooperation to dismantle networks engaged in trafficking in women.

■ Armed Conflict

Peace is a prerequisite for the attainment of equality between women and men. Unfortunately, armed and other types of conflict still persist in many parts of the world. Aggression, foreign occupation and ethnic and other conflicts are an ongoing reality affecting women and men in nearly every region, aided by excessive military expenditures and the arms trade.

Though women rarely have any role in the decisions leading to armed conflicts, they work to preserve social order in the midst of the conflicts. They also make an important contribution as peace educators and resolvers of conflicts.

The Platform recognises that rape, which is common during armed conflicts, is a crime, and under certain circumstances is an act of genocide. It condemns "ethnic cleansing" as a strategy of war and rape as one of its consequences. Such practices must be stopped and their perpetrators punished, it asserts.

The Platform recommends action to:

- Increase the participation of women in conflict resolution at decision-making levels;
- Reduce excessive military expenditures and control the availability of armaments;
- Work towards the universal ratification of the anti-mine Convention and Protocol by the year 2000;
- Recognise the important roles and contributions of women in peace movements throughout the world;
- Recognise the need to protect women living in situations of armed and other conflict or under foreign occupation, or who have become refugees or displaced.

■ Economy

Women contribute significantly to economic life everywhere. Their share in the labour force continues to rise, they are becoming more invloved in micro, small and medium enterprises and their income is becoming increasingly necessary to all households.

However, women are largely excluded from economic decision-making. They face low wages, poor working conditions and limited employment and professional opportunities. Though women contribute to development through paid as well as unpaid work, their unpaid work, such as domestic and community work, is not measured in quantitative terms and not valued in national accounts.

Discrimination in education and training, hiring, and remuneration and promotion, as well as inflexible working conditions, lack of access to productive resources and inadequate sharing of family responsibilities, contribute to restricted employment, economic and professional opportunities for women.

The Platform recommends action to:

- Promote women's economic rights and independence, including access to employment and appropriate working conditions and control over economic resources;
- Facilitate women's equal accees to resources, employment, markets and trade;
- Provide business services, training and access to markets, information and technology, particularly to low-income women;
- Strengthen women's economic capacity and commercial networks;
- Eliminate occupational segregation and all forms of employment discrimination;
- Promote harmonisation of work and family responsibilities for women and men.

■ Decision-making

Women's equal participation in decision-making is not only a demand for simple social justice or democracy. It is essential for achieving transparent and accountable government. It will also provide a balance that more accurately reflects the composition of society.

Despite the widespread movement towards democratisation in most countries, women remain largely underrepresented at most levels of government, especially in ministerial and other executive bodies or in reaching the target of having 30 per cent of decision-making positions held by women by 1995, as endorsed by the UN Economic and Social Council. They have achieved little progress in attaining political power in legislative bodies. Globally, only 10 per cent of legislative positions, and a lower percentage of ministerial positions, are held by women.

Similarly, the underrepresentation of women in decision-making positions in the arts, culture, sports, the media, education, religion and law have prevented women from having a significant impact on many key institutions and policies.

The Platform recommends action to:

- Ensure women's equal access to and full participation in power structures and decision-making in governmental bodies and public administration entities, including the judiciary, international and non-governmental organisations, political parties and trade unions;
- Increase women's capacity to participate in decision-making and leadership positions.

■ Institutional Mechanisms

Most countries have established institutions for the advancement of women. These are diverse in form and uneven in their effectiveness. They are often marginalised in national government structures, without a clear mandate, and lack adequate staff and resources as well as support from national political leadership. At the regional and international levels, mechanisms and institutions for the advancement of women encounter similar problems.

Many organisations have development methodologies for gender-based policy analysis. Unfortunately, they are applied either sporadically or not at all.

The Platform recommends action to:

- Create or strengthen national machineries and other governmental bodies; ensure that responsibility for the advancement of women is vested in the highest possible level of Government;
- Integrate gender perspectives in legislation, public policies, programmes and projects; ensure that before policy decisions are taken, an analysis of their impact on women and men is carried out.
- Generate and disseminate gender-disaggregated data and information for planning and evaluation; measure, in quantitative terms, unremunerated work that is outside national accounts.

■ Human Rights

All human rights are universal, indivisible, interdependent and interrelated. Their full and equal enjoyment and the United Nations and is essential for the advancement of women.

Governments must not only refrain from violating the human rights of all women but work actively to promote and protect these rights.

Recognition of the importance of women's human rights is reflected in the fact that three quarters of the UN Members States have become parties to the Convention on the Elimination of All forms of Discrimination against Women. However, the gap between the existence of rights and their effective enjoyment derives from a lack of commitment by Governments in promoting and protecting those rights and the failure of Governments to inform women and men alike about them.

The Platform recommends action to:

- Promote and protect the human rights of women by fully implementing all human rights instruments, especially the Convention on the Elimination of All Forms of Discrimination against Women;
- Review national laws to ensure implementation of all international human rights agreements;

- Ensure equality and non-discrimination under the law and in practice;
- Achieve legal literacy.

■ Media

Today, many women work in the media, but few have reached positions at decision-making levels. In most countries, the media continue to project a negative and degrading image of women and do not reflect women's diverse lives and contributions to society. Violent and degrading or pornographic media products in particular affect women negatively.

Everywhere the media have the potential to make a far greater contribution to the advancement of women. They can create self-regulatory mechanisms that can help eliminate gender-based programming. Women can also be empowered by having greater skills, knowledge and access to information technology.

The Platform recommends action to:

- Increase women's participation in and access to expression and decision-making in and through the media and new technologies of communication; Governments should aim at gender balance through the appointment of women and men to all advisory, management, regulatory or monitoring bodies;
- Promote a balanced and non-stereotyped portrayal of women in the media. The media organisations, NGOs and the private sector should promote the equal sharing of family responsibility and produce materials that portray diverse roles of women leaders;
- Develop within mass media and advertising organisations professional guidelines and codes of conduct and other forms of self-regulation to promote the presentation of non-stereotyped images of women, consistent with freedom of expression.

■ Environment

Through their management and use of natural resources, women provide sustenance to their families and communities. As consumers and producers, caretakers of their families and educators, women play an important role in promoting sustainable development.

The deterioration of natural resources results in negative effects on the health, well-being and quality of life of the population at large, especially girls and women of all ages.

However, women, who are rarely formally trained as natural-resource managers, remain largely absent from decision-making and have their experience and skills too often marginalised. Despite the leadership role played by women's organizations, institutional coordination with national bodies is very weak.

The Platform recommends action to:

- Involve women actively in environmental decision-making at all levels, including as managers, designers and planners, and as implementers and evaluators of environmental projects;
- Integrate gender concerns and perspectives in policies and programmes for sustainable development;
- Strengthen or establish mechanisms at the national levels to assess the impact of development and environment policies on women.

■ The Girl-Child

In many countries, the girl-child faces discrimination from the earliest stages of life, through childhood and into adulthood. Due to harmful attitudes and practices, such as female genital mutilation, son preference, early marriage, sexual exploitation and practices related to health and food allocation, fewer girls than boys survive into adulthood in some areas of the world. Due to lack of protective laws, or failure to enforce such laws, girls are more vulnerable to all kinds of violence, particularly sexual violence. In many regions, girls face discrimination in access to education and specialised training.

More than 15 million girls aged 15 to 19 each year give birth and face pregnancy-related complications. Girls are also more vulnerable than boys to the consequences of unprotected and premature sexual relations, including HIV/AIDS.

The Platform recommends action to:

- Eliminate all forms of discrimination against the girl-child; enact and enforce appropriate legislation that guarantees equal right to succession and ensures equal right to inherit, regardless of the sex of the child;
- Eliminate negative cultural attitudes and practices against girls;
- Eliminate discrimination against girls in education, skills development and training;
- Eliminate discrimination against girls in health and nutrition;
- Eliminate the economic exploitation of child labour and protect young girls at work;
- Strengthen the role of the family in improving the status of the girl-child.

■ Institutional and Financial Arrangements

The Platform for Action establishes a set of actions that should lead to fundamental change. Immediate action and accountability are essential if the targets are to be met by the year 2000.

Governments are primarily responsible for their implementation. However, success depends also on various national, regional and international institutions, public and private, which require clear and strong mandates, authority and resources.

- At the national level, commitment at the highest political level is essential for the successful implementation of the Platform. By the end of 1996, all Governments should have their own national strategies or plans of action. Governments should establish or improve effectiveness of national machineries for the advancement of women, and seek the active support of a broad range of other actors.
- At the regional and sub-regional levels, the regional commissions of the United Nations should promote and assist national institutions. Regional institutions should develop and publicise regional plans of action for implementing the Platform within given time-frames and resources.
- At the international level, all entities of the United Nations system should have the necessary resources and support to carry out follow-up activities. International financial institutions are encouraged to review and revise policies to ensure that their investments and programmes benefit women.

To ensure system-wide implementation of the Platform and to advise on gender issues, the Secretary-General of the United Nations is invited to establish a high-level post in his office. The Platform also calls for committing adequate financial resources from all sources and across all sectors.

For further information contact:
Department of Public Information
United Nations, Room S-1005
New York, NY 10017, USA
Fax: 212-963-4556

United Nations Department of Public Information.

3
WFS Articles on Critical Areas of Concern

Poverty ~ We're Hungry, Cold and Underpaid

Scotland: Outraged by British officials' assertions that poverty does not exist in the United Kingdom, a plucky group of Scottish women are planning to argue otherwise on the world stage.

The women who come from a wide range of religious, cultural and class backgrounds, have written their own Scottish Plan of Action to take to the United Nations' Fourth World Conference on Women in Beijing next fall. Under normal circumstances, their contributions would be included in a comprehensive British government report.

In their report, the Scots contend that oppressive poverty shapes many women's lives in their country and they criticise British officials' failure to recognise and address the problem.

"Poverty in Scotland is as bad as anything in the Third World," says Norma Hurley, the researcher who reviewed all the data and wrote the final report for the women's groups.

According to statistics released by the UK Department of Social Security last year, the number of people living in poverty in the UK increased from 5 million in 1979 to nearly 14 million in 1991.

"The very real problem of poverty and the lack of affordable childcare are, arguably, the most serious obstacles to the advancement of women in Scotland," the alternative report says.

"The scale, extent and seriousness of poverty is not addressed in the UK report. This is an error which needs to be corrected."

With 5 million people located in the northern reaches of the British Isles, Scotland became part of the UK after it agreed to share a common Parliament with England in 1707. But the long years of administrative union have done nothing to diminish the fierce national pride still burning in the hearts of many Scots.

Scotland maintains its own legal and educational system and many Scots continue to mistrust London's administrative rule. This division was reflected in the Scottish report, which said that Britain's Value Added Tax on fuel placed an unfair burden on the frigid northern region.

"The tax has a more deleterious effect on the poor and vulnerable in Scotland—the majority of whom are women—than on the poor in areas of the UK which have a less harsh climate," the report points out.

There are clear differences in salary levels between Scotland and the wealthier regions of the UK as well. While the average weekly wage for men in the UK is 353.50 pounds per week, Scottish men earn an average of just 326 pounds per week. The average weekly UK wage for women is 252 pounds, while the Scottish women's average wage is 246 pounds.

Work on the alternative plan began in 1992, when Scottish women's groups grew frustrated with their lack of input into the official British plans for the Beijing Conference.

They were also upset when British officials decided that the official delegation to the European region's preparatory meeting for Beijing would be lead by UK Employment Minister Ann Widdicombe, who publicly left the Church of England last year to protest the Church's decision to ordain women as priests. Widdicombe subsequently joined the Roman Catholic Church, which continues to bar women from becoming priests.

With Widdicombe's appointment as a signal of the government's intentions, Scottish women opted to write their own independent report drawing attention to their concerns.

A network of diverse groups, ranging from the Women's Committee of the Scottish Trade Union Congress to the Church of Scotland's Women's Guild, held forums and discussions around the country where women expressed their most pressing worries.

These meetings found that women in Scotland are often in poor physical and mental health, without social or recreational contacts. Many live in overcrowded, damp housing with inadequate heating and do not have a well-balanced diet, warm clothing or sufficient bedding.

With few opportunities for remunerative work due to Scotland's lack of industry and lack of affordable childcare, most women spend their working lives in on-going struggle to make ends meet.

Half of Scotland's full-time working women have jobs that are officially classified as low-paid and only 13 percent of Scottish mothers with a child under 10 work full time—half of the average for the European Community. Meanwhile, the Child Poverty Action group estimates that 62 percent of adults on income support in Scotland are women.

As a result of this, elderly women have minuscule pensions, if any. According to the Glasgow Women's Health Working Group, Scotland has the fourth highest premature death rate of the 35 countries worldwide that keep such statistics.

Yet at a public meeting held by Widdicombe last fall as part of the official Beijing preparatory process, a high ranking British official from the Department of Social Security denied that poverty was a relevant topic for discussion in the UK. "Globally speaking, there is no poverty in the UK," the civil servant said.

Scottish women's groups plan to point out otherwise at the Beijing meeting. They are raising money to send their own delegates who will challenge the official government position.

"There was a real commonality of concern over the issues of importance," Hurley says. "They were repeated over and over again by women and groups from every background."

Women's groups say that the experience of preparing their own report taught them how they could work together to achieve common objectives. They hope in the future to jointly tackle some of the problems that they have identified.

"Women are pragmatic about the possibility of making changes. They want straightforward improvements," she says. "It is very positive and very heartening. But the question has to be asked: is there the political will to make them?"

Grace Franklin

Poverty ~ Living Paycheck to Paycheck

Czech Republic : Like many single mothers, 45-year-old Alena Kucerova, hasn't had it easy. After marrying in 1970 she and her husband moved from a small village to Kromeriz, a medium-sized town in the eastern region of the Czech Republic. By 1974, she was divorced and left to raise her three-year-old son virtually alone.

"My son and I somehow managed, but it was much worse before," she says, the toughness she has acquired showing in her sharp mannerisms and tone of voice. With the money she earned from her job as a hairdresser, Kucerova had to pay off loans, pay rent and support herself and her son.

Kristina Tesarova, 36, a high school German teacher, has also been painstakingly counting her crowns to support her 14-year-old son and invalid husband. "Financially we live from paycheck to paycheck," she says.

According to reports produced by the Prague Gender Studies and Single Mothers Club, there are 687,671 widows and around 8,000 single moms within the Czech Republic's 10.3 million people.

Three years after the Czech Republic split from Slovakia in 1992, many changes have taken place. The country has had to brace itself to bear some unpredictable growing pains in the face of privatisation, free market economy and the entrance of foreign investors.

These changes have seeped beyond the surface, bringing changes within families and young couples. They have also left one in every four women living alone—widowed or divorced.

Alena Svobodova was married and a mother by the time she was 20, but six years later she was divorced and left to raise her daughter alone. Working as a nurse at a psychiatric hospital, she earns US $146 a month. With one fourth of that going toward rent, she always finds herself short of cash at the end of the month.

"I try to save US $ 11 a month which really is very little, but at least it is something. At the end of the month, I have nothing. Sometimes I have to borrow money from my parents or friends just to pay for the basic needs," says the 36-year-old Svobodova who lives with her 13-year-old daughter in a studio flat in a mid-sized Czech town.

The government determines the minimum that a family can live off depending on the family size and how many members work. According to their figures a single adult can live on US $89, one adult with a child under the age of three can survive on US $143, two adults with two children need to earn US $273 and parents with three children must have a minimum of US $335. The average salary earned by Czechs is US $315 before taxes.

If a family earns less than the government thinks they can live on then they can apply for aid. For most women supporting their families, their pay often falls short.

Surviving isn't easy for these women. Female breadwinners who juggle child rearing, household chores and a job have not been welcomed into work force according to Drahomira Chytilova, director of the economic department of a medium-sized town employment office.

Married or single mothers from Kromeriz stand in lines at this employment office, hoping to find a position which has flexible working hours.

"Our clerks shouldn't ask about the women's marital status and whether or not they have children, but they do," says Chytilova. Often because of the woman's limited working hours, she doesn't get the position.

"It is never written that she didn't get the job because she is a mother of two children, but because of 'her situation'," Chytilova says.

Jitka Sterbakova, mother of two, has been looking for a job after being on maternity leave for two years. She says, "The first question the person interviewing asks is, 'Do you have any kids?' If I say yes, the second question they ask is, 'Are your parents alive?'"

In addition to money not stretching far enough for many women, the Czech Republic has a housing shortage. Houses are assigned by the government, but sometimes they have to wait years.

Svobodova had to wait six years for the small studio she and her daughter currently share. "I was supposedly a high priority case and I still had to wait 6 years. It was awful," she says. "My ex-husband wasn't willing to give up the flat so my daughter and I had move out."

While waiting she rented three different flats. "We were as nomadic as gypsies," she laughs looking back now. But Svobodova remembers that she was a nervous wreck and under tremendous pressure trying to find a place.

Tesarova feels the government could do more in the area of housing. "I walk through the town and I see dark windows. There are flats that are empty that people are keeping for when their children are grown. There should be some law for these situations," she says. "Applicants should be prioritized by how many children they have."

Svobodova agrees, "I suppose the government could do more in the area of housing. I was in such a desperate situation living on the street. I was renting out places and I never knew when these people would throw me out. We were definitely a social case."

Women living on their own rose 51 percent within 3 years. In 1991, 21 percent of marriages ended with women getting divorced or widowed, but by 1994 it had jumped to a dramatic 72 percent, according to the Prague Gender Studies and Single Mothers Club.

However, Kucerova believes that women who are divorced and have children are looked after by the government. "In general, the government isn't bad about providing for single mothers," she says. "Some people don't know what is available and the clerks at the welfare office don't voluntarily inform them of the other kinds of aid they may qualify for. They think that it's your problem so you go find out."

Tesarova would like to receive assistance, but her salary is 73 cents over what the government considers the basic minimum for a three-person family with one wage earner. Even if her paycheck slid under the minimum she would not get aid from the government.

"The officials would come here and say, 'You have a telephone, don't you? So if claim you don't have enough money, then have your phone disconnected.' They would calmly say they don't consider a telephone as a basic need. It is above standard. Next they would say, 'Sell your television.'"

Kucerova doesn't believe things have changed much since the 1989 revolution when the Republic shifted into a free market economy, and she doesn't believe they will either. "We have been receiving more welfare money than we had before the revolution, but the prices of goods in stores have gone up as well."

Tesarova agrees but insists that she is quite happy in her role as the family breadwinner. "It is true that we have very little money, less money than others have, but there is nothing that can be done about it. The situation is the way it is and we cope."

She firmly believes that things will improve. "I don't foresee us ever having money stowed away or being able to buy more expensive shoes. But someday it won't be this hard."

Svobodova has similar hopes about the future. "I would say it will better," she sighs. "But if not we will always find a way to hang in there. It always works out somehow."

Debby Tomecek

Education and Training ~
Teen Mothers Back to School

Kenya : The Kenyan government has made a radical departure from the norm: it has launched a programme to re-admit girls who drop out of school because of pregnancy.

"This is now a policy. Sensitisation will be carried out among all education officers to allow girls to continue with their studies," explains Elizabeth Masinga, a senior officer in the Ministry of Education.

Though the details of the policy are still sketchy, this is certainly a major step forward.

Despite the great strides Kenya has made in education since its independence in 1963, girls continue to remain disadvantaged. Most parents begin the discrimination at home, where by observing the traditional division of labour, they overburden girls leaving them very little time for study.

The drop-out rate of girls is high at every level of education. Nationally, the enrollment rate is the same for girls and boys joining primary school. But only 35 percent of girls—as opposed to 55 percent of boys—complete primary level. This is a figure far below the 70 percent for both sexes targetted by the government by the year 2000.

At secondary school level, pregnancy becomes the main culprit, leading to girls being expelled from school and thus terminating their education.

In recent years the number of pregnant schoolgirls has reached alarming proportions. In one study, it was established that over 10,000 Kenyan girls drop out of school annually due to pregnancies. This translates into roughly one out of every three girls admitted to secondary school.

Besides the trauma of being thrown out of school, many parents disown their unmarried pregnant daughters in order to avoid social stigma.

It's an open secret that a large number of schoolgirls get abortions with or without the knowledge of their parents, so that they can at least finish their education.

Other factors too have contributed to the falling numbers of schoolgirls in Kenya.

Economic constraints exacerbated by the effects of structural adjustment programmes, have forced many parents to choose the children they wish to educate. The sons, who will never get pregnant, invariably win.

Educationist Dr.Eddah Gachukia adds that the emphasis on mathematics and science subjects in the new syllabus also keeps girls away from schools. She also argues that very little has been done to eliminate stereotyping of gender roles in school textbooks.

"Most teachers of technical subjects which are erroneously referred to as 'non-traditional courses', are male, and hence girls have no role models to inspire them," Gachukia points out.

The number of girls entering Kenya's four public universities has thus steadily declined from 29 to 20 percent last year. Currently, among Kenyan women who make up 52 percent of this East African country's population, only 40 percent are literate. And if things do not improve for girls, this figure will further drop.

Which is the reason that spurred the government to formulate the re-admission policy for school mothers. However, it has not gone down well with everyone.

"Does this country have any sense of morality left?" is the rhetorical question posed by Martin Shikuku, a legislator and secretary general of the opposition, Forum for the Restoration of Democracy.

A practising Roman Catholic, Shikuku advocates a return to traditional values. He says that our forefathers prided themselves if a daughter was a virgin when she married. "There is no difference between our forefathers and ourselves," states Shikuku. "This talk of modern times is nonsense."

He firmly believes that if student mothers are allowed back in school, they will set a bad example and more girls will have children.

Shikuku is sceptical too about the policy's benefits to society. According to him, only girls from rich families will gain. "It's only the daughter of a rich man who can have a child and continue with her education because there will be hired hands to take care of the baby," he points out.

Shikuku, a father of eight daughters, says that just as he advises his own daughters, he tells all girls to choose between education and marriage. "I have always preached to my daughters that sex before marriage is immoral."

The League of Women Voters concurs. So, in fact, does Gladwell Mungai, deputy headmistress of a girls secondary school in Nairobi.

"If we rule that when a girl gets pregnant she goes from the school for good, others will think twice before engaging in sex," says Mungai. She also feels that it would be unfair for the girl to be re-admitted to the same school where she will be teased and perhaps lose interest in education altogether, thus defeating the whole purpose. "Such a girl should go to another school where she is unknown," she says.

Margaret Mwaniki of Kenya Catholic Secretariat analyses the problem from the single parent angle in African society.

Single motherhood marks a major deviation from the accepted African social and moral norms, she says. It also subjects young women to great emotional and psychological stress, social alienation and deprivation.

"This practise of blaming the victim is quite unfortunate because it ruins many innocent lives," notes Mwaniki, adding that she would rather see education interpreted and applied in a wider context, to bring about the overall development of an individual.

She does not want the new policy "to end at just re-admitting school mothers to school but also to ensure that each secondary school has at least one counsellor who can relate to these students—and others—at a personal level."

But this kind of a dialogue also needs to be replicated within families. And more pertinently, with boys in families.

"We must take away the myth that it's only the girl who is guilty," says Mwaniki. "And the practise of expulsion from school for pregnancy is a condemnation of women."

Many others like her feel that Kenyans need to seriously assess just how much damage has been caused by trying to solve the pregnancy crisis by expulsion. And now with the government's liberal measure of re-admitting school mothers, it's time to make amends and strive for a more sensitive, all-encompassing policy.

Rebecca Katumba

Education and Training ~ Tribals Turn Away From Sex Trade

India: As you enter Abhiuday Ashram in Morena, Madhya Pradesh, you are greeted by a group of school children smartly turned out in dark blue uniform.

This is a boarding school with a difference. All the 150 boys and girls are children of Bedia women, who follow a form of ritually sanctioned caste-based prostitution.

Abhiuday means 'a new sunrise'. The school is the first government funded institution set up to rehabilitate the Bedia tribe of this central Indian state.

The task at hand is herculean. It involves transforming the Bedia mind, their customs, their traditions. And making Bedia men work for a living, instead of soliciting for their sisters.

Among the Bedias, the daughter of a family is introduced into prostitution by her own parents. She is the principal source of income. Males either solicit clients, engage in petty criminal activities or remain idle.

Bedia women have catered to the lust of rich landed men, politicians, administrators and businessmen for centuries. The Bedia population now numbers 16,682 people belonging to 3124 families.

Article 23 of the Indian Constitution, which relates to rights against exploitation, prohibits traffic in human beings. The Supreme Court of India in 1989 had directed all state governments to strictly enforce the Article, bring all inmates of red light areas to protective homes, and provide them with education and training so that they can choose a more dignified way of life.

Though the Jabalpur High Court had also passed strictures against the flesh trade, these orders have remained on paper. P.V. Rajagopal, Inspector General of Police, Gwalior city says the Prevention of Immoral Traffic Act is extremely difficult to implement. The law does not prosecute the sexworkers though it is strict with the pimps.

Om Prakash, a Bedia man teaching in a government school, says almost all Bedia families are engaged in the profession or struggling to leave it. Bedias permit daughters, sisters or mothers to be sexworkers but it is a sin for the wife to be initiated into this profession.

The Bedia father celebrates once his daughter attains puberty. At the age of 13, a ring is inserted in her nose, signifying that she is ripe enough to entertain customers. On the day of initiation, there is feasting and merry-making and a large gathering of clients collects at the young woman's home. Whoever offers the highest price for the night gets her. Having lost her virginity on this night, she has to entertain a new man every night from then on.

When the woman conceives for the first time, she is formally married to a one rupee coin. Most women bear several children.

However, many of the women are unhappy being in prostitution. In one Bedia village in Morena, several came forward to say there should be an end to this social evil. "We were not born prostitutes," said 26-year-old Baby who earns around Rs 10,000 (US $ 322) a month, "We are thrown into this by our parents."

She added, "If someone is willing to marry me I would leave this profession without a second thought."

Saroj Bai left the trade hoping to be integrated into society. But her two educated sons are unemployed and frustrated. "We left the old ways, looking forward to a dignified way of life, but the feudal mentality of the people here prevents our acceptance in the social mainstream," she said.

There is historical evidence to suggest that the custom evolved at the end of the seventeenth century. Before this the Bedias, who lived in the jungles and foraged for food, supplemented their existence with dacoity and loot. They were declared criminal tribes by the British. The Bedias began to move continuously, seeking the protection of rich landlords, but were frequently caught and jailed.

The burden of managing the family fell on the women who sold themselves for sustenance. After initial resistance, the men compromised with this and the community restored to the defensive mechanisms of ritual and tradition to make prostitution an acceptable avenue of livelihood.

Today, some members of the community feel a need for change. There is a movement for reform, but it is not yet strong enough.

Ram Snehi Charri, 62, runs the Abhiuday Ashram, the children's home in Morena. Charri who is unmarried, has devoted 40 years of his life to activities like rescuing women and offering them alternative sources of employment.

The first women's home in Madhya Pradesh was founded by a voluntary organisation in Gwalior in 1959. It raids notified red light areas with police assistance and brings women to the home which offers vocational courses and provides employment. Some women have been helped to marry.

R.C. Charri, a senior police officer who belongs to the community, say the Bedias have internalised their degraded social status. The Bedia woman is not forced into this profession. From her earliest socialisation she is taught that on her rests the responsibility of supporting her parents and brothers. The men have little reason to seek change because the system earns them an assured livelihood.

Yet, with education, the younger Bedia has grown up with a strong urge to join the mainstream. The attitude of society towards Bedia children is harsh, because they are considered illegitimate. This rejection has inculcated in them a strong hatred of their social system.

One reason why many Bedia women want change is the fact that generally the family abandons the woman when she can no longer earn. If she has a daughter then she is expected to take care of the mother. But the mother, being a victim of the system, longs to free her daughter from this vicious cycle.

The process of transition is going to be long and arduous, says Minister of State for Home Affairs Satyadev Katare. He feels that the administration should identify educated, younger Bedias who can be recruited as effective change agents.

The state government has drawn up a four-phase action plan, known as the Jabali project, for rehabilitation of the women. The first phase proposes setting up of homes for children between 6-14 years where they would be provided basic education. Such homes are running effectively in a few districts. Abhiuday Ashram in Morena is a part of this programme.

The other three phases for women in the age groups of 15-19, 20-49 and 50 plus exist only on paper.

Yet the critical age group is 15-19 when the young woman, having attained puberty, is left to struggle on her own to free herself of this spider's web. Recently Alka, 19, committed suicide because she was not permitted to marry someone she loved. She and her lover died hand in hand. There are many such victims.

In Shivpuri, in the first ever gathering for shared introspection of Bedia families, a young boy stood up and said, "I am the illegitimate child of a businessman of this town who will never acknowledge me. My mother and sister have brought me up through prostitution. This must end."

In a similar gathering in Morena, a girl barely in her teens said, "It is not caste but one's actions and character that determines one's future. I am going to prove this to the world."

In voices such as these one can already hear the breaking of the shackles.

Sharmila Banerjee

Education and Training ~ Stay in the Kitchen and out of the Lab

Argentina : "It is a known fact that in women, intellectual development is accompanied by a decrease in their reproductive capacity. As the brain expands, the ovaries contract," an eminent nineteenth century biologist once concluded.

Have attitudes really changed? Not in Argentina, many women claim. Only two years ago, Argentina's Finance Minister publicly suggested that a female researcher from the National Council for Scientific and

Technical Research (CONICET) "go and wash the dishes".

Although this incident was soon forgotten, several women researchers recently decided to find out what happens when women enter the male-dominated world of the "hard sciences".

They conducted an informal study into the academic achievement of both sexes during their school years. The results showed that women generally have higher levels of achievement. They complete courses within the stipulated time and they obtain higher grades.

However, once they graduate, women take longer to enter the job market and they tend to apply for posts on the lower rungs of the professional ladder. They also remain in these posts longer than their male colleagues would.

This pattern is evident in CONICET, Argentina's most important state research institution. At the beginning of their research careers, men and women enter on an equal footing. But as the researchers climb the professional ladder, the number of women begins to decrease, until at the most senior levels they occupy only five percent of the posts.

Men usually take over the scientific and technological research posts, leaving the "softer" social sciences and humanities to women. To understand the reasons for this situation and organise to modify it, a group of women scientists has created the "Science and Technology Gender Network."

The group allows women scientists and researchers to exchange ideas and experiences, analyse the role of women in science and technology and develop an awareness of gender issues that will help them pinpoint specific problems facing women scientists.

Diana Mafia, a philosopher and specialist in feminist epistemology, is one of the network's founders. Mafia herself has suffered many of the types of discrimination she analyses in her research papers.

"When I began to do research on feminist epistemology, I was able to do it because I had spent 15 years teaching logic and traditional epistemology. That's how I managed to avoid the most common prejudice: that I was engaged in feminist philosophising because I had never been able to come to grips with logic or do a formal analysis of a theory," Mafia explains.

"In any case, I'm regarded as something rather exotic at round-table discussions, like a comic strip character. They all think, 'Let's see what Diana Mafia has to say today.' I use humour and irony to overcome these attitudes."

But Mafia notes that all the women scientists interviewed to date by the network—of all ages and backgrounds—claimed that they had never suffered any kind of discrimination in their jobs. They also insisted that in their particular discipline there was no differentiation between the sexes.

"But then, when they began to talk about their own lives, they recalled encountering a number of difficulties that their male colleagues have never faced," Mafia says.

There are many examples of the kinds of obstacles faced by Argentina's female scientists. One woman who applied for a research post at CONICET was turned down simply because she had small children.

The interviewer decided she had pressing family responsibilities that could not be delegated and refused to give her the job, ignoring her academic merits and experience.

Another case concerned a married couple, both researchers, who received scholarships to study science abroad. While the husband received the full award, the wife was paid only half, because as a married woman she was considered to be economically dependent on her spouse.

When the couple returned to Argentina,

after completing the same courses, they were both interviewed for jobs at CONICET. Despite the fact that their professional level was the same, the husband was appointed to a post that was two categories above his wife's.

Mafia claims that part of the reason that this situation continues is because women who have reached high positions within the system show little inclination to change it.

"You only reach this point when an important group of women come together to exchange points of view, and they begin to discover common patterns of discomfort," Mafia adds.

The Science and Technology Gender Network intends to make long strides in that direction.

Valeria Belloro

Health ~ Toning Up Health care

Canada: Responding to a growing concern that women are being shortchanged by Canada's health care system, the Canadian government is setting up a Center of Excellence for Women's Health. It's a new idea that promises to deliver better information to Canadian doctors and health professionals working in the complicated field of women's health.

"There is ample evidence that health care systems—in Canada as in other countries—have not given as great attention to women's health issues as to men's health issues," the Liberal Party said in a book of promises during last fall's election campaign. When the new government was formed at the end of October, Prime Minister Jean Chretien announced he'd set up the Center of Excellence for Women's Health, which would be operational in about a year.

While it will not be the country's first centre of excellence, it will be the first dealing specifically with women's health issues. The other existing centres have been promoting better research in fields like environment and high technology.

"The purpose of the Center of Excellence on Women's Health is to get some clearer understanding of what most significant women's health issues are and prompt the whole health system to be more responsive to addressing those concerns," says Abby Hoffman, a former Olympic athlete who now runs the government's Women's Health Bureau and will be responsible for setting up this new centre.

Canadian women are poorer than Canadian men and research has shown a clear link between poverty and poor health. The salaries of working women, while increasing, are still 28 percent lower than that of men. And while women in Canada outlive men by an average of seven years, they have more chronic diseases and disability than men. This, together with their role as childbearers, makes Canadian women the greatest users of the health care system. Yet, according to women's health advocates, female patients are often not adequately informed or consulted about treatments.

"They don't feel they are active partners in the process," Hoffman says. "We want the centre to be involved with non-professionals as well as health care professionals."

One of the priorities of the centre—and of the Women's Health Bureau—is to develop a 'report card' on the health status of Canadian women. This information will be useful to both health care professionals and the government as it formulates health policy.

Hoffman and her staff of four are hammering out the details of the centre's mandate and operation now. The centre, which will be established at a Canadian university yet to be named, will take a multi-disciplinary approach to women's health. Priorities will probably include mental and reproductive health, violence against women, chronic and degenerative health problems, female cancers, nutrition and occupational and environmental health.

While a lot of progress has been made in terms of women's equality in Canada, it has been mostly focused on legal and economic issues. "The health system has been a relatively underdeveloped area," says Hoffman. "There's a general feeling that something needs to be done about women's health and the way the system deals with the health needs of women."

The biggest problem in recent years has been lack of research. The government says the study of breast cancer has been underfunded in Canada, as in the US. But even in studies of ailments afflicting men and women equally (such as heart disease) most of the research has focused on men. And in medical procedures specific to women, such as hysterectomies, treatment of osteoporosis and caesarean sections, doctors and patients often complain of significant gaps in knowledge.

The women's health initiative comes at a time when Canada's world-renowned health care system is near crisis. Most economists say it will be impossible for the government to significantly cut its $ 46-billion (US $ 34-billion) budget deficit without dipping into the money it spends on health and social services. Many expect the government to freeze the money it gives to Canada's 10 provinces to help pay for health services.

Canadian federal and provincial governments spend about $ 70 billion (US $ 52 billion) a year to support the country's generous system, which guarantees every Canadian access to the same standard of medical care. Marcel Masse, the federal government's intergovernmental affairs minister, has suggested that spending could be cut by as much as 20 percent without significantly reducing the range of services.

The provinces have already taken steps to curb their health spending by closing hospitals, freezing the salaries of provincially-paid health care workers and exempting some medical procedures from government funding. Meanwhile, the average age of Canadians, and their dependence on health care is rising steadily.

"As people are more conscious of the social and health issues related to an aging population, it's becoming better known that while women are still outliving men, the kinds of chronic conditions that beset older women are ones that we've not made a hell of a lot of progress on," says Hoffman. "So increasingly there is a large proportion of the elderly female population whose health is really quite poor."

Against this backdrop, the first women's health collective was formed in Vancouver on Canada's west coast in 1972. It maintains a resource library, conducts self-help groups, offers birth control counselling and publishes material on health issues. Since then, many other collectives have sprung up around Canada, including a black women's health group in Toronto and a Canadian women's health network, through which the groups share information. Canadian women, evidently, have started taking their health concerns into their own hands.

Jill Vardy

Health ~ Mothers Battle "Nuclear Monster"

Ukraine : In a way, it was really 5-year-old Serhij who was the impetus for the Ukrainian environmental group, Mama-86. Serhij was born in 1989, three years after the meltdown of a reactor at the Chernobyl Atomic Energy Station, 60 miles outside Kyiv, released vast quantities of radiation into the atmosphere.

Like many Ukrainian children born after the disaster, he suffers from an immune system weakness which leaves him highly susceptible to colds and other infections.

The realisation that her child and the children of her friends

Faced a lifetime of physical illness as a result of radiation poisoning, jolted Anna Syomina. Out of her anger, Mama-86 was born. "My activity in the organisation was driven by the very fact of my son's birth," says Syomina, 30, who now serves as the executive director of the group. "This event awakened my civil consciousness and made me more receptive to information on Chernobyl."

Members of the Mama-86 group, which is officially named 'Mothers of Kyiv for Children's Protection', seek to draw young mothers' attention to the link between their children's health and environmental degradation in the post Chernobyl-era.

In the five years since they began, the group has collected enough donations to equip a medical laboratory, where physicians offer medical examinations of children's internal organs and recommendations to parents for their care and treatment. The laboratory also informs parents about the causes of their children's illnesses.

"The main goal is to raise awareness of environmental issues through concrete assistance to children with health problems," says Syomina. "We are open to all mothers. Any mother whose child has serious medical problems will be put in a list for examination in our laboratory."

As Ukrainains mourned the ninth anniversary of the disaster this week, Syomina talked about her plans for the organisations future projects.

Soon they will offer evening childcare services so that mothers, especially single mothers, can have a few hours for themselves. In addition, they intend to develop children's environmental education projects and vacation programmes to take kids to the cleanest part of the Ukraine.

Syomina, who studied architecture at the Kyiv State Academy of the Arts, never had any intention of going into environmental or social activism. But shortly after her son was born, the Ukrainian media published the first accurate information about the impact of lingering radiation in the environment on children.

Furious, Syomina became the epicentre of a spontaneous young mothers' movement in her community. The group began agitating for radiation monitoring and decontamination of the places where children live and play.

They chose the name Mama-86 with its reference to the year of the meltdown, because it "symbolises a shift in the ecological consciousness of the Ukrainian people."

Accurate information was sadly lacking in the initial days after the Chernobyl disaster. Initially, communist officials, including the then-minister of health, "continued to assure people that everything was normal".

"It was a real crime that because the government was afraid to speak the truth, our children continued to play with sand in the playgrounds during the days after the catastrophe," Syomina says. "It was much later that we found out that the Chernobyl explosion was equal to the effect of thousands of Hiroshima bombs."

One of the group's primary goals has been the closure of the crippled power station, which has continued to operate despite ongoing radiation leaks.

At first, Ukrainian officials argued that the country's need for energy outweighed the dangers of another nuclear accident. Last month, however, during a visit of the French Minister of Environmental Protection, Ukrainian officials pledged to shut down the plant within the next five years.

Members of Mama-86 viewed this as a major victory. But Syomina says that the group will continue to apply pressure to ensure the government keeps its word.

Already officials have hinted at possible delays, warning that closing a nuclear power station "is not like turning off a light in a room". They have said they need billions of dollars to shut down the three reactors now operating and to clean-up contaminated areas.

However, Mama-86 members are determined to brook no excuses. "The Chernobyl disaster has shown the whole world the price that people pay for negligent nuclear consumption," Syomina says. "It's high time to stop the nuclear monster that has been poisoning our kids."

When Syomina talks, it is clear that she is deeply committed to her chosen cause. "Children have been the most helpless, unnecessary victims of the tragedy," she says. So far, she says, the laboratory has examined 2,000 children. "We haven't found a single healthy child among them."

According to the laboratory's statistics, after the disaster, Kyiv's schoolchildren showed a 6.5 percent increase in cases of childhood pneumonia, a 4.8 percent increase in cases of liver disease and a 3.5 percent increase in cases of brain cancer. The Ukrainian Ministry of Health has also reported a tripling of cancers among children since the 1986 disaster.

Last year, the parents of 130 children with cancer formed the charity foundation 'Oncolog' (oncologist) to help each other cope with their grief and burden.

Meanwhile, Syomina, with her son in tow, frequently spends her weekends in the Mama-86 office, thinking up new ways to serve children and their parents. ""We realised that nobody could help us cope with Chernobyl's consequences," she says. "We must rely only on ourselves."

Oksana Kuts

Violence ~ Horrific Home Violence Prompts Controversial Law

Costa Rica : Zeidy is only 34 but she appears ill, exhausted, fearful and a nervous wreck. She says she wishes that her husband would drop dead so that she could escape the daily torture she has endured the past 16 years.

Sitting on a bench in the crowded waiting room of the Women's Office here, this thin, frail mother of three children recalls that a year has passed since she filed charges against her husband at a local court. He had savagely beaten her, disfiguring her face and causing a detached retina in one eye. "Where's justice?" she asks.

" If I don't die from this I'm going to go crazy," she whispers as she wipes her tears. Help may soon be at hand for Zeidy and women like her suffering through an epidemic of domestic violence in this small Central American nation of 3.5 million people. Thousands are routinely beaten, humiliated, threatened, raped and brutalised by husbands, partners or male relatives.

Between January and October of 1995, the Women's Office, attached to the Interior Ministry, received 3,600 complaints from victims of domestic violence, compared with 1,736 during the same period in 1994. Each month, two women die as a result of violence at home.

According to Zaira Salazar, director of the Women's Office, more than half of last year's victims were housewives and 60 percent were married. The victims were of all ages, social classes and occupations.

After years of silence, an increasing number of women are coming forward to talk, and the Costa Rican Congress is finally debating stronger legislation on the problem.

They have been prompted by two horrific cases that recently hit the headlines. Costa Ricans were shocked to learn of a woman called Silvia whose husband kept her and their three year-old daughter locked up in a hen-house for three years, eating one meal a day and sleeping among ants and scorpions.

Last September, the newspapers were filled with pictures of Fatima, whose right arm was completely severed as she tried to protect herself from her machete-wielding husband.

These cases and others have served to highlight the failures of the Costa Rican state, the courts, the laws and society in general to protect women and children from abuse in the home.

The new bill before Congress will be voted on in the next few weeks. It incorporates proposals submitted two years ago by women's rights groups that define measures to protect women and children from domestic violence.

Although welcomed by feminists, the bill has also become controversial. Feminist groups insist that specific approaches should be used to tackle violence suffered by the different members of the family, such as the elderly and adolescents. But these are not covered by the new law.

Ana Carcedo, Director of the non-governmental National Women's Centre (CEFEMINA), warns that the bill could become a double-edged sword, since it could also be used against women.

One of the most controversial aspects is article 5, which allows a judge to order the victim's removal from the home to a relative's home or shelter "away from the common home, to protect the victim from future aggressions".

According to Lidia Martin, a lawyer at the governmental Women's Ombudsman's Office, such a measure would make women "double victims" since they would be deprived of their home and sent to a shelter.

Francisco Pacheco, a former education minister and deputy of the ruling party, counters,

"The family is a unit, especially in Latin American countries, where in practice many people live under the same roof.

Some people have a very narrow vision, an irrational attitude that comes from an exclusive feminism that seeks to restrict the law only to (favour) women."

The new law provides judges with 16 different measures to choose from to protect a victim of violence. Victims can ask the judge to apply the measure that seems most beneficial to them, according to deputy Maria Lidia Sanchez, of the ruling party.

In a bid to secure approval for the bill, Sanchez managed to include a clause that guarantees "special protection in cases of violence between couples and where incestuous sexual abuse occurs". However, feminist groups argue that this application is too wide.

"There is a fear of legislating especially for women," says opposition deputy Mary Alban, who supports the feminist organisations' case to revise the bill.

Despite the fact that in June Costa Rica ratified the Inter-American Convention to Prevent, Sanction and Eradicate All Types of Violence Against Women, the new legislation does not contain the required penal, civil and administrative provisions to comply with this commitment.

Salazar considers the bill "inadequate" because it does not classify domestic violence as a crime and does not adequately protect victims.

"The bravery of the women who dare to report domestic abuse, despite the threats and dangers they face from partners, is sharply at odds with a legal process that victimises them once again," says Salazar.

Under the existing law, Maria's husband had been fined on several occasions for mistreating and battering her. Some 18 months ago, after yet another quarrel, he shot Maria dead and then committed suicide in front of their three children.

"Family violence is regulated but not forbidden. Our laws are full of misconceptions and do not offer real legal support to desperate women who report their cases," explains Rebeca Alvarado, who specialises in counseling battered women.

Many distraught and desperate women who see no way out of their daily torment attempt suicide or even try to kill the aggressor.

"He makes me feel hatred, bitterness. I feel such a strong impulse to kill him that I go into the kitchen and pray to God. I just wish he would die," says Zeidy.

Zeidy confesses that she has put up with all the abuse for the sake of her three children. Two months ago she was raped by her husband in front of her three children, and now, she mutters almost inaudibly, there is a fourth child on the way.

Isabel Sanchez

Armed Conflict ~ War Brings Increased Tension to Sri Lanka's East

Sri Lanka : The rumour spread down the platform where passengers had been waiting three hours for the train to Batticaloa to move. "The boys have blocked the tracks."

The 'boys', the Liberation Tigers of Tamil Eelam (LTTE), have been fighting the Sri Lankan army for 13 years to establish a separate Tamil homeland on the island, including Jaffna in the north and Batticaloa in the east.

Unlike the north however, Batticaloa has no dividing line; no - man's land separating the army and the LTTE. Here the Tamil and Muslim population are particularly vulnerable.

"People are afraid," says Monica, a local human rights activist in the town. "Even myself. When I hear a noise at night I move to a safer part of my room."

For their own safety, human rights activist no longer speak out for fear of retaliation from both the LTTE and Sinhala security forces.

Since the defeat of the LTTE on the Jaffna peninsula, fighting has increased in the east as the Tigers recapture areas, and the army launches new offensives which will increase Batticaloa's heavy burden of human loss.

It's estimated in local human rights statistics, that since 1989 between 15 and 25 thousand people have been killed, disappeared or extrajudicially executed by the army, police and the LTTE.

Since mid-1995, there has been an increase in civilian casualties and a distinct deterioration in observation of human rights in the district, again by both sides but particularly by Sinhala security forces.

Last year villagers were used by the army to clear land mines; and detentions, beatings and torture continue to be reported, according to Monica, along with disappearances.

The LTTE's threat of suicide bombers has increased the level of checks and body searches—particularly of women.

Still, the people of Batticaloa go about their everyday business within the army's circle of steel posts and checkpoints.

Daily shelling and fighting in the area surrounding Batticaloa continues and unofficial curfews have been imposed between 6 p.m and 6 a.m., creating acute tensions.

It's in the day to day lives of women where these tensions manifest clearest. They are the ones who have to shop and travel into town from rural areas, facing aggressive body searches from the army at several check points.

"Women suppress it, but sometimes they take (their frustrations) out by beating their children. They get irritated easily, and their whole mental balance is damaged," says Monica. Non-government organisation field workers have also reported an increase in domestic violence against women.

"There's not much law enforcement. People don't like to go to the police station which is militarised, and not part of the civil administration," says Monica. She also cites an increase in the number of unlicensed video shops showing pornographic films in villages in the district. "Women are dealing with home and the outside," says Jeyanthy, a project officer from Suriya Women's Development Centre (SWDC). SWDC conducts workshops for women on development, domestic violence, health, counselling, legal rights and the images of women in Tamil cinema. The emphasis of their programmes has changed from direct assistance to education.

"People need to find out their own needs, they have to think," says Jeyanthy.

SWDC also helps the YMCA register marriages in the villages so if a woman is widowed, she can collect the government's US $1,000 compensation. Since 1990 five to six thousand women have become widows in Batticaloa district.

"They are tied to the sea or the land. They don't run away, they don't have somewhere else to live when the trouble starts. They are poor," says Monica.

In a town where violence and ethnic identity have gouged deep scars, a woman whose motivation is non-violence is an anomaly.

Amara Hapuarachchi works with torture victims and families of detainees. She has been working and living in Batticaloa since 1993. She is one of only a handful of Sinhalese, the country's majority ethnic community, living in the Tamil district.

"I think it's possibly my own search for meaning, a deeper identity, not just an identity given by the fact that you are born into a Sinhala speaking family and you happen to have this religion, and you are from this town," says Hapuarachchi.

Given the town's history it is not surprising that there are those who think the idea of non-violence is impossible. "There are people who say it won't work. But although they don't intellectually agree with it, somewhere in them they are willing to give it a try," says Hapuarachchi.

People have spoken more out of anger than a feeling of resistance, and not in an organised manner. After the LTTE attack on a police station December 1995, 23 civilians were killed. People spoke of the high civilian traffic at that time of day. 'Why can't they do it at night?', they asked.

While the people are generally afraid of the LTTE and occasionally express their anger, their mistrust and anger toward the Sinhalese security forces is far greater.

"Most of the people we go to meet in the military, the top rank, say you have to win the hearts and minds of the people," says Hapuarachchi. "But sometimes an incident takes place, a colleague has been killed and you are not able to think rationally so you take your anger out on an innocent civilian."

For those who speak out against the army and police excesses, there is the uncertainty as to how much support the government, far away in Colombo, will give them.

"Earlier we felt we were safe on one side at least. But now that hope is shattered. We have a bitter feeling," says Monica.

President Chandrika Kumaratunga won 83 percent of the vote in the east during the presidential election. But with abuses increasing, the government is fast losing its support, including those who spoke of an end to the conflict.

"Now," says Monica, "in the perspective of the LTTE and the Tamil psyche, people who are talking peace are talking the same language as the government. The government has appropriated our language."

A sense of isolation and alienation spikes Monica's words as she explains why Batticaloa doesn't receive the assistance needed.

"There's a great need for relief work in the north, but there is a big problem here also. It's a hidden problem," she says. "Because there's no influx of refugees, there's nothing for a video camera.

It's not a spectacular thing, but people think they're not being cared for."

In this atmosphere, political solutions to the ethnic conflict have little meaning. "The villagers hardly talk about it. They don't even want to consider it because the LTTE has not considered it," says Hapuarachchi.

The overwhelming sense of the people in the district is to get on with their lives, quietly adapting to their circumstances.

"You get women who have only lived in Batticaloa, sometimes not even in the town of Batticaloa, who are willing to take the risks when their sons are in detention in Colombo. To take that journey.

You get women who seem timid taking very bold steps."

With military activity increasing in the area as the army regains ground, that boldness will need to hold fast for some time to come.

Melissa Butcher

Armed Conflict ~ The War Must Stop

Sudan : Last month five East African heads of state met in the Kenyan capital Nairobi, to share their concern and express the need to end the 11-year-old civil war in southern Sudan.

The Nairobi talks were part of a series of peace talks that have taken place since 1987 in various African capitals. But the war is yet to end.

Civil war in southern Sudan started in 1955 and continued till 1972 when a peace agreement was reached. But in 1983, internal and external factors sparked it off again leading to continued conflict between government troops, the rebel army and tribal militias.

The recent talks were slightly different. Initiated by the Inter-Governmental Authority for Drought and Desertification, they mainly focussed on the urgency of delivering relief aid to the war-affected people.

The consequences of war have been drastic, heightened as they are by drought and desertification in the region. Increasing costs of war and decreasing productivity have led to virtual disintegration, limiting social services and driving millions into poverty.

Besides the suffering of the displaced who unwittingly add to the burden of their host countries, in the war zones of southern Sudan, hospitals, clinics, schools and all other services are either curtailed or closed. Commercial activities and communications are disrupted and therefore food security systems do not work.

In the region, over 900 primary schools, 148 intermediate schools and 35 secondary schools have shut down. The University of Juba – the only university in the south—has shifted to Khartoum.

Fleeing rapidly deteriorating conditions, approximately half a million Sudanese sought refuge in neighbouring countries. Three and a half million headed for major cities in southern and northern Sudan, with the majority coming to Khartoum.

Inevitably, the impact of war on women and children has been devasting. Those who survived the war were forced to flee leaving behind everything they possessed. Hundreds of thousands were rendered homeless, children were orphaned and the elderly became totally vulnerable, without families to care for them.

"Women have witnessed the death of their children, husbands and relatives. And children have experienced the shocking death of parents," says Alawia Farrag, a leader from southern Sudan.

As a deputy in the Transitional National Council (the parliament), Farrag is among those who continuously campaign with politicians and in the media, calling for peace in the region.

It is easy to see why. According to a study by reseacher Dr. Samia Al Hadi, "The direct impact of war is not only on health, education and economic conditions, but ...(on aspects related to) cultural uprooting."

Moving into a different social environment has meant a loss of people's cultural symbols, identity and familiar patterns of behaviour. Psychological disturbances are obvious among many of these women. Algore Malaik from the Dinka tribe of southern Sudan is just one example.

Malaik's husband joined the rebels and died in the bush. She moved north to Khartoum with three children. One of them died during the long journey. Her 9-year-old she says "just disappeared in this city, I don't know where." Only her three-year-old remains with her. Malaik is stunned into a numbness that she cannot emerge from.

Adding to the trauma of these women is the lack of appropriate employment. Women are moving to an environment where their acquired skills are irrelevent. Consequently, they are forced into domestic chores.

Statistics provided by the National Relief Organisation point to the very fundamental changes among the women from the south.

In their homeland, 40 percent of women were farmers, 30 percent herders, 10 percent fisherwomen, 15 percent craftswomen and 5 percent did other jobs. After displacement, 60 percent work as domestics, 20 percent are vendors, 5 percent factory workers, 3 percent take to begging on the streets and 2 percent do other work.

Children who once helped their parents herd cattle and farm, now wash cars, sell cigarettes and do marginal jobs in markets.

Increasingly, kidnapping of children is reported. It is said that they are taken by rebel forces who force them to fight. Many of them die in the bush from fatigue, hunger and disease.

Sudan has already brought to the notice of the international community the fact that 30,000 children have been kidnapped from their families in the south.

During the last months of 1993, the United Nations High Commissioner for Refugees (UNHCR) transported 98 Sudanese children to Ugandian capital Kampala. They had returned from Cuba where they had undergone military training. The eldest of them was 19 years old while the youngest was only 11 years old. They had been sent for training three years ago.

The need for quick and effective action is all too clear. The director of planning and operations at the National Commission for Relief and Rehabilitation assures that they plan to establish a number of institutions to cater for widows, orphans and those psychologically affected by the civil war.

Steps are also being taken to resume production through projects located in areas not directly affected by the war.

For instance, many schools for displaced students at the camps around Khartoum and other cities have started. Women in displaced camps are undergoing vocational education and efforts are on to establish small projects enabling family units to continue their productive role.

Refugees are also trickling back to lands that are recaptured by the government army. Most of them receive some means of agricutural production, financial subsidies and food items.

The Peace and Development Foundation which was established to rehabilitate war-affected people, has redistributed land in the Upper Nile region for returnees to begin agriculture. And many national and international organisations like Unicef, the Red Cross and UNDP have resumed their relief activities.

Still, recurring conflict continues to hinder relief aid. Clearly, it's imperative that all sides concerned come together to give peace a chance. There is too much at stake for Sudan's people—and especially for Sudan's women and children—if this does not happen.

Neimat Bilal

Economy ~ Coastal Women Find Their Worth

Philippines : On the morning you will see her spreading fish on bamboo slats to dry in the sun. In the afternoon, you will find her in the town market selling the dried fish.

Her sunburnt, wrinkled face and skin belie her real age of 29. Virginia Castillo looks like 40. But in her bright eyes, you can read the new-found pride in being able to earn money all her own.

Nearby is a barn-like structure where Castillo cleans and salts fish in large aluminium basins. Some of her neighbours, too, are in the same business. Bamboo slats propped by crudely cut wood in their front yards are full of drying fish.

Castillo is one of the 1,049 beneficiaries of a programme of the United Nations Fund for Population Activities (UNFPA). The programme is being undertaken in the Pangasinan area of the Central Luzon province and in Capiz in Visayas province. It aims to improve the status of women in small-scale fishing in the Philippines.

Castillo lives in village Maniboc in Central Luzon, some 200 kilometres north of Manila. Here 15 women availed of the loan component of the programme, enabling them to start small businesses of their own such as fish vending and tinapa (smoked fish) making.

Launched three years ago, the programme aims to financially empower women who were housewives before. It also tries to promote family planning among them. In Pangasinan, 48 barangays (villages) have been reached by the programme.

Philippine rural women traditionally manage the family budget, with money mainly provided by the husband and sometimes by the wife.

Before joining the programme, project members could decide how much to spend on food and household items but they did not have equal say in the purchase of major assets. With access to independent income, the situation started to change.

Norma Manuel, a beneficiary who used her loan for tinapa-making, said: "Although I was managing the family budget, I couldn't freely buy things for myself because I didn't have my own income. It was so constricting."

Increased contributions to the family budget provided the women a say in family economic decisions. Earlier Emma Tiangson needed her husband's permission to give extra money to their son. "Now I can give without asking," she said.

Earning income means also earning the husband's respect. Norma Orjeda commented that before the project her husband treated her as a 'household good'. "After being selected president of a women's group, I conduct meetings and my husband respects me."

Though their businesses have not made them rich, they have definitely improved their status. The UNFPA programme has also developed their confidence to join community actions. Those who admitted to being shy and ignorant before are now involved in village affairs. A group even collected signatures on a petition demanding the prohibition of dynamite fishing near their village.

Luz Muego, head of the provincial population office which spearheads the project in Pangasinan, said the opportunity to earn and invest in children has changed the women's attitude towards family planning.

"The increasing cost of raising a family and educating children are their major reasons for wanting fewer children," she said.

Younger women cited the experiences of older group members with many children. A member who has six children said that if she had fewer she could have sent all of them to college.

In rural Filipino society, women are usually seen by husbands as childbearers and caretakers of their needs. They are often not consulted regarding the number of children they will have.

Lala de Guzman, at 29, has three children below the age of three. Asked how she convinced her husband to allow her to have an Intra Uterine Device (IUD) inserted, she simply said: "I insisted."

While the project has succeeded in financially empowering the beneficiaries, it still has to overcome problems such as lack of accessible family planning services. But according to Muego, the situation is being corrected by assigning some women members to coordinate with Rural Health Units in their towns to get supplies of pills and condoms.

Before the programme was launched three years ago, Castillo tended a "sari-sari" (variety) store whose capital she borrowed from loan sharks. Although a secretarial graduate, she was not able to find employment in this country where few of the 800,000 who graduate from college annually are absorbed by the labour market. Her husband, also an unemployed graduate, supported the family by buying and selling bagoong (salted fish sauce), the main industry in the area.

Castillo's income from the sari-sari store could hardly meet the 20 percent interest on her loan. Although they had two children, they could not afford a house of their own, staying instead with her parents-in-law.

When the UNFPA programme was launched in 1991, Castillo immediately joined. From then on, life looked brighter. She used her loan of US $ 452.80 to buy fish from Bulacan which she dried and marketed in the town for US$ 1.50 a kilo. Thrice a week, she goes to Bulacan, 150 km away, to buy a jeep-load of fresh fish to supply to her co-members.

What is ironic is that the barangay where she lives is only a few steps from the sea. She has to buy fish from another province as, "there is no more fish in Lingayen Gulf because of blast fishing".

Last year, Castillo and her husband were able to build a three-by-four metre house of bamboo and wood. She is even thinking of buying a black and white TV set "for the children". But she has not saved enough yet and does not want to dip into her capital.

The family planning aspect of the UNFPA programme, however, has not hit home yet with Castillo. Since the programme was launched, she has had three more children. Now she has five, which is still considered few in rural areas where a family usually has eight children.

Castillo said she tried pills but her abdomen and back "ached terribly." She is finding, through a population worker, a family planning method that will suit her.

Just at that moment, Castillo's four-month-old woke up and wailed her lungs out for her mother, bringing an end to her mother's confidences.

Yolanda Sotelo-Fuertes

Economy ~ Rural Women Build a Bank

Sri Lanka : The Indian Ocean laps the shore of Hambantota at the southernmost tip of Sri Lanka. This is a sprawling district with a climate so harsh that it does not rain for years at a stretch. The ground is unyielding and vegetation is scarce.

Most rural folk here live below the poverty line. They subsist on Janasaviya, the government's poverty alleviation scheme which provides each family unit earning less than Sri Lankan Rs.1,200 a month (US$ 25) with a basket of essential foodstuffs and a cash stipend of Rs 450 (US$ 9) per month.

The recipients are expected to save the money and start a self-employment venture when the assistance ends in two years.

Janasaviya expects the families to be self-supporting by then.

The cash stipend all too often ends up in food or in drinks for the men or to repay loans. Islandwide, the assistance has been used effectively by few and Hambantota was no different. Not till a handful of women got together and pooled the money to put it to good use.

"They wanted to outwit the moneylender who charges exorbitant interest," explains G.A. Premalatha, one of the initial group. The money grew till they had to find a way of using it effectively. Advice came from the government agent, M.G. Mithraratne, who explained to them the mechanics of rural banking.

"This was his brainchild. Now we know it is a modified version of the Grameen Bank of Bangladesh," says Chitrani Amarakone, an enthusiastic farmer.

A group of five women formed a Kantha Samithi (Women's Society) and others followed suit. Today 26 Samithis have affiliated themselves into the Women's Development Foundation, with its own modest office and staff—all women.

The Foundation has opened a Janashakti Bank for each of the 48 villages. The word Janashakti means people's empowerment. But the scheme is in every sense a woman's venture—and loans are given only to women, at minimal interest.

"It is a bank with a human face. Though only four years old, the scheme is the real achievement of the women. They all come from the poorest of the poor, Janasaviya beneficiaries, food stamp holders, the landless, often stricken by drought, assailed by inadequate nutrition and debilitating levels of health. These women have stoutly built up these institutions by placing one 10-rupee note over another, as it were," says Mallika Wanigasundera, journalist and development worker.

With loans only a short walk to the village bank, women have an amazing self-confidence. They tell you proudly that all credit goes to the Government Agent who is their guide, philosopher and friend but that the banks belong to them!

The few women trained to handle the work of the Foundation come smartly clad in saris, riding scooters. They are used to visitors, from other districts and abroad, who come almost weekly to see how Janashakti works.

At the bank in Nonagama, two women manage the work. The bank is a small room, part of a village house. There are two desks, three chairs and a steel cupboard. A big sign outside proclaims the bank.

"Every village has an office like this," explains Premalatha who acts as a liaison officer. "The two women who manage the bank are paid a stipend by the Foundation."

"Now whenever we want a loan we walk to the bank. No bus trips and no trips to moneylenders," smiles Seela Gamage, who has brought Rs.200 and her passbook to repay the monthly instalment on her loan.

"We have modified the Grameen system to suit us...ours is a system for women to get a loan for any economic activity while subsisting on the Janasaviya allowance. It has worked very well," explains K.A.Gnanawathie who works in the bank.

The women can now turn their backs on mainline banks and the moneylender who charges 240 percent per year.

"The Bank's aim is to combat the heavy indebtedness of the people of Hambantota and stimulate saving. These women have skills and just need small financial support to get on their feet," says Mithraratne.

We see for ourselves Atiya Edirisuirya's house with red brick walls and verandah, standing bang against the mud hut she lived in just a year ago. She and her husband Wimal came to Hambantota one night with their three small children. They were fleeing Tamil militants who were killing Sinhala villagers in Trincomalee district.

The family that gave them shelter took them to the Janashakti Bank for an emergency loan of Rs.5,000 (US$ 100) to settle down and another Rs.500 to start goat rearing.

"We had nothing when we came here. Now we owe the bank quite a lot but we have some poultry and paddy in addition to the goats and can pay back the loan," says Edirisuirya looking at her new house built with a Janashakti loan, tears glistening in her eyes.

Chitrani Amarakone lives by a muddy stream that provides a more or less steady supply of water for her home garden. She has a flourishing two-acre plot.

"My husband does all the work on the plot which brings us enough money to live on. With the Janasaviya assistance I pay the loan installments and the electricity bill," says Amarakone, whose home now has electricity—something that was a dream four years back.

The story of Seela and Ranjit is not such a happy one. They married when both were 16 and joined his parents' fishing venture. But with three children to feed, Seela is among the four percent to have defaulted on loans. "The fishing nets were stolen many times and they couldn't find money for fuel for the boats," explains Ranjit's father.

There is also C.Nonahamy whose family has been beset by illness. Her husband died and her elder son went missing after militant attacks. She has no means of paying back.

"We look carefully and sympathetically at these few instances and see what we can do to help them," says Mithraratne. "We will never force payments," he adds.

The bank workers are sturdy cyclists, holders of A-levels who walk a couple of miles in the morning to fetch water and cook the morning meal before they come to the Foundation office in the city, or to the village banks. They are the women who move the wheels to give loans to poor women just like them.

"They are our real change agents," says R.Weerasinghe, Deputy Director, Planning. Each of them keeps the accounts in line, supervises five banks, sorts out ledgers and strengthens the financial structure of the few weaker banks.

"Women take the loans but the benefits pass on to the whole family. Only the poor can become constituents, not the affluent. Trust is their only security and teams of five guarantee each others' loans," explains Priyanthi Ranjani, President of the Foundation.

The rationale of the Janashakti Banks is to develop a viable credit culture based on self-reliance, and wean people away from dependence on subsidies and handouts.

As Premalatha says, "The empowerment of women is the greatest byproduct. They have become self-confident, speak for their families, discuss problems openly and when necessary stand up to husbands and fathers."

Vijita Fernando

Decision-Making ~ Running Away From Politics

Czech Republic: Writer and former dissident Eda Kriseova made heads turn in 1989 when newly elect President Vaclav Havel—of the formerly communist Czechoslovakia—appointed her as his adviser. His choice made her one of the highest ranking women in the government.

Then in 1992, when it seemed the Czech and Slovak Republics were destined to split, heads swivelled again as Kriseova, a 55-year-old mother of two, stepped down from Havel's side after three short years in politics and returned to writing.

Since the political shift from communism to democracy took place in the Czech Republic seven years ago, the number of women in public office has dropped. With the third free general elections taking place from May 31 to June 1, and over 10 parties competing to get their candidates in parliament, the question on peoples' minds today is, 'Will there be any women?' And if not 'Why?'

In 1989, there were 28 Czech women deputies in parliament, from a total of 200, and one woman minister. This year, the number of women deputies stands at 19 and there are no ministers.

"Today they've disappeared," says Petra Jedlickova, at the Gender Studies Center in Prague. "I'm not sure why. Maybe they're oppressed or pushed down. Maybe they don't want to (have high government positions)."

During and after the Velvet Revolution (when the Czechs took their country back from the USSR), Marie Cermakova, president of the Gender Studies Foundation says women were equally represented in civic and non-political movements, contributing to the establishment of the new democratic structures.

"It was not until the lists of candidates for the first post-89 elections were composed that women lost their positions, mainly because they were placed in the non-electable positions on these lists," she says.

The authors of the list gave men a preference she says, "believing that men were more competent and therefore more electable. Women were effectively removed from politics."

The low percentage of women in Czech politics, however, might have reasons rooted deeper than time. Within their family, Czech women don't receive much support to enter public life.

"In the public (sphere), women accept their complimentary role to the position of men," says Milena Cerna, who served as an adviser to the Ministry of Education from 1990 to 1993. "They don't have enough self-confidence to see that their opinion is very valuable in society."

Even when Czech women do enter politics, they seem to stick to health and social care issues, which are considered "women's issues." Cerna, for one, tried to bring a new health education curriculum to Czech schools, which had to be approved by a committee of 12 men.

But she too found the political arena an undesirable place. Today she is the executive director of the Good Will Foundation, which does outreach and nonprofit work in the Czech Republic.

Jirina Siklova, founder of the Gender Studies Center and a sociology professor at Charles University, says many women prefer grassroots activities to politics. Most Czech women, she says, simply aren't interested in "the extremist political attitudes, where there's a right wing and a left wing and nothing in between."

"While Czech women may claim to hold an aversion to politics in general, their proclaimed attitudes don't always correspond with their behaviour," says Cermakova, a senior researcher in the Sociological Institute of the Czech Academy of Sciences.

Cermakova feels that women tend to choose careers in education, health care and administration because this is "where women gained dominance during the socialist regime".

Cerna agrees that women follow career paths leading to jobs in teaching and social work. "I'm very unsatisfied with the position of women in this society because they're very passive. This society is so strongly a male society. Contributing to this is the fact that women are considered complementary to men without any influence on economics," she says.

Asked if Czech male politicians would support more women in government, Cerna says, "Men don't even think about this. They'd like to see more women in mini skirts, bringing coffee."

"Women continue to be subtly undervalued. It is very difficult to reform the unequal gender relations confirmed by generations in five years," adds Cermakova.

But a recent survey indicates times could be changing. A public poll taken by the Czech Research Institute of Public Opinion in 1991 and again in 1995, shows that Czechs are becoming more open to women in public office.

The survey, in which 1,008 Czechs over the age of 15 were questioned, reveals that 81 percent of the woman and 70 percent of the men said it would be beneficial to have more women in public life. Those interviewed said they valued different characteristics in men and women in top political positions. For example, men are considered to be decisive, authoritative, and able to manage well and make good decisions. Whereas women are prized for their ability to resolve conflicts between people and for their perfectionism.

Despite what the survey may indicate, many women here still question how much has really changed when it comes to their status in politics.

"I think this is a macho society," says Kriseova. Speaking of her two years in Prague Castle as President Havel's adviser, she says that her male colleagues' compliments often sounded hollow. "She's right, but she's only a woman," Kriseova recalls them saying, or, "That's a good idea, even if she's a woman."

Rachel Sarah

Decision-Making ~ From Torture Victim to Minister

Ethiopia: Tall, elegant Tadelech Haile Michael, 43, heads Ethiopia's Women's Affairs Office and holds the rank of a minister in the Prime Minister's Office.

"I never imagined that life in prison would end up in such way, and that I would survive, let alone be a minister," confesses the former political detainee.

Tadelech is one of the survivors of a tough and heroic struggle against the fascist Dergue government, which comprised rebellious army officers who had abolished the previous monarchy, proclaimed the republic, suspended the constitution and dissolved parliament. All political and administrative functions had been taken up by the Armed Forces Coordination Committee, called the Dergue.

Tadelech lost her husband and many friends to the crusade against the Dergue. Today, she is a champion for the rights of her country's women.

Tadelech was born in Ethiopia's capital Addis Ababa. On completing high school, she was sent by her parents to Switzerland to pursue studies in social sciences. It is here that she met the renowned, progressive leader Berhane Meskel Redda, who would become her husband and change the course of her life.

"I met Berhane Meskel through a friend and somehow got involved in politics— always discussing the then land holding system, the question of nationalities, women's issues, etc," remembers Tadelech.

Meskel was a leader of the students' movement of the Haile Selassie University in the early 1970s. He was also a co-founder of the Ethiopian People's Revolutionary Party (EPRP), which opposed the Dergue's policies.

In September 1976, Tadelech returned to Ethiopia from Switzerland with her nine month-old daughter and began to work for a radio station. Meskel was then in hiding because the Dergue government wanted to kill him.

Tadelech recounts how the EPRP split and Meskel became leader of one splinter group. Meanwhile, she got into trouble when people realised she was the wife of a man wanted by the army. She left her child with her mother and went underground, joining her husband in Merhabiete Province, in Central Ethiopia.

Their objective was to agitate and mobilise the peasants in their struggle against the dictatorial regime. But mobilisation was not easy, and besides, the military government had stepped up its search.

"Although we were in the bush for two years and tried to reorganise ourselves under the leadership of Berhane, to promote the cause of justice and democracy, the situation was not favourable and we fell into the hands of the brutal enemy," says Tadelech.

It was in February 1979 that Tadelech and some comrades were apprehended, while on a mission in the Wello region in North Eastern Ethiopia. A few months later, Meskel too was captured in an exchange of fire with the army.

Tadelech is bitter about the lack of respect for human rights shown by the government. Her husband was killed because he refused to abandon his principles and bow down before the dictatorial regime.

"The rest of us were mercilessly tortured with the motive of exposing our members and sympathisers and making us give up our cause. We persistently resisted whatever was done to us, and therefore were condemned to death," she says.

At that time, Tadelech was pregnant with her third daughter.

"To my surprise, when they realised that I was expecting, they stopped beating me up. They were also hesitant to kill me. I survived and delivered my child in prison," recounts Tadelech.

The prisoners keenly followed the news of military victories of the EPRDF and its advance towards the capital, says Tadelech. When they realised that the government was losing, they were afraid they would be exterminated.

To their relief, on the eve of the EPRDF's take over of Addis Ababa, on 7 May 1991, all the prisoners were released. "Had this not been the case, I would have been dead by now or be serving life-long imprisonment," says the minister.

With the establishment of the Transitional Government of Ethiopia (TGE), democracy was set into motion. The TGE was recruiting progressive thinkers to help in the task of recons-tructing the nation, and Tadelech was assigned charge of women's affairs.

Tadelech says that it was extremely difficult in the beginning to recruit experts, to get organised and start the actual work, with special attention to drafting a women's policy.

Tadelech was promoted to the rank of a minister in March 1993. She finalised the National Policy on Ethiopian Women and launched it in September of the same year.

The policy is considered the basis for the improvement of the living and working conditions of Ethiopian women. It promises to liberate them economically, socially and politically, eliminating legal, cultural, traditional and attitudinal obstacles to their progress.

Over 85 percent of Ethiopians are rural and earn a living from subsistence farming. Most rural women work 13 to 18 hours a day within the household and in the farms.

Tadelech points out that the national policy is being implemented mainly by the Women's Affairs Office in the Prime Minister's office. But to avoid the marginalisation of women's organisations and issues, she says, they have also established 14 women's affairs departments in different ministries and commissions, and 10 women's affairs bureaux in regional governments, with their respective offices at lower levels.

"It's a great honour to be assigned this post. It's a pleasure to work for the betterment of the Ethiopian people, especially women, who suffered untold oppression and exploitation during the previous regimes," says Tadelech.

She says her office has been empowering women to actively participate in Ethiopia's national reconstruction, to take up leadership posts, and to be involved in decision making at all levels. For instance, last May, 12 women were elected as representatives in the federal government, and another 79 in the regional governments.

Tadelech's colleagues recognise the value of her work. In August 1995, when there was a reshuffle following the formulation of the Federal Democratic Republic of Ethiopia (FDRE), Tadelech retained her post.

"I'm delighted to see that my dreams have come true—dreams of peace, justice and democracy prevailing in Ethiopia," says Tadelech.

Hadera Tesfay

Decision-Making ~ One Woman's Campaign for Democracy

Cambodia : Doctor, politician, diplomat and social worker rolled into one. That is Kek Galabru, president of a Cambodian NGO that is striving to bring peace and democracy to the troubled nation.

Galabru, who heads LICHADO (in English the Cambodian League for Promotion and Defense of Human Rights), sees three steps to bringing full democracy to the people of Cambodia. The first and second, holding free elections and creating a democratic Constitution, have been accomplished.

The third, and most time-consuming task, she says, will be educating the public to understand and respect the new system. That is where LICHADO comes in, with its wide array of educational projects.

Galabru grew up in the thick of the political turmoil which plagued Cambodia in the 1950s and '60s, with her father serving as a minister in the government and eventually as general secretary of the executive council, and her mother a member of parliament.

As a child she never had ambitions to go into politics. At the age of seven I nearly died of malaria while my father was posted in one of the provinces," she said, " I decided then I would become a doctor and help people in the provinces."

After attending medical school in France, Galabru returned to Cambodia and worked in a Russian hospital. She married a Frenchman, then his country's ambassador to Cambodia. In 1970, the couple left Cambodia and moved to Canada, Brazil, Angola, and eventually France.

"When I left Cambodia," she said, "I wanted to raise awareness of human rights connected to health care. But then there was war and it was difficult to start anything. So I set up an NGO in France to bring medical equipment to Cambodia." In 1989-90, she twice organised airlifts of medical equipment to her war-torn country.

Galabru and her husband were instrumental in setting up the first meeting between Hun Sen, then leader of the Vietnamese installed government in Cambodia, and Prince Rannaridh, now prime minister of the Royal

Cambodian Government. This meeting led to a conference between King Norodum Sihanouk and Hun Sen, which eventually led to the Paris Peace Accord in October 1991.

"I am very proud of that," said Galabru with a smile. "I never declared my role to a newspaper because my husband and I want to work with our hearts. We don't want to make these efforts just for show. It is really my best wish to get peace for Cambodia."

After the peace accord was signed, Galabru returned to Cambodia to establish an NGO to teach human rights. After waiting six months she received permission in March 1992 to set up LICHADO, primarily to help the UN Transitional Authority in Cambodia (UNTAC) hold fair elections.

"We played an important role with UNTAC in the process of national elections. We had 26 offices in 21 provinces, funded by the then European Community. We sent almost 900 people as national observers and others were trained by UNTAC to be defenders."

Problems arose and complaints were made because certain villages were deemed too dangerous to monitor, but UNTAC eventually went in, "and we went with them" said Galabru.

LICHADO's greatest contribution to the voting process was its publication of a small purple voting manual, written in Khmer and illustrated with cartoons for the illiterate, explaining the electoral process. A million copies were printed and distributed.

A subsquent publication, 'The Voice of Cambodia', discussed the rights of women and provided information about hygiene and nutrition.

Now that elections are over and the UN has largely pulled out, LICHADO continues its quest to educate the people. "My organisation focusses on human rights," said Galabru "but there is always a focus on health care."

For example a group of four women are currently travelling throughout Cambodia's 11 provinces to hold informative sessions on women's rights, hygeine, and family planning.

LICHADO does not have the funding to distribute birth control or ensure it is administered properly, but,"we start talking to them to show them there is a method for birth control, just to give them the idea that they have options for family planning," Galabru explained. The group also distributes a cartoon style manual to teach women hygiene in raising children.

Besides, they also hold regular lessons about the Constitution, explaining to people, the rights that have been promised to them.

In October 1993, Tet Vichet, a general in the government army, asked LICHADO to teach the almost 2000 Khmer rouge defectors about democracy and human rights. And the group recently received permission from the Ministry of Education to hold similar courses for high school students.

The Minister for Religion and Culture recently suggested a training session for Buddhist monks so that they can pass on the message to their followers. He describes democracy and Buddhism as "two wings of the same bird."

Now under production is a booklet which explains how the government and justice system work and illustrates the promises of the Constitution, including freedom of speech and religious orientation and the right to elementary and secondary education.

Other endeavours include a UN-guided training programme for police, a fund raising project for university students, and a health care service for prisoners at Phnom Penh's five prisons.

As if overseeing these projects were not enough to keep her busy. Galabru is also an adviser to Prince Rannaridh, Minister of Foreign Affairs, on diplomatic and international issues. She said modestly: "I make reports, stay in contact with diplomats and push France to continue helping Cambodia."

Galabru also hosts a television talk show, "Pinis Pinus" (This and That), which discusses social, political, economic and cultural issues such as freedom of the press, the threat of AIDS, and relations with neighbouring nations.

Sitting in her office, wearing her signature Khmer style dress, she can barely get through a sentence without being interrupted by one of her four western workers and almost 30 Khmer teachers. What gives Galabru the energy for all of these projects? "It is my dream," she says, "to bring peace to Cambodia.

Gretchen Peters

Human Rights ~ Awarded for Fighting Rape

India : Frail and emaciated, she has been rendered speechless by an attack of typhoid. But after two long years, Bhanwari Bai's cry for justice is being heard as she prepares to receive the Neerja Mishra Award for Exemplary Courage and Devotion shown by Women on Duty.

"The award is the victory of all my colleagues and women activists," says Bhanwari Bai in a feeble voice. She will probably use the award amount for the benefit of women seeking justice like her, but at the moment she is non-committal. "I will have to discuss it with my sisters," she says.

Economic and social boycott and constant threats have not diminished the zeal of this unlettered 42-year-old Sathin (change agent), employed in the Rajasthan Government's much acclaimed Women's Development Programme (WDP), who was gangraped two years ago.

"I was working for the Government against child marriage. What reward did I get? I was raped," she says with tear-filled eyes.

In 1992, the State Government decided to observe the two weeks before Akha Teej (a day when hundreds of children tie the marital knot in Rajasthan) as an anti-child marriage fortnight. The District Collector directed the Sathins to prepare a list of those who were going to perform child marriages on the auspicious day.

In Bhateri village near Jaipur, the list included the name of Ram Karan Gujar, a ward panch. Bhanwari Bai had tried to dissuade him and other members of the community from conducting child marriages.

On May 5, the police stopped the wedding of Ram Karan's one-year-old daughter. The Gujars blamed Bhanwari Bai for this and swore revenge.

She was totally isolated. The Gujar community stopped selling her milk and refused to buy her pots. Even the women of Bhateri were not prepared to support her. She was expelled from the Kumhar Jati Panchayat. Her father-in-law and brother-in-law boycotted the family. Mukesh, her teenaged son, found that classsmates would not talk to him.

Worse, on September 22, 1992, Ram Karan, Ram Sukh, Badri, Gyarsa (all Gujars) and Shravan Sharma allegedly attacked Bhanwari and her husband Mohan Lal while they were working in the fields. Mohan Lal was beaten up. Bhanwari was allegedly gangraped by Badri and Gyarsa while Ram Sukh Gujar held her down.

Even a crime as heinous as rape did not deter her. The next morning she and her husband rushed to Patan village and related their story to Sathin Krishna.

Krishna, together with another worker Rasila Sharma, accompanied them to Bassi to register a complaint. Here began a long fight for justice, and further humiliation in the process by the Police, medical and judicial departments.

Deputy Superintendent of Police Rajendra Joshi lodged the FIR after much reluctance, saying Bhanwari Bai was making false allegations because of personal animosity. He even asked her if she knew the meaning of rape.

The doctor at the Primary Health Centre refused to examine her and referred her to a Jaipur hospital, with a slip requesting that she be checked for her age—there was no suggestion of a rape examnation.

In rape, examination delayed is evidence destroyed, but she could only get a medical examination 48 hours after the crime. This, when doctors know that rape is a medical emergency where the victim may require urgent treatment. In India, rape still has the lowest conviction rate as the guilty always gets the benefit of doubt during investigation.

On October 10, members of the National Commission for Women, which has the powers of a civil court, visited Bhateri. They condemned the police behaviour and concluded there had been a major attempt to tamper with evidence.

The Sathins of WDP and other women activists organised a rally to express their anger. On October 22, 1992 some 2,000 women marched through Jaipur. The rally exposed the enormity of the obstacles facing women who want to pursue a case of rape. It questioned the seriousness of the Government's intention to achieve gender equality. Women workers within development programmes are often victims of the same oppression they are trying to fight.

The failure of the state to take action on behalf of Bhanwari Bai, particularly when it has been using women like her to pursue its policies, reveals its duplicity. It purports to promote women's rights, without facing the consequences that such change provokes.

Bhanwari Bai ran from pillar to post, including a trip to Delhi and a meeting with the CBI chief, to get justice. When the villagers got an inkling that she might win the case, they approached her for a compromise.

It took one year for the chargesheet to be filed. Gyarsa was arrested in November last while the other four culprits 'absconded' till December 17, 1993, often in the protection of politician and community leaders. Ram Sukh and Shravan were granted bail in April 1994, while Badri and Gyarsa are still in custody.

Things were really hard for Bhanwari Bai and her family. Her husband, who earned some money as a rickshaw-puller in Jaipur, was compelled to stay at home to protect her. They survived on meagre earnings from their one-acre plot and Rs 10,000 granted from the Prime Minister's relief fund. The Sathins also raised money for her.

Today the dust has settled over Bhateri and a lull prevails as the prime accused are still in jail. Bhanwari Bai is determined to fight the battle till the end and ensure that the court sends those bailed out back to prison. "People are again talking to me except the culprit's families for whom I don't care anyway," she adds.

Phoolchand, a resident from a nearby village, observes, "At least now the villagers admit that Bhanwari belongs to Bhateri. Two years ago they said that they didn't know such a person."

This, when Bhanwari Bai had been working for the WDP since 1985 and had the reputation of a committed worker. She had taken up issues relating to land, water, the public distribution system, literacy, health and payment of minimum wages at famine relief works. In 1987, she was the first to pursue a case of attempted rape. The accused admitted his crime in front of the entire village and sought pardon from the victim.

Sexual violence is a time tested technique for beating women into submission and the Sathins want this ugly truth acknowledged publicly at a policy level.

In this case the Sathin was working at the instance of the state. The state trained her to do it. The state even trained her on how to respond to rape. But the state neglected to train her against its own ignorance, incompetence and negligence in giving her redress when she herself was raped for performing the state's work.

Bhanwari Bai's is one of those rare rape cases where there are two credible witnesses to the crime, she and her husband. What more evidence does the state require to prosecute the rapists?

As television crews move their spotlights to Bhanwari Bai and arrive in Jaipur, local women activists wait for the next hearing of the case, which was scheduled for September 21 but postponed as the judge was taken ill.

Neena Bhandari

Human Rights ~ A Writer Forbidden to Read

Israel: How much courage does it take for a woman to walk out after 10 pregnancies and 20 years of marriage? Yehudith Rotem knows. A decade ago, after a difficult and suffocating marriage, she divorced her husband. She could not have known at the time what she would become: a successful journalist, publisher, ghost writer and author.

In her new book 'Ahot Rehoka' (Distant Sister), published earlier this year by the Steimatsky press, Rotem returns to her earlier life and the 'haredi' society in which she lived with her husband. The haredi world forms part of the ultra-conservative community of Jews scattered around Israel.

Haredi scholar-husbands spend their time studying the Torah and the Talmud, the Jewish holy books, while their wives toil both in and outside the house to support the family. Since devoting themselves to study will reward the men with eternal life in heaven, the women are supposed to see themselves as partners, and therefore not feel exploited.

Haredi communities follow a circumscribed lifestyle that includes strict observance of religious rituals, arranged marriages and large families. Followers live in separate neighbourhoods and dress in traditional clothing.

In 'Ahot Rehoka,' Rotem reveals that haredi men maintain their dominance partly by forbidding their wives to read. All orthodox Jews revere the written word, and fear human susceptibility to improper books. The haredi attitude to secular texts is ambivalent, ranging from the suspicious to the openly hostile. For haredi wives, reading books on the sly is a private form of rebellion, to which only the most tolerant husbands turn a blind eye.

Born of Hungarian parents who came to Israel because of the Holocaust, Rotem was brought up in an orthodox but not haredi household. She entered the latter after a semi-arranged marriage. A voracious reader since her childhood, she soon found it difficult to accept her husband's assumption that the intellectual life is only for men. "How can you compare your studies to my studies?" he once asked. He forbade Rotem to write, or to attend the university. All the reading was to be done by him, and him alone.

Today Yehudith Rotem lives in an apartment lined with books and journals. Some are in English; the majority in Hebrew. Interspersed are the photographs of her seven living children. Rotem enjoyed all her pregnancies and the nurturing of her children because that was the only form of creativity allowed her.

However, she says emphatically, "The fire of the library that burned in my heart could not be quenched. All the water with which I scrubbed the floors, did the dishes and washed the laundry couldn't put it out."

'Ahot Rehoka' is the work of an insider and is based on interviews with at least 40 women, all contacted through word of mouth. Rotem did not advertise in newspapers for fear of rabbis who would have forbidden haredi women to speak to her.

Several women refused to talk anyway because they were afraid of their husbands. Those who finally agreed to speak are perhaps more broad-minded than the majority who refused to be interviewed. They admit quite candidly that while for them their lifestyle is a burden, for the women who really believe in it the haredi life is a religious mission.

Many of Rotem's observations regarding haredi communities apply to orthodox Jewish communities everywhere. When masses of men study rather than work, the burden of both earning and nurturing falls on the woman.

In a brief but moving chapter, Rotem describes the plight of an Israeli woman who enters a hellish life when she marries a haredi student in New York City. Besides dragging her and their many children from city to city without enough money to support them, the husband begins imposing stringent religious observances in the home and beating her when these are not met. Though Rotem does not say so in the book, she admits in person that the woman portrayed is her sister.

'Ahot Rehoka' has created a stir in haredi circles, although Rotem deliberately refrained from condemning the community outright. "What right do I have to pass judgement on a lifestyle which obviously works for thousands of people?" she says. What upsets her is that people should be forced to remain in it when it does not make them happy.

Since the book's publication, Rotem has received dozens of calls and letters. While some people are grateful for her disclosures, others have pointed out that haredi men are also oppressed. Rotem agrees. Those who are accomplished students of the Torah are respected, but others are unsuited for study. Their frustration can have disastrous consequences for the family. Many would like to leave the haredi life, but the community will not let them.

It is significant that more men than women have contacted Rotem after the publication of her book. When asked why, Rotem can only guess. "Perhaps it is because men in essence created this way of life, and therefore feel less guilty when they respond to signs of change," she says. "Women, on the other hand, want so much to be good girls, and fear the disapproval of the term 'drop out.'"

Rotem says those who have left the community have mostly been men. Women suffer more, but, paradoxically, it is they who often internalise the yeshiva life most deeply and work to maintain it at any cost.

Change is always difficult, even soul-searing. As Rotem freely admits, it has not been easy for her either. Occasionally she wonders if she has done something wrong. "Walking out on something does have negative connotations," she says. Many readers have commented that her deep empathy for her sisters still trapped in the haredi world means that she misses it. Rotem counters that she simply identifies with them and understands the difficulty in making the choice she herself made.

She admits that her decision has caused problems not only for herself but also for her children. While her three elder daughters, those who knew their father best, are no longer observant, the three living with her still accept the religious framework and attend a religious high-school. Her only son chose to remain with his father after the divorce and has since married a haredi woman.

Despite everything, Rotem feels herself empowered. "A deeper and richer personality," is how the author describes herself. And one with no regrets.

Preeti Singh

Human Rights ~ Fundamentalism's War on Women

USA : An Italian woman was beatified by the Catholic Church for honouring the marriage sacrament. She died at the hands of her abusive husband instead of leaving him. Three women were killed in the US by a scripture-quoting gunman opposed to abortion. Algerian women are shot in the streets for refusing to wear the veil.

At the final preparatory meeting this week for next September's United Nations Fourth World Conference on Women, participants agreed that the rise of religious fundamentalism is inciting violence against women and reversing human rights advances worldwide.

The fundamentalist backlash will be part of the Conference's Platform of Action.

Panels on fundamentalism and women's rights held last Tuesday included speakers on Catholicism, Protestantism, Islam and Judaism, as well as on Buddhism, Hinduism and Native American Indian religions.

A common theme was how extremists use religion to achieve a political end, and that the rise of fundamentalism can in most cases be attributed to worsening economies and escalating nationalism.

"Religion is the most powerful force in the lives of most people," explained Frances Kissling, president of Catholics for a Free Choice, a group that supports the right to choose abortion. Kissling recently won a battle against the Vatican which tried to deny her certification as a delegate to the UN Conference.

"At best, religion represents goodness and charity," she continued. "At worst it occupies the fear and hatred within people."

Panels sponsored by the American group The Project on Religion and Human Rights included 'Witnesses on the Situation of Women's Human Rights in Various Religions' and 'Fundamentalism and Violence against Women'.

The project is described by founding co-chair Reverend Dr. Donald W. Shriver, Jr., as "a new effort to overcome the gap between people who swear by religion and those who swear at it". Women's Feature Service, USA sponsored an evening discussion titled 'Counter-Attack: Women Stand Up To Fundamentalism' to emphasise the courageous measures that women are taking to maintain rights they have gained over the last two decades.

Reports on the brutality women have suffered were mixed with discussions of why such attacks are occurring.

Joan Ferrante, a professor of medieval religions and one of the keynote speakers for The Project on Religion and Human Rights panels, said the use of male imagery encourages patriarchal religions.

"If the male is set up as the authority figure and the female as a figure to be dominated," she said, "it is a small step from controlling what a woman does to beating her. We have to change basic attitudes of religion to equalise women's lives."

Kissling said that controlling women's behaviour is essential to the fundamentalist ideology. "Why does the Catholic Church reserve its passion for issues of sex, reproduction and women's rights?" Kissling asked. "Where's the passion for civil rights? Why do they rage against women?"

The Church, she added, seems "lost in the pelvic zone."

Dr. Susanna Heschel, a professor of Jewish studies, said that all religions are connected to human rights violations against women. Women cling to their religious beliefs, she explained, "because they think sexism was created by men, not God".

In 'The Project on Religion and Human Rights' panels, Muslim women from Sudan and Pakistan criticised the American media for portraying their religion as specifically fundamentalist and evil. "There is nothing in my religion against women," Dr. Asma Mohamed Abdel Halim, a Sudanese speaker, said. "What women need is a feminist interpretation."

Halim added that in Sudan, interpretation of the Koran is in the hands of a few people. Women are not part of that group.

Shazia Rafi, a Pakistani, said Islam was liberating for women in the sixth and seventh centuries. "Polygamy was outlawed and women had rights of inheritance," she explained. At that time, she explained, "lawyers and judges set the rules. Nowadays it is done by people with little education."

Karima Bennoune, an Algerian-American

lawyer and activist, prefaced her remarks by encouraging the audience not to blame Islam. "I am speaking of a political movement, not Islam as a whole," she said, as she described how organised violence against

Algerian women, including gang rapes and murders, is rapidly escalating.

There are some bright spots for women and religion. Yoden Congdon described Tibetan Buddhism as an equalising force. "We believe in reincarnation, where form is transitory. Anyone can come back as a male or female so religion has a positive effect in our society," she said.

Radha Kumar, a fellow at the Institute of War and Peace Studies at Columbia University, described two successful Indian campaigns on behalf of Muslims and Hindus during the 1980s.

"The court ruled that religion was not allowed to intervene in human rights," Kumar said as she described the result of successful campaigns to give Muslim women the right to financial maintenance from their husbands and free Hindu women from the pressure to commit suicide after their husbands' death.

Kumar explained that when feminists involved in the campaigns were criticised for being too Westernised, they searched for and received support from some traditional sections of Indian society.

"This shows great promise for such campaigns in the future," Kumar added.

In spite of the horror that is currently occurring in Algeria, Bennoune said women should not lose sight of the progress being made. Algerian women are fighting against the fundamentalists both individually and collectively.

"Women activists continue to meet in secret and speak to the foreign press," Bennoune said. "They continue to write, to publish, to work and not to wear the veil. Women have gone into hiding to continue their work even though they face death at every moment."

Marsha Talcin

Media ~ Men on Women

Zimbabwe : So women think they can come out of the kitchen, dare to wear pants and be men?

A group of 20 black male journalists who gathered here recently to discuss gender say this will happen only over their dead and buried bodies. Most reflected the deeply ingrained resistance among Zimbabwean men to women's equality.

"Women want a situation where they become men. But that is not possible. That can never be," said Innocent Madawo, a journalist with Zimbabwe Inter Africa News Agency, the national wire service.

He grumbled, "This gender issue is getting out of hand."

"Women do not know what they want from us men. They have an inferiority complex," chimed in Ben Chavundura, an officer with the Ministry of Information. "They want the power and men have power. Women should not fight to take over men's positions or to be like men. That is where the resistance to this gender issue started. This is a war against men."

The gathering was organised by Ecumenical Support Services (ESS), a Christian NGO involved in community development, and an organisation called Padare.

In Shona, the main language in Zimbabwe, Padare means a court session for men to decide on crucial issues affecting the family or community. Padare was established three years ago as a forum to encourage men to work for women's equality.

Despite tremendous legal gains made by Zimbabwean women since the country became independent from white minority rule in 1980, male chauvinist attitudes are prevalent in all walks of life.

Two male members of Parliament last year argued in the House of Assembly that because women are biologically different from men, they cannot be equal. The debate took place only months before the Beijing Fourth World Conference on Women, at which Zimbabwe was well represented.

John Vekrio, a Padare executive committee member, said, "We want to agitate for change. We believe reporters should change their way of reporting. Padare's motto is, 'Real men do not abuse women'."

Dr. Tafataona Mahoso, a senior lecturer at the prestigious School of Mass Communication who helped lead the gathering, added, "There are many men in Zimbabwe who believe that the oppression of women does not exist. They tend to see the demands of women's emancipation as imposed from outside. "We should come to a stage when men see the liberation of women as a social need," he said.

The journalists examined newspaper stories and magazine articles. They found that Zimbabwean women usually make news headlines only if they have been raped or are victims of some sort of sexual assault; are commercial sex workers being accused of spreading sexually transmitted diseases; have dumped their babies; have murdered a man, usually their husband; or have been killed themselves.

In a role-play session the men were asked to pretend they were women and say how they felt about such stories.

Despite admitting that women are unfairly represented in the media, the journalists were not convinced that they needed to change their style of writing.

Tichawona Mukuku, deputy editor of the monthly political magazine Moto, commented, "Activists in the gender forum are divorcees. They are women we cannot respect."

Arnold Msipa, editor of a rural community newspaper called the Makonde Star, said he felt, "uncomfortable about covering women's meetings." He added: "There is nothing special about gender. We might be different, she might have breasts and so on, but why all these questions about gender? Why should we have gender? We should just have people."

Shaking his head, Mukuku noted, "Suddenly you have women saying that is sexist, this is sexist. Even my father does not know how to approach his wife any more. The other day there was a call for women to present the weather report. It's just a weather report. Does it matter who presents it?"

Vekris remained adamant that it is important to continue challenging such deeply entrenched views. "Women have a job to do for their own emancipation, they must be at the forefront," he noted at the close of the workshop. "But what part are we playing as men in that emancipation?"

Isabella Matambanadzo

Media ~ Changing The Media's Maxim

Jamaica: With her fishnet stockings, skimpy G-strings, a head of dyed red and blonde hair and a pierced nose, Carlene has become a national 'mascot' of sorts. Dubbed 'Queen of the Risque', many an exclusive corporate party becomes a non-event without her scantily clad presence.

Carlene, who prefers not to use her surname, is a strikingly attractive mulatto of 25 and one of the worst nightmares of the Women Media Watch (WMW), an organisation dedicated to cleaning up the image of women in media.

As increasing competitiveness has caused several media publications in Jamaica to lower their standards, Carlene frequently appears in local newspapers, television commercials and calendars, baring almost all for quick and sub-stantial money.

The maxim that sex sells is the unspoken credo of many advertisers. Women's organisations have lobbied long for putting an end to the use of women as sex objects in advertising, but with little success.

Sometimes the women get more assertive.

Dr. Carolyn Cooper, noted lecturer and Chair of the Women and Development (WAND) Studies at the University of the West Indies, recently tore down all the pinups of semi-nude women on the walls of the Senior Common Room and replaced them with posters of semi-nude men. She earned the wrath of the male community but she made her point.

"When the shoe is on the other foot, it's a completely different story," she says. "None of those men wanted to see male posters on the walls, yet they never objected to the posters depicting naked women. We are talking about a principle here."

Meanwhile, the WMW, a 15-member strong organisation carries on with its seven year campaign to clean up the image of women in the media. The portrayal of violence against women, or women as sex objects, have been its main issues of concern since its genesis in 1987.

Despite the absence of an organisational structure the group has counted many successes and despite its limited membership and shortage of financial and human resources, it maintains a visible profile.

In 1993, the group hosted a weekend regional conference on mainstream and alternative media, began work on a booklet on media and gender issues and started a documentary 'Crushed Faces' which explores the work of WMW. The production of a 12-minute video called 'Behind the Images' a fictional drama on domestic violence and the media, is regarded as its major achievement.

The WMW also protested against the treatment of a rape scene in a popular local television drama called 'Sarge in Charge' starring the island's most popular comedian, Oliver Samuels. WMW felt that the episode dealt trivially with rape and made the victim an object of derision. An apology was demanded on behalf of the women of Jamaica. The producers did, in fact, comply, apologising through the national media and promising to be more sensitive to gender issues in future.

The group was not as successful, however, in getting the Jamaica Chamber of Commerce (JCC) to withdraw a poster depicting the bare posterior of a woman to lure visitors to this Caribbean island. The poster, which won the JCC annual Tourism Poster Competition, was made by an 18-year-old boy, whose teacher defended the poster with the comment that the female body was "saleable".

With a visible national profile and an undeniable contribution to gender issues, WMW features prominently in the National Report on the Status of Women in Jamaica, being prepared for the Fourth World Conference on Women to be held in Beijing in 1995.

For the group, it all began with a research conducted by Sistren Theatre Collective, which identified violence against women at the personal, community and national level as a serious hindrance to development.

"Because of this, a group was established to monitor the media and to assess the link between violence and the overt or implicit message which is communicated in media programmes and presentations," says the National Report.

WMW has busied itself with a public education programme that includes lectures, discussions, drama workshops, educational displays, films and videos. The group also lobbies through letters to the press and key media persons, radio call-in programmes, letters to companies and advertising agencies and meetings with women's groups.

It also networks with other groups in the region concerned with similar issues like the Women's Crisis Centre and Women Inc., Belize Women aganist Violence, Sistren Theatre Collective and the Association of Women's Organisation in Jamaica (AWOJA).

"Our aim," says executive member Pat Donald, "is to raise public awareness of the causes of sexual violence in our society and to improve the image of women in the media as one way of reducing sexual violence."

Indeed, violence against women is one of the critical issues that Caribbean women's groups are focusing on for the Beijing Conference.

"Violence against women is a feature of the lives of Jamaican women of all social classes and age," the Report states. "Some of it is domestic, but violence in the society has increasingly been directed against women—through lyrics of popular songs, through radio messages, through sexual harassment, through sexual abuse, through battering, rape and murder."

The Women's Crisis Centre alone reported an increase of 545 cases of domestic violence over the 1992 figure. The police also reported an increase of rape cases over the 1992 figure. The WMW views these trends with a lot of frustration.

"We have come a long way, but we still have a long way to go," notes Jennifer Grant, the current and first woman president of the Press Association of Jamaica. "The media in Jamaica still suffers from fear of addressing gender issues in a structured way despite the fact that women are their biggest audience."

Grant does not feel that the Jamaican media pays sufficient attention to the effects of violenc on women and children. The WMW, in their constant effort to sound the alarm on these issues, therefore, play a significant role.

Carol Narcisse, president of AWOJA admires the WMW for maintaining a very consistent campaign to portray a positive image of women in the media.

"They have done this largely because of their strategy, which does not take a confrontationalist approach," she points out.

"Instead, they attempt to meet with media managers and encourage them to look at their work from a gender perspective."

Recognising that despite the WMW's attempts not enough has changed, Narcisse talks about the concerted efforts needed till Beijing and beyond. Until society as a whole redresses the condition of women in all areas, their status will not be elevated to that of "valuable human beings".

"The issue of the negative portrayal of women in the media is not to be separated from the conditions of women in society," she says, "for one is only a reflection of the other."

Grace Virtue

Environment ~ Women Take Over Wastelands

India : If people are poor it is because they have access to only that which society designates as worthless. In the rural areas of the south Indian state Andhra Pradesh, it is wasteland.

An NGO called the Deccan Development Society (DDS) is trying to capitalise on that sole resource of the poor, by introducing agricultural techniques to make wastelands productive.

In Karibemula village, Zahirabad block, a woman called Narsamma decided three summers ago to lease 16 acres of wasteland lying uncultivated with a rich farmer. As a member of her village sangham or union (the village level unit of DDS) she was assisted with a loan for a pump and motor and guided in permaculture. Narsamma's harvest of 60 bags of millet, some wheat, sugarcane, sunflower and groundnut provided food for her family, fodder for the animals and a surplus for sale. And the demonstration encouraged members of sanghams in neighbouring villages to lease experiment with permaculture.

Today land has been leased by members of sanghams in 20 villages. At Raikode 70 acres is being purchased by members of 60 sanghams through government schemes.

Permaculture is the organic cultivation of land with designed inter-cropping, forestry and water harvesting. It is educated farming and farming for education, introduced into this drought-prone district five years ago by its demonstration on a three-acre DDS farm at Pastapur.

With harvests of food, fodder, fuel and fruit and yields comparable to rainfed chemical agriculture, permaculture—the core of DDS philosophy—is the transforming inverse of market oriented monoculture which results in erosion, epidemic and endangered productivity.

Today the DDS training centre on the Pastapur farm, with cooking facilities for 500 people at a time, boasts of surplus fuel. Besides nurseries there has been an increase in production of vegetables, cereals, pulses and oilseeds.

Where local farmers have with chemicals produced around five quintals of oats per acre, harvests here have recorded yields of 11.9 quintal per acre, with about 20 kg of mustard as intercrop.

Most important, there has been an increase in biomass, so essential to soil fertility.

DDS's rural development programme in Medak district is wholly foreign funded. On the face of it, its projects are mundane and devoid of innovative rhetoric. Like the other 300 organisations listed in a recent study of voluntary agencies in Andhra Pradesh, DDS, which is not mentioned, is devoted to agricultural extension, education, health and child welfare. What makes DDS different is that its members are mostly women. The list mentions only 10 grassroots women's organisations while DDS has over 60 sanghams and the number is growing. The four DDS directors have decided to keep ongoing contact with the sanghams.

Satheesh, a DDS director who lives in Pastapur and has himself bought an eight acre farm for permaculture, will tell you, "Permaculture is care for the earth, a permanent culture." You know from the gentle tone in his voice that care cannot be fragmented. Choices have to be made and his has been to work in an anti-poverty programme primarily with children. Under a creche project 14 centres for pre-schoolers are run by committees of mothers. Teachers drawn from the villages underwent an intensive training programme. They learnt to teach through song, dance, drama, craft and innovative materials. Each month teaching activities focus on a specific topic, like fruits or leaves or water or the summer or winter season.

Satheesh reports that, "The mothers' committees estimate the quantity of cereals, pulses, oil and vegetables needed for the creches. It's touching to see members carry bags of provisions for four to five kilometres to inner villages....we look forward to the day when they will also supervise the learning activities." He devotes a great deal of time to the School for Sustainable Development that DDS recently started on a five-acre farm at Machnoor, 10 km from Pastapur. "There are 80 children between 10 and 15 years old at the school and not surprisingly 80 percent of them are girls. You know that the sanghams have mainly women members." The school is full-time but closes during harvests so the children can work and earn wages in kind—a vital contribution to the family. The school teaches carpentry and pottery, swimming and cycling, social forestry and permaculture, besides reading, writing and counting.

Satheesh is confident that the students will be able to take the class ten school-leaving exam with ease. Among the students is 12-year-old Anil from Algol, who talks enthusiastically of "rounding up all the children from the village and filling up the bus to bring them to school". Anil lost an arm in early childhood but that no longer makes him feel maimed. He learns carpentry and pottery like the others and permaculture as well. DDS tries to integrate work, environment and education. Inspired by its philosophy, 400 members have planted over 60 varieties of trees around their homes. 100,000 saplings have been raised and a contract signed for raising 20,000 mango grafts for a public sector company.

A scheme for growing trees in public places has met with great enthusiasm. Devised to enable the person growing the tree to earn, it has brought incomes of US $ 150- 250 to about 40 members. In 1991 DDS was given the K.P. Goenka memorial award for environmental protection.

Healthcare is part of DDS strategy. Health workers have surveyed the villages and identified people suffering from tuberculosis and leprosy. They have identified handicapped children, pregnant women and lactating mothers. The choice of treatment they say is not between allopathy and the traditional Indian system ayurveda.

"Even ayurvedic medicines bottled and brought from outside are no solution. Any system of healthcare, to be sustainable, has to be from the people's own milieu," says a recent DDS report. "Hence we have listened carefully to local healers, understood the usage of local herbs and medicinal plants, tried codifying them. Our medicines are largely composed of these plants and herbs which are accessible to the people." Vegetables did not form part of the daily diet of the poor and efforts to encourage every member to raise a kitchen garden failed.

"The women go out every morning for the daily wage and come back late in the evening....there is no one to protect the vegetable plots. Stray cattle, intrusive chicken and curious children upset all their efforts...." says the report. Another method was found to foster nutrition. Loans were given to women to buy vegetables and sell them in poor areas. Not only were the loans returned but fresh loans were taken to continue the business. Medak district is drought prone and recurring famine conditions in the past two years, with skyrocketing prices of grain and fodder, led sangham women to undertake buying and selling grain and negotiating wages in kind.

Loans were also extended to 10 small plotholders of US $ 30 per acre to enable them to cultivate their land rather than leave it fallow. Four had a good harvest and repaid the loans, three return small sums every week and three have suffered losses. There have been no miracles.

Zahirabad is not thickly wooded or green. But if people were to talk about it today they would not tell you stories about forests that were but about trees that will be.

Buchy Rao

Environment ~ Future Cities Need to be Gender-Aware

United Kingdom: At four minutes past midnight on December 5 in the year 2006, the majority of the world's population will live in cities. Of these, one billion will live in absolute poverty. By the year 2025, 19 of the world's 25 megacities will be in developing countries with scant resources to meet even their people's basic necessities.

Far from being a doomsday prediction, this is the apocalyptic future that cities are headed for, say experts. The phenomenal growth and expansion of cities is changing urban landscapes: hillsides are cut, valleys and swamps filled with rocks and waste water, and groundwater levels plummet.

As cities grow, so does urban consumption and waste generation. In the magnificent gothic Town Hall in the heart of Manchester in UK, nearly 1000 delegates from 50 major cities of the world, are trying to draw up plans to cope with—and perhaps improve upon—this disturbing urban scenario.

The occasion: Global Forum 1994, the largest environmental meet since the Earth Summit in Rio de Janeiro two years ago. The delegates—drawn from citizens groups, trade unions, international aid agencies and municipal authorities the world over—have assembled for a 4-day jamboree (June 24-28).

Among a myriad issues, they are discussing resource use, urban poverty, finance for sustainable development, governance, environment and health, transport and communications.

It's not quite the carnival atmosphere of Rio, say conference regulars. But Manchester, the world's first industrial city, is an apt venue for a brainstorming on cities and sustainable development.

What is very evident at every level of the debate—perhaps for the first time in a conference of this magnitude—is the need to factor in women's concerns in sustainable development.

"You cannot talk of urban health without first talking of pregnant women, the health of the mother and child," says Bimala Shrestha of the Institute of Medicine in Tribhovan University, Kathmandu.

"We are discussing the role of urban agriculture in sustainable development," says Jac Smit, President of the Urban Agricultural Network, Washington DC. "There is no way you can do this without women. They form 80 percent of urban farmers all over the world.

In Mexico, Peru and Tanzania, they decide the kind of food that will be grown around their homes....We are trying to see how these experiences can help other cities design sustainable development programmes. Women are at the very heart of sustainable development."

Global Forun 1994 is likely to come up with another first by recommending special means by which poor urban women can gain access to credit facilities.

Housing, integral to any urban devlopment plan, is one area where women's needs are increasingly felt.

Patricia Matolengwe, one of South Africa's many homeless, who is now part of a housing savings scheme started by the poorest residents of Cape Town, points out: "Women are the ones who need the money, because they build the houses. But they are never given a loan unless they are married and their husbands can show some security with which they can pay back their loans. The system needs to be changed."

Yves Cabannes from Brazil, who has been facilitating the workshop on finance and development in cities, is clear that "women have got themselves together in community-based initiatives and are forcing the lending institutions to rethink their entire approach." Cabannes cites the example of Grameen Bank in Bangladesh where 94 percent of the people given loans are women. "Increasingly, more and more lending institutions will have to move in that direction," he says.

In Columbia there has been a sharp rise in female headed households and an increase in female ownership of homes. By the dint of sheer numbers, they have influenced institutions to offer them loans to improve their homes.

"There is considerable debate on the extent to which current living standards in affluent cities and among affluent groups within cities can be maintained while also meeting sustainbable development goals," say Diana Mitlin and David Satterthwaite of the Human Settlements Programme, International Institute for Environment and Development, London.

The debate centres around the different concepts of sustainability among experts, and becomes bitter when North-South differences come to the fore. City planners from developing countries, however, are clear that their goal is to achieve a basic standard of living for all their residents.

But even as town planners agonise over the urban nightmare to come, the key factor repeatedly emerging is that half of those affected are women.

It's pointed out over and over again, that the way cities develop affect women far more than men.

In most third world countries, for instance, it is women who fetch water, gather fuel, look after children and grow food. They have to bear the brunt of lack of sewers and safe water, cramped living spaces, domestic pollution and disease. Women the world over bear primary responsibility for household-management. Poor quality houses, insecure surroundings, proximity of schools and health centres make a major difference to women's work.

In the towns of sub-Saharan Africa, 80 percent of urban families use wood fuel for cooking. "But there is not a single city in the region which has planned its wood fuel supply," Diana Lee-Smith, secretary of the Nairobi-based Women and Shelter Network, points out. "On the contrary, most cities with carefully drafted plans of sustainable development do not allow the use of wood fuel."

Laws do not change reality and women in informal settlements go through extreme hardship, trudging miles to fetch wood. They break the law, but they have no other way of putting food on the family table. The city planners do not consider this basic necessity.

Lee-Smith admits that she herself is not clear of what the alternative can be except that it will be different in different regions. "The point is, that the planners need to think of the alternatives which they do not do at the moment," she says.

As migration from the villages to towns grow, the problem of squatter colonies becomes more intense with devastating impact on women's lives in developing countries. But women's concerns have remained marginal to the urban development debate till now.

"The gender-aware city has hardly been a part of the public discourse on sustainable development," says Lee-Smith.

The situation, however, is changing, as

more and more harried women organise themselves in urban ghettos around the globe and demand a say in how resources are being managed. There is too much at stake if women are not brought into the debate.

Everywhere, women are affecting the way cities develop. And when the Manchester meet winds up, this is the primary message that will go home.

Patralekha Chatterjee

The Girl-Child ~ Children Face Crisis

Peru : Forced to work from an early age to contribute to their family's income, working-class girls in Peru face an uncertain future.

Once they quit school, chances to get educated become remote for most. There is also a high risk of early pregnancy, sexual abuse and both mental and physical health problems.

According to the National Plan for Children 1991-2000, out of every 100 Peruvian children between the ages of 6 and 11, 60 have to work.

"For many parents, children's participation in the family's budget is part of their upbringing, because it helps to teach them discipline and responsibility," says sociologist Jeannine Anderson, who has done research in marginalised areas of capital Lima.

Anderson says that among certain groups such as people from the Andean highlands and rural migrants, more than economic necessity it is deeply ingrained customs that force children to work. "In many rural societies children are incorporated into the family business, in farming activities or domestic work", explains Anderson. Thirty percent of Peru's 22 million people live in the countryside, and many migrate to poor urban areas.

Anderson, however, admits that given the current state of Peru's society there is a positive side of the situation: working children can earn money and escape the tension-filled environment that is often their home. Nevertheless, she warns that working girls face many disadvantages.

"Often girls help with domestic work, both at home and outside," says Anderson. These tasks are often not recognised as actual work and pave the way for all sorts of abuses. Moreover, it frequently entails quitting school and missing out on opportunities for a better life.

Sociologist Violeta Sara La Fosse's research, done over 10 years ago when Peru's social decay was not as marked, showed that lower-income girls tend to start working before they were even five years old. Boys did not start before they were seven.

Another study done during the late 1980s revealed that over half the girls between in the age group of 14-19 years worked as domestic helps. Current statistics from the Ministry of Labour also show that around 70 percent of girls between the ages of six and 14 who work do so as domestics. The remaining 30 percent work as street vendors.

But it is difficult to estimate accurately how many girls work as domestics, because of an Andean tradition of parents handing over girls to richer "godmothers" or relatives who are supposed to provide the children with a home, food and education in exchange for "small services".

Isabel Chirinos is a typical case. Born in the Andes town of Huancayo, she was handed over to her "godmother" when she was eight.

"My godmother was a doctor, but how awful she was!" says Isabel in halting Spanish. "I slept on a mattress on the floor in the kitchen and spent the day working, sweeping, washing clothes. My hands used to bleed."

At 15, with the insistence of the parish priest, her godmother sent her to school. But Chirinos found it difficult to study. Her "godmother" refused to help her with the homework and her heavy workload did not leave her much time to study.

At 17, Isabel ran away when a friend got her another job. "They treated me better and they even paid me," she remembers, "but I still could not get beyond third grade."

Sociologist Walter Alarcon, an expert on working children, has found out that on an average girls in Lima join the labour market when they are eight to nine years old. But in downtown Lima it is common to see five-year-old girls selling candy or begging late at night.

"What do you want me to do, miss? There's no work," says Rosalia Camasca when asked why she allows her three girls to beg on the streets. "My husband can't find a job, and I can't get anything either. If you work as a maid you get nothing. Here at least people see the girls and give them money," she says.

Camasca's youngest daughter is three-year old and the eldest is ten. Between the four of them the family manages to earn about 20 soles a day (US $ 10 dollars). While almost half is spent on food, a good deal is used in going back and forth from Lima to a shanty-town down south where the family lives.

It is unlikely that her daughters will ever go to school. But this does not worry their mother. "If only they were boys," she sighs.

The official report of the Ministry of Education says that of the total number of illiterates in Peru 73 percent are women. While many start going to school very late, other quit early. In some parts of the highlands, over half the girl students leave before graduating from primary school. Moreover when the costs of education are high, poor families prefer to educate their male children.

Psychologist Maria Eugenia Mansilla, who has conducted a survey among children who work at a market in Lima says that most children of both sexes want to go to school. "In spite of the tremendous effort involved in doing schoolwork and carrying out the duties of their regular work, children are willing to study," says Mansilla. "They have this vision of school as a space where they can become children again."

Twelve-year-old Ines, who lives in what is called "Southern Cone", one of the largest shanty-towns in the capital, is one such enthusiastic student. But her gruelling schedule at work hardly gives her time to study.

Early morning at four Ines buys fruits from the wholesale market, prepares breakfast for the men there and then leaves to sell the fruit. "I don't get back home till eight at night. How could I want to do homework then ?" she asks.

Sociologist Alarcon says that boys generally work for eight to 10 hours a day, shining shoes or carrying sacks in the market. They manage to earn US $ 11 to 15 per day. Girls, meanwhile work on an average 12 hours a day but earn only US $ three to five. Almost 30 percent of them work for over 13 hours a day and do not get any salary, just food and shelter.

As if that were not enough, lawyer Ana Maria Yanez points out that many girls, specially young domestic helps, end up pregnant. Women's legal aid services report that the girls in the age-group of 11 to 15 years of age are most vulnerable to sexual abuse.

"There's ample evidence to suggest that many of these abuses were carried out by the father, the stepfather, close relatives or employers," says Violeta Bermudez, a lawyer.

But caught between economic necessity and old traditions not many Peruvian girls will be able to evade these risks by not working.

Zoraida Portillo

The Girl-Child ~ A Plan to Stop Child Labour

India : Eleven-year-old Mary gets up every morning at 3 a.m.. She dresses listlessly and trudges to the bus stop where she is huddled into a vehicle carrying 70 children some 30 km away to a match factory.

The factory is in Sivakasi, a town in Ramnathapuram district of Tamil Nadu in south India. Mary and her co-workers spend 12 hours at the factory each day, applying chemicals on match sticks and putting them in boxes.

For every 1,000 sticks she fills Mary gets a few cents. Her fingers move deftly as she tries to better her daily target of 2,000 sticks.

Paradoxically, Mary's parents are landowners. They have three acres in their village in Madurai district. But as the region suffers from frequent droughts and there are inadequate irrigation facilities, they are heavily in debt. They have had to send their daughter out to work to make ends meet.

Mary initially worked as a domestic servant in her own village but her earnings were meagre. So, like many others, she migrated to Sivakasi where she currently earns the equivalent of US$ 5-6 a month, depending on her output.

Mary's skin has peeled at several places due to the chemicals she works with. But the eyes in her otherwise dull face burn with an almost fanatical light. She is determined that her younger sister will not suffer the same fate. "I will somehow make enough money to send her to an English medium school, learn to type and work in an office instead," she says.

Mary is only one of several million child workers in India. These children work mostly in small-scale industries like match and fireworks, handloom, lock-making, carpet-weaving, glass and gem-polishing and fishing.

Employers have no qualms because the children come cheap, work long hours and pose no problems. Some as young as three years are pitted into trades. Many of these children are girls.

The government of India is well aware of the problem. Last month it announced its intention to abolish child labour and launched an ambitious US$ 283 million programme to cover 2 million children employed in hazardous industries.

Welcoming these efforts, Joseph Gathia, director of the Centre Of Concern For Child Labour (CCFCL), however, regrets that current government programmes are weighed in favour of the boy worker more than girl workers like Mary.

"This has not been done deliberately, but because the boy labourer is more visible," he says. The girl worker tends to be invisible as she works in home-based or small-scale industries.

According to figures compiled by the Ministry of Labour, girls account for 33.57 percent of child labour in the country. In six Indian states girl workers outnumber boy workers.

In 1985, the Madras Institute of Development Studies found that girls are universally employed in piece rated work. They are not generally given supervisory tasks or work allowing skill formation. Men and boys do work which is more remunerative and skilled while women and girls do routine, unskilled, low-paid jobs.

Gathia says the best way to alleviate the sufferings of girl workers is to make them visible. "We must recognise the economic value of girl workers." He underlines the need to create programmes specifically geared to deal with their problems, particularly health problems.

"Often, before the age of 10 a girl worker has developed diseases as a result of the pitiable conditions of her workplace. By the time she reaches adulthood, her body is already damaged," he says.

In Lucknow and Sitapur districts of Uttar Pradesh in north India, for instance, girls suffer from asthma and eye problems, because they work indoors in poor lighting and strain their eyes while bending over embroidery.

At a preparatory committee meeting in New York for the World Summit on Social Development to be held in Denmark next year, the Indian government announced that it would set up a National Child Labour

Elimination Authority (NCLEA) headed by the Labour Minister.

The announcement came as a surprise to social activists and voluntary organisations, as the government's policy hitherto had seemed to focus only on regulating child labour and making it more humane. The approach indicated in the National Policy on Child Labour (1987) was to eliminate child labour only from the most hazardous occupations and processes.

The sudden reversal of policy has led to speculation in different quarters. Political observers believe that threats from the United States to ban imports of products made by child labourers could have pressured the Indian government to re-examine its stand.

According to sources, US government officials and NGOs had, at the New York meeting, indicated to the Indian delegation that the US could get a ban on imports involving child labour enforced through the North Atlantic Free Trade Agreement (NAFTA).

NAFTA is a powerful trade bloc consisting of the US, Canada and Mexico. If NAFTA imposes a ban, that could create a chain reaction, since it has a trade treaty with the European Community (EC) as well as the Indonesian bloc. Such a move could even lead to the collapse of major export-oriented industries in India, like carpet manufacture.

An official at the Ministry of Labour, speaking on condition of anonymity, said the NCLEA's thrust would be to end the exploitation of 2 million children employed in hazardous industries, though the total number of child workers in the country is much higher.

A report prepared by the Ministry of External Affairs, which is to be released at the Denmark summit, says the US$ 283 million programme would be implemented in states having large concentrations of child labour in hazardous industries.

Citing poverty as the main problem, the report says the emphasis would be on bringing families out of poverty. The parents of child workers would be given employment through existing programmes like the Employment Guarantee Scheme, the Integrated Rural Development Programme and the Artisans' Tool Kits Programme.

Special schools would be set up for the children, to provide vocational training in skills they can use when they become adults, the report adds.

Nitin Jugran Bahuguna

4
The End of the Long Road: Consensus and Commitment

Mallica Vajrathon

For anyone who is new to the workings of the United Nations, attending a UN-organised world conference for the first time can only be a daunting experience. Here, things are usually not what they seem; important outcomes often do not emerge from rooms where important people gather but from informal working groups where non-VIP delegates discuss and negotiate issues on the agenda.

The Fourth World Conference on Women at Beijing was no exception. To put it mildly, the event must have been puzzling to many! At the Plenary, where Heads of States, or governments, spoke, the room appeared to be half empty with not too many listeners. In contrast, the crowds headed towards the working groups and the numerous informal meetings. Delegates rushed from room to room and many were closetted in closed session. Only delegates could participate in the negotiations; the UN staff who were allowed into the rooms were there merely to facilitate the process and keep detailed records of the negotiations.

The styles of negotiation vary from one conference to another. The negotiation process seems endless, carrying on not only through the day, but late into the night, checking and questioning every word in the text of the Draft Platform for Action that might have some hidden meanings. Negotiating the outcome of a UN world conference is an exercise in compromise. The language has to be weighed, debated and challenged before any consensus can be reached. Voting is used only when no consensus is reached. And decision-making comes only after lengthy general debates on specific issues before the text is adopted by the conference.

Over the last two decades, the UN has organised four world conferences on women. These were a part of mobilisation of support for the two UN Decades for Women that were declared by the General Assembly as a result of the Conference of the International Women's Year. The largest of all these was the Fourth World Conference on Women held in Beijing in 1995.

Preparations for the Beijing Conference need to be seen as a continuum of previous UN conferences. Even if each one of them had its unique characteristics, there were also some common aspects. For instance, UN rules and procedures for negotiations had to be followed in accordance with adopted guidelines; the ways of conducting the Plenary or working group sessions had to be agreed to in advance during one of the PrepComs, by a bureau or a Steering Committee in accordance with General Assembly Resolution 40/243.

Methods of participation of inter-governmental organisations and non-governmental organisations were decided by ECOSOC and endorsed by the General Assembly. Dealing with the UN system, inter-agency coordination mechanisms and working with the media had to be planned ahead of time. A

Steering Committee for the Conference was set up and chaired by the Secretary-General and/or Deputy Secretary-General of the Conference, to discuss working methods between different departments. This Committee also had to determine resource requirements; organise technical services; schedule planning missions to the host country to look at the Conference site chosen by the government; ensure media and communication coverage; and coordinate security matters. The UN General Assembly, in its resolution 45/129 endorsed the recommendation of ECOSOC to have the Commission on the Status of Women (CSW) act as the preparatory body for the Beijing Conference.

Since its inception in 1945, the CSW played a central role in the UN towards improving the status of the world's women. From 1985 onwards, its responsibilities were enlarged by the General Assembly to include promoting the implementation of the Nairobi Forward-Looking Strategies, as well as monitoring the work of all relevant bodies of the UN system. The Beijing Conference was not meant to repeat the work of its predecessors; its objectives were to evaluate the work done in implementing the Nairobi Strategies, and to address a limited number of key issues identified since 1985 as reflecting fundamental obstacles to the advancement of the majority of the world's women.

In doing so, the Conference was expected to create impetus for women—as half of the world's population—to move forward, well-equipped to meet the challenges of the 21st century in political, economic, scientific and technological development. It was expected that the outcome would be a concentrated and concise Platform for Action, leading to feasible, effective action on the selected critical areas of concern by the year 2000.

Austria was the first country to express an interest in hosting the 1995 World Conference on Women. But later in March 1992, China sent an official invitation to the CSW, offering to hold the Conference in Beijing. The General Assembly, in its resolution 47/95 of December 1992, expressed appreciation to the Government of the People's Republic of China for its offer.

And thereafter began the long and complex process of official preparations!

The UN Planning Mission went to China in June 1993, headed by Gertrude Mongella, Secretary General of the Conference. The team consisted of senior representatives from divisions and departments of the UN system involved in the preparations—i.e., the Division for the Advancement of Women, Secretary of ECOSOC, Planning and Meeting Servicing Section, Office of Conference Services, Radio and Television Section, Promotion and External Relations Division of the Department of Public Information and the Coordinator of the NGO Forum.

The Department of Public Information had a two-fold role. It was to provide information and services to all media covering the Conference, and to produce its own daily radio, television and print coverage. It was estimated that there would be between 9,000 and 10,000 participants for the official event and 20,000 UN accredited NGOs. Moreover, about 3,000 journalists were expected to attend the Conference.

The Mission reviewed several possible sites for the Conference and the NGO Forum, based on an initial set of proposals by the Chinese government. On the basis of this review, it was decided that the Conference would be held at the Beijing International Convention Centre, with opening ceremonies at the Great Hall of People preceded by the NGO Forum which would be held at the Beijing Workers' Sports Service Centre.

Other matters discussed by the Planning Mission were security, protocol, hotel accommodation, financial arrangements and draft

Conference Agreement to be completed and agreed to with the host country at its second Planning Mission in 1994.

The second Mission met with the host country between 29 May-3 June 1994 and was headed by Ebrima Jobarteh, the Deputy Secretary-General of the Fourth World Conference on Women. Discussions with the Chinese Organising Committee were a follow-up to the first Mission on all policy and technical matters. The Host Country Agreement document, NGO accreditation, privileges, immunities and resource requirements were reviewed by the UN team and the Chinese Ministry of Foreign Affairs. Staff requirements for servicing the Conference were revised. It was estimated that 309 UN staff were needed for the Conference. The rest of the persons needed for servicing the Conference would be local Chinese staff.

The Host Country Agreement was signed by the then UN Secretary-General, Mr Boutros Boutros Ghali in September 1994 during his official visit to Beijing—exactly one year before the Conference was to begin. Following this, two Chinese technical teams came for a visit to UN headquarters in New York to further discuss related technical and logistical issues.

The third UN Planning Mission was in Beijing between July 12-16, 1995, to wrap up the myriad details that needed attention before the Conference actually began. Loose ends were tied up in accordance with the Host Country Agreement. Questions of protocol and security were discussed with the Chinese counterparts, and technical communications and media facilities were checked. The team also visited the Great Hall of People that was to be used for the opening ceremonies.

At the request of the CSW, the UN Secretary-General set up a Secretariat for the Conference with additional new staff from developed and developing countries at the Division for the Advancement of Women (DAW) — at that time based in Vienna. Towards the end of 1993, because of some restructuring within the UN system, the Secretariat was moved to New York and became part of the Department of Policy Coordination and Sustainable Development, under the leadership of the Under-Secretary General, Mr Nitin Desai.

The CSW also recommended that the UN Secretary-General appoint, not later than 1992, a woman as Secretary-General for the Beijing Conference. She would need to have an international stature in relation to the advancement of women, as well as experience of the UN system to assume primary responsibility for the preparation of the Conference.

In December 1992, Mr Boutros Boutros Ghali appointed Gertrude Mongella of the United Republic of Tanzania as Secretary-General of the Conference. She was then serving as her country's Ambassador to India. Prior to that, she had been a cabinet member in President Julius Nyerere's government and had served at various times as Minister for Natural Resources and Tourism, Minister for Community Development, Social Welfare, Culture and Women's Affairs.

As Secretary-General of the Conference, Gertrude Mongella had to implement all General Assembly legislative mandates relating to the preparations of the Conference and its outcome. She was also responsible for the management of DAW, accountable to the Secretary-General of the UN in respect of the Conference and through Mr Nitin Desai, to the UN Secretary-General in respect to the management of DAW.

An ad hoc UN inter-agency meeting was held in New York from August 9-11, 1993, where Nitin Desai introduced Gertrude Mongella and discussed the status of national and regional preparations, host country arrangement, the draft guidelines for national preparatory activities, NGO participation and criteria for accreditation.

In addition to resources allocated from the UN's regular budget, the Secretary-General of the Conference had to organise fund-raising for voluntary contributions to the Trust Fund for Conference Preparations. Governmental donors to the Trust Fund were Austria, Belgium, Canada, Denmark, Finland, France, Germany, Italy, Japan, Liechtenstein, Malta, Netherlands, Norway, Portugal, Spain, Sweden, UK and the USA. Other contributors included the American Association for the Retired Persons (AARP), Carnegie Foundation, China Women's Federation, Ford Foundation, Rockefeller Foundation and UNIFEM. UNFPA and UNICEF contributed senior level staff to the Conference Secretariat. The total amount in the Trust Fund was approximately US $4 million and the total professional staff at the Conference Secretariat numbered about 25.

The CSW recommended that governments establish a national committee, or designate a national focal point, to initiate and promote preparations for the Conference by organising and coordinating national activities. These activities would also include increasing public awareness and assembling information and gender-desegregated statistics for the elaboration of national reports on the situation of women. It urged organisations of the UN system at the national level to cooperate with country efforts in preparing for the Beijing Conference and to coordinate their activities through the UN's Resident Coordinator.

The purpose of preparing national reports was to take stock of the present situation of women, analyse the progress made since the Nairobi Conference a decade ago and prepare for future action. This complex exercise was done in almost every country by national machineries for the advancement of women together with other technical ministries, governmental agencies and NGOs, with assistance from the UN's Resident Coordinator.

The CSW sent guidelines on the preparation of national reports to achieve some standardisation. This would help increase the country's analytical input and would improve the capacity for building consensus at both regional and global conferences. Some general suggestions were that the main body of each national report should be short (maximum of 50 pages), featuring the most important national priorities and issues for the advancement of women, and could include reports prepared for the Committee on the Elimination of Discrimination against Women, as well as those for the World Conference on Human Rights; the Intenational Conference on Population and Development; and those prepared for specialised agencies and organisations of the UN system. A total of 174 national reports were prepared for the Beijing Conference.

The CSW set an agenda for various meetings worldwide. During 1993-1994, 17 meetings were held among which were also the various regional preparatory conferences. Regional preparations for the Conference included the examination of the regional implementation of the Nairobi Strategies, the analyses of national situations and reports, the planning of future actions and the organisation of preparatory conferences for each region by the Regional Economic and Social Commissions.

In the CSW Resolution 36/8, the Commission requested the regional conference to identify regional trends, priorities, obstacles and also innovative suggestions for future action. The results of these regional conferences were to be provided to the Commission not later than at its 39th session. It also recommended that the regional conferences include in their agendas the issue of women in public life, emphasising their role in politics and decision-making. Later, the Commission added in its request, the issue of entrepreneurship and the advancement of women, emphasising the need to facilitate an overall entrepreneurial activity through appropriate economic policies, training, access to credit, information and other support systems.

Moreover, the CSW recommended that a public information strategy for the Conference be designed, based on the Conference themes and using information mechanisms that would reach the largest number of people. The Commission also requested the Secretary-General to plan and implement an information campaign, issue a news bulletin entitled "Conference 95" twice a year to disseminate information on the preparatory activities, and to include the Conference as part of the UN's 50th anniversary celebrations.

The Conference was specifically mandated to cooperate with NGOs, both during the Conference itself and at the parallel NGO Forum. The NGO Forum '95 was originally to be held in close proximity to the UN Conference. The CSW invited the Committee of NGOs to arrange the NGO Forum as a parallel activity to the Conference. National and regional activities of NGOs would provide information, including media arrangements. The Commission emphasised the importance of unrestricted participation by the media in covering the NGO Forum. At the early stage of preparations in 1992/93, Marlene Parenzan was designated Forum Coordinator operating out of Vienna.

During the UN's Decade on Women, a specific instrument that protects women's rights and is binding in international law was developed. This instrument—the Convention on the Elimination of All Forms of Discrimination against Women (CEDAW) — was adopted by the General Assembly in 1979 and the first signatory ceremonial event took place at the Mid-Decade Women's Conference in Copenhagen.

The Beijing Conference placed emphasis on CEDAW as an important document which underpins the full range of women's rights – an international bill of rights for women. At the time of the Beijing Conference, 145 States had ratified CEDAW.

Twenty-three members of the Committee on the Elimination of Discrimination against Women under the leadership of Ivanka Corti of Italy actively participated at all levels in all regions in the preparatory process and at the Beijing Conference itself in 1995. On 7 September, Ms. Corti made a statement at the Plenary Session of the Conference urging members states which had not ratified CEDAW to do so. She emphasised that CEDAW does not merely focus on respect for equal rights per se; rather, it aims to ensure the equal enjoyment of these rights. (By June 1996, 153 states had ratified the Convention.)

As momentum for the Beijing Conference built up, the General Assembly decided that the documents before the Conference would comprise:

- Draft Platform for Action
- A report of the Secretary-General on the second review and appraisal of the implementation of the Nairobi Forward-Looking Strategies for the Advancement of Women.
- 1994 World Survey on the Role of Women in Development.
- Updated edition of the World's Women 1970-1990: Trends and Statistics.
- Outcome of regional preparatory meetings for the Beijing Conference.
- Updated compendium on the implementation of CEDAW.
- National reports to be prepared by governments as a basis for future national action.

The preparation for drafting the Platform for Action itself was a long process. It was initiated by the CSW as early as in 1993 at its 37th session. A draft outline of the Platform for Action had to be sent for approval by

ECOSOC. The outline would have to be concise and accessible, aiming to accelerate the implementation of the Nairobi Strategies in critical areas so that equality becomes a reality by the 21st century. The Structure and Guidelines were set in the annexure of CSW Resolution 37/7 for the Secretary General to prepare the first draft of the Platform for Action. It contained eight areas of critical concern:

- Inequality in the sharing of power and decision-making at all levels
- Insufficient mechanisms at all levels to promote the advancement of women
- Lack of awareness of, and commitment to, internationally and nationally recognised women's rights
- Poverty
- Inequality in women's access to and participation in the definition of economic structures and policies and the productive process itself
- Inequality in access to education, health, employment and other means of maximizing awareness of rights and the use of their capacities
- Violence against women
- Effects on women of continuing national and international armed or other kinds of conflicts.

Many key factors from the second review and appraisal of the Nairobi Strategies were further diagnosed in the process of drafting the Platform For Action. It was diagnosed, for instance, that women continued to be almost completely absent from decision-making at all level in the majority of UN member states in issues relating to peace and development. Despite increasing democratisation and access to education and employment, women had made little progress in attaining political power in legislative bodies, or in government, and in achieving the "critical mass" target of 30 per cent. Women constituted only 10 per cent of parliamentary membership and an even lower percentage held ministerial and sub-ministerial positions in government, except in the Nordic countries; women were not put up as candidates for public office in almost all countries.

In the economic sphere, women were not well represented in decision-making in large public or private corporate structures or in national economic policy formulation and programme development. They were segregated in certain occupations and their average remuneration remained lower than that of men. Women faced many obstacles in their efforts to rise to decision-making levels in government and large corporations (including in UN agencies, organs and bodies) largely due to the dominant male culture in these organisations and subtle discrimination in hiring and in career development.

The review indicated that the political will to integrate women's concerns in all aspects of public action was lacking. There was also a lack of awareness of gender issues and commitment to internationally and nationally recognised women's human rights. Clear-cut guarantees against sex-based discrimination were often absent in national constitutions or fundamental laws. Where they did exist, they were often undermined by the absence of implementation mechanism, or by the persistence of negative customary norms and practices that subordinate women. Mechanisms to enforce rights were often absent or were difficult for women to access.

Greater priority was given to the problem of violence in the family and in society. An increasing number of countries have modified their laws to make violence against women in the family a crime with appropriate sanctions. The Declaration on the Elimination of Violence Against Women was adopted by the UN General Assembly in 1993, recognising that "violence against women is a manifestation of historically unequal power relations between men and women, which have led to domination over women by men and to the prevention of their full advancement, and that violence against women is one of the crucial social mechanisms by which women are forced into a subordinate position compared to men".

Women were the main victims of armed conflicts across the world—conflicts, in the planning of which they played no part. They had only begun to be included by the UN in peace-keeping and international conflict resolutions. Increasingly, as a result of family disintegration and war-related violence, women were turned into refugees, single heads of household and displaced persons. Rape and other types of abuse were used as "weapons" to humiliate adversaries.

In the area of health too, many traditional practices harmful to women's health and their human rights continued unabated in many parts of the world. Morbidity and mortality rates of women due to reproductive health related causes, as well as due to early and frequent pregnancies remained unnecessarily high. Although many countries had made significant advances in primary health care, general and maternal health care and treatment of complications from pregnancy and child birth was very inadequate. HIV/AIDS was rapidly increasing among women due to the difficulties they face as a result of their lower status, economic situation and lack of information.

Poverty among women was directly related to their lack of rights and access to institutional resources. The greatest poverty was found in households where women with dependents were sole earners. Equal access to education had been achieved in some regions, but in many others, a variety of reasons impeded the education of girls and women.

From early in the preparatory process, among the key persons in the CSW who had influenced the Structure and the Guidelines of the Platform for Action were: Mervat Tallawy of Egypt, Chairperson of the 37th CSW Session; Vice Chairpersons Achie Lululima of Indonesia, Olga Pellicer of Mexico and Joke Swiebel of the Netherlands, and the Rapporteur, Victor Tkachenko of the Russian Federation. Other members of CSW closely involved during those early days were: Evangelina Garcia Prince of Venezuela, Wang Shuxian of China, Avonne Fraser of the USA, and Patricia Licuanan of the Philippines (later elected Chairperson of CSW for the whole period of preparations for the Beijing Conference 1994 and 1995).

The drafting of the Platform for Action required close interaction between members of the CSW, Secretary-General of the Conference, staff of UN specialised agencies and organisations, and the Conference Secretariat. The CSW recommended that an inter-sessional work group be convened in early January 1994 to have more time to go through the draft Platform for Action that was drafted under the leadership of Gertrude Mongella. The draft addressed the need to achieve more balance in the roles and relationships of men and women rather than focusing on women as a separate group.

Forty states members of the CSW attended five meetings of the working group under the chairperson Ms. Djenebou Kaba of Cote d'Ivoire . Ms. Olga Pellicer of Mexico, Vice-Chairperson was appointed coordinator for consultations on the draft Platform for Action. Twenty-six NGOs also attended the session discussing the structure of the draft Platform for Action.

The final outcome of the inter-sessional working group was an adopted version of the structure of the draft Platform for Action as follows:

I. Statement of mission.
II. Global framework.

Five Regional PrepComs

Regional activities were organised as part of official preparations for the Beijing Conference. In 1994, the regional preparatory conferences were organised by the Regional Commissions of the UN to evaluate the implementation of the Nairobi Strategies and to set regional areas of concerns and priorities for action to achieve equality between men and women.

Five senior staff of the Conference Secretariat in New York were assigned regional responsibilities—Rose Arungu-Olende from Kenya, Nora Galer from Argentina, Mathilde Vazquez from Spain, and Rashida Selim from Bangladesh. They worked as a team in which I was Principal Adviser to Gertrude Mongella. Dorota Gierycz, staff member of DAW from Poland later joined and strengthened the team for the East European region. Ishan Bouabid, a journalist from Morocco, took responsibility for liaison with regional press and media at all the regional conferences.

From early 1994, we identified in each region a network of people, institutions and organisations involved in sectoral and inter-sectoral issues relating to the themes of the Conference, and for strategic inclusion into the draft Platform for Action. We liaised regional-focused activities with focal points of the UN Regional Commissions in organising the Regional Conferences. Large numbers of NGOs, inter-governmental organisations and regional financial institutions working within each of the regions participated in the regional conferences.

Asia and the Pacific

For the first of these regional conferences—the Second Asian and Pacific Ministerial Conference on Women in Development—the team worked closely with senior officials of ESCAP and Regional Focal Point on Women, Meena Patel and Thelma Kaye. The Conference was held from 7-14 June, 1994 in Jakarta, Indonesia, resulting in the adoption of the Jakarta Declaration and the Plan of Action for the Advancement of Women in Asia and Pacific. The Conference was attended by 58 countries. They chose ten areas of concern for the region: the growing feminisation of poverty; inequality in women's access to and participation in economic activities; inadequate recognition of women's role and concerns in environment and national-resource management; inequitable access to power and decision-making; violation of women's human rights; inequalities and lack of access to health; negative portrayal of women in the media; inequalities and lack of access to education and literacy, inadequate mechanisms for promoting the advancement of women and inadequate recognition of women's role in peace-building.

Latin America and the Caribbean

The regional preparatory meeting for Latin America and the Caribbean—the Sixth Regional Conference on the Integration of Women into Economic and Social Development of Latin America and the Caribbean—was held in Mar del Plata, Argentina from 20-25 September 1994, under the auspices of ECLAT. We worked closely with the Women Focal Point of ECLAT, Miriam Krawczyk, who shouldered all the substantive and administrative details in convening participants from 38 countries, considering country reports and negotiating texts of the draft Platform for Action in Mar del Plata. However, the final discussion was completed at the 16-18 November meeting in Santiago, Chile, when the regional plan of action was officially adopted. The region identified eight strategic areas of concern: gender equity; economic and social development with a gender perspective: women's equitable share in the decision, responsibilities and benefits of development; elimination of poverty among women; women's equitable participation in decision-making and in the exercise of power in public and private life; human rights, peace and violence; shared family responsibilities; recognition of cultural plurality in the region; international support and cooperation.

Europe and North America

For Europe and North America, the High-level Regional Preparatory Meeting was organised by the Economic Commission for Europe, held in Vienna, Austria from 17-21 October 1994. We worked closely with the Deputy Executive Secretary, Dunja Pastizzi - Ferencic, and Focal Point for Women and

Development, Patrice Robineau, in preparing the Conference. Fifty-four member countries of Economic Commission for Europe (ECE) adopted a Regional Platform for Action - Women in a Changing World - Call for Action from an ECE Perspective. Seven areas of concern for Europe and North America were: insufficient promotion and protection of women's human rights; feminisation of poverty; insufficient de facto gender equality in employment and economic opportunity and insufficient policies and measures to reconcile employment and family responsibilities; insufficient participation of women in public life; insufficient statistical systems, databases and methodologies to inform of policies and legislation and to secure equal treatment of women and men; and insufficient intra-and inter-regional networking and cooperation on the advancement of women. The Preamble of the Platform for Action committed governments in the region to achieving, by the year 2000, a more equitable and sustainable society where women's knowledge, potential and contributions are recognised and taken fully into account in all policy and decision-making.

The Arab Region

The regional preparatory conference for members states in the Arab region was organised by the Economic Commission for Western Asia (ESCWA), the Economic Commission for Africa (ECA), and the League of Arab States from 6-10 November 1994 in Amman, Jordan. We worked with Fatma Sbaity Kassem, Focal Point on Women in ESCWA, on the content of the draft Plan of Action with regional experts and the Centre of Arab Women for Training and Research and the Secretariat of the League of Arab States. The representatives of governments and NGOs negotiated the text, and the Arab Plan of Action was adopted at a high-level meeting. Arab women's priority concerns based on areas of vital importance, and measures to be taken were: safeguarding the right of Arab Women to participate in power and decision-making structures and mechanisms; alleviation of poverty; ensuring equal opportunity for Arab women at all levels of education; ensuring women's equal access to health services; strengthening the capabilities of Arab women to enter the labour market and achieve self-reliance; overcoming the impact of war, occupation and armed conflict on women; elimination of violence against women; participation of women in the management of natural resources and the protection of the environment; and effective utilisation of communications to effect changes in roles in society and achieve equality between the sexes. The Arab Plan of Action for the Advancement of Women to the Year 2005 urged Arab governments to establish policies quickly and to take action with a view to providing the appropriate environment and setting up the necessary elements in order to meet the urgent needs of Arab women in an effective manner.

Africa

The last in the series of regional preparatory conferences for Beijing was the Fifth Regional Conference on Women in Africa held in Dakar, Senegal from 16-23 November 1994. Regional preparations were handled between the regional team from headquarters and the regional focal point on women of EA, Mebo Mwaniki. Fifty-one states in the region adopted the Africa Platform for Action focusing on eleven areas of concern: women's poverty, insufficient food security and lack of economic empowerment; inadequate access to education, training, science and technology; women's vital role in culture, the family and socialisation; improvement of women's health, reproductive health including family planning, and integrated programme; women's relationship and linkages to environment and natural-resource management; involvement of women in the peace process; political empowerment of women; women's legal and human rights; mainstreaming of gender-desegregated data; women, communication, information and arts; and the girl child.

The conference declared commitment to forge a new ethic for sustainable development based on the equal and active participation of women, men and youth as agents of change at family, community, national and international levels and committed to integrating women's concerns in balancing political, economic, cultural and social policy options; harmonising and reconciling economic growth with social equity; and emphasising the interdependence and partnership of women, men and youth of Africa, in an atmosphere of peace and well-being.

III. Critical areas of concern.
IV. Strategic objectives deriving from the critical areas of concern and action to be taken:
- Introduction containing the themes: Equality, Development and Peace;
- Strategic objectives deriving from the critical areas of concern;
- Action to attain each strategic objective and responsibility for implementation.
V. Financial arrangements.
VI. Institutional arrangements for implementing and monitoring the Platform for Action.

The open-ended committee under the leadership of Ms. Olga Pellicer presented a Conference Room paper containing a summary of its discussion based on the informal paper prepared by Ms. Mongella and her staff at the Conference Secretariat. This paper would be worked on and submitted as a document for the 38th session of the CSW in March, 1994.

A number of suggestions were thrown up. Many representatives emphasised that the statement of mission be concise and dynamic, depicting women positively and recognising their potential and their positive role as agents of change, not as objects.

They also suggested that the draft should include: new technologies and communications and their impact on trade, investments, job opportunities and security; the impact of democratisation on women's advancement; achievements in the advancement of women since 1975; the international economic situation and national policies, such as structural adjustment and debt which have an impact on economic empowerment of women; new opportunities (and not just obstacles) for the advancement of women; results of the regional reports and results of other international conferences.

They felt that the critical areas of concern section should be diagnostic, supported by objective, concise and quantitative data and the basis for the Platform for Action remain the CSW resolution 37/7. The results achieved by other world conferences before 1995 should be taken into account as well as the previous work of CSW, particularly its consideration of priority themes under equality, development and peace. The importance of a life-cycle approach in all critical areas of concern was stressed. Some delegations proposed reordering the sequence of the eight areas of concern by importance, starting with sharing of power and continuing with economic and social rights. Some delegates suggested additional areas of concern such as the girl child, the important role of the media and information. Several delegations wanted "to inspire a new generation of women and men working together for equality" as set out in CSW resolution 37/7, to be added as another critical area of concern. Detailed comments were made on each of the critical areas of concern by the delegates at this inter-sessional working group session.

The 38th session of the CSW held in New York in March 1994, considered the draft Platform for Action that was attached to the report of the inter-sessional working group and made further improvements based on its suggestions and recommendations. CSW participants strengthened the section on strategic objectives. NGO participation at this first PrepCom had expanded to over 200. The CSW prepared a draft Platform for Action setting out the structure of the document, its main lines and instructions to be followed in a further revision of the draft. It requested the Secretary-General to develop the draft further for consideration by the CSW at its 39th session, taking into account the results of the regional preparatory meetings. It further requested the Secretary-General ensure that the draft of the Platform for Action be made available in all languages at least six weeks before the beginning of the 39th session. The revised draft Platform for Action was to be circulated no later than 1 February 1995.

The session also adopted a key resolution on Gender Equality in Population Programmes reaffirming the goal of universal access to safe motherhood, to family planning and reproductive health services and facilities for those who wish to use them, to assistance in preventing and overcoming infertility, and to full and timely information about all aspects of reproductive health and sexuality.

To further develop the Platform for Action, the Secretariat considered findings of the second review and appraisal of the implementation of the Nairobi Strategies, the results of regional preparatory meetings (*see box*) and other international conferences, as well as inputs from organisations of the UN system and a variety of other diagnostic documents.

Additionally, the Secretariat took into account the results of the World Conference on Human Rights, the International Conference on Population and Development, and the second preparatory meeting for the World Summit for Social Development. It also looked at suggestions and recommendations coming from NGOs and inter-governmental organisations, as well as many aspects of the results of expert groups and seminars held between 1993-1994.

The 39th session of the CSW acted as PrepCom II for the Conference. Negotiations continued over three gruelling weeks, on the 68-page heavily bracketed text of the Platform for Action. Delegates could complete only 60 per cent of the negotiation on the text. In fact, instead of shortening the text as originally intended, they added more words and issues onto it. As a result, by the end of the session, the text had expanded to 150 pages, with a profusion of brackets!

There were two categories of brackets in the texts of the draft Platform for Action at this stage of the preparations: those which had to be worked through because of the questions regarding details; and those which were subject to basic disagreement. Over 90 brackets were on health issues. The difficulties in negotiation in the area of concern on health were on the subject of family and religion. Other difficult areas for negotiations were:

- the system of national account of women's unpaid work and the measuring of women's unpaid work;
- education on sexual and reproductive health and freedom of religion;
- reaffirming that reproductive rights rest on the recognition of all couples and individuals to decide freely and responsibly the number, spacing and timing of their children, and to have the information and means to do so; on whether to include sexual orientation as one of the grounds on which discrimination should be prohibited; on culture and national sovereignty; and whether the term "universal" should be used in reference to human rights.
- new and additional resources that are both adequate and predictable;
- girls should have the same, equal rights to inheritance as boys;
- armed conflicts in the peace section that included issues such as disarmament, and ending the use of nuclear weapons, land mines and the arms trade;
- the use of the word "gender" and the word "equity" in the context of the principal of equality;
- international arrangements in establishing the high-level post in the Secretary-General's office.

The ECOSOC, in its decision of June 1995 authorised the Chairperson of the CSW, Ms. Patricia Licuanan, to conduct open-ended informal consultations from 31 July to 4 August, 1995 to further consider the draft Platform for Action, especially those portions that remained within brackets. It further decided that the results of such consultations would be transmitted in the form of a non-paper to the Conference in Beijing for its pre-Conference consultations. The Secretariat staff had its hands more than full ! They had to group brackets by issues and subjects, to facilitate delegates' negotiation in removing as many of them before sending the text to Beijing for final negotiations before its adoption.

At the end of two weeks of lengthy negotiations in Beijing, the draft Platform for Action was adopted by consensus. Many countries spoke on their reservations after its adoption on many issues like reproductive health, human rights and ensuring equal inheritance rights. But many countries also made commitments. For instance, India committed to increase education investment to 6% of GDP with focus on women and girls; USA committed to pursue the ratification CEDAW and to establish Presidential Inter-agency Women's Council; Ghana committed to have legislation to protect women's property rights, and adult literacy class for women; Denmark committed to continue 1% of GNP development assistance focusing on poverty elimination. At the end, the UN Secretary-General was invited by the Conference to establish a high-level post in his office to act as his adviser on follow-up activities in the UN system.

5
1975–1995: Creating A Tapestry of Concern

Anne S. Walker

A remarkable transformation has occurred. A transformation in the way women worldwide now organise around United Nations' world conferences and summits, impacting the way the UN develops and produces plans of action at the end of these meetings. The seeds of this transformation date back to the late 1960s.

It was then that women's non-governmental organisations (NGOs) across the world began lobbying the UN to name 1975 as International Women's Year (IWY). It took a while, but the year was finally declared so by the UN in 1973, and the first world conference on women, called the IWY World Conference, was held in Mexico City in July 1975. Parallel to this conference was the first NGO Forum for women, called the IWY Tribune.

Women came to the IWY Tribune in record numbers. It was as if a call had gone out to every corner of the world, rallying women activists from towns and villages, cities and continents, to come and organise for change. Around 6,000 women packed the halls of the Centro Medico in Mexico City at the largest consciousness-raising session for women ever held. They wanted to reach out and share resources; to find support for the activities they were undertaking in their communities, often against seemingly insurmountable odds. Women discovered they didn't need to be isolated any more.

Across town at the World Conference, representatives of international NGOs participated as observers, banding together to put up resolutions at plenary sessions, sitting in on working groups whenever possible, trying to make changes in the draft Programme of Action that would be the end result of the Conference. It was a thankless task for these women, who collectively represented many millions of members of their organisations. They were made to feel that they were peripheral to the real action, and that their lobbying distracted delegates from what governments felt were issues of greater importance and relevance.

Meanwhile, at the IWY Tribune a remarkable thing was taking shape. The organisers had planned for six major panels each day, held in three large auditoria at the Centro Medico. Each auditorium held around 1,000 to 1,500 people. In addition, there were a multitude of other activities planned, including art and craft displays, workshops, music, films and slide/tape presentations, and street theatre. The scene was festive, colourful and full of excitement.

Media coverage concentrated almost exclusively on North-South differences and conflicts. But despite this, participants found they had a great deal to discuss with women from other parts of the world who were actively involved in similar issues. They found that they had a great deal in common, whether they came from the mountains of Kenya, the plains of Argentina or the cities of North America and Europe.

Requests for space to hold small group discussions and workshops began to pour in to the organisers. Hasty consultations took place and more areas were made available. A daily list of additional workshops appeared in each of the Tribune's morning newspaper. The workshops became focal points for women organising around specific areas of concern, and to the organisers' amazement more than 200 workshops were held by the end of the 10-day period.

The seeds were sown of what was to become a revolution in the way NGO fora were organised. Women were organising, strategising, synthesising and mobilising. And they were demanding to have input into the Conference across town, where governments were taking decisions that would affect their lives and the lives of their daughters.

During the last week of the Tribune, a march was organised where some hundreds of women marched through the streets of Mexico City to present their demands to the world's governments meeting at the World Conference. They sat down with their government delegations and discussed ways in which they could play a more active role in decision-making that would lead to an improvement in their lives and the lives of all women in their countries. The world's women were taking a stand on all development issues and nothing would be quite the same ever again.

At the conclusion of these momentous meetings in Mexico City, the IWY Tribune Committee returned to New York with the purpose of finishing the necessary reports and accounting of activities for donor agencies, and closing down the space where the Committee had met. But the mail would not stop! In fact, it multiplied as the weeks went by. Soon there were mountains of mail from women across the globe asking for help and asking to be kept in touch. In the mail also came project proposals, materials produced and requests for names and addresses of women met at the IWY Tribune.

Across the road at the United Nations, wheels were moving towards the declaration of the next ten years as a Decade for Women. Member states were under pressure from women in their countries to undertake research around the needs and concerns of women, and for the development of programmes and projects that would tackle some of the major social and economic inequities that women faced everywhere. A treasure chest had been opened and nothing could get that lid down! Finally, at the General Assembly of the UN in December 1975, a Decade for Women: Equality, Development and Peace, was proclaimed.

From all of this, the IWY Tribune Project was born, with the express purpose of developing strategies for sharing resources of all kinds from, by and with women worldwide. Regional resource kits for women were developed in collaboration with various women's networks, mirroring the way the NGO process of work was also developing at the UN. Women were reaching out and sharing, developing strategies and techniques for advocacy and networking, finding ways to break through barriers of isolation and lack of access. A participatory process of technical assistance and training, of communication support services and networking, and of information collection and dissemination was underway and it would soon reach out to tens of thousands of women in every corner of the world.

The second world conference on women called the World Conference of the Decade for Women was held in 1980 in Copenhagen, again with a parallel NGO Forum. What began as the IWY Tribune Project was now the International Women's Tribune Centre (IWTC). With its growing data base of women and groups worldwide, IWTC played an important role in the information and communication process leading up to the Copenhagen conference and NGO Forum, and undertook to organise an information and communication centre at the Forum itself, called Vivencia!

In this space, containing a resource centre of materials, a card file of participants, and areas for small groups to meet, women took part in a multitude of workshops and small group discussions, signing up for emerging networks around issues, or organised by region, or ones that focused on language. Altogether, 10,000 women and some men turned up at the NGO Forum—a vivid and colourful illustration of the growing momentum towards a truly global women's movement.

The connections between the NGO Forum and the World Conference were beginning to be built in a much more systematic way in Copenhagen. The lobbying undertaken by women at the World Conference across town — still only International NGOs in Consultative Status with the Economic and Social Council (ECOSOC) of the UN — was becoming more organised, though each women's group still lobbied for its specific concern. For instance, peace issues were advocated by women's peace groups, religious issues by religious groups, business and professional women's groups fought for economic issues, and so on. Occasionally, representatives from several women's groups would collectively place resolutions on the floor for circulation among delegates. Coordination of these activities was worked out through the UN NGO liaison service and resolutions were generally typed up on official UN stationary, translated into the five UN languages and placed in delegates' "pigeon-holes".

It was difficult, laborious and time-consuming work for NGOs, frequently with not too much to show for their efforts. At the same time, women participating at the NGO Forum on the campus of Amager University were increasingly feeling left out of the UN process and frustrated at not being able to have more input into the main documents under preparation.

The third world conference on women was held in Nairobi, Kenya in July 1985. Known as the End of the Decade of Women World Conference, here, a parallel NGO Forum was again held, this time at the University of Nairobi. A far larger crowd than was expected turned up, with 15,000 participants at the Forum instead of the 10,000 for which the NGO Forum Committee had planned. Actually, there were closer to 20,000 because thousands of African women did not register, but came to events such as Tech and Tools, the appropriate technology event co-sponsored by IWTC, the World YWCA and the Kenya Appropriate Technology Action Committee, which was off-campus and did not require an official pass. Women came by the busloads from Kenyan villages and many of them were never counted in the overall total.

Forum '85 was a more activist-oriented meeting with women's networks organising, mobilising and strategising in every corner of the Nairobi University campus. Organisations such as Development Alternatives for Women in a New Era (DAWN) and The Institute for Women, Law and Development were born. Women were more confident and skilled at organising, mobilising, raising funds and developing loosely structured worldwide, regional and national networks.

Additionally, women were beginning to want a larger say in what their governments were planning on their behalf. Strategies for breaking down the barriers between government delegates and NGOs were being developed. Meetings were held at the NGO Forum to discuss ways this could be done and daily briefings became the order of the day. UN officials and government delegates would travel each morning to the Forum site and brief NGOs on progress made the day before at the Conference. Problem areas of the document would be discussed, bracketed paragraphs revealed and explanations given of why certain words could or could not be used. NGOs were becoming more and more knowledgeable in the UN's ways of work. NGOs with consultative status who were able to participate in the conference as observers, took their concerns and issues across town to the conference and put them before delegates as resolutions that were circulated on the floor, or placed in "pigeon holes". Still, the input of NGOs was very marginal and peripheral to the work of the delegates and the Conference itself.

From Nairobi came the Forward-Looking Strategies (FLS) for the Advancement of Women to the Year 2000. Since this document was more straightforward and outlined more issues and concerns faced by women across the world than was the case before, women took ownership of it in new ways. The FLS became somewhat of a women's movement treatise, particularly in regions of the Global South where they began to use it for lobbying their governments and as launching pad for new projects.

The next major stage in this new era of NGO organising and influencing at the UN, got off the ground in the early 1990s. The fledgling Women, Environment and Development Organisation (WEDO) and its founder, Bella Abzug (a former US Congresswoman), called for a conference of women to strategise around environmental needs and concerns. The major objective was to influence the document that would come out of the UN Conference on Environment and Development (UNCED), better known as Earth Summit in Rio de Janeiro, Brazil, in 1992. Entitled Agenda 21, it had been formulated through a series of hotly contested preparatory meetings in New York and in the regions, but still had remarkably little that was specific to women's issues and concerns. Therefore, a women's action agenda was planned.

The Women for a Healthy Planet conference took place in Miami in December 1991 and 1,800 women from 80 countries participated. The first day was organised like a tribunal with a panel of judges, a jury and a series of witnesses who spoke about wastage of the earth's precious resources and resulting degradation in all regions of the world.

On the second day there were workshops, with a report at the end of each workshop on the specific action each group wanted to take around each area of concern. These reports were collected and a committee of women worked throughout the night to consolidate them into a final document.

On the third day we arrived in the Plenary Hall to find the document entitled Women's Action Agenda 21 on everybody's seat. Shortly after, Maurice Strong, the Secretary General of the Earth Summit, arrived on stage to be presented with a copy before 2,000 cheering women. He made a commitment to see that this Agenda would be taken seriously into account during the Rio Conference.

It would be difficult not to be impressed with this level of organising and strategising. From this experience came the 90s model of caucuses at UN meetings that revolutionised the way NGOs in general and women in particular organise to advocate major issues and concerns at each preparatory committee, each regional ministerial meeting and each UN World Conference. Caucuses of women representing all organisations and groups, all regions and countries and all issues and concerns have become part of the UN/NGO landscape. They have been given considerable credit for the increased level of importance being accorded to recent UN plans of action and strategy documents that result from world conferences.

UNCED was the first of the UN world conferences of the 1990s. It also became the first to have a formally organised Women's Caucus, with the new WEDO group carrying the lion's share of the organising. Femea Planeta—as the Women's Tent at the NGO Global Forum in Rio was called—became the central place for women to get together and strategise, with each day allocated a different focus of concern and organised by women's organisations representing that concern. It was here that the Women's Caucus met daily, with another caucus meeting across town for representatives of organisations that had accreditation and could participate at the UN conference as observers.

There was another important outcome of the meetings around the Earth Summit which is not often mentioned but is increasingly assuming major importance. With the NGO Global Forum in Rio situated so far from the Earth Summit, it was difficult for NGOs to participate in the conference itself, and many new ways of participation began to emerge. The fax revolution was just getting underway and NGOs were more aware of the possibilities. A faxed briefing was sent daily from the UN Conference to the Forum and various NGOs began to use this new technology to fax their input into the emerging document across town.

NGOs were also discovering the Internet and work had already begun in setting up networks such as Greennet, Econet, Peacenet and others organised around environment, peace, human rights and women's issues. The network that spearheaded much of this not-for-profit electronic networking was the Association for Progressive Communications (APC), which led the way in providing channels that linked together the advocacy and activism of NGOs worldwide. This new emerging electronic information highway was utilised extensively in Rio for communication between the two sites and for keeping in touch with all those who could not participate but were watching developments back home. It has since snowballed into a truly international highway and the documents from all the UN conferences of the 90s are placed on it, making them accessible worldwide. People everywhere are becoming better informed and able to have substantive input into the agenda-setting for international meetings and events.

The next conference of the 90s was the World Conference on Human Rights in Vienna in 1993. Women's human rights groups met regularly in the years leading up to Vienna, developing strategies to involve women in every part of the world in a campaign to bring the reality of violations against women's human rights onto the international agenda.

At PrepComs for the Vienna Conference, at regional ministerial meetings in each of the five world regions and at the Commission on Human Rights, women's caucus met daily. Task forces for each issue areas were formed and each task force reported back to the full caucus daily, with a caucus statement developed and produced that each woman could use when talking with delegates.

At the World Conference itself in Vienna, caucuses were held in both the government conference area as well in the NGO Forum area. In the conference area, government delegates, international agency personnel, UN staff and leadership, as well as NGOs who had consultative status to ECOSOC and were participating at the conference as observers, came to the caucus held in a room specially set aside by the UN Development Fund for Women (UNIFEM). Usually a speaker would start off the daily meeting, then there would be in-depth discussions around the topic of the day, the drafting of the Plan of Action, and anything else that might have come up during the previous day's plenary sessions and working groups.

Downstairs in the same building, women's caucuses were held daily for NGOs, who crowded into whatever space could be found, to be briefed on the day's meetings, and for discussions on all issue areas. Strategies were developed to meet new situations; women lawyers gave reports on debates over words and paragraphs, and discussed legal issues; rosters were drawn up so that there would always be representatives of the NGO caucus outside the door of each UN conference working group, who could talk with delegates and make suggestions as to new words, new paragraphs, new ways of including important women's human rights concerns and issues into the UN document.

Additionally, a Rights Place for Women was established with space for women's groups, networks and organisations to display materials on women's human rights, meet and organise with women from all regions. In the preceding two years, across the world public hearings had been held, where women testified to violations of their human rights. Representatives from each of these hearings came to Vienna to be part of a Global Tribunal on Women's Human Rights.

This Tribunal was held on the first day of the World Conference. Its impact was evident from the fact that even government delegates from the conference upstairs, slipped away throughout the day to join the hundreds of participants who listened for over ten hours to testimonials from women who had faced gross human rights violations in their own countries and homes, and to the emerging statements from the panel of four judges. By bringing the practical realities of women's lives into the domain of government officials and statespersons, women had turned the agenda upside-down. A new process had begun that placed women at the very core. Women's human rights took centrestage as one of the world's most serious and pressing concerns.

There is no doubt that the participation of women at each of the Preparatory Committees for the Vienna Conference was a major factor in the NGO input to the final documents from the Conference. However, the Global Tribunal; the presentation on the Conference floor of one million signatures contained in a petition that had circulated worldwide during the years leading up to Vienna; the demonstrations (particularly by the women from Bosnia and Herzegovina); and the organised lobbying by the women's caucus, also played an important role in dramatically changing the outcome of the World Conference on Human Rights. Not only do the Declaration of Vienna and the UN Plan of Action on Human Rights contain major sections on women's human rights, but the UN announced at the Conference the appointment of a Special Rapporteur on Violence Against Women.

In 1994, the World Conference on Small Island States was held in Barbados and a women's caucus was active again, lobbying for women's perspectives, issues and concerns to be integrated into the final document. As in Rio, there was a meeting of minds between advocates on behalf of women and environmental activists. The merging of these two passionate and practical groups resulted in a changed perspective on the needs and concerns of small island states.

Later in 1994, came the International Conference on Population and Development (ICPD) in Cairo. Years of active lobbying by women's caucuses at every PrepCom and regional ministerial meeting leading up to Cairo, and the daily Women's Caucus meetings at the NGO Forum held parallel to the ICPD, achieved considerable success in influencing the final Plan of Action, moving the issues of women's health and reproductive rights centrestage. It was in the preparation for this Conference and at the Conference itself, that women faced the most virulent and organised attacks from religious and political fundamentalists—in itself a recognition that women were finally being taken seriously as players on the world stage !

In March 1995 at the World Summit on Social Development in Copenhagen, the women's caucus grew in strength and experience and gained increasing respect from delegates and other NGOs alike. Here, the issues were what are often regarded as more 'mainstream' : economics, industry, armed conflict, peace and security matters. NGOs lobbied hard for serious consideration to be given to women's essential role in all development, but most particularly, in social and economic development. They presented facts and figures on the effects of structural adjustment policies on women, and showed clearly how the World Bank and other international agencies were frequently oblivious to these concerns in their drive to balance budgets and have loans repaid by struggling nations.

In September 1995, the Fourth World Conference on Women (FWCW) was held in Beijing, China, along with the NGO Forum on Women, held in Huairou, 40 miles outside of Beijing. In the two years preceding the FWCW, PrepComs had been held in New York at the UN and regional ministerial meetings had taken place in every world region. This time, women's caucuses were held at every regional meeting along with every PrepCom.

Women in Asia and the Pacific were the first to gather in Jakarta, Indonesia, picketing arriving government delegates, with placards that announced every major issue and concern that they wanted included in the Regional Plan of Action and the global Platform for Action. Then came the meetings in Mar del Plata, Argentina, for Latin America and the Caribbean; in Dakar, Senegal, for Africa; in Amman, Jordan, for West Asia; and in Geneva for Europe and North America. Each women's caucus followed carefully the progress of the draft regional Plan of Action and the global Platform for Action. Each also developed a Caucus Statement that delegates now eagerly solicited as a major player in the development of both the regional Plans of Action and the Platform for Action. In every region, women focused on issues and concerns of major importance to women in that region. Moreover, strategies and networks were established for regional follow-up actions.

At the final PrepCom for the Fourth World Conference on Women in New York, the Women's Linkage Caucus was formed. It was an outcome of the women's caucus that had met at each world conference and summit, now with an even stronger focus on linking the gains obtained by women at each of these previous meetings held during the 1990s. Women were determined that there would be no going back on any of the commitments made by governments in Rio, Vienna, Barbados, Cairo and Copenhagen.

The first Women's Linkage Caucus Statement in March 1995 at the final FWCW PrepCom in New York, was probably the most comprehensive of all of the caucus statements, containing both new issues and concerns as well as commitments and decisions made at previous conferences. It was a wake-up call to governments and to the UN that women were not going to let them forget the commitments on which they had promised to take action.

Most of all, the Women's Linkage Caucus Statement was the end result of years of activism by women all over the world. Within its pages were the hopes and dreams of literally thousands of women, each working towards a world where everyone would have the opportunity to live in peace and prosperity, free of violence and free of the inequities that stifle and weaken women's creativity and productivity.

In the years leading up to Beijing — and particularly in the final year — IWTC once again assumed the role of global information provider. Initially, it was with a focus on providing information to women that would allow them to be key players in the agenda-setting for their regional meetings, and then as a key provider and support for women actually planning to participate in the Beijing meetings. As time for the meetings drew near, this role also included assistance with registration and visa difficulties, assistance with hotel accommodation forms, and access to breaking news regarding the site for the NGO Forum.

This was a time of rising and falling tides and some of these tides came remarkably close to swallowing us whole! There was a need to keep women informed on a daily basis of hurdles and obstacles being erected to confound. Greatest among these was the hurdle presented when the China Organising Committee (COC) announced the change of site for the NGO Forum from downtown Beijing to Huairou, a small town 40 miles outside of Beijing and a considerable distance from the World Conference site. Happening as it did just six months before the Forum was to open, there was precious little time for protest. It was clear that the Beijing authorities were becoming nervous at the thought of 50,000 women activists arriving in their land.

IWTC immediately faxed women's media networks worldwide to alert them to the news. With this information in hand—followed almost immediately by a petition that included addresses for the UN in New York and the COC in Beijing—women in every region mobilised. Letters and petitions began flowing into the office of the UN Secretary General and to the headquarters of the COC.

Women sought the support of their governments, of the UN itself, of other NGOs and of each other.

Though we were not successful in bringing the Forum back to downtown Beijing, the campaign did alert the UN and the world that women are a force to reckon with. We now have the means to make instant contact with each other and will use these means in whatever ways necessary to secure our place as partners in decision-making.

Finally, there was Beijing, the largest of all the UN world conferences with 17,000 participating in the Fourth World Conference on Women itself and another 35,000 at the NGO Forum on Women in Huairou. At the conference, the Women's Linkage Caucus joined with the NGO Forum Office and with members of the Conference of NGO's (CONGO) representing international NGOs who had consultative status with ECOSOC, to form Equipo. This was a combined caucus and organising body that created spaces for NGOs to meet and discuss issues and concerns, and kept them informed of the progress of the Platform for Action.

The Fourth World Conference on Women, following a tradition born with UNCED, allowed an additional 2,500 NGOs to get accreditation to the Conference, making the representation of NGOs as observers to the Conference the largest ever at a UN conference. Equipo was established to provide guidelines for all of these new representatives, and to assist them in finding their way around a confusing scene of UN World Conference meetings, work groups and plenary sessions.

The preparatory work of the prior three years—including caucuses and task forces set up on each critical area of concern at each PrepCom and regional meeting, the world conferences and summits of the 90s, the hearings, tribunals, demonstrations and activism of women across the globe, and finally, the dedicated, persistent and informed lobbying at the FWCW itself—all came together to produce the final Platform for Action, one of the most comprehensive and realistic documents to come out of this most recent series of UN conferences. It is a document that women worldwide are able to mobilise around.

And this they are doing, both as monitors and watchdogs of its implementation by governments, and as initiators of new projects that work towards the achievement of its purpose.

Through all of this, the organising and strategising by the world's women has led to a strengthened and much-expanded women's global network—one that is constantly shifting and changing shape as needs arise; one that links with local, national, regional and international networks that are based on issue areas, sometimes on regional concerns, frequently defined by language.

Each network is a silken strand in a tapestry of concern that binds women together in a common bond of activism and support for an equality that will touch every aspect of society. The international arena on which many of today's dramas are played out, is being rearranged in subtle yet practical ways. Women are beginning to take their rightful place as key players in deciding the destiny of our planet.

6

The 'Yin' and 'Yang' of a Political Process

Soon-Young Yoon

Let's not be modest. With about 50,000 participants, the Fourth World Conference on Women in Beijing qualified for the Guinness Book of Records. We were the largest number of women activists working together at any one place, ever. If we had all jumped at once on the same spot of Huairou ground, we might have knocked the earth off its orbit!

The NGO Forum on Women began days before the official Conference. For 10 days, participants chose from about 4,000 workshops and panels. They participated in the daily plenaries that highlighted speeches from feminist activists and visionaries such as Aung San Suu Kyi. As preparation for the UN meeting, nothing could have replaced this building of collective energy. Themes such as institutional and financial arrangements, political participation, religion and spirituality, and the girl-child were highlighted in plenaries. Regional tents became centres of networking and political preparation for lobbying.

Electronic technology was also used effectively to link the Forum to the UN conference and to a global "townhouse". NGOs used the well-equipped computer centres for electronic lobbying and inputs into the Platform for Action. Many NGOs who were not in Beijing made excellent use of these facilities from afar. During the period, there were more than 60,000 E-mail messages sent and received, and around 100,000 visits to the NGO Forum World Wide Website. There was no doubt about it—in virtual and real space, this was a global conference like none other.

The international women's movement in Beijing appeared stronger, more diverse and more committed to influencing the UN than ever before. The interaction between NGOs and governments had passed many milestones since the first UN women's conference in Mexico in 1975. We saw the evolution of the NGO Forum, from being the rebel camp outside the UN grounds, to a legitimate partner. Political modalities also changed from confrontation as a means to getting our points across, to successful lobbying. Paradigms and international consciousness evolved as well over two decades and by the time the FWCW was held in Beijing, the discourse had shifted from viewing women as "victims" to an assertion of women's rights as "citizens".

More than at any other UN conference, the Huairou NGO Forum belonged with the official meeting. Indeed, the success of the FWCW depended on the strong interaction and mutual commitments between NGOs and governments. It was this interaction that shaped the political dynamics leading to a global consensus document known as the Platform for Action. This document was a historical statement of diverse, sometimes conflicting purposes and commitment. At the same time, it was also evolving a paradigm infused with a new collective ideology and vision for civil society.

One point should be made at the outset.

The women's conferences were not just "events". They were highlights of a long political process which shifted its leadership from women of the North to a global, more regional-based movement. Nor was the Platform for Action that emerged from the Beijing Conference just another UN document. What distinguished this lengthy document from previous texts was the invisible transformation of the NGO/GO political process leading to the compromises represented within it. The real post-Beijing legacy, thus, was the structural change in the relationship of a social movement to the intergovernmental process.

How did all of this actually happen? It was evident early on that the size, scope and goals of the Beijing Conference required a new kind of organisational structure and facilitating body. To meet this challenge, the Convener of the NGO Forum, Supatra Masdit and the Executive Director, Irene Santiago were determined to organise regional facilitating committees and coordinate these through a fulltime Secretariat in New York.

A critical factor leading to the success of the NGO Forum was the role of the facilitating committee working with a new NGO Forum Secretariat structure. While a handful of women had organised previous women's conferences representing international NGOs based in the US, this NGO Forum was regionally based and culturally diverse. Regional focal points, backed by representatives from the Conference of Non-governmental Organisations (CONGO), and the NGO Committees on the Status of Women, worked with the New York Secretariat. With a 200-organisation Planning Committee, this group raised funds, organised the regional NGO fora, helped coordinate the women's caucuses and provided technical support to the regions. A newsletter kept all regions informed and guidelines concerning how to draft amendments to the UN documents were shared widely.

In New York, fewer than 15 persons constituted the Secretariat along with a group of dedicatDominican Republicinterns. Using the best of high-tech equipment and communications, this group was able to deal with most of the complexities the Conference was to bring. Most of us had left our own jobs to join the team, little realising that we had entered an endless maze of new challenges!

At the beginning, it appeared that things were going smoothly. The 14-member facilitating committee had returned from their first visit to China with a written agreement which even provided for freedom of speech on NGO Forum grounds. With the site issue settled, we turned to the problem of raising our own funds as the UN does not sponsor the NGO Forum. Here, too, there was reason to be upbeat. Many corporate, government and UN funders and foundations contributed generously; the Chinese government agreed to provide the main logistical support in Beijing.

However, the crisis of the site change suddenly transformed the euphoric mood. I still remember the shocked look on Supatra Masdit's face when she read the telegramme from the All-China Women's Federation that the site was to be shifted from Beijing to Huairou, 40 miles away from the UN conference.

What followed was a flurry of global NGO protest and fax campaigns which demonstrated the force of the women's movement. Pressures on the UN and governments were persistent and widespread. On June 8, a new letter of agreement was signed with compromises. The Chinese accepted the increased number of participants, guaranteed a shuttle service and a satellite site near the UN conference in Beijing.

We tossed out the old maps and rushed to establish new ones, realising that we had only two and a half months to organise a new NGO Forum. Hotel reservations and visa obstacles were only part of the problems. It was clear to us that the real cost was being paid by participants whose dreams were crumbling in a logistic nightmare of late visas and hotel reservations.

For us, life changed completely. Sleep was what you did between crises and insomnia took up the remaining night hours. What kept us going was the realisation that thousands of women counted on us to stick together, work out problems with the Chinese organisers and keep the event threads together. All we had to do was keep a united front and hold open opportunity until the women of the world came to Beijing to weave it all together. And so we did.

Fortunately, the NGO Forum's role in the lobbying process had gained strength throughout the period. The Beijing Conference was unique partly because of its national preparations. Never before were so many NGOs involved in drafting amendments to the Platform for Action. In many countries, NGO preparation for Beijing had started at the subnational levels. For example, in Botswana, one women's group organised village conferences for over two years in preparation for a national meeting. Palestinian camps had a series of meetings at which women's groups made their recommendations to the next level of camp organisation, until all of the camps became involved.

The women's movement had also established higher standards for NGO access to negotiations. NGOs and the women's movement demanded greater participation in government and UN decision-making and financial support for their movement. While in 1975, there were few NGOs on official delegations at UN conferences, at Beijing in 1995, almost every delegation included one. Moreover, NGOs pushed for and succeeded in ensuring that more women were included in and even headed official delegations.

For the first time in the history of women's conferences, during the preparations for Beijing, five regional NGO fora were organised parallel to the UN preparatory meetings. These fora produced NGO amendments to the Platform for Action. At all the regional conferences between August 1993 and November 1994, women displayed exceptional abilities at NGO/UN negotiations and lobbying. There was no doubt of the high level of interest: in each case, the number of participants who attended was twice the number expected. Grassroots women were most strongly represented and all fora included the involvement of youth, the disabled, indigenous women, lesbians and older women. But, perhaps, the biggest surprise was the large number of official delegates.

The planning committee sought new ways to balance diverse voices with unity. Thus, it decided that during the final March PrepCom of 1995, the NGO Consultation would concern itself with the UN Platform for Action. (Previous consultations were largely workshops, leaving lobbying to a "women's caucus.")

The meeting of a 35-person Editing Committee before the March PrepCom in 1995 was a critical preparatory activity organised by the NGO Forum office in New York. This was another "first" in the history of UN women's conferences where NGO regional amendments to the Platform for Action were drafted into a single global document. Editors representing regional as well as diverse experiences and NGO committees working on the Twelve Areas of Concern, met for two days to synthesise NGO documents including the regional NGO Platforms, caucus documents, and agreements from previous UN conferences such as the International Conference on Population and Development (ICPD), the Children's Summit, UNCED in Rio, the Human Rights Conference and the Social Development Summit.

Certainly, the process of drafting the amendments, negotiating their language and completing a balanced document was not perfect. Nevertheless, at the NGO Consultation held just prior to the Committee on the Status of Women (CSW) meeting, 1,400 women representing hundreds of NGOs from all regions, met to finalise the document. (We joked that they finished in two days, what the UN CSW could not complete in three weeks !) NGOs added language to focus on the central themes of diversity, economics, women's rights as human rights and the right to education with a gender perspective.

Last-minute negotiations meant that many portions of the text introduced by NGOs could not be fully agreed upon or checked with home governments. Still, 60 to 80 percent of the NGO amendment document was included in the official UN text. The next task was to remove the many brackets (nearly 60 percent was in brackets) around the "good text" which resulted from the rapid introduction of new text and controversial language.

When I met Mrs Gertrude Mongella in the halls on the last days of the March PrepCom, I said to her: "We have done you a great favour because, for the first time, every woman in these halls has read the UN document and they are ready to carry forth the document when the meeting is over." She laughed and agreed.

With the Platform for Action largely negotiated through "informal informals" and pre-consultations, in Beijing, NGOs worked primarily on the controversial text and remaining brackets. Attention was also turned to the drafting of the Declaration and towards political pressure for government commitments. Many NGOs felt that the lobbying process and influence on the draft Platform for Action was highly successful. As one woman put it: "We can hardly believe it. Everything we wanted is there. This Platform went beyond Cairo's ICPD and gave us more ground to pressure the governments."

With a great deal of focus, perseverance and intelligence, NGOs refused to be distracted by logistic and political obstacles. Instead, they charged on to make sure that their energies were directed towards lobbying. A few governments supporting the Holy See were unable to derail the strong language that supported sexual and reproductive health and rights. Similarly, some states finally adopted most of the Human Rights NGO amendments with reservations. Issues such as the girl child, violence against women and structural adjustment were given adequate attention, thus forging stronger commitments to the "critical areas of concern".

What were some of the gains?

- The international movement of women asserted its right to speak on all issues as women's issues. Women want to redefine the structures, culture and values of development. They no longer see themselves as "victims"; instead, they are establishing their rights as "citizens".

- There was a search for greater commonality between women from rich and from poor countries to work together, as they acknowledged that solutions to global poverty, environmental degradation, negative impact of the media and new information technologies involve us all.

- At the UN Conference, delegates recognised that the true enemy of peace was not war between nations; that before there can be lasting peace between nations, there must be an enduring peace in family life. There cannot be an end to global ethnic violence while domestic violence persists. There cannot be a moral separation between private and public spheres. Responsibility for domestic violence is no longer private, but is a public, legal issue.

- Women's health—particularly since the ICPD in Cairo, it has been closely tied to women's empowerment and education.

Important emphasis was given to health information and prevention of ailments and it was reiterated that health services should deal with women's "complete state of well-being"—mental and physical—throughout their life-cycle, addressing the needs of girls, adolescents and the aged.

- Human rights emerged as a new moral instrument for women's rights. It stands not only for legal reforms, but for the rights of women as citizens, covering a wide diversity of women and their needs.
- Gender—as a social construct of the relationships between men and women—was debated and entered into the new Platform for Action. This controversial concept affirms that "biology is not destiny". There are socially and culturally defined differences which define gender inequality.

Most definitely, we should be proud of the gains achieved. But the most important accomplishments of the Platform for Action are invisible. Even after governments returned home and went about business as usual, the women's movement has the potential to carry this document and, with their votes, make governments accountable.

Furthermore, this constituency is now better organised and more global than ever before. Mobilisation around the Beijing Conference and the Platform for Action has strengthened NGO networks in a "spider web" structure from grassroots to regional level. Leadership has diversified and regional, sub-regional, national and sub-national structures have emerged with working groups and issue caucuses. These "spider web" structures will continue to evolve and grow stronger much beyond Beijing.

Another gain not readily seen is the political experimentation which appeared during the Beijing Conference. One of these was a "first" for any NGO Forum—a facilitating team which ran the lobbying process representing regional and issue caucuses as well as international committees. Called 'Equipo' (Spanish for "team"), the formation of this global representative team was timely and politically strategic. 'Equipo' was a facilitating body composed of members of the NGO Forum Facilitating Committee, the NGO Committees of the CSW, CONGO, regional and diversity caucuses. It was a new model of how to mobilise representative groups at an NGO Forum.

Another facet of the invisible legacy was the way in which diversity became the foundation of unity. Women at the NGO Forum struggled with the issue of cultural differences and unity and came up with notable solutions. As Rebecca Sevilla, a Latin-American lesbian advocate put it: "I want to speak about the ethic of diversity which is to meet you halfway." So, giving up some space, learning about another culture, allowed the women's movement to move toward a common ground.

Two years later, the flurry of post-Beijing activities were another phenomenon—the largest number of meetings after any UN conference. Post-Beijing events are popping up everywhere. As early as November 1995, many national consultations between NGOs and governments had already started "bringing Beijing home". And that was just the beginning.

Of course, the Beijing Conference did not come with a written guarantee. There is no historical inevitability to assure that the international women's movement will succeed. There are plenty of obstacles. Fundamentalist movements alone, with their obsessive need to control women's bodies and the family, are significant threats.

Internal threats are no less real. For instance, competition for scarce resources between larger, established NGOs and grassroots groups can undermine the movement. Taken to extremes, intramural rivalries

From Nairobi to Beijing

"National was more like an outline, a framework. Here in Beijing, the whole tapestry is being enriched, we're putting in the design, the colours, the specifics," Leticia Ramos-Shahani of the Philippines said in an interview this week.

In 1985, Shahani was director-general of the Nairobi conference on women. In Beijing, she is chairing the Group of 77, now composed of representatives of 132 developing countries. In her own country, Shahani is president protempore in the Philippine Senate and chair of its committee on women and the family.

"Looking back at my experience in Nairobi, the negotiations then were simpler. There was the cold war, apartheid, there were mega issues that held us together. Now in Beijing, you don't have that glue.

"The women are more active, more specific. Domestic violence is coming out strongly even in plenary. They are now revealing what happens in the bedroom."

Shahani says more attention must be focused on women's economic contribution, as did the UNDP's 1995 Human Development Report, which was released last month. The report measures not only quality of life but establishes a measure also of women's empowerment.

But she also said that much dissent remains about what constitutes a fundamental right for women.

"In the Group of 77, the most contentious so far is the reproductive rights issue," she said. "There is a mini-Cairo debate going on. You have the fundamentalists and the 'surrogates of the Vatican' within the group. They are a small minority but we go by consensus. If there is none, they can make their reservations in the main committee and in the plenary. In Nairobi, there were so many asterisks, so many footnotes.

"We have to make sure consensus is really arrived at in Beijing. Every delegation wants to go back to their country and say that this Platform For Action has been arrived at by consensus. That is the bottomline for any international conference. Any dissenting voice is like a crack. Otherwise, we fall back to the language of Cairo, Copenhagen, Vienna," Shahani explained.

On the issue of resources, the G77 is calling loudly for "new and additional" resources while the US wants to limit the document to "existing" resources.

After Beijing? "It will depend on the political will, it will depend on those wonderful NGOs who will lobby for its implementation. Don't blame the UN if it is not implemented.

"When you change the role of women in society, you revolutionise society. The 21st century is the century of women. There has to be a change, although the men have to be our allies. We have to do away with this mindset that women are weak.

"Mahbub Ul Haq says that the 21st century will be the second industrial revolution. And women will have a greater role. But there are disadvantages. In the Philippines, export processing zones prefer women to men. Why? Because women have a large capacity for boredom. Imagine that."

Shahani also says that changing women's status will require more than changes in society. It will also require internal changes and a spiritual searching by every individual.

"The UN is looking at empowerment in external terms—legal, educational. Unicef is always looking for programmes on the outside vaccination, breastfeeding. But we should also teach the child to be cooperative. Conventions are expressions of moral values. Human identity is partly spiritual.

"Empowerment should come from within. I don't have the answers myself. How do you do it universally? We must have a vision. What do we want? Education for what? Not to recreate the same violent world. In the Philippines, I'm promoting this moral recovery programme. We must be able to create an alternative structure. We have to make the choice."

Anita Anand and Olivia H. Tripon
Beijing Watch

could drive many activists to join cynical bystanders watching from the sidelines. One high school student at a Beijing preparatory meeting put it this way: "The older generation of feminists has given feminism a bad name. You fight for power among yourselves. You think power is out there waiting to be taken, but we young women, believe in the power from within."

Most worrisome of all, diversity as a code of ethics within the international women's movement could be put aside as more mainstream leadership takes over. The danger is that NGOs representing diverse groups such as women of colour, indigenous women, lesbians and women with disabilities may feel alienated from the very movement they helped to build. All these problems, and more, could well sweep away this "spider-web" structure.

But the good news is that for the time being, none of these obstacles seems insurmountable.

Like the 'Yin' and the 'Yang', NGOs and governments may be opposites, but they are also complementary parts of a single political process. There is real potential for this NGO/GO partnership to succeed. Nevertheless, to make this work, we need stronger official support for NGO autonomy with substantial financial backing. We have had major disappointments after the UN conferences on environment, population and human rights. Post-Beijing celebrations are already marred by fears of more cutbacks in funding. At the very least, a stance of healthy skepticism is clearly warranted. At future rallies, at least one banner should prominently wave an important message saying: "Vigilance, vigilance, vigilance."

SECTION THREE

At Beijing

1
Introduction
Anita Anand

The stage was set for the Fourth World Conference on Women. The last months were anxious and exciting. Passports, tickets, visas and accommodation in Beijing had to be finalised. In the already bulging suitcases decisions—about what paper to discard, food to take, and the size of umbrellas—had to be made.

All this was compounded by rumours that visas were going to be difficult to get, literature taken to the conference would be screened, no demonstrations were to be allowed, and lesbians were not going to be looked upon kindly, among other things.

Some countries and delegations of countries, talked about boycotting the conference due to the perceived oppressive methods of the Chinese government in terms of free speech and movement. The international press and news agencies wrote about how the government was going to cordon off the local population and not spare any means to keep foreigners in line.

Since April 1995, many NGO participants were extremely anxious at the Chinese government announcement that the site of the NGO Forum was moved to Huairou 40 miles away from the previous Beijing site, due to a technical flaw. Rumour had it that the negative experience of Li Peng, the Chinese Premier, at the World Social Summit in Copenhagen earlier in the year was the reason behind the move. He wanted the outspoken Forum participants far from Beijing, and the UN conference location.

With this background, thousands of women and some men travelled to Beijing, where the challenges were enormous. Participants arriving at the airport were greeted by efficient Chinese staff, stamping passports and whisking groups through customs. Buses waited to take participants to hotels and hostels, in Beijing and Huairou, free of cost.

This section includes editorials from the daily publication BEIJING WATCH produced by the WFS, during the 10 days.

To get a daily paper out was a feat, due to the size of the Conference, the distance between Beijing and Huairou (40 miles), high cost of taxis, unreliable and slow buses that shuttled between Beijing and Huairou, incessant and unexpected rain, and general exhaustion which accompanies such events.

However, as the contributions in this section indicate, the WFS was not alone in having to face these challenges. Everyone attending the Conference encountered them.

In this section we also provide a glimpse into the thinking of the youth. Selected articles from Beijing watch, show in a nutshell the aspirations of the next generation.

In the earlier section, Mallica Vajrathon described the regional conferences which set the tone for the finalisation of the twelve areas of concern and the draft Platform of Action. In this section, we asked representatives of various regions active in the preparations (some of them coordinated the groups) to write about their experiences during Beijing. They have included facts and anecdotes about the regional experiences, before, during and after Beijing. And these are necessary to situate the contributions.

We also asked individuals who had been in leadership or key positions in institutions organising the Conference, from the UN and the NGOs, to write of their experiences. All this for readers who were and were not in Beijing, and cannot imagine the hard work that goes on behind the scenes to bring about such an event.

The section highlights the amazing achievements of the individuals, organisations and women's movements all over the world. It features experiences that changed women dramatically.

From Latin America to the Pacific, in each region there are commonalities of experiences. One example is the difficulty of language many women faced. And it was not with Chinese. English, which is one of the languages of the conference and many of the NGO events and documents, posed a problem. Thai, Indian, African and Latin American women, especially those from the grassroots, had to creatively resort to gestures and other measures to get around.

Almost all contributors write of their discomfort with Chinese security, and resentment at feeling they were being watched, photographed and eavesdropped upon. Some write of the inadequate facilities in Huairou. But all agree that the event was worth attending and was a great common denominator for collective action of governments and women's movements. Some feel that in a sea of words and documents not much gets done, as governments lack the political will and commitment to gender and women's empowerment.

From Latin America, Virginia Vargas writes about how the NGO process got off to a stormy start when regional women's groups refused to accept the facilitating committee's recommended person to chair the group. Instead they chose her. It was in this region that the group 'Equipo' was formed six months before the Beijing Conference, in the Dominican Republic, to shepherd the process through difficult, and not so difficult times.

Vargas writes about strategies Equipo adopted, but laments the weakness of the media strategy. She points out that while alternative media and communications largely used by women's organisations and movements are strong, they still do not replace the need to be in touch with and get the message into mainstream media. And this continues to be a challenge.

In Latin America, as in other regions, the level of activity was at all levels. Local, national, sub-regional, regional and global. The players were large and small NGOs, networks, all expressions of the women's movements, governments, the UN and its agencies, the Conference Secretariat, the Forum Facilitating Committee, the churches, media, etc. In Latin America, the presence of the non-Spanish Caribbean was a complex challenge.

The government dynamics of the region was uneven, says Vargas. The Caribbean is more advanced in democratic institutions, whereas Latin America varies—from democracies sensitive to women's interests to fundamentalist, authoritative and conservative regimes.

The Economic Commission for Latin America (ECLA or CEPLA the Spanish acronym) was the official space for building consensus. The NGO work relied, as in other regions, on the existing networks and their constituencies, that had experience in the previous UN conferences.

By the time Beijing came around, NGOs experts and representatives were on the official country delegations of all the Caribbean, and almost all Latin American delegations. There were support teams and organised networks to give delegations thematic and political assistance. This helped the lobbying at the Conference and incorporated women's movements proposals into the Platform for Action.

According to Vargas, Beijing was a victory, and new parameters were established between civil society and the State, giving a concrete and flexible content to women's alliances, yet indicating their limits. Resolutions were achieved a little differently, and tensions between women and official dynamics were perceived in unconventional ways.

Much of the success of women's movements through the Beijing process, Vargas says, was because the movement broadened its canvas to include multiple expressions, for example young people and indigenous women. And a significant development has been the realisation that channels of negotiation and follow-up with the State must be widened.

The scene shifts to Europe, where Georgina Ashworth says the politics, shape, composition and diversity of the region changed dramatically during the five years preceding Beijing. The fall of the Berlin Wall and the various 'velvet' revolutions in the countries which had been independent but within the Soviet orbit, impacted not only the countries concerned but all of Western Europe.

Ashworth points out that the women's movements of Western Europe had not been deeply involved in the previous three world conferences on women. The reasons for this was insularity and preoccupation with local issues (and sometimes conflicts); disinterest in the UN as a source of women's liberation; a vague desire not to be imperialist towards the Third World; and resources (feminism is not funded in Europe).

Ashworth focuses on the preparations at the UK level and the preparatory meeting in Vienna in 1994. The NGO Forum, she points out, was the first European (and North American) meeting of women's movements. There was also some dread among Europeans at the potential dominance of US organisations with their better funding and sense of superiority towards others, although the US social provisions—childcare, equal pay for work of equal value—are far behind Europe's limited infrastructure.

Ashworth describes lucidly the human frailties of participants of different countries with their agendas and how these were handled. She describes the role of the European Commission which committed funds to large numbers of women from the "developing countries" and East and Central Europe, administered by Women in Development Europe (WIDE) and CHANGE, respectively. And Ashworth makes an important point, in that no funding was available for NGOs in Northern countries from their own donors.

From Africa come two contributions. One which describes the African preparations, and the other, a sardonic look at the 'Beijing Game' in the region. Njoki Wainaina was Chairperson of the African Women's Development and Communication Network (FEMNET) during the preparatory process, and describes the activities starting from 1984, when 100 women came together for what was the first African women's NGO Forum.

In a fashion that is not atypical to other parts of the world, the group attending the Arusha meeting got propelled into action for the forthcoming Decade End Conference for Women which was held in Nairobi, Kenya in 1985. An African Women's Task Force was created and mandated to ensure that the numerous tasks of mobilising and sensitising women for Nairobi took place. In 1988, this Task Force became FEMNET.

It was also the NGO coordinating activities for Beijing. Wainaina recalls the daunting task to get the region organised for Beijing, complicated by the barriers of language and poor communication between the countries of the region. But those attending the African region's preparatory meeting in Dakar, Senegal in 1994 will recall that despite the logistical and organisational nightmare, the women of the region were well represented.

Wainaina concludes by stating that the value of shared responsibility, of recognising and using the comparative advantages of diverse groups, was an important experience.

Sara Longwe has a different take on the African participation, and makes no bones about this in her contribution. She says that ten years after Nairobi, from the national and regional reports prepared for Beijing, it was obvious that all African countries had made little or no progress in pursuing the Nairobi Forward Looking Strategies (FLS).

Longwe suggests that governments dominated by men sign international agreements because they want to look good, and thereby gain international respectability to access donor funding from Northern countries. She proposes an alternative 'feminist project' in which the women's movement must use its elbows to make a space and increase a space for itself, and not accept the space made for it.

Moving to West Asia, Fatima Kassem describes the process initiated by Economic and Social Commission for Western Asia (ESCWA) and UNIFEM. In 1993 the ESCWA organisers began by visiting all the 13 members countries it represented, encouraging the governments to form preparatory committees which included NGOs. This was followed by national meetings in nine countries, with reports and recommendations submitted to ESCWA.

The regional preparatory meeting held in Amman, Jordan in 1994 was the largest meeting ever organised by ESCWA. It received wide media coverage, and owed its success to the collaboration of all parties, says Kassem. The most significant development in this region was the composition of the Arab delegations to Beijing. Ten of the 20 heads of Arab delegations were women, and 10 of their deputies were either of ministerial level, high officials, or presidents of NGOs.

Haifa Abu Ghazaleh one of the Coordinators of the NGO Forum Facilitating Committee of the region, writes of the far sightedness of the Arab region to prepare proposals for post-Beijing organising. These consist mostly of setting up infrastructures that bring different groups together to take forward the Plan of Action.

From India, S.K. Guha, who was active in the Beijing process as a bureaucrat in the Department of Women and Child Development—responsible for formulating the country paper—feels that Beijing was important because of what happened before and after it. And the open ear of the government in devising the paper was not a conscious process, but one it deserves credit for, in not resisting the input.

Guha describes the process which unfolded, organised by the Coordination Unit (CU) which pulled together all voices into the process. It worked with the government in holding meetings in different parts of the country, bringing women out who had never been out of their homes, villages and communities, and taking the message of Beijing to them. In turn, it heard from them and took the messages back to the government and other NGOs.

As a result of this process, several initiatives have been introduced in Parliament for women's empowerment with direct input into policy making at the national level. Suneeta Dhar, Coordinator of the CU, points out that the most significant factor for women who went to Beijing was the tremendous appreciation they got from their communities when they returned home.

Southeast Asia was no less active. From Thailand comes a contribution by Shashi Ranjan Pandey and Darunee Tantiwiramanond, who say that women's NGOs were successful in the international arena by using the opportunities provided to them by international organisations and conferences, and finding allies in various bureaucracies. Also, by mobilising their human and financial resources.

As in other regions, they point out that the most dramatic development of the Beijing process was the coming together of rural women under an umbrella organisation. They cite the example of the November 1994 meeting organised before Beijing which was attended by 200 women—in which for the first time, grassroots women in traditional sarongs outnumbered the conventionally dominant group of middle class NGOs, academics and donors.

In the same region, for Cecilia Young Dong-ling of Hong Kong, the Beijing Conference was a catalyst in that the colonial government established the Equal Opportunity Commission on Sex and Disability, and terms of reference to address employment issues. An important learning of the Beijing Conference, says Dong-ling, is that in order to be heard, women need to become good negotiators.

Onto the Pacific and last regional contribution. As in West Asia, Bernadette Rounds Ganilu says that the Beijing Conference had a special significance for women in the Pacific. For the first time in 20 years women participated, not just in an international conference, but in events leading up to it.

She says that in the previous conferences (1980 and 1985) Pacific governments and NGOs were not involved at the decision making level. Their issues and input were lumped along with the broader canvas of the 'Asia and Pacific' region, with Asia usually taking the lead.

This regional report traces the developments in the region, the various organisations that came together to build consensus on issues that would be priorities, strategies to get them in to the Platform for Action, as well as get Pacific region women involved. They did this with the assistance of monthly Peacesat satellite conferences, recording the activities of NGOs and their needs. In addition there was a bi-monthly newsletter called S'Pacifically Speaking, and regular reports in the national Radio Fiji and Pacnews for regional dissemination.

There were 400 Pacific women in Beijing. France, at the same time, resumed its nuclear testing in the region. The women attending the conference took the opportunity to denounce this testing.

Sixteen governments from the Pacific attended the Beijing conference, including New Zealand and Australia. In preparation for Beijing, the Pacific region was together with Asia. The NGOs strategised together, and this was very useful says the report. For example, the group strategising on issues of structural adjustment and violence against women had representatives from Malaysia, India and the Philippines (South and Southeast Asia).

Besides the regional contributions, we asked Charlotte Bunch to make a contribution on how she saw the Beijing process. The result was a piece on a global referendum of human rights, authored with Mallika Dutt and Susana Fried. They describe the Beijing process through their eyes, as coordinators of activities and campaigns related to women's human rights.

Bunch, Dutt and Fried say that of the multitude of issues discussed, certain themes resonated across regions. The prevention of violence against women; advancing women's health and reproductive rights; reversing the negative impact of international economic policies; countering the rise of religious and secular conservatism, and giving women a greater voice in policy making.

Despite successes, they point to the gaps. The lack of strong interaction between development and human rights discourses. And they mention losses. There was no explicit reference to sexual rights or orientation; there was the replacement of explicit reference to race and ethnicity with "demographic factors" in some sections; there was inadequate inclusion of internally displaced women as in need of international protection, and there was weak language about the various forms of "family."

In a conversation with John Mathiason who has for a very long time been the man in the women's unit, I thought it important to ask him to make a contribution to the book. He reviews the history of the Department for the Advancement of Women (DAW), the Commission on the Status of Women (CSW) and the Beijing Secretariat — the three UN pockets which were responsible for pulling off the Beijing conference.

More than this, he describes how the dialogue and debate in the three bodies developed, how issues are resolved, ideas taken forward to gain wider acceptance, and eventually find a place in the Platform for Action. For those who wonder why it takes so much time for UN agencies and processes to reach consensus, this contribution is worth reading!

2
Beijing Watch *Observes*

(These editorials appeared in the daily paper produced by WFS during the Conference.)

The Icing, Not The Cake

September 6: Women gathered at the Conference in Beijing said today that they had come to ice the cake and not bake it. They were referring to the amount of money that will be needed to implement the Global Platform for Action, which will be adopted at the end of the Conference. Other UN international conferences have had a tag, which may not have been met. This time around there is not even that. Adding insult to injury, women have been told that finances to implement the recommendations should be found in existing resources. But the existing pie has already been sliced without consulting or favouring women. In this, defence spending ranks high. How much would it cost to implement the Platform for Action? While no figures have emerged in a concrete way, an attempt has been made. The 1995 UNDP Human Development Report puts a figure of US $20 billion, just five percent of the total size of public sector budgets in developing countries. Where could this money come from? By reordering existing budget priorities, the report suggests, especially through judicious cuts in military spending and elimination of inappropriate development projects. For at least a decade conferences have called for cuts in defence budgets, or at least a freeze. And while there is some agreement that good development equals sustainable development, there are no clear, quantitative criteria of inappropriate development. And while women wait for these cuts, is anything due to them?

Since 1975 at the First World Conference on Women, and before, women have argued that their work is unrecognised, undervalued and underpaid. For the first time, a value has been ascribed to this work—$11 trillion a year according to the UNDP report. What would it mean if resources were not allocated to implement the Platform for Action? A piece meal approach to women's empowerment.

This would affect not only women, as it is commonly thought, but men and children as well. In the meanwhile, women who have travelled from the far corners of the globe to be in Beijing want more than platitudes. They want concrete policy plans with implementation strategies attached.

Most of all they want a figure for the finances. It has been at least a decade of baking cakes. Let's see the icing.

Working Woman, Working Man

September 7: Carol Bellamy, executive director of UNICEF, says she is intrigued by the term working woman. What do women do at home, she asks. Relax?

Many women who are full time homemakers, when asked what they do, often say 'nothing' as they are 'housewives'. This is because the world of work in which men live, is outside the home. Or so we have been told.

Many women who work outside the home

do it at a cost. And they always feel guilty, having been taught that no one can take care of the children as well as they do. Hillary Clinton speaks of the 3 pm anxious mom syndrome, when women at their jobs worry about what is going to happen to their children who are getting home from school.

Mary Ann Glendon, the Vatican representative says that women who stay at home have been ridiculed and not given a fair hearing at the Conference. She reminded delegates to remember the women who dedicate their time and energy to motherhood and family life. Had Glendon read the Platform for Action, she may not have said this.

Women's movements, believe it or not, are made up of women who live in families, carry out their responsibilities (often more than their share), and work outside the home. The input from the regional preparation meetings in the last two years has stressed the needs of women at home, in the workplace and on the streets.

The Platform for Action addresses this, but not in a manner that will allay the acute anxiety that some men, women and institutions have about the place of women. This is the difference between the women's movement and the Vatican and fundamentalists, who want women to stay home, so that men can 'work outside the home'.

Hillary Clinton, Benazir Bhutto, Gertrude Mongella, began their speeches by situating themselves as mothers first. No matter how high an office a woman occupies, she feels she must justify her work outside the home as secondary to her role as a mother.

If men would work in the home in much larger numbers than they seem to be doing, they might discover just how much work it is to maintain a home and raise children. And the definition of 'working woman' might change to include work at home.

Maybe then, we could call them working men.

Money, Money and Money

September 8: In the meeting rooms and halls of the conference centre, the subject eventually turns to money. Sometimes the word commitment is used. Two days ago, the delegates agreed to remove the annexure which would list the governmental commitments that would pay for implementing the Platform for Action.

Did the delegates think they could get away with this? With the NGO Forum over, thousands of women are installed in the Beijing International Conference Center. They are combing the plenary speeches to get a figure they can put on the commitment score board. With this they hope to lobby the country delegates to keep to their word. Let's face it. Without the money, what good is the Platform for Action?

Ten years ago in Nairobi, no price tag was put on the Forward Looking Strategies. In 1995, as the last decade is reviewed, it is clear this was a mistake. This year, the United Nations Fund for Women (UNIFEM) found itself in a strange situation - out of money. In 1994 the annual income of UNIFEM was US $13 million. For an organisation whose mandate is to work with women in developing countries, this amount is a drop in the ocean.

Evidence from development practice over the decade indicates that there is a popular belief that small is beautiful, especially where women are concerned. Small credit programmes, boost the informal sector, and working on expand micro projects. Governments and funding agencies have also set aside money for women in this premise.

But the kinds of changes the Platform for Action spells out are going to require more than micro funds.

Noeleen Heyzer, director of UNIFEM, sees the future of the Fund in the political and economic empowerment of women. If this is going to be done with $13 million, then we all have a surprise coming.

And the NGOs are not going to give up that easily. From now till the last day of the Conference, they are going to struggle to get a figure from the delegates. And if the Platform is going to be enacted, the sums need to be said out loud.

The conferences of the last five years have stressed that women are key to development and that their empowerment is essential for social progress. This thinking is a shift from that of the 1970s and 80s. But if the UN wants to think big, as women want to think as well, then the sums being discussed have to be large and committed.

Come on folks, you have nothing to lose but your guns.

Content Discontent

September 9: A UFO landed on earth and Martians inside wanted to study the feelings of Earthlings by watching TV, listening to the radio and reading newspapers and magazines. This is the report they sent: "There are major differences between the male and female of the human species. He is active, decisive and obviously in control of his work. His recreation and what he says are all important. He has his emotions under control and often has to tell the female what to do. We found it harder to get information about her. She seems to be a passive creature, interested mostly in the home and family, and in making herself beautiful to keep her man happy. There are a few females who seem to be as successful as men, but they are rare. The female is highly emotional, and yet seems to get great pleasure from cleaning and cooking. She does little outside the home, and is less intelligent than the male..." Well, this may be a tall tale. Or maybe not. A handbook called Content Discontent released today by INSTRAW (UN International Research and Training Institute for the Advancement of Women), shows that women feature less than men in the world's media, and in some areas are completely invisible. In no country is the news about women more than 20 percent. And in some countries the percentage falls as low as 4 percent. While this may not be new to most women, what is disturbing is that this is despite the increasing numbers of women who have been entering media in the last 10 years.

Not surprisingly, these women are in the lower level positions in media, and in all parts of the world the media power brokers are overwhelmingly male. And a trend toward more concentrated ownership by fewer people has a negative effect on the portrayal of women. If fairness, equal time and balance don't make sense, at least commercial considerations should. Women are not only half the media public, but control the purse strings making up to 80 percent of all purchases. Many media men and organisations say they don't know how to get the 'gender thing' into their corridors, copy and tapes. Try reading the handbook. It's easy to read, won't offend the male ego and may even lead to content, content.

Keen Youth and Anxious Adults

September 11: Monday was Youth Day at the Fourth World Conference on Women. As young people and their advocates tell us about problems and needs, another discussion in the Contact Group on Health is key.

On Sunday the issues of the Contact group were parental rights and responsibilities, sexual rights and the review of laws containing punitive measures against women who have undergone illegal abortions.

It's not surprising that all these 'contentious' issues - in brackets and those that delegates have to negotiate around - relate to the sexual act.

Here is a deja vu of the International Conference on Population and Development (ICPD) held in Cairo in 1994. UN member nations passed by consensus a document that was far reaching when it came to these 'contentious' issues.

It is true that member nations are not together or totally on board when it comes to sexual matters. There seems to be a view that if young people or adults don't know about sex - clinically or socially - this ignorance will be bliss.

In this discussion the operative word is punitive. And everyone is punished. Men, women, adolescents and children. While parents may be given rights to protect children at home, how do they ensure physical and mental safety of children outside? Attempts to control people's sexuality results in people doing what they want, behind closed doors. And punishing women who have illegal abortions will not stop them from seeking and having them.

Youth, we hear and say, are our future. And sustainable development, the world community has agreed since 1992, means that the children inherit an earth that the present generation can be proud of. Somehow, when it comes to sexual matters, the worst kind of adult anxiety is perpetuated on youth.

What is being said to young people is that sex outside marriage is wrong, that women do not have the right to terminate a pregnancy, and that parents have the right to decide what youth should know about sexuality.

Young people know about sex. But they don't get this information from their parents whose responsibility it is. They learn from their peers and the media. And women will need access to abortion because of early and unwanted pregnancy due to rape, incest and failed contraception.

It's time that the issues were faced squarely. Young people should have information that will make them sexually responsible, and parents are responsible for providing this to them. And if women have to be punished for having illegal abortions, let's also punish the perpetrators.

All in the Family

September 12: Yesterday, there was a small stampede in one corner of the press room. The delegates of the Holy See were giving an ad hoc press conference on the work of the Contact Group on the family. Reporters crowded in, elbowing one another, falling over each other, and breaking a work station or two.

The Holy See, its supporters and countries with strong fundamental movements, are openly suspicious of the language in the draft Platform for Action on the family - which reflects the changing nature of relationships between men and women, parents and children, and proposes a definition based on present reality.

What indeed is a family? A place in which there is love and caring, nurturing and encouragement to grow and evolve in an open and respectful atmosphere. The nature of families has changed - from extended structures that included various permutations and combinations of relationships to nuclear units and single heads of households.

This is because of change - wars, migration, aspirations of people and relationships between men and women. Traditionally it was assumed that emotional, financial and physical support was lodged firmly in the family. But modernisation transformed this. And people began to realise that a family is more than a blood tie.

Fundamentalists believe that if women and men did not know about these changes, they would live happily in defined families.

But the evidence is that women want to define their relationships - to other women, men, society and children. They don't want to be told by the state and holy men what to do. There is one single reason that women have not rebelled earlier in exploitative relationships - and it is economic.

As women have more access to the workplace and earn a wage, the situation has changed. And with laws to protect and promote their rights, they will define the kind of families they want.

Real families are those in which love is given unconditionally. Fundamentalists believe that everything is conditional - love, obedience, marriage, children, relationships, authority - and non-negotiable. In short - women's lives are also conditional and non-negotiable.

Mother Teresa, in a message to the Conference, says that families that pray together stay together. But families, first and foremost, have to be together to pray and stay together. Since neither the church nor any fundamental movement can assure that, they should stop insisting that they know best.

In a world of views, the attempt in Beijing is to bring views together. For a start, the reality of families - broken, abandoned, violent, and sometimes loving - have to be acknowledged. This is the family.

Inheritance, For a Start

September 13: Wally n'Dow, Secretary General of HABITAT, the UN conference to be held in Istanbul next year, says that the focus of the last UN conference of the century will be on how people live. He elaborates and stresses that the issues of gender and land will be central to the discussion and debate between the conference on women and Habitat. Group 1, at the Fourth World Conference on Women, has been discussing succession and inheritance rights. Egypt has stated that countries of Islamic faith could not accept the idea of 'equal inheritance.' Many people are confused about the concept of equal inheritance. In traditional societies it was assumed that men would always protect and provide for women. Therefore, inheritance and succession for women was a non-starter. As times changed and women got opportunities to live without the patronage of men, they began to demand equal rights to inheritance. Since we live in an unequal world, what would it mean if women inherited property and money? They would have the same rights and responsibilities as men. In a system that favours men, women fear that they will lose the protection of men in their families, and be reduced to penury and abandonment in their old age. But this is happening already. Despite the inheritance laws that favour men in most parts of the world, they do abandon women and children. The large number of widows and orphans testifies to this. While men have the legal right to inherit, they only have a responsibility to protect. Even in some countries where women have equal inheritance rights, they are often tricked out of this, or willingly give over their share to men in the family. If women were given a choice - to be protected by men or have equal inheritance rights - what would they choose? Both choices have their repercussions, which they would have to live with. But to give up their right to inherit would mean a life of dependency and subservience. Equal rights would mean choices and responsibilities beyond their dreams. If men shared inheritance with women, the burden of protecting women would be shed. They could develop strong relationships with women based on mutual sharing and trust. Women, on their part, could breathe easier knowing they are persons in their own right and not appendages of men. Studies in poorer countries, where most women live, reveal that what women want most is land they own and can use as they want. If HABITAT is to be a success, let's say yes to inheritance and succession, for a start.

Men on Men

September 14: Of all the paper in the press centre at the BICC, probably the most popular book is *Men on Men*, a contribution by the Swedish government to the Conference.

In the foreword, Ingvar Carlsson, prime minister of Sweden, says he believes that men have great stakes in equality between the sexes. But a lot needs to be done before men become good partners with modern feminism and women become partners in men's search beyond the traditional role.

Carlsson also says that distancing ourselves from the old patriarchal macho image has a liberating effect, particularly for men. It means being able to choose a personal attitude and relationship which is not predetermined by tradition.

This can probably apply to women too. It is true that feminism may have left most men behind. But many women also need to move out of their traditional roles and goals.

For both men and women who have benefitted from the changes that feminism has brought about, a central issue is that members of the other sex have not travelled with them, and if they have, they have not been happy travellers.

The basis of this concern is the issue of space. Men who cannot or refuse to recognise feminist women are afraid that their space will have to be shared by women in the workplace, outside the home. And women who have such terribly high standards of maintaining homes and raising children, refuse to recognise feminist men and drive them away from what they consider their terrain.

If men and women agreed privately and publicly to negotiate for space things might be different. And if they made space for each other, in and outside the home, they would find themselves enjoying the spaces they occupy more than they presently do.

There would be balance in their lives. They might become better human beings, better partners and most important, like themselves a lot more.

Much is said about tradition and culture being an obstacle to change. But if men and women really wanted to cross this hurdle they would. There is plenty of evidence to support this.

Men who are looking to move beyond patriarchy will find women who will support them. For this, men will have to most of all do more - to maintain the home, raise the children, and free up the time and energy of women to participate outside the home, in society. They will have to make space for women in corporations, parliaments and decision making positions.

Let's hear it for these men.

It has Made a Difference

September 15: On the last substantial day of the Fourth World Conference on Women, exhaustion and fatigue have truly set in. Delegates, NGOs, UN staff and the press are ready to go home. The Working Groups of the Conference have completed their work and the Main Committee meets to go through the Platform, chapter by chapter, on the issues and language that the working groups are proposing. By and large there is agreement on the Platform for Action, with some 'contentious' issues being settled as member states express reservations. This means that while states have accepted the basic principles of the debate, they are not accepting the universality of it. And this is registered in the final session of the meeting, on the last day. The NGO lobby is winding down, with some individuals and organisations still making an effort to get the attention of the press and observers. Calls for press briefings, follow up action sessions, and some guerilla theatre in the conference centre, keep the press and security guards busy. NGO networks which promise to monitor the Platform for Action are forming every other hour. For those that have been organising and preparing for Beijing for several years, the sentiments at the end of the Conference are mixed. This is a historic Conference, not just for women but for society as a whole. The thousands of men and women who are here will not be the same again. What can be said of the Conference? It is the largest UN Conference ever, with an impressive mobilisation of women from all parts of the world. The process leading up to Beijing was equally significant in that governments and NGOs worked together, as they never had before. And while the NGOs may not be completely happy with the Platform of Action that will be adopted tomorrow, they can celebrate that the document reflects, by and large, most concerns of women. Each person, country, NGO, the UN and governments have tasks spelled out for them in the Platform, starting with the individual. Each must make a personal commitment to change starting with themselves. Resources — financial, human and natural — are essential to the process. While firm sums of money have not been committed, the goodwill expressed can be noted and built upon. The most worthy learning in the Conference is that the 'contentious' issues of sexual rights and orientation, definition of gender, and inheritance are on the international agenda. The Conference has made a difference as issues cannot be addressed without coming face to face, across the table, and it has given the trare opportunity that people, NGOs and government do not get. But this process of participation has to be more than word smithery at the international level and related to people daily lives. This is the challenge.

Three Weeks in China

September 16: The tables were taken away, the chairs stacked on top of one another. UN agency staff packed their literature in cartons to be shipped away. Some were already on the plane. As delegates took the floor in the early evening on the last day to register their reservations to the Platform for Action, otherwise adopted by consensus, the press gathered around the TV monitors for the last haul.

A major surprise of the day was an address to the plenary by President Fujimori of Peru. In a succinct and strong statement, he talked about how the hierarchy of the Catholic Church was preventing the Peruvian state from carrying out a modern and rational policy of family planning.

But Fujimori and Peru were not going to be stopped. Unfortunately other countries and coalitions have not shown such courage. There has been an attempt all day to lobby for the 'family, motherhood, church, morality and chastity', and to accept the Platform with reservations.

The government of China, the UN and Secretary General Gertrude Mongella, were all thanked for ensuring the success of the Conference. The Chinese people have worked hard at being good hosts to the 40,000 people here. While there may have been inconveniences, hardships and problems, it was not for lack of trying. And it was not easy for the Chinese. Relatively new to the world of international conferences, especially one in China, it was difficult for them to meet at least 40,000 demands a day.

The added attraction for participants at this Conference was China and Chinese people. Of the cultures of the world, China has been least accessible, until recently. International media has not been kind to China. And Chinese are wary of the media. Hopefully this will change.

The Chinese Organising Committee (COC) has followed every regional meeting and PrepCom since 1993. They have admitted that they have much to learn, as they have little or no experience with NGOs or with issues that the Forum and the UN are addressing. Yet, they have tried to create an equitable society for their citizens. Like other nations they may not have got everything right. And, an outcome of the conference is an individual and collective learning for all gathered here.

The Chinese people who have been close to the Conference will not be the same again. The level of preparation for the Conference - the volunteers, the security and the mobilisation of the women - it is truly remarkable. It is said that there were almost 5000 student volunteers at Huairou and at the UN conference.

The three weeks in China have been an eye opener. It is with this new vision that the Platform for Action will need to be implemented by each person, NGO, government and the UN. Let's go forth from Beijing with a new sense of purpose to make the world a better place.

3 The Experience of Youth

Youth Say Our Future is Now

Ten-year-old Marbre Stanly-Butts first realised she was a feminist when she challenged the history books.

Rather than sitting placidly in class learning "his-story," the precocious girl from California frequently interrupted class to complain about the sexist language in the textbooks.

Her mother was called in and eventually a deal was made. Stanly-Butts made it quite clear that she would have a standing objection to the sexist language, so that the class could get on with the lessons.

But already tempered in the fire of activism, the young girl and her friends wrote letters to the editors of their textbooks to complain about the inherent bias towards men. They got no response.

"Women don't really want to say, 'I'm a feminist,' because of the stereotypes," said Stanly-Butts, who was wearing a button which read, 'Commit to All our Daughters.' "In order to say, 'I'm a feminist,' I think you have to have a lot of pride."

The youth at the Fourth World Conference on Women, like Stanly-Butts, have combined pride, vision and activism to present a strong presence here.

"We are tired of being referred to as the 'future,'" said Karolina Vrethem, 27, president of the Council of European National Youth Committee (CENYC). "We are the actors of today."

To honour youth participation in the Beijing process, the Division for the Advancement of Women celebrated Youth Day with a series of panel discussions.

While the experts spoke about affecting youth worldwide, young activists made sure that their voices were not drowned by their elders.

"We want to be a part of shaping society," said Vrethem. "It sounds nice when people say the youth 'are the future,' but things are happening now. We don't want to sit and wait."

Young women and men between the ages of 15-24 constitute over 20 percent of the world's population. Eighty percent of the world's youth live in the developing world.

Already, young women have felt the pains of discrimination in education and health, and many know what it means to be poor and homeless.

Rather than continuing to be the victims, young people say they should also be seen as problem solvers.

"Many of those in power only refer to the 'problems' of young women...Yet, we are not 'problems' to be reckoned with; we are partners in progress," the Youth Declaration says.

Over 60 countries attending the Beijing Conference have youth on their official delegations. And throughout the regions of the world, they have been involved in national and regional preparations.

This is a big step forward, Vrethem said, but it is not something that the youth should be "thankful" for. "We should be a part of the process!"

Five regional youth meetings were organised by the UN Conference Secretariat before the Preparatory Regional meetings. These sessions provided more than 100 young women and men from all over the world a chance to contribute to the regional platforms and plans for action.

The Beijing Platform for Action makes specific references to youth in various sections, and the Girl Child is one of the priority issues of concern.

Young women like Vrethem and Stanly-Butts have already taken up the mantle of feminism and are speaking out against discrimination. For them, Beijing has not been a waste of time.

"I think that the Beijing Conference matters, because 10 years ago we never thought about discrimination against girls," said Stanly-Butts, whose mother is a psychology professor and testifies in court on behalf of battered women. "We always heard about discrimination against women, but the discrimination has to start somewhere."

Pat Made
(Beijing Watch, September 12, 1995)

Children's Express

The more than 2,000 journalists covering the NGO Forum here probably pay little attention to 9-year-old Brendan Quirk as he walks around the grounds looking for news.

Quirk, who comes from California, is the youngest journalist covering the Forum for the United States-based syndicated children's news service, Children's Express.

Clad in bright yellow-and-red T-shirts bearing the name "Children's Express News Team," the seven children, who range in age from 9 to 16 years old, are scurrying about the Forum with their ever-present tape recorders to press briefings and interviews. Quirk is the only boy among the California team of young reporters whose mission is to give children a voice.

"We are needed here because they say we (the children) are going to take over the world," said Chela Delgado, the 13-year-old editor for the news service. "But adults always try to say what is best for children or what is wrong for children. Yet they are not the ones who can talk about the experiences of children."

"We can talk for ourselves," said Madeline Blair, a reporter with the team. "Children's Express gives children a significant voice in the world."

The 20-year-old news service began with one man's vision of publishing interesting stories for children in New York. But when lawyer Bob Clampet took a group of children to cover the 1976 Democratic Convention in New York, he quickly learned that children had their own news agenda and the ability to create their own stories.

"Clampet thought that the children could interview the janitors and the other people who make conventions work, but the children went off and were talking to Senators and delegates," said Rosanne Marmor, who joined the organisation 15 years ago when she was only 13.

"He (Clampet) realised that the children could do whatever they wanted and that they could make Children's Express what they wanted it to be," said Marmor who is now a coordinator at the children's news syndicate.

There are now six bureaux in the United States - two in New York, one in Washington, D.C. (the largest bureau), one in Indianapolis,

Indiana, another in Marquette, Michigan and the Oakland, California branch. Children's Express has also spread its wings internationally with bureaux in Australia, New Zealand and London.

Some 35 newspapers across the United States subscribe to the free syndicate, which is entirely run by children.

Delgado says the service has covered issues such as violence against children, drugs and health, especially Acquired Immune Deficiency Syndrome (AIDS). Nine-year-old Quirk said he is interested in AIDS, because "my father has AIDS."

The Children's Express has also organised children's hearings on violence and abused children, with the most recent hearing held in Washington, DC and attended by US Attorney General Janet Reno.

Children's issues have become a major area of concern internationally. In 1991, the United Nations held the World Summit on Children, and children's hearings on the environment and other human rights issues have been part of the UN process since the 1992 United Nations Conference on Environment and Development (UNCED).

"The media is a strong way to give children a voice around the world," said Marmor. "Through our wire service, we get their voices to millions of people."

The syndicated news service was a part of the US-based international news agency, United Press International (UPI), but has been an independent wire service for over 10 years.

Not only is the Children's Express an example of how media can provide access for other voices, it also as its own unique style of operation. "You don't have to be able to really read and write to join Children's Express which is why we have children as young as 8 or 9," said Marmor.

Once the children graduate from high school, they can no longer be a reporter or editor for the syndicated service, although many like Marmor come back to work as coordinators and to work with each new generation of children to get their messages out to the world.

The children practice what they term "oral journalism." They sit and discuss their areas of interest, design questions together and then head off with only a tape recorder to get their stories. The tapes are then transcribed by the senior editorial staff and then sent off on the wire to their subscribers.

Delgado also points out that the children are not really strict about deadlines and schedules. "We usually meet at least once a month, and the children are given ample time to finish their stories."

Only the California team of Children's Express made it to China after months of fund raising and preparations. The Centre for Urban Family Life in Oakland, California is the umbrella group that provides grants and helps to raise money for the California branch of Children's Express.

For many of the children, this is their first big trip overseas, and like most journalists here, they are having their good and bad days.

"This is my first trip with Children's Express. I usually know what day it is and what time it is, but here, I find that I'm loosing track of the days and the time," said 13-year-old Tamentanefer Lumukanda.

Sixteen-year-old Haylene Sandler said that she and the other children on the team were also disappointed with the way some workshops on children's issues had been organised. "We went to a workshop on Southern African youth and there were no youth there. Only adults talking about youth. It doesn't make sense for others to talk about and for us."

'By Children for Everybody' is the motto of the service which according to Marmor attracts very few youth to the journalism profession. "About 80 percent of the children in Children's Express do not want to be journalists," she said. "Many become interested in community work or education and they give back what they have learn to their communities.

"The children learn how to use the media to get their point of view across, and they also learn about the rights of children or the fact that children have no rights," Marmor said.

Pat Made
(Beijing Watch, September, 1995)

Girl Feminists Surf the Net

Danika Pranik-Holdaway and her younger sister Madeleine begged their mother to bring them with her to Beijing, when she first told them she would be attending a Women's Conference there.

At 13, Danika already has a long history of feminist activism behind her. Her first campaign was in her middle school history class, when challenged her teacher's failure to mention an important woman inventor in a book he wrote on the history of the cotton gin.

"I was the only person in my class who thought he was wrong," said Danika, who wears a peace ring and braces and attends Marin Country Day School in San Francisco.

Madeleine, 10, who is poised beyond her years, chimed in, "If he had left out a man, they would have said, 'Yes, he should be included'."

The two sisters got their wish. Their mother, a science writer and feminist, brought them with her to the Conference. And on Monday, the two girls were participating in UN Youth Day festivities.

Over the course of the last two weeks, the girls have attended forums on topics ranging from the rise of religious fundamentalism to how aging women in Japan care for their parents.

They have also been promoting GirlNet, an electronic e-mail network for girls to provide a forum for young women around the world to discuss topics that concern them.

"We started it about three months ago, and we are going to write to girls around the world," said Danika, as she and Madeleine shared a bag of Skittles and waited to meet their mom.

Already they have met future e-mail pals from Nigeria, Switzerland and China at the Conference. They decided set up a girl's group on the Internet because they think it's important for girls to learn about science, technology and math.

"A lot of times boys are educated, while girls are left to clean the house," said Madeleine, who admitted she was glad her younger brother was left at home with her dad.

Both girls agreed that last week's NGO Forum, with its protest marches and colourful programme, was more lively than the discussions now taking place at the Beijing International Conference Centre.

"Here everyone claps like this," said Madeleine, as she imitated a cautious, polite round of applause.

The two sisters have had a whirlwind week. They were scheduled to climb the Great Wall with US First Lady Hillary Clinton but had to settle for a photo when the trip was rained out. The two girls were patient as journalists clambered to interview them Monday.

After a television interview with CNN's Richard Roth, the two turned to each other and rolled their eyes. "All he asked me about were boys," said Danika in disgust.

(GirlNet's e-mail address is: *Girlnet@aol.com* or *Girlnet@linex.com.*)

Jennifer Griffin
Beijing Watch

Give Us a Bright Future

Young women from around the world urged conference delegates to protect their rights and implement the Platform of Action once they return to their native countries.

"We want a future in which every girl and young woman will have a right to education, free of discrimination, a free access to health care and to related information and a right to control their own body," Sara Ramamonjisoa, of Madagascar, told delegates during the last Plenary Session Friday.

Ramamonjisoa was speaking on behalf of the thousands of young women who attended the NGO Forum in Huairou and the official conference in Beijing. Sixty-four countries have young women on their official delegations.

Young people formed a Coalition of Youth, which conducted its own lobbying over the course of the conference.

Ramamonjisoa said that many people pay lip service to investing in girls and young women for a better future. But she said that "we need to be listened to not because of what we will become but because of what we already are."

(Beijing Watch, September 16, 1995)

4
From the Regions

Latin America:

A Diversity of Dynamics

Virginia Vargas

Perhaps in a manner typical of the region, the launching of the Beijing process in Latin America was volatile too! The UN had decided to name a Facilitating Committee for the Beijing Conference which, for the first time, would be composed of regional representatives. One of the first hurdles we came up against in Latin America and the Caribbean, was when the UN tried to impose a non-feminist coordinator for the region. It was an appointment made without consulting either the regions or the networks involved. A significant section of the women's movement and the NGOs of Latin America as well as the Caribbean refused to accept this appointmment. It was amazing to see the reactions: in a lightning manoeuvre, lasting less than a week, hundreds of faxes were sent off to the UN demanding a replacement by a woman from the women's movement. We were successful. I was given the honour of becoming the new coordinator for the region.

Since ours was the only region to effect such a change, right from the start it gave the region a great legitimacy vis a vis the UN and the global networks. Besides, it also gave NGO participation the "style" of a movement and a dose of defiance—both of which were expressed at many other times throughout the process.

After a difficult experience at the March PrepCom in New York, the idea of holding another meeting in the Dominican Republic came up. At that time it seemed necessary to encourage a space for discussion that would permit us to overcome various limitations, as well as to fully realise our collective capacity for Beijing. The regional and global networks became our "spokespersons" par excellence. Together with them we set forth many joint strategies and created 'Equipo' (Spanish for Team), a space where the networks, global institutions and streams of the movement came together to organise daily lobbying at Beijing. This initiative turned out to be not only extremely united but one that was politically very effective as well.

Out of the Dominican Republic meet emerged a document which set out the strategies to be followed at both the UN Conference as well as the NGO Forum at Beijing. This grew out of the conviction that all networks shared a vast experience in principal lobbying strategies. Directions were also set up for pre-Beijing lobbying and for dealing with the media.

In my opinion, our media strategy was,

perhaps, one of the weaker aspects of the process. While I believe that the importance of alternative communication is clear, nothing can take the place of the mainstream mass media where, unfortunately, women's voices still do not reach. Not much of the regional mass media was seriously interested in Beijing. Of course, the big, international media gave ample coverage but often we were left with the feeling that they neglected writing about the more significant topics in terms of what women were achieving or proposing. And here is a challenge for the movement: how do we get our topics to reach the world of communications whose parameters of what makes news are different from ours? Nevertheless, the communicators were present and did act, maintaining a permanent link with the movement.

We formulated a communications proposal, the objectives of which were to establish both effective communications in the regions, as well as to create public awareness of the importance of the Beijing Conference as a forum for debate in changing women's conditions in our countries.

In the regional process, we moved at multiple levels. There was a permanent to-and-fro movement from the local, national, sub-regional, regional and upto the global levels. The actors, male and female, the institutions and movements were also multiple—large and small NGOs, networks, diverse expressions of the women's movements, new streams which outlined new autonomies and identities, governments and government coalitions, the UN and its agencies, the Conference Secretariat and the Forum Facilitating Committee, the churches, the media, etc. All these formed a fascinating spectrum of alliances, confrontations and negotiations which wove the social and political fabric for the multiple dynamics that became the whole Beijing process.

In order to relate to this enormous diversity of dynamics, we organised ourselves into six sub-regions with teams responsible for each sub-region and each country within it. The regional networks were a fundamental part of this flexible structure. The presence of the non-Spanish Caribbean was a complex challenge but it enriched the regional perspective enormously and offered us a more friendly and homogenous ground for lobbying.

Our agenda was as multiple as the identities and interests of women themselves: we did not negotiate only the specific agendas of this diversity but the movement's entire agenda which was enriched by the achievements of the earlier UN conferences of the decade.

The government dynamics of the region were uneven. For instance, the Caribbean is far more advanced in democratic consolidation and in gender agendas on the public level. Latin America contains the diversity of mixed political eras—from democracies sensitive to women's interests, to even fundamentalist, authoritarian and conservative regimes. At any rate, the actors in these official spaces were also broadening their frames of reference as they negotiated. Their greatest learning experience was, doubtless, that of being able to dialogue (although some never managed it at all) in an intense fashion with civil society and its women.

It must be said here, that the Economic Commission for Latin America (ECLA, or CEPLA by its Spanish acronym) played an extremely significant role. It was here that differing positions with regard to women's issues—of the more conservative and more progressive governments—were outlined. It was here that the Vatican exerted diplomatic-political pressure which caused one highly placed Central American government functionary to openly protest the interference. It was here that the governments' first contacts with the movement's regional structure were made.

CEPAL became the official space for building consensus. This implies that despite the ferocious resistance on behalf of some of the region's official delegations, the official document — 'Action Programme for the Women of Latin America and the Caribbean, 1995-2001' — that came out of the Regional Conference at Mar Del Plata, was a very advanced one.

The office of the Regional Coordination itself moved in several directions. We relied on health networks which had made advances at the Cairo Conference, as well as on the movement's groups of Catholic women (among them Catholics for a Free Choice) which did an excellent job of clarifying the issues, giving inputs and revindicating the plurality of viewpoints within the Church. We also sought and obtained alliances with women and men from other, more democratic churches who raised their voices and thus, broke the Vatican's conservative hegemony.

All these strategies gave us legitimacy and visibility as well as permitted us greater latitude to act as a region and better use our relative advantage: that of being the best linked region and of being able to dialogue with and be a connecting point between the South and the North—between networks, regions and positions that have been opposing and contradictory.

We, therefore, arrived at Beijing organised not only into teams with successful lobbying experience; we arrived with high-level official delegates and NGO experts in the official delegations of almost all the Caribbean and most of the Latin American countries. We arrived with support teams and organised networks that would give the delegations inputs as well as thematic and political orientation. This was of emormous assistance to the lobby effort within the very core of the Conference and also helped the movement's proposals being incorporated into the Platform for Action.

The results of the Beijing Conference are well-known: we won a lot. We established new parameters in the relationship between civil society and the State, giving a concrete and flexible content to women's alliances but indicating their limits. We began to resolve things differently, to look dialectically at the tension between the movement's dynamics and official dynamics. The profiles became more fluid. Some fundamental questions were, of course, left pending, such as that of the freedom of sexual preferences. And one of the movement's immediate tasks now is to create consensus in civil society regarding these democratic demands.

But on the whole, the entire process was a milestone for the women's movement. Beijing was a learning experience in regard to the strength of this movement, because through the process, the movement's action and political proposals were expressed as not just regional threads but as a global pattern. What the process really demonstrated was the movement's capacity to take over and permeate official, national and global spaces, and by so doing show itself to be a global, political movement.

Much of the success of the movement's achievements through the Beijing process occurred because the movement broadened its canvas to include multiple expressions. As the discourse moves forward, these new expressions—such as those of indigenous women and young women — must be incorporated, not merely as a formal presence but firmly, into women's agenda.

The dialogue between the movement and the State is becoming urgent for locating common agendas for our countries and the region. It's also imperative to design mechanisms for the allotment of funds in order to avoid competition between the government and civil society, and also because it is of utmost importance to strengthen the NGOs'

Recognising Cultural Diversity

The 1990s in Latin American so far have been a period of rapid economic development coupled with the persistence and intensification of widespread poverty and serious social problems.

The debt crisis of the 1980s set off a period known throughout the continent as the "lost decade," when most people suffered a serious erosion in their basic living standards.

With the imposition of structural adjustment programmes (SAPs) by the International Monetary Fund, there was a sharp downturn in economic and social investment, which affected basic public services such as health, education and housing.

Overall, during the 1980s, Latin America and the Caribbean became the region with the least equitable distribution of incomes, according to the Economic Commission for Latin America and the Caribbean (CEPAL).

Now, many Latin American economies are again growing. But as the Latin American and Caribbean Regional Action Programme acknowledges, "accelerated economic growth does not necessarily translate into better levels of well-being for all the population."

Specific actions will be necessary to improve women's standards of living and help them to integrate into and benefit from the existing process of economic growth. It was just such actions that women called for last year during the Sixth Regional Conference on Women's Integration into the Economic and Social Development, held in Mar de Plata, Argentina.

The programme adopted in Mar de Plata is designed to "accelerate efforts to achieve gender equality and the total integration of women into the development process, as well as the full exercise of their citizen rights within a framework of sustainable development with social justice and democracy."

The programme focuses on actions necessary in eight priority areas: gender equality, economic and social development with a gender perspective, the elimination of poverty, women's participation in the decision-making process and in positions of power, human rights, peace and violence, shared family responsibilities and recognition of the region's cultural diversity and international support and cooperation.

Many feel that the recognition of Latin America's cultural diversity is one of the most important achievements of the document.

Rosemarie Madden, a member of the region's advisory team a member of the Latin American Committee for the Defence of Women's Rights (CLADEM), believes that recognising of the region's cultural diversity will help in more effectively addressing the problems that affect Latin American women.

"For example, when we talk about illiteracy, what do we mean? Are we talking about illiteracy in Spanish or other languages spoken in the region," she asked.

In fact, gender limitations in other spheres are often aggravated and exacerbated by cultural differences. For example, indigenous and black women suffer the most from discrimination and poverty, which may not affect other women as much.

During the regional discussion of the Platform, many of the controversies that plagued the negotiations during the final preparatory meeting in New York last March were in evidence.

Countries such as Ecuador, Guatemala, Honduras, Argentina, Perú, El Salvador and the Dominican Republic questioned the use concepts previously recognised at other United Nations meetings, such as the diverse nature of families and women's human and reproductive rights.

However, other concepts which might have proved problematic were readily accepted by all delegates, including the notion that women should participate on an equal footing in the decision-making process and in positions of power, both in public and private life.

> The Latin American Platform was drafted on the basis of a series of regional and international documents aimed at strengthening the role of women in the international arena, beginning with the 1977 Regional Action Plan for the Integration of Women into the Economic and Social Development of Latin America and the Caribbean and the agreements reached in Nairobi in 1985.
>
> Latin American women's organisations were also able to exert a significant influence on the final regional platform for action, according to the regional NGO coordinator, Virginia Vargas, a Peruvian.
>
> "The government report which came out of the Preparatory Conference at Mar del Plata is a good report," Vargas said. "It is not a complete document, and perhaps does not contain all that we would wish, but civil society, through its own organisations, was able to permeate the document with its demands."
>
> The document constitutes an important instrument for the women of the region. But Madden argued that its implementation by governments must be closely followed up by women's groups and NGOs.
>
> "At a time like this, when official national and international institutions such as the United Nations are in decline, and no longer have the weight of previous times, the organisations of civil society must become new mechanisms for working with women," she said.
>
> **Thais Aguilar**
> (Beijing Watch, September 7, 1995)

capacity to capitalise on the achievements of the Beijing process.

Beijing's achievements force us to consider a policy towards women's citizenship so that women's rights as citizens are acknowledged and respected. The most important challenge that we face is to have the recommendations from Beijing accepted not as isolated measures, but rather as citizens' rights. And to achieve this, civil society, the women's movement and, of course, the State must all commit themselves to meeting the demands.

Many of the movment's contributions are contained in the Platform for Action that emerged from Beijing. Many others are still to be obtained from each nation's civil societies, from global civil society and from feminists and/or government allies.

Any reflection on post-Beijing must have as its axis the fashioning of a "political agenda" in order to continue the region's political process. A series of key themes in building the women's movement in the region has been discussed. One of the most significant develoments has been the realisation that channels of negotiation and follow-up with the States must be widened. We must be conscious that we are constructing a democracy that includes women. For this, it is necessary to establish strategic alliances with governments, with other movements and with sectors of civil society.

Europe:

A Confused Experiment that Worked

Georgina Ashworth

The politics, shape, composition and diversity of Europe changed dramatically during the five years immediately preceding the Fourth World Conference on Women. The fall of the Berlin Wall and the various 'velvet' revolutions in countries which were previously independent but within the Soviet orbit, impacted not only the countries concerned but all of Western Europe. Suddenly contact—both negative and positive—was possible between generations of peoples previously fed on hatred and propaganda about each other by their governments.

The European Union moved spasmodically towards consolidation through economic standardisation and very masculine political posturing. And the railway linking the continent of Europe to England opened. Although Mrs Thatcher lost power during this period, individual countries restructured their economies still further on the Thatcher model, cutting social costs and cheapening the labour force by feminising it and reducing union power, particularly attracting Japanese multinationals keen to have production units within the European market and therefore, not subject to import quotas. Poverty and unemployment increased throughout the region and a savage, nationalist-religious war was waged in the centre, in which women were 'discovered' to be victims for the first time.

While capitalism 'triumphed', many forgot that in the late 1980s there had been much debate about the 'crises of capitalism', because of its failure to reduce exploitation of the environment as well as people.

The more established social welfare women's organisations had paid the previous three world conferences for women, a little, rather arrogant attention. However, women's movements—that is groups with varied feminist politics—throughout Western Europe, had not been deeply involved. The reasons for this lack of interest were insularity and preoccupation with local issues (and sometimes conflicts); disinterest in the UN as a source of women's liberation; a vague desire not to be imperialist towards the 'Third World'; as well as resources (feminism is not funded in Europe).

However, a host of new reasons brought new actors and activism into the preparations for the Fourth World Conference. There was the missionary enthusiasm of those who had been involved in the UN Decade for Women and veterans of the Nairobi Conference. There was also greater cooperation between feminist groups and the 'traditional' women's organisations. After the Chernobyl disaster and the realisation that frontiers are flimsy in the face of nuclear disasters and war, new possibilities opened up for East-West exchange. And finally there was anger at governmental deceptions, and a little more institutional money.

The Economic Commission for Europe (ECE) which embraced East and West even before these changes (and which includes the US and Canada for post-World War II historical reasons), also experienced a modest revival in this time. Diplomats were no longer instructed just to oppose each other on issues of coal, iron and steel and other cross-border transactions, coinciding with new officials in the ECE secretariat who had an interest in civil society. Under pressure from the women's international NGOs headquartered in Geneva, the ECE organised the first ever World Conference Regional Preparatory meeting in Vienna, mid-way between East and West, in November 1994. Combined with its own Forum, this event accelerated interest throughout the 54 countries as never before, not least because it was full of dramatic stresses revealing the new realities of the UN, of government-NGO relations, and of the need for women's movements to be effective in lobbying and persuasion on their own concerns.

Western European governments, especially the UK, had tended to treat the Decade for Women, its events and instruments, as for 'women out there' rather than for domestic implementation. The Scandinavian governments had far more progressive affirmative action policies than others, and indeed elements of the Danish women's movement opposed membership of the European Union (EU) because its social legislation was behind their own. But for British women, membership of the EU brought far more progressive law than existed.

For representatives of all of these governments it was something of a shock to meet together for the first time to negotiate a regional Platform for Action at the Vienna Regional Meeting that would belong to and be rooted in their own political cultures, rather than dismissable as applying only to 'Third World' countries to 'help them catch up', as British officials used to say. While some had taken the meetings of the Commission on the Status of Women seriously, and therefore had clear mechanisms for domestic consultation (if not always fully satisfactory in the view of the women's movement), others had not. They took for granted that there would be no interest from their citizens or passive acceptance of what was said in their name. They were, therefore, in for a greater surprise as critics emerged from every side about their style, the content of their interventions, and their accessibility. The Vienna Regional Meeting thus became a considerable learning experience for many Western governments' women's bureau representatives as well as for those from East and Central Europe.

Its NGO Forum was also the first European (and North American) meeting of women's movements — this, despite their apparent frequent travel, exchanges, contacts and international experience, was an opportunity they had been deprived of over the previous two decades. Most international contact had previously been between North-South, or between English-speakers and the US, from where much of the early feminist literature had emerged. Therefore, there was a sense of confused innovation when several thousand women travelled to Vienna to experience this novelty. There was also some dread among Europeans at the potential dominance of US organisations with their better funding and definite sense of superiority towards others, although US social provision—such as childcare, equal pay for work of equal value, etc. — is very far behind even Europe's limited infrastructure. Women from countries formerly dominated by the Soviet Union tended to share some of these apprehensions—but towards the Russians—preferring to relate to Western Europeans and to speak English.

A caucus system emerged from those who made themselves busy, organising daily briefing sessions, and the effective drafting of amendments to the regional Plan of Action, negotiating with the UN over access and rooms for sub-regional caucuses and meetings. Some mistook these volunteer administrators for power-hungry megalomaniacs which, mostly, was far from the truth.

There were differences of style between the Europeans and the Americans and some interpersonal conflicts. But the great confused experiment worked. There was a great deal of

> ### History of the Facilitation Initiative:
>
> A lesson learned from the Nairobi Conference in 1985 was that there was lack of coordination between the groups involved in the conference preparations, and there was no overview of the funds required for the preparations.
>
> The OECD/DAC Expert Group on Women in Development (chaired by the Netherlands from May 1993 - May 1995) took the initiative to coordinate DAC Members' support to developing countries with regard to preparatory activities for the 1995 Beijing Conference. This initiative was titled the OECD/DAC Expert Group on WID's Facilitation Initiative. The overall objectives of the Facilitation Initiative were:
> - to ensure an equitable spread and optimum use of the scarce human and financial resources available for support to conference preparations in developing countries;
> - to provide coordinated support to national and regional level preparations.
>
> In order to achieve these objectives different bilateral donors acted as regional coordinators — so called regional lead donors RLD) — for different regions of the developing world. Denmark was the RLD for South Asia, Sweden for South East Asia, USA for Latin America, UK for the Caribbean, France and Canada for Francophone Africa, and the Netherlands for Anglophone Africa.
>
> The RLDs were to collaborate with Regional Focal Points which preferably would be local organisations that were capable of establishing working relations with government agencies, national machineries, NGOs and the local donor community as well. These Regional Focal Points (RFPs) would act as a technical resource and coordination platform for the RLD. Their function was expected to be three-fold:
>
> i) to provide a technical support facility to the RLD in its function of ensuring an equitable spread and optimum use of the scarce human and financial resources for support to the conference preparation;
>
> ii) to act as a facility for personnel from a wide range of organisations from different countries within the sub-region to exchange ideas and discuss strategies;
>
> iii) to enhance national preparations by the various countries through dissemination of information and support for (and organising of) seminars, workshops, and providing training.
>
> This was meant to be the basic general set up of the Facilitation Initiative worldwide. Each RLD worked within and adapted it according to its own standards and experience in the region of which it was RLD.
>
> In early 1993 a Consultant Coordinator was appointed by the DAC/WID Group to coordinate the whole Facilitation Initiative process, facilitate the dissemination of information on the conference preparations and the development of the Facilitation Initiative between the members of the DAC/WID group and the RLDs/RFPs in particular. She reported regularly on the progress made and distributed new information that came from the UN Conference Secretariat.

interaction between groupings and networks, some newly funded by the European Union, such as the European Women's Lobby and the Older Women's Network Europe, and the formation of some new coalitions like a Balkan group which went on to tackle the Dayton Peace Agreement from a feminist perspective.

The Regional Meeting adopted a Regional Plan of Action, the first of its kind, which took effect immediately and has been studiously ignored by governments since. The background papers had concentrated on access to 'public life' which is still limited in Western Europ, with the exception of the Scandinavian countries, and is deteriorating very quickly in East and Central Europe. The fact that this focus was chosen, reflected a preoccupation with the male dominated realities of democracy in both East and West. More controversial were the sections applauding economic 'globalisation', which the women's caucuses removed from the Plan. But these were small gains in the face of strong forces.

The Council of Europe, newly expanded with members from Central Europe, also organised a major conference in February 1995 and successive smaller events, emphasising the generation of independent NGOs and civil society. While the Council has far fewer financial resources than the Commission, the commitment in the Committee for Equality and its Secretariat is very dynamic. These are relatively staid events, but they provide a legitimate space for politicians and civil servants to meet women's movements.

The Council has the European Convention on Human Rights as its idealistic base, but the Convention contains no guarantees of gender equality or the equal exercise of rights by women as well as men: it is the document that the world would have had, instead of the Universal Declaration on Human Rights, if Bertha Lutz from Argentina and Eleanor Roosevelt from the US had not struggled for women in the late 1940s. So, 50 years on, the Equality Committee argued for a Protocol to amend the Convention and make it more women-friendly. The Council of Europe also promotes non-sexist language and 'parity democracy': the physical sharing of political space-both not really heeded in the 40 or so member-states.

No two people—even from the same country and age group—will have experienced all the 'Beijing' processes in the same way. Few had the same motives for going there, many still being ignorant of what might be expected from a Forum or a UN Conference. Some still expected to read papers to a silent academic audience; some to attract an immediately devoted collective to their issue; some to march or demonstrate; some to influence their government daily. Some went because they were born in China or Hong-Kong.

It is difficult to assess, therefore, whether they satisfied their motives. There was also some boycotting of China as a location, either over the issue of Tibet, or the evidence of Tiananmen Square or—more rarely—the repression of women. Some, however, went specifically in the hope of meeting Chinese women.

In the nine months between the Regional Meeting and the Beijing events, there was unprecedented activity in Europe generated by European institutions, increasing the interest in going, despite difficulties in finding funding and especially obtaining visas.

The European Commission, having taken no interest in the three prior Conferences, committed funds to large numbers of women from 'developing countries' and East and Central Europe, administered by Women in Development Europe (WIDE) and CHANGE respectively. Parliamentarians became interested and joined the 400 or so present in China. The 'Francophonie' (the French organisation supporting the contribution of French language and culture through former and existing French dependencies) channelled resources to its member states, and the British Council made resources available to a dozen Conference Lobby and Advocacy Training courses in Africa, the Middle East and elsewhere. The Overseas Development Administration of the UK put resources into a development NGO network, and into workshops in China itself. But there were no resources for domestic NGOs.

There was, thus, still a tendency in many countries to relate the issues and instruments of the Conference to foreign rather than domestic policy. The European Women's Lobby, however, had a clear mandate from its members to make the decisions within the final global Platform for Action, relevant to

A Woman's Place is in the Economy

Sheryl McCullough, an American postal worker, knows what issues are important to her.

"My concerns are equality in the work place as it relates to wages and working conditions," said McCullough, a 42-year-old African American administrator for the U.S. Post Office and the mother of a 16-year-old son.

"Women are still the primary caretakers and the work environment should be more conducive to that." Child care, elder care and equal pay for equal work are issues she would like to see addressed, said McCullough, who ran a post office educational booth at Huairou.

McCullough's feelings reflect the economic issues that are at the top of the agenda for many European and North American women at the Beijing conference. Of particular concern to the region's leaders is the growing number of women who live in poverty as a result of the economic stagnation and political change in the northern economies.

"Economic problems affect women first," said Yves Berthelot, executive secretary of the Economic Commission for Europe, who led the regional Preparatory Conference in Vienna last October.

Women tend to receive lower wages than men for similar jobs, even in Scandanavian states which are often looked to as models of gender equity.

Manuela Ferreire Leite, the Portuguese Minister for Education, notes that in her country, which has one of the highest rates of female employment in Europe, "women still occupy the least qualified and most precarious jobs."

Many Americans are concerned about the issue of unwaged work, and the fact that women receive no benefits—such as pensions or health care—for the work they do when raising a family.

Many American NGOs would like to see the Platform of Action recognise all unpaid work at home and in the informal economy and to take a strong stand on guaranteeing women access to economic opportunities.

"Jobs and the economy are very important," says Susan Davis, director of the Women's Environment and Development Organization. "The kind of benefits you are entitled to are related to your class of employment."

The current language in the platform talks about the need to balance paid work with responsibilities at home.

"In the Platform for Action, the most diluted section concerns access to economic structures," Davis says.

Berthelot said the issue of poverty is of particular concern in the former Soviet Union, where economies are now in transition from state controlled economies towards a capitalist system. As a result, women's life expectancy has dropped, maternal mortality rates are increasing and the number of women living in poverty has escalated.

Jan Peterson, the North American focal point person for GROOTS, an international grassroots organisation, said programmes to address women's poverty must be designed to empower the people who receive the aid.

"Women's poverty has to be looked at from a development perspective," she said. "You can't talk about welfare reform without talking about how grassroots women will be given help to build their own self-support organisations."

Another issue of key concern among women throughout North America and Europe is safeguarding—and expanding—their reproductive rights in the face of a growing religious fundamentalist movement that opposes abortion.

Berthelot says that "the Vienna Platform of Action demands that women's reproductive rights should be fully recognised and respected."

> But abortion is illegal in Poland, Spain, Ireland and Switzerland and has been raised as a contentious issue by Catholic conservatives in many other European countries.
>
> Many American NGOs are concerned that the document agreed to in Beijing will take a weaker position on reproductive rights than the document signed at the population conference in Cairo.
>
> "It's going to be a struggle," said Jacqueline Jackson, chair of the National Board of Directors of the Planned Parenthood Federation of America.
>
> Conservatives opposed to abortion are here in greater numbers than they were at the Cairo conference, and they have adopted a new strategy, she observed.
>
> "We now hearing more about the nurturing role of motherhood," she said. "But it ignores the reality of women's lives, the burdens they face on the way to that nurturing role."
>
> Equal-sharing of political power is also a key issue in Europe. While countries like Sweden and Norway are models of gender integration - with more than 40 percent of their parliament seats filled by women, other countries still have a long way to go.
>
> In France, just 6 percent of the seats in the National Assembly are filled by women and in Turkey, the rate is just 1 percent. Overall, only eight countries have parliaments with more than 20 percent of the seats filled by women.
>
> Women are, however, being encouraged to enter politics. "We are already focussing measures on women and decision making," says Padraig Flynn, European Commissioner for Social Affairs and Equal Opportunity.
>
> Berthelot says that while Europe does have many laws to protect women "the gap needs to be filled between law and reality." In many cases, women are not even aware of the laws that have been passed to protect them, such as the anti-sexual harassment laws in effect in many countries.
>
> "The situation in Europe is good de jure, but not de facto," Berthlot says. "The ideas are there and even the laws. Nevertheless, thousands of women in the region suffer from similar tragedies as women elsewhere."
>
> *Natacha Henry and Samme Chittum*
> *(Beijing Watch, September 9, 1995)*

European women as well, and worked to that end.

Therefore, apart from the multitudinous workshops that were organised by NGOs in the Forum, there were daily meeting in the Conference with the political leadership of the European Union (which rotates among member states every six months, and was at that time, with Spain). As leaders, the Spanish delegation spoke on behalf of the other 14 members in the Conference. These meetings were crowded, confused and often conflictual, more due to the pressures of time, location, weather and occasionally the pre-emptive Spanish style, than real differences of opinion. However, monitoring agreements when they were presented in the drafting processes, was much harder, and there was sometimes a sense that the daily meetings were more cosmetic than real. Relatively few East Europeans had access to the Conference itself, but those that did were well-organised in caucuses, and those that did not received briefings about the status of events from CHANGE.

The stresses of commuting between the city and Huairou, and of coping with the authorities, caused at least miscarriage and heart attack; and there was a very high rate of colds and respiratory problems among Europeans both while they were in China and on return. Perhaps this was also the case amongst other regional groups. Departure also brought tensions among those less used to the patience necessary for travel in 'developing countries'.

Most events organised since the Conference have been entitled 'Beyond Beijing'. In these, there is a mixture of hope and a certain sadness, almost cynicism. As elections approached in various countries, there were hopes that government could be held accountable to implement the Platform for Action. But the same approach of elections actually pushed to the side the importance of internationally-inspired documents, which only have 'moral' force. 'Social integration' and unemployment became important issues, and the European Union, under the influence of the Irish presidency in the second half of 1996, may begin to turn the tide of human- less economics with which we have been so afflicted in the past decade.

At the ECE Annual Conference in 1996, it was back to normal discussion of transport and trade standards. Only two NGOs made interventions, reminding member states that they adopted responsibilities in Beijing, and pointing out the political and economic losses still being suffered by women in Eastern Europe, under the influence of male Western advisers. It is a revisiting of all the 'women in development' phenomena of the 1960s for women in these newly 'liberated' countries.

There will be, however, an 1ECE Beyond Beijing' conference in Bucharest organised jointly by UNDP, the UN Division for the Advancement of Women, and the small ECE Secretariat, mostly attended by East European NGOs. The Council of Europe has continued its series of civil society and post-Conference meetings at its headquarters in Strasbourg and various cities in Eastern Europe.

As in the two decades before, the chief gains have been in connections made, stereotypes replaced by direct contact, networking, and the politicisation of some women who previously tended to deny the discrimination, harassment and violations in their lives. Younger women have been brought in, and to some extent the 'baton' of necessary perseverance, determination, inventiveness and solidarity within the women's movements has passed on to them. Campaigns have succeeded in ensuring the War Crimes Tribunal for Former Yugoslavia has female judges, and deals with the rape and violation of women as seriously as other massacres.

Yet, new dangers face us all with the medicalisation of many health issues, with genetic engineering and technological developments unconstrained by social consultations. And, of course, there is still the drastic political under-representation of women through most of the continent.

Africa:

A Mission Accomplished

Njoki Wainaina

For African women, the road to Beijing was the continuation of a journey that started in Arusha, Tanzania, way back in October 1984. At that time about 100 African women met for what was the first African women's NGO Forum. It was the NGO meeting prior to the African Regional Preparatory Conference, held in Nairobi in July 1985.

That NGO meeting was convened by the NGO Forum office in New York. At the end of the meeting some issues arose that spurred African women into action. The key issue was that while the rest of the world was already prepared, or was in the process of getting ready to come to Nairobi for the UN conference and the NGO Forum that year, the majority of African women did not even know that there had been a Decade for Women, let alone that it was ending in a global conference on African soil ! Thus, the need for urgent action to ensure effective representation and participation by African women, became paramount.

An African Women's Task Force was created and mandated to ensure numerous tasks such as: mobilising women in large numbers across the continent to attend the UN conference and the NGO Forum '85; sensitising and preparing them to bring their issues to the forefront of the global agenda; preparing them for their role as host; setting in place mechanisms that would enable them to work together, build solidarity and advance their common issues and concerns beyond the NGO Forum and UN Conference. The African Women's Task Force finally fulfilled its mandate with the foundation of FEMNET in April 1988.

With this history in mind, FEMNET was selected to be the coordinating NGO for Africa's process to Beijing, in a hotly contested campaign in Vienna in 1993. As women from over 40 African countries came together in the African Tent on the first day of the NGO Forum '95 in Huairou, we witnessed the realisation of that dream we had in Arusha ten years before.

In January 1994, FEMNET convened the first meeting of the Africa Regional Steering Committee (ARSC). This Committee had been constituted through a process of consultation, interaction and networking with FEMNET members and other international organisations. The Committee had, of necessity, to be broader than FEMNET's own membership, based on criteria which included special interests, professional, geographical, linguistic and thematic representation. Despite efforts to make it broadly representative, there were still many who felt excluded. The next hurdle was to get responses from the organisations selected to the Committee. But the greatest challenge of all was to get and maintain the committee of organisations selected.

At the first, well-attended meeting of the ARSC, a coordinating structure comprising national, sub-regional and regional coordinating bodies was created and approved for implementation. A programme for the preparatory process and the African NGO Forum on Women was developed, and the responsibilities of the different players including national focal points, thematic coordinators, sub-regional committees, the regional secretariat, the Nairobi Planning Committee, the Dakar Planning Committee and the ARSC were defined.

FEMNET was well aware that communication was one of the greatest challenges of networking in Africa where communication systems are highly inadequate and language barriers only serve to complicate matters. Further, the cost of sending information is enormous. An even bigger problem was sharing of information by those who received it. However, judging from the turnout in Dakar for the African NGO Forum on Women, in November 1994, it was clear that our network worked.

The road to Dakar proved a major challenge in terms of ensuring the widest possible dissemination of information, as well as mobilisation of organisations to contribute to the preparatory process. The mobilisation of necessary resources to organise the Forum, maintaining continuous communication with interested organisations, individuals and groups, and coordinating the process and content also proved to be a daunting task.

A number of factors combined to make coordination fairly problematic. The end result was severe logistical and organisational problems which made the Forum far less effective than it could have been. On the positive side, however, it must be said that African women rose to the occasion, overcame a lot of the difficulties and participated fully in the Forum activities.

The African NGO Forum attracted unprecedented numbers of African women from diverse categories, geographical representation, professional and socio-economic levels, including grassroot groups, persons with disabilities, young women and girls. In spite of such a motley group, important issues of women's advancement and gender equality were discussed by over 4,000 participants.

The Dakar Forum was a first experience for most of those who participated and it provided an opportunity to strategise for Africa's participation in the NGO Forum at Beijing. There was renewed commitment from participating organisations, networks and individuals. The roles, responsibilities and obligations of different players were clarified and the identification and analyses of key issues for African women concretised our Beijing agenda.

The period between Dakar and Beijing was exciting, as national focal points, thematic coordinators and the ARSC Secretariat at FEMNET all networked closely to continue mobilisation, consolidate issues and contribute to the on-going process of "removing the brackets" from the Global Platform for Action. The dissemination of the African Platform for Action, and preparations for Beijing went on simultaneously.

The design and coordination of the programme and contribution to the African Tent was one of the key preoccupations at that time. Every opportunity to discuss, refine and mobilise ideas and contributions from Network members was utilised. The meeting of the Commission on the Status of Women (CSW) in March 1995 and of the African Women Leaders in Addis Ababa, in July 1995 were used to firm up the plans for an African NGO and government partnership, solidarity and participation in Beijing.

African women's participation in the NGO Forum and the UN Fourth World Conference on Women at Beijing was, in our assessment, highly satisfactory. The preparatory process had sharpened our negotiation skills and raised our levels of conceptualisation, clarity and articulation of issues. It also improved networking and communication between the diversity that is African women. At both the Forum and the Conference, African women interacted with women from across the world with confidence and clarity.

Given the economic status of many African countries and the scramble for limited resources, the numbers of African women who made it to Beijing was also a source of satisfaction. The solidarity that women of this region craved for a long time was evident in all African activities at Huairou and Beijing. For many of us, this was the fulfillment of a mission with which we have struggled for more than a decade.

Beijing was a great experience for us. Apart from the enhanced knowledge of issues, priorities and strategies for the future, we also had a chance to compare our situation and performance with that of women in other regions. We learnt more about our own women elsewhere in the continent and discovered ways to overcome differences and build solidarity around common concerns.

The value of shared responsibility, of recognising and using the comparative advantages of diverse groups was another key experience. As African women organised before and during Beijing, their enormous energies and talents were mobilised. Together we affirmed that Africa's women can be the solution for the continent's crises and we must continue to work for this recognition.

As we look beyond Beijing. African women recognise the major challenges involved in translating words into action. This has been a common theme in all activities since the Dakar meeting. The challenges to hold governments, the UN, NGOs, societies and ourselves responsible for implementing the actions proposed in global conventions, remains critical. Maintaining the momentum achieved in Beijing and spreading the proposals for action to every level and front is a challenge that will keep all of us on the alert. Our promise is that what happened to the Nairobi Forward Looking Strategies must not be allowed to happen to the Platform for Action for Equality, Development and Peace. We have already moved into action!

Playing the Beijing Game

Sara Hlupekile Longwe

Three years before the Beijing Conference, I happened to be at a meeting in Vienna where the venue of the next World Conference on Women was being discussed. Beijing had been proposed but this choice was vehemently opposed by many Western delegates. They argued that China did not have a democratic political system and had a disgraceful human rights record, and therefore was not a suitable place to hold a conference on women's rights.

I took the lead, from among the African women at the meeting, in countering this argument. It seemed that North-South politics were influencing the discussion. Furthermore, we saw this as politics of men, whereas we women were a global sisterhood. We also saw an implication that women of the North were dictating to us on women's rights and treating the Third World as an unclean place. If we move the conference to a country where women have equal rights, we asked, then where is such a country? Would they prefer the United States of America where the culture was overtly sexist and the government had not even ratified the 1979 Convention on the Elimination of All Forms of Discrimination Against Women (CEDAW)?

I was proved wrong even before the Beijing Conference began. Five months before the Conference, the Chinese government announced that they had found a 'structural fault' in the Beijing Stadium which was to have been the site of the NGO Forum. The Forum would, instead, be moved to the town of Huairou, 30 kilometres from Beijing.

This was an example of a political move masquerading as a technical issue. In moving the NGO Forum to Huairou, there was an obvious coalition of interest with the UN organisers—the move would limit the capacity of the NGO Forum to lobby government delegations and thus influence the final Conference document.

If I was proved wrong before the Conference even started, I really had to eat my words when I reached Huairou. The site was small, unsuitable and overcrowded. Much of the accommodation was in unfinished buildings—more like a building site. Worse than that, the place was crawling with the army, police and secret police who constantly followed, watched, harassed and filmed.

When the Chinese government first came up with its story about the Stadium's 'defect', the NGO Forum sent its own inspection team to China to look at the facilities in Huairou. They reluctantly declared that Huairou would have to do. In effect, the Chinese had presented the NGO Forum with an ultimatum. The only alternative would have been to move the whole UN Conference to another country which was virtually impossible at this late stage.

This story is not just a story about China,

Delegates Fight to Preserve Regional Gains

African women will be fighting hard at the Fourth World Conference on Women to ensure that gains made at a regional level are not diluted in the global decisions taken here.

They are convinced that the African Platform for Action, adopted at the preparatory meeting in Dakar last fall, is stronger than the Global Platform for Action (GPA) that delegates to Beijing will discuss.

"Our task in Beijing is to ensure that the GPA includes as many of the issues from the Africa Platform as possible," says Kenya's Njoki Wainaina, chairperson of FEMNET.

The Nairobi-based NGO coordinates African NGOs attending the meeting. "The most critical action for us is to safeguard what has been bracketed in the draft GPA document."

African women are anxious for their governments to use the Conference to take concrete steps to redress gender imbalances.

Presenting the African regional perspective at the plenary of the NGO Forum, Winnie Karagwa Byanyima, coordinator of the Women's Caucus in the Uganda Constitutional Assembly, warned of being deceived by recent changes in the continent.

The wave of multiparty elections in Africa, she said, are characterised by "a few powerful men in previously one party systems, who split up the old structures into several parties.

A multiparty system can function in just the same way as a one party system or military junta—entrenching power and privilege for a few elite, rich men."

According to a study by the Addis Ababa-based Economic Commission for Africa (ECA), which has coordinated preparation by African governments for the Conference, the representation of African women in Parliament around the continent stands at a paltry 7.7 percent.

The African Platform for Action notes that as a result of unfavourable international terms of trade, drought and civil war, the majority of African countries are now some of the least developed in the world.

The document notes that African women are worse off than they were a decade ago.

On the face of it, the APA is a milestone for African women. It highlights the central issue of poverty and need for economic empowerment. African countries played a key role in having poverty placed first in the list of the twelve "critical areas of concern" in the GPA.

African negotiators between now and the close of the Conference will seek to knock away the brackets inserted in this chapter by northern countries who want to tone down criticism of IMF and World Bank-sponsored structural adjustment programmes.

They will also strive to secure commitments to debt cancellation for the poorest countries.

African countries lobbied at the global preparatory meeting in New York in March for the inclusion of the twelfth area of concern, the girl child. The issue was first discussed at the Dakar conference.

African women argue that problems of gender inequality stem from negative attitudes towards girls. They are less educated than boys, are married at young ages, and are subjected to harmful traditional practices such as genital mutilation.

Unlike the GPA, the African Platform carries a section on Culture, the Family and Socialisation. The section has been criticised for not sufficiently addressing the dichotomy between constitutional provisions for gender equality, and the many negative forms of traditional discrimination against women that still prevail.

But it does attempt to tackle the sensitive and complex issues of culture and socialisation, which the global document shies away from.

African countries have also argued consistently against the Vatican on the fraught issues of reproductive health, contraception and abortion.

> The Vatican will lobby against the language used in last year's Cairo population conference document. It urges governments to reduce the incidence of unsafe abortions, ensure that services are safe when they are not against the law, and provide humane care for all women who suffer the consequences of unsafe abortions.
>
> "Our role in the Conference is to ensure that women's health issues are pushed forward to ensure that the gains of Cairo are not lost," says Afua Hesse of Ghana, a paediatric surgeon and member of the Ghana Medical Association.
>
> In the heavily bracketed section of the GPA on promotion and protection of women's human rights, thrown into question by the Pope and fundamentalist Muslim countries such as Iran, African governments have insisted that advances reached at the global conference on human rights in Vienna two years ago be upheld.
>
> The African Platform states: "Women's rights are universal and indivisible from human rights. The equal status of African women and their legal and human rights should be integrated into the mainstream of African governments' legislative, judicial and administrative bodies."
>
> But Sudan joined conservative voices in opposing the use of the term "gender" in the GPA, on grounds that it implies acceptance of homosexuals. A working group has since recommended that the word be retained.
>
> In her address at the NGO Forum, Byanyima highlighted the rise of religious fundamentalism in African countries such as Algeria, and the ethnic strife in countries like Rwanda. "These cases are turning back the clock for women," she said.
>
> With reports by Rosemary Omale, Millie Phiri and Ivy Morna.
>
> **Colleen Lowe Morna**
> (Beijing Watch, September 5, 1995)

or even about the Beijing Conference. It is a story which illustrates two different levels of the conference game—the technical level, masking the underlying political level. On the surface, everybody is apparently following the Technical Sequence, which is about reports, policies, goals and implementation. It has its own accepted behaviours, diplomacy, organisation and vocabulary. Underlying all this is the power struggle of the Political Game. This is the hidden agenda, with its own coded discourse. But let us first look at the Technical Sequence of the Beijing process.

From the technical point of view, the Beijing process is very easy to understand. It mirrors the process of the earlier (1985) Nairobi Conference, a routine now well-established for all UN world conferences on women. In summary, the process is as follows:

1 *Situation Analysis:* Individual governments write a pre-conference situation analysis to identify the main outstanding gender issues and progress in meeting previously agreed commitments.

2. *Regional Plan:* Government delegations have a regional conference to identify the major regional, gender issues and make a regional commitment to address these issues.

3. *World Plan:* The world conference puts together the picture from the regions and all governments agree to a declaration of principles and a plan of action on major issues.

4 *Plan Implementation:* All governments spend the next ten years pursuing the strategies and goals of the agreed plan of action.

The above process is technical in the sense that no politics are visible. There are no competing interests; no differing points of view. Apparently, each government and everybody in each government, is committed to implementing policies for women's advancement.

Many of the participants seem to believe in this process. This is evidenced by the enormous time and effort which is put into achieving consensus on text, including even lengthy arguments over the use of a single word! Such lengthy wrangles must surely be built on the faith that once the word is agreed upon, then it will be followed. But lengthy wrangles over a single word are a sign of the underlying political tensions.

Can we believe in the Technical Sequence as summarised above? One reason for the prevalence of belief is that it is a ten-year process. So you have to be with it for a long time before you begin to suspect that it does not work! How many of us in Beijing had been in Nairobi ten years earlier? But I have now seen a full ten year sequence from Nairobi to Beijing. The Nairobi Forward Looking Strategies (NFLS) were simple, forthright and radical in the way they committed governments to addressing gender issues. Governments were committed to establishing national gender policies based on the Nairobi Strategies and to set up national machineries to pursue the policy.

Ten years later, looking at the national and regional reports in preparation for the Beijing Conference, it was obvious that for all African countries, little or no progress had been made in pursuing the Nairobi Strategies—not even window dressing!

For example, taking the example of my home country Zambia, where the government had established neither a gender policy, nor any national machinery for women's advancement. Over the past decade the proportion of women in Parliament remained at the same five percent; the number of females among university students remained at the same 25 percent. Despite a revision in 1991, the Constitution continued to give the same protection to customary law, which provides for legalised discrimination against women—in access to land, in marriage, in the continuance of brideprice, an so on.

This lack of progress in Zambia is part of a global pattern. The Beijing Platform for Action was almost entirely concerned with trying to pin down governments and UN agencies to more specific identification of the gender issues which need to be addressed, and more detailed plans of actions in order to achieve the earlier Nairobi commitments.

Why was there virtually no progress on the Nairobi Strategies? Here, we need to look at the underlying political game. Most Third World governments are male dominated and very concerned with maintaining male privileges in societies which are very patriarchal. They are absolutely not interested in pursuing policies of gender equality.

Then why do governments sign these international declarations? Because they need international respectability, especially when donor funding from the Northern countries depends upon a semblance of respectability on human rights. Therefore, the political game involves signing international declarations and conventions, but actually doing little or nothing about implementation.

In other words, the Technical Sequence is shadowed by the Political Game which lies hidden within the process. The Political Game version of the Technical Sequence looks something like this:

1. *Situation Analysis:* Governments write a pre-conference situation analysis which overlooks major gender issues and uses a selective approach to the data to make claims that gender gaps are closing. Any lack of progress is attributed to the backward and traditional attitudes of the people who resist enlightened government policy.

2. *Regional Plan:* Governments send a low-level delegation to the regional conference, with a brief to water down all vocabulary so as to avoid definite commitments.

3. *World Plan:* Governments send another low-level delegation to the world conference. This is headed by a junior minister in charge of an area of social welfare, such as community development. This allows the interpretation that any agreements are concerned with improving women's welfare (rather than women's rights). The junior status of the minister implicitly casts doubt on the validity of any government commitment to the final conference declaration.

4. *Plan Implementation:* Governments establish a small Women's Development Department in the Ministry of Community Development. This Department is established under donor pressure and is entirely financed by donors. Its functions are not clear and it has no influence over other ministries. Ten years later, there is still no gender policy.

This is the type of political game that summarises the participation of most African governments in the Beijing process. In other words, they go through the motions in such a way so as to ensure no progress or result.

In the more dictatorial regimes, there is no real attempt to even play the political game. The more dictatorial the regime, the less its accountability to its citizens and the more explicit the message to women that they can forget about equal rights. For example, the delegates from one African country came home from Beijing to find that government officials confiscated their Beijing literature at the airport. Later, the President told them: "Don't bring your Beijing talk back here." In such a country there may be no space for the women's movement. It has been put behind the Chinese Wall.

A national NGO women's movement, however, has a chance of making something of the Beijing process where a government claims to be in favour of equal rights for women. In other words, it makes these claims not only in Beijing but also at home (and therefore, allows the Beijing Platform for Action to be brought into the country).

This is the situation in much of Africa. Outside of the Islamic countries, patriarchy is the ideology that dares not speak its name. The principles of male domination are in obvious contradiction to all principles of democracy and human rights. It is this contradiction between respectable democracy and covert patriarchy which causes the awkward dichotomy between the Technical Sequence and the Political Game.

But to the extent that a government maintains the claim of being open and democratic, the existence of the patriarchal Political Game cannot be admitted. It is a dark game which exists in empty words and proceeds by dirty tricks.

It is this ideological contradiction between the Technical Sequence and the Political Game which can be exploited by the women's movement. The women's movement must pursue the Feminist Project, which is to reveal and exploit the contradiction. This involves following the Technical Sequence step by step. At every stage the gap between the Political Game and the Technical Sequence must be exposed.

Sometimes the women's movement needs to produce their own alternative version of the steps in the sequence to show what it really should look like. So the Feminist Project would look something like this:

1. *Situation Analysis:* NGOs produce their own national situation report on progress in closing gender gaps, and evidence of government policy, action and administrative machinery for women's advancement. The NGO 'shadow report' reveals any inadequacy, cover-up and lip-service in the official government version.

2. *Regional Plan:* A national NGO delegation attends the regional conference to lobby its own government delegation on recognition of gender issues and commitment to action. Back home, the delegates inform all

other women of government commitments and demand action on them. In regional collaboration, NGOs map out strategies of international cooperation in dealing with priority regional gender issues and for pushing reluctant governments.

3. *World Plan:* National NGO delegations extend the regional strategy to lobby their government delegation to push for definite commitments, and to ensure that the World Plan pays sufficient attention to priority regional issues (for example, in Africa, status of the girl child, female genital mutilation, inheritance). NGOs, North and South, strategise on global alliances in this struggle for equal rights for women.

4. *Plan Implementation:* The world conference was only the beginning. Now the NGOs must work together, nationally and regionally, to push governments into action on national commitments. This also involves monitoring and evaluating government and regional progress on major, common gender issues. NGOs also need to take independent NGO action to implement programmes in areas where the government is dragging its feet.

This is the optimistic version of the Feminist Project. It is based on the faith that governments can be influenced and that there is political space for independent political action. Perhaps some space exists in many Third World countries. The women's movement must use their elbows to make the space and to increase the space.

The Feminist Project involves making the space to operate. It does not mean accepting the space given to you. It does not mean accepting Huairou. It means marching to Beijing!

West Asia:

Building a Common Agenda

Fatima Kassem

In West Asia, the Women and Development Unit of the Economic and Social Commission for Western Asia (ESCWA) acted as the regional coordinator. It was way back in November 1993 that ESCWA, aided by UNIFEM, began its phased preparatory activities at various national levels. These efforts were further forged at the regional level during the Regional Preparatory Meeting in Amman, Jordan in November 1994 and the Regional Beirut Workshop of July 1995. This entire process culminated in the daily Arab Group meeting held during the Beijing Conference.

In the first phase of preparation, between November and December 1993, a team from ESCWA (which serves 13 Arab countries) visited Bahrain, Egypt, Kuwait, Lebanon, Oman, Qatar, the Syrian Arab Republic, the United Arab Emirates, Yemen, Jordan, Iraq and Palestine. This phase was essentially geared towards encouraging governments to form joint national preparatory committees for the Beijing Conference with a balanced representation from both government and NGOs. Once these committees were established, they were entrusted with the task of preparing national reports on the situation of women in the context of the 1985 Nairobi Forward Looking Strategies. In the light of their findings, the committees then formulated national plans for the advancement of women.

In the next phase, during May-October 1994, ESCWA, in collaboration with these committees, organised and moderated nine national workshops in Bahrain, Jordan, Lebanon, Oman, Palestine, Qatar, the Syrian Arab Republic, the United Emirates, and Yemen. This was followed by a revision of the national reports and plans of actions and the committees then submitted the new reports to ESCWA for use as inputs into the preparation of a regional assessment of the status of Arab women, and the formulation of a regional plan of action.

The third phase saw the culmination of all preparatory activities, when the Arab Regional Preparatory Meeting for the Fourth World Conference on Women: Peace for the Advancement of Arab Women was convened in Amman from 6-10 November 1994. This was organised by the League of Arab States, with patronage of HRH Princess Basma Bint Talal, Chairperson of the Jordanian National Committee for Women and the Joint National Preparatory Committee, as well as members of the UN Secretary General's Advisory Group of Eminent Persons on the Fourth World Conference on Women.

The Regional Preparatory Meeting was held in two segments. One was the Expert Group Meeting for the formulation of the Plan of Action, which finalised the draft regional plan of action on the basis of national reports and plans of action, incorporating the recommendations of the Amman NGO Forum and the Youth Consultations. The other was a high-level segment of the Arab Regional Preparatory Meeting which adopted the Arab Plan of Action for the Advancement of Women to the Year 2005.

The Arab Plan of Action identified the following priority areas for Arab women:

i) Safeguarding the right of Arab women to participate in power structures and decision-making mechanisms

ii) Alleviation of poverty among Arab women

iii) Ensuring Arab women equal access to health services and to all levels of education

iv) Promoting Arab women's economic self-reliance and capacity to enter the labour market

v) Overcoming the effects of wars

vi) Participation of women in natural resource management and safeguarding the environment

vii) Using the media effectively to bring about changes in traditional roles in society and to promote equality between men and women.

The Regional Preparatory Meeting was the largest meeting ever organised by ESCWA. Later, from 6-8 July, 1995, as a wrap-up, a regional workshop was held in Beirut, on Leadership and Lobbying Skills and Coordination Among Arab Official Delegations to the Conference. This workshop, attended by 13 Arab states, culminated in the Beirut Declaration for the Advancement of Women. It also greatly helped the official delegations polish their lobbying skills, and to coordinate their positions vis-a-vis the divisive issues in the draft Beijing Platform for Action.

The promptness in setting up the joint national preparatory committees, the preparation of national reports and plans of action, and the organising of national preparatory meeting for grassroots women, clearly indicated the importance given by ESCWA and governments to women's issues and concerns.

The Regional Preparatory Meeting which received wide media coverage, owed its success to the dynamic interaction between governments, the joint committees, NGOs, experts and officials of UN agencies, as well as to the presence of Arab countries from the ESCWA region (Mashrek) and North Africa (Maghreb). As Ms Nadia Hijab, a researcher and authority on Arab women, put it: "A major step forward was taken at the Arab Regional Preparatory Meeting .... There was

Muslim Women Stand By Their Differences

An interpreter's mistake during a panel discussion this week caused a furore among Muslim delegations. An English interpreter misquoted French parliament member Nicole Catala saying that Islam is the only religion that discriminates against women.

Egypt's Ambassador to Japan, Mirwet Al-Tallawy called a press conference to clarify the French speaker's position on Islam.

"Madame Catala did not touch on Islam negatively," said Al-Tallawy. "On the contrary, she said that it was a tolerant religion."

As the conference draws to a close, Muslim women are reflecting on how it addressed their concerns and how they were perceived by other delegates.

Non-Muslim women see Islam as a religion that does not treat women equally, said Al-Tallawy. She says this misperception is reinforced by the Western media.

Islam is a progressive religion which was concerned with human rights even before the Magna Carta, said the Egyptian envoy. It gave women the right to maintain their maiden names and granted them inheritance rights long before Western women began talking of these issues.

Islam, she said, is a comprehensive socio-economic system that protects everyone in the family.

But some Muslim women say that what began as a progressive social system has been turned into an instrument of repression by some conservative mullahs, or religious leaders. These women say that the interpretation of Islam by some theocratic governments and fundamentalists groups is actually a distortion of the Prophet's words.

In predominately Muslim parts of Nigeria, for example, Shari'a law is sometimes used to reinforce male dominance.

"In the constitution, all Nigerians are equal, but this is only on paper. In the Shari'a courts, the judges select what is favourable to men, whether it is Western, traditional or Muslim," said Mariam Jamilah Mohammad, Dean of the Faculty of Education and Science at Kaduma Polytechnic in northern Nigeria.

Divisions among various Muslim countries were readily apparent in the conference debate over inheritance rights. Under Islamic law boys are entitled to twice the inheritance their sisters receive because boys and men are assumed to be financially responsible for the women in their family.

Under these conditions, it is only fair for a woman to receive less than an equal share, said Ebtissam Al-Dofri, a female human rights activist from Yemen.

During the debate, Muslim countries such as Bahrain and Morocco insisted on a literal application of the Shari'a to determine inheritance. Others, such as Egypt, wanted a compromise which guaranteed girls "equal access to inheritance rights."

But Pakistan and Turkey, which both have Muslim women as their heads of state, strongly advocated giving girls and boys the right to an equal inheritance.

Pakistani female delegates were extremely disappointed with the compromise language because they said it would perpetuate Muslim women's economic dependence on their husbands and brothers.

Muslim delegates also differ on the degree to which a woman's dress should cover her body. While most agree that a woman's clothes should be modest, there is little consensus as to what "modest" means.

"It is a matter of personal choice," said Soheila Sadegh, a member of the National Council of Resistance, a Paris-based umbrella organisation of Iranian opposition groups.

But in Iran a woman is given 74 lashes if she does not observe a strict dress code, which requires women to be covered from head to toe.

Some Muslim women say they prefer to cover up, even without the threat of punishment. Al-Dofri from Yemen wears the black "niqab," which covers everything but her eyes and hands. She says her choice of dress shows she is in "worship of God."

Leila Deeb
(Beijing Watch, September 15, 1995)

interesting dynamics between the different groups ... a watershed in the way women's issues in the region are discussed."

The region's governments built a common agenda (as is clearly reflected in the Statement of Mission of the Arab Plan of Action), where the parameters were well-defined: "The Arab Plan of Action emanates from the tenets of Arab civilisation and the divine religious and human values that respect the rights of women as human beings."

Thus, women's issues and concerns were viewed within the broader framework of Arab heritage, civilisation, culture and religious convictions. The extent to which the region values the role of women in the family and the role of the family as a social institution, were also well articulated in the Arab Plan of Action.

All these preparatory activities succeeded in raising awareness about the critical areas of concern to women and their advancement. Moreover, they were also instrumental in encouraging member states to put women's issues high on their agenda.

On the recommendation of the Beirut Workshop and the initiative of the Ministry of Social Development in Jordan, Arab official delegations met daily in Beijing. These meetings were organised by ESCWA in collaboration with the League of Arab States and the chairmanship of Jordan (as the 1995 Chair of the Arab Group). The purpose of these meetings was to brief the delegations on the progress of negotiations and reach a common position regarding the bracketed parts of the draft Platform for Action. The meetings were characterised by high-level representation, excellent attendance and very strong commitment. In fact, the success of Arab coordination during the Conference can be largely attributed to the attendance at the daily meeting: 17 out of the 20 Arab countries participating in the Beijing Conference attended the meetings.

During the last of these meeting held on 15 September, the Arab Group decided that they would hold annual regional coordinator meetings for the next five years to monitor implementation of the Arab Plan of Action and the Beijing Platform. They also decided to establish the Arab Group as an internationally recognised entity for UN purposes and to request their respective permanent missions to the UN to take immediate measures thereof.

Perhaps the most significant development was the composition of the Arab official delegations to Beijing. It was a true example of practising what was being preached: ten out of the 20 heads of Arab delegations were women at the level of First Ladies or Ministers, and 10 of their deputies were from either ministerial level, high officials or presidents of national NGO federations;

For the first time, the Arab Group had a spokesperson—Jordan — in formal and informal negotiations within the Group of 77 and the Islamic Group. The support provided by the states to each others' positions in the various groups went a long way in forging cooperation, confidence and effectiveness in reflecting Arab concerns—but more importantly, Arab women's concerns—in the draft Platform for Action.

But it would be meaningless to talk about the Arab Group's successful coordination at Beijing without mentioning the commitment of Arab governments. This was amply reflected in the seriousness with which they prepared for the Conference and their determination to follow-up their Conference promises.

The thought that went into the whole process was quite clear. For instance, it is known that women's issues are sensitive in the cultural setting of this region and need to be handled with a great deal of care and insight. These sensitivities, combined with political instability and marginal roles that

NGOs still play in the region, constituted another major bottleneck. Therefore, the Arab Plan of Action adopted 'Peace for the Advancement of Arab Women', thereby, strategically targeting democratisation and grassroots participation for development.

Since the Beijing Conference, activities in the region have continued. The weakness—and in many cases, the absence—of national machineries for women to monitor and follow-up the implementation of Beijing's recommendations, was an area of grave concern. Among the 13 ESCWA countries only Egypt, Jordan and recently, Lebanon, have established permanent and autonomous national machineries and mechanisms for women. Bahrain, Oman and Yemen have separate departments for women's affairs housed within social affairs ministries. However, several ESCWA countries have organised national workshops to formulate national strategies and draw time-bound, prioritised programmes for implementation of the Beijing resolutions.

Attention was also drawn to the paucity of gender-disaggregated data and indicators on women and family. ESCWA has designed its 1996-1997 Work Programme and structured its 1998-2001 Medium Term Plan in the Area of Women and Development (WAD), keeping in view the Beijing recommendations. The WAD programme is designed to provide a gender perspective on issues related to the full integration and greater participation of women in the development process with a holistic, systemic approach, and with emphasis on the core themes of awareness-raising, capacity building, poverty alleviation, partnership with NGOs and community development.

Further, ESCWA continues to undertake research and operational activities and provide technical and advisory services to member states to enhance their capacity to achieve a number of objectives. One of the major targets is to reduce the persistent and increasing burden of poverty on women. In addition, there will be ongoing efforts to compile and analyse laws, policies, measures and programmes that impact women.

Work will also continue to strengthen institutions of civil society, national machineries and mechanisms, as well as NGOs. One of the most important tasks ahead is to develop a status of Arab women index that will be region-specific and culturally-sensitive. If all these various activities can be initiated, the path will be sufficiently cleared for the advancement of Arab women into the next century.

The Outcome and Beyond

Haifa Abu Ghazaleh

Even prior to the Beijing Conference, UNIFEM West Asia, submitted a proposal for a post-Beijing follow up (through the European Commission in Jordan) in five Arab countries — Jordan, Lebanon, Syria, Yemen and Palestine. The project's main objective was to strengthen the capacity of governments and NGOs alike, to pursue the implementation of Beijing's Platform for Action through a two-phase programme.

In October 1995 the EU indicated their interest in phase I of the project. After a lengthy period of negotiation to formulate an agreement compatible with both the EU and UN financial regulations, the project was effectively launched on March 1, 1996.

Starting from that day, the consultation process with governmental and NGO committees, as well as with donor communities was intensified. However, during the period immediately after Beijing, there was some

Equality Should Include Religion

By declaring that religious principles "do not contradict equality between the two sexes or exclude women's rights," Arab women hope to protect women and help them reclaim Islam, says Hoda Badran, co-coordinator of Arab NGOs at the Beijing Conference.

"Arab NGOs advocate that religions in the area must be understood correctly as the source of development and tolerance," says Badran.

Religious conservatism has moved to the forefront in this region where some countries, most notably Algeria, have also seen a rise in violence directed at girls and women.

Religious extremism there has sparked a campaign of terror, said Zahira Yaji of Algeria. However, "despite fear and terror, intelligent strategies are being worked out by women to achieve their rights".

But while many Arab groups here denounce extremism, they also insist that the Platform for Action respect religious values.

"We emphasise that the implementation of the Beijing Declaration can only be done under the umbrella of respecting divine religions," said Haifa Abu Ghazaleh, Arab NGO co-coordinator.

In the run-up to the Beijing Conference, several religious clerics denounced the draft document as anti-religion and anti-family.

"The absence of religion in this document is very obvious," said Sanaa Mahmoud Abdulla, a Saudi Arabian woman who attended the NGO Forum wearing a niqab, a veil that reveals only the eyes.

"The importance of religion to all societies must not be neglected because we can never live without it...Islam gives solutions to all women's problems," she said.

Several Arab countries supported the Vatican's stand on reproductive rights in Cairo last year and look set to do the same here.

"Arab groups are opposed to the idea that abortion should be legalised or considered a human right," says Badran. "They are also very suspicious about sex education in school."

The 22 Arab countries may run into trouble on the issue of early marriage, according to Badran. Countries with spiralling population growth rates oppose the practice. But others with smaller populations encourage large families and are reluctant to set a cut-off age.

Because of this, said Badran, "You can't have a consensus. But you can talk from a health perspective. A girl's age shouldn't be that low (at marriage) because that can lead to health problems."

Violence against women has only recently come out of the closet in some Arab countries. Kuwait recently set up a hotline for victims of violence. But shelters for abused women are still an alien concept. And many still consider violence a family affair.

The draft document lists Female Genital Mutilation (FGM) as a form of violence against girls. But Badran says FGM is not practised in all Arab countries. Where it is a problem—in Egypt and Sudan—it's a "symptom rather than a structural problem," she said.

"When women are educated, when they are aware of their human rights and understand those words, they will refuse to circumcise their daughters," Badran said.

Educational problems run deep; 65 percent of Arab women are illiterate. Several countries have set up massive literacy campaigns. But activists say it will take decades to wipe out traditional biases, particularly in poorer countries, where families spend their meagre resources on educating their sons.

Arab women's groups also criticise their governments for failing to apply constitutional rights to equality to family law, which favours men when it comes to divorce and child custody.

Finding a unified voice on this point could prove difficult; civil and political rights vary widely.

(Cont. on page 162)

> *(Continued from page 161)*
>
> For example, Tunisian women are often envied for having a progressive constitution that outlaws polygamy, while Kuwaiti women cannot vote.
>
> The theme of the regional meeting (preparatory to the Beijing Conference) in Amman was peace, and groups are emphasising the negative effects of armed conflict on women.
>
> They point to the continuing Arab-Israeli conflict, the UN sanctions on Iraq and Libya and the Kuwaiti prisoners of war that the Gulf state says Iraq is still holding.
>
> Badran said economic changes had lowered the standard of living for many people in the Arab world, where the numbers of women supporting their families has increased during the past few years.
>
> Finally, Arab women are calling on their governments to ratify CEDAW. Only eight Arab countries have joined the Convention so far. Those have expressed reservations, particularly on the concept of equality, have done so on the grounds that it violates their religious and cultural values.
>
> *Mona Eltahawy and Leila Deeb*
> *(Beijing Watch, September 11, 1995)*

dissension between the members of the official and NGO committees in most of these countries. The project therefore, could not move smoothly into the post-Beijing planning process. Undeterred, UNIFEM contacted the relevant representatives once again to trigger off another round of forming committees. As a result, the following were set up:

- **In Jordan:** The Jordanian National Committee for Women (JNCW) was formed to include representatives of the official and NGO sector in the country. Among its organisational framework, the JNCW has a coordinator, who in her turn has formed a small committee of the leading NGOs in Jordan.
- **In Lebanon:** Two National Committees were formed in Lebanon. The Lebanese National Committee for Women (official sector) and the Lebanese Civil Committee for Women (NGO sector). Although the Lebanese Civil Committee is not yet formally registered, the process is being initiated. During this transitional period, UNIFEM decided to establish an administrative agreement with the Friedrich Ebert Foundation which will act as an institutional channel to the committee for the implementation of NGO activities in Lebanon.
- **In Syria:** The Syrian Women's Union was formed, which included both the official and NGO sectors.
- **In Palestine:** The official coordinating committees of the Ministry of Planning and International Cooperation (official sector) and the Palestine Women's Union (civil sector) were formed.
- **In Yemen:** The Yemen National Committee for Women official sector) and the Yemen NGO Coalition were formed.

The primary objectives of the project's first phase are:

1. Identifying the partners in the Arab countries which will carry out the implementation of the project.

2. Strengthening the capacity of the leading governmental and non governmental organisations.

3. Defining the priorities of women on the national level.

Basma Urges More Political Integration of Arab Women

The most "pressing need" of Arab women is to share power and decision-making at all levels, says Princess Basma Bint Talal, the head of both the official Jordanian and NGO delegations to the Conference.

In general, Arab women's political activity is very low, said Bint Talal, who was at the forefront of a push to allow women to sit on municipal councils. That effort resulted in the election of the first woman to head the village council of Khirbet Al-Wahadneh in Northern Jordan.

Alleviating poverty among women and boosting their economic participation is another major area of concern, says Bint Talal, who assists the Queen Alia Fund for Social Development. She is also Chairperson of the Jordanian National Committee on Women, established in preparation for Beijing.

"This includes giving women equal opportunities in education and vocational training to help them become economically self-sufficient," she says.

"They should also have equal access to and a chance to participate in the definition of economic structures and the productive process itself."

As chairperson of the Arab Association for Women and Development, Bint Talal has helped this pan-Arab NGO strengthen the role of Arab women in development. Other needs, she adds, include access to health services, protection from persecution, armed conflict and all forms of violence.

The Arab Plan of Action, incorporated into the Global Plan of Action, takes these needs into consideration and includes mechanisms to address them.

Some of the most important of the nine areas of concern in the Arab plan include supporting women's economic self-reliance and ability to enter the job market. The plan also addresses the need for women to control natural resources and effectively use the media to promote equality between sexes.

Internationally, Bint Talal is a leading figure, appointed as a member of the World Health Organisation's Global Commission on Women's Health. She was a key player in linking the NGOs with delegates at the ministerial meeting during the Amman Prepcomm last November.

"NGOs have a very important role in development and peace building as they provide the vital link between governments and the people," she says. "This role needs to be strengthened and new means of cooperation between NGOs, governments and the bodies of the United Nations need to be found."

For example, she said, in Jordan, the NGO sector was developed early and has an outstanding record of cooperation with the government. The government can benefit from the expertise of the NGOs in social development, she adds.

After Beijing, she says, "it is very important for the success of the Conference to have time-bound mechanisms on the national, regional and international level for the implementation of the Platform for Action."

The UN is expected to help monitor the execution of national implementation strategies.

Regional UN agencies should also help prepare regional plans of action, she says. They should also, in conjunction with UN women's units, promote the platform and be responsible for regional monitoring.

"In Jordan, we have an excellent mechanism to ensure the implementation of the plan," says Bint Talal, referring to the Jordan National Committee for Women, a national policy making and supervising forum.

Bint Talal said she is optimistic about the potential unleashed by these two parallel international events. Besides creating an international Platform for Action for women, the Forum and Conference, she says, are "excellent opportunities for the exchange of expertise and viewpoints on a global scale."

Leila Deeb
(Beijing Watch, September 13, 1995)

4. Enhancing the participation of women in socio-economic life.

5. Preparing national strategies and workplans for women.

6. Strengthening and consolidating the roles of the national networks—both, the official and civil sectors—in order to translate the Beijing Platform for Action into national workplans in each country.

7. Organising workshops to study the strategies and workplans.

8. Holding a general meeting to adopt the national strategies and workplans.

9. Designing entrepreneurial projects based on the country's priorities and needs.

10. Organising meetings with donor and funding agencies which support such projects.

In each of the countries, the project coordinator assisted the partners and encouraged them to organise and implement a series of workshops on Beijing's twelve areas of concern, so as to reach a consensus on country-specific priorities and work out the mechanisms to be adopted for each of these areas. This was the first step in preparing for the countries' national strategies for women, which in turn will enhance the status of the region's women.

South Asia:

India: It's a Long Haul, But We'll Make It

S.K.Guha

The Beijing Conference was important, first and foremost, because of what happened before and after it. This continuum was one of the key factors of the Conference. In India, it brought about a tremendous mobilisation of women's groups, the government, state governments, government departments. In addition, it brought about heightened awareness and advocacy; a great deal of churning of issues and discussion. It was an immensely stimulating process.

Secondly, governments made commitments in Beijing—specific commitments which became the part of the document. This has given something concrete to be waved at governments in seeking policies and programmes and in monitoring them.

Moreover, the Conference sent a very strong signal that there are many players in the whole process—the government, the NGOs, the UN system and the national financial institutions. So, we are seeing a process in which every agency is seeking what they are supposed to do; whether or not they are clear about where they stand. To some extent, it becomes people's responsibility.

When the Indian government launched the preparatory process in mid-1993, we were not sure how we would go about it. There is a set pattern for the preparation of an international conference—prepare a paper, get experts to look at it, consult various ministries, participate in meetings, etc.

This is how it happened for the 1985 Nairobi Conference, for UNCED, for ICPD and all the others. This is what the government thought it would do for Beijing too. But somewhere along the line in preparation for the Beijing Conference, it found itself part of a much wider process involving hundreds of organisations and doing a lot of listening.

It was a period in which the government did the maximum listening in the nodal

Department of Women and Child Development. To be frank, it was not a process that was consciously visualised and I think the government deserves credit for not resisting this kind of change.

It was a change that, in fact, started during late 1993-early 1994, when the Coordination Unit (CU) and other organisations throughout the country contributed. This was the actual beginning. No other conference had ever spawned this kind of a process. The UN had given a time table and the country paper had to be submitted by April 1994. In early '94 we had a draft before the Jakarta and ESCAP meeting. But seeing the mood in the country we made a decision within the government that this would have to be a draft, and we informed the UN that it was a draft.

When asked about the final version of the country paper, I said that I did not know, but it would be before Beijing as so much had to be done. We felt that with so much churning going in the country, this could not be just a government paper. On many of the gender issues in the country (as in the Mathura rape case or the women's reservation bill) there had been an on-going process of interaction between the women's movement and the government. Therefore, it was felt that the country paper should be a country paper and not a government document. And that was quite unique.

I think this happened for the first time in the history of UN conferences. It was a result of the mood in the women's movement, the enthusiasm and the expectations that were being articulated and generated, as well as other factors like the economic liberalisation process India was going through. India had gone through two budgets was going through many fiscal corrections. There was a lot of concern and debate on this issue. Women's organisations and women from various walks of life wanted a say.

The CU really went out to the grassroots, not limiting their discussions mmerely to academics in Delhi or in the various states. In 1993, as a response to the kind of expectations generated, the government also decided that it would hold a series of regional meetings throughout the country, to bring in the voices of women. As a result of very large consultations and meetings, the efforts of the CU and the government complemented one another.

In fact, there were a number of papers produced by NGOs too. One was primarily on structural adjustments and there was this other paper which the NGOs and the CU brought out. The process which the UN had laid down gave scope for this: there would be a country paper and there would be a separate NGO Forum. The NGO forum committee got together and contributed their inputs.

Besides this national process, there was a lot of international interaction taking place over the document itself. Some contentious issues were discussed for a period of two years. These issues spread across several sectors. For instance, in the sector on poverty, the contentious issues were structural adjustments, economic liberalisation, market orientation. In health, it was the whole issue of not only reproductive health but all the aspects of health. In environment, there was the entire question of bio-diversity versus monoculture, women's traditional knowledge and the issue of intellectual property rights. And in human rights there were concerns such as the use of violence, uniform civil code on strengthening international monitoring and international machineries on handling the issue of violence, conflict, arms expenditure, etc.

Many contentious issues were based on development in the international community—disarmament or the new international economic order, North-South dialogue, trade issues—all these came up in Beijing. I remember many of the countries said they agreed with all this but that Beijing was not the

THE COORDINATION UNIT

Reaching Out to a Broad Spectrum

The Coordination Unit was set up in December 1993 and was to play a very catalytic role in terms of information dissemination. It was an India-level project, which I coordinated. All the countries in the South Asia region chose different mechanisms for the work, and each country in the region evolved creative and innovative ways of mobilising around Beijing. In India it was done through the structure of a collective. It goes to the credit of the women's organisations of the country that they chose to have a collective to structure and carry out the coordination of the entire process towards Beijing.

The Coordination Unit was a collaborative effort. It focussed on specific issues so that it was not just a secretariat but it also initiated generic information and consultation. In Beijing, as a region, we had a common feeling of something tangible; of issues that were being taken up. Indian women came back from Beijing feeling that the agenda of the South had been dealt with adequately.

We had never organised anything on this scale before. The regional conference at Manila was our first taste of a really huge event. But we all worked very hard and kept learning as Beijing neared. The Coordination Unit did whatever was humanly possible and we all worked to our very best ability. It was difficult work to coordinate the activities and processes that were going on simultaneously at regional, state and national levels. And given the time constraints the Unit managed it extremely well.

In our preparatory process towards Beijing, we experienced many challenges. There was a mass-scale mobilisation of women from every region and with concrete issue-based work. It was a multilayered process—of constantly linking the micro to the macro; of bringing different kinds of women together (women from the desert, hills, peasant women, trade unions political organisations, women's groups, minority communities, etc.); of consciousness-raising and formulating new visions; of transparency, openness and accountability; of demystifying existing feminist concepts and international mechanisms and procedures.

In trying to mobilise women from diverse backgrounds and walks of life and across geographical boundaries, we were attempting to make the women's movement more inclusive. In this respect, it was a recognition that women were struggling in different spaces all over the country and wanted to be a part of the movement. Also that the women's movement itself needs to spread out and reach other constituencies The process thus acknowledged the need to formulate new spaces and paradigms based on women's historical lives—it was an effort to 'strengthen the force' and not to narrow it down.

One of the most significant features of this process was that it believed in giving a lot of support to each other, in listening to each other and building tolerance towards each other.

We realised early that not all of us could go to Beijing, so we thought why not bring Beijing here. We tried to bring the essence of what happened at the macro level, to the micro. The Beijing experience was especially momentous for grassroots women. A significant detail for most of them was the tremendous appreciation they got from their communities upon their return home.

They came back far richer in experience. Some had never even stepped out of their villages. After Beijing, they started seeing things from a different perspective. For instance, International Women's Day, March 8, took on a whole new meaning for them. They had celebrated March 8 but now they came to understand the reasons in a broader way. And most important of all, they saw the linkages of issues in their villages to the more macro level there in Beijing.

Another critical experience for them was to see how governments work. They had, till then, experienced only how local government operated. In Beijing they saw the strategising, the lobbying, the discussions—all of which we were bringing to them in a language they could understand. The need to build solidarity with women from elsewhere in the region, in other countries, became clearer to them.

Post-Beijing, efforts have been ongoing in the region. Some of our best workshops have been centred around issues that emerged in Beijing. There has been a continuation of the processes that were set in motion; a commitment to the Plan of Action. The region's women saw the need for 'strategic' links among the various groups, given the political divides that exist in South Asia.

Certainly in South Asia, there has been an effort at strengthening all that was achieved at Beijing. The networking has grown stronger and even information sharing has been tremendous. This was a very large commitment at Beijing — to see oneself as a part of the whole process and to do whatever was necessary to strengthen and continue that process. So there is a reaching out, not just to women's organisations, not just to the converted but to a far broader spectrum.

Suneeta Dhar
[As told to Gouri Salvi]

---

forum; that it should be discussed at some other meeting. However, the response would be: 'Why should this not be the forum? This is the conference where these issues will come up again and again. It is an area where the women's movement is. So let's talk about these issues.'

The consultative process continued even beyond Beijing. Here, in India, from November and December 1995 till today, the issues around which consultations took place were the commitments which the government made. One of these was to have a national policy — something that was high on the Beijing Plan of Action. Then, there were consultations related to the UN system; some UN agencies started looking at the Beijing work and what the Beijing mandate should be for them.

The World Bank, UNDP and the UN system as a whole started looking at the Plan of Action and set up groups to look at how this could become part of their agenda, keeping in view the commitments which were made at Beijing—institutional strengthening in terms of new programmes, monitoring programmes, in terms of committee action as a policy stance.

In India, the issue of reservations for women in parliament and assemblies came up just before Beijing and in fact, there was a session in Parliament where ministers were asking about it. The Speaker urged the government to look into it very carefully. Immediately after Beijing it came up in a big way. By the end of '95-early '96 the draft bill was being debated in the law ministry. There was no specific commitment on that but affirmative action got focused in a big way.

Then there were the discussions on India's Ninth (Five Year) Plan. If you look at the working report of the Department of Women and Child you will find quotes from Beijing. Here is a working group document which says that it owes a lot of this mandate to Beijing. The discussions ultimately led to an approach paper in which empowerment of women is a Plan objective. I see this clearly as an outcome of the Beijing process.

There were also specific commitments that were mentioned at Beijing—universalisation of the integrated child development scheme. All of this has been happening; some has not been ratified, but the process is on and the momentum continues. With Beijing the whole style of functioning changed in government department, and that too still continues.

Beijing spoke of many things—paradigm shifts, empowerment of women, relationships between men and women—and how all these things were everybody's business. These shifts in thinking are basically processes which will eventually lead to changes in mindsets—of individuals, governments, organisations. And the Beijing Conference, through its sheer size and process, contributed in a large way to a change of mindsets.

For example, soon after Beijing, India went into a general election. The manifesto of every single political party spoke of empowerment of women. Whether they actually empowered women or not is a different matter. But to speak of empowerment was perceived as good politics. At the end of the day we found that the number of women nominated was small, but there was something in the air; something which made political parties make promises.

From Mexico to Beijing, the women's conferences have to a very large extent stimulated public action and political thinking, and have laid the foundation for paradigm shifts. I do not think that a paradigm shift is like a mathematical shift—it has to be seen how it gets translated into practice and action. Certainly, it is long haul. But Beijing definitely created the kind of ambience where at least everybody is talking.

(As told to Anita Anand)

Strengthening the Beijing Process

Asha Ramesh

The Coordination Unit was initiated by a group of donor agencies who came together, called the Inter Facilitating Committee for Beijing (IFCB). There were about 14 donors in IFCB. NGOs too felt that there should be a unit, since in earlier conferences information on and about the conference had not reached everyone — and was limited to metropolitan areas. There was a feeling that there must be an effort to reach grassroots women NGOs who, while they are doing tremendous work, did not get the recognition or visibility they needed and deserved — only because they are away from the power centre.

The Coordination Unit was set up in December 1993, and I joined in August 1994 as convenor on the issue of women and political participation. There were six of us who handled sectors — health, education, media, economic empowerment and livelihood, violence against women, etc. In India, political participation was a relatively new issue in the sense that the 73rd and 74th Constitutional Amendments (giving women quotas at local governance) were passed in 1992. Thus, women had just come into electoral politics in a big way almost all over the country. We had to address the issue of women's participation in local governance, trade union activity, decision-making positions in the bureaucracy, and most important, mobilisation of women.

We held over 60 meetings all over the country in all levels — village, district, state, and national. We identified groups working on issues and they took the initiative of organising meetings with support from the Coordination Unit. It was decentralised to a large extent. We tried to get representation from every area of the country to participate in the Beijing Conference — even from regions like Jammu and Kashmir and the Northeast.

Moreover, these local groups were working with grassroots women, so we were able to draw them into the process. Nearly 189 women went to Beijing. Language did not prove to be an obstacle, because the Coordination Unit had decided that in Beijing, grassroots women would speak in their own language, and we would serve as translators. The basic attempt was to try and get as many of them to go to Beijing and contribute to the process through participation in workshops — and it was very successful. For most it was a first time experience, and they came back more empowered and better equipped to reach out to larger numbers of women.

For the Coordination Unit, Beijing was a mixed experience. We faced a lot of flak and accusations that our agenda was donor-driven. However, from my own experience as part of the Unit, I think there was absolutely no pressure from the donor. They did not take any of the decisions on people, venues, issues, etc. That was all left to us. And let's face it. This process would not have been possible without the resources of donors. The resources were adequate so hundreds of women could participate in the Conference. However, by the time Beijing came along, people did understand that the process did make a difference.

In December 1995, the National Alliance of Women (NAWO) was formally constituted. After Beijing, this Alliance was given the task to help take forward the achievements of the Conference. About a month before Beijing we had a Conference of Commitments in India, attended by most officials of the Ministry of Human Resource Development and many other groups, where the Government was asked to make commitments. In all fairness, the Government of India made commitments at Beijing. All groups pledged at this Conference of Commitments that the process initiated for Beijing should continue. The group felt they had a responsibility to all women it had reached out to, to keep the process alive. Therefore, it was decided that post-Beijing, NAWO would do that work. Specifically, it would pursue the implementation of the Government of India's commitment as well as the implementation of the Beijing Platform for Action. NAWO would serve as a monitoring body, as a body that would make interventions. It would also, from time to time, seek interaction with government departments and provide inputs for policy changes. For instance, a think tank has been formed to provide input into the forthcoming Five Year Plan and three members from NAWO are part of it.

A major aim of the Alliance is to take micro issues and concerns to the macro level. For this, we must get the voices of women from every remote corner of the country heard, especially if we are to impact government policy. We have 12 focal members around the country, who have responsibility for the different states of India. Since then, state level teams have emerged, and there have been several consultations at various levels since Beijing.

For the first time in India, this exercise was attempted and a coalition of groups came together, reaching out to smaller groups. This initiative now needs the support and encouragement of as many groups and persons as possible. We need to stop competing with each other and join hands to strengthen the Beijing process. This is the most important challenge before the women's movement today.

(As told to Gouri Salvi)

ASIA-PACIFIC

Real Regions Value Women

More women live in the Asia Pacific region than anywhere else. They have organised into some of the strongest and most active women's movements in the world. During the preparations for Beijing, they fought to have their voices heard by government delegates and to ensure that official wisdom was debated at the grassroots.

There has been much to discuss. Asia Pacific is a region of vast economic and cultural diversity. Some of the world's poorest nations are here: Bangladesh and Nepal. So are some of the fastest growing economies: China, Korea, India. And one of the richest: Japan.

Amid the political and economic insecurity that accompanies these contrasts, "Women are the pawns," said Gita Sen, an economist with Development Alternatives of Women in a New Era (DAWN). Sen spoke at the NGO Forum's opening plenary, and drew a grave but brave picture of where the women of the Asia Pacific region are coming from.

Sen added, "The growing crises of debt, of food, of fuel and water and of livelihoods place women at the crossroads between economic activity, production for income and the care of human beings."

As the Fourth World Conference of Women opens in Beijing, delegates from governments and NGOs are feverishly holding caucuses and lobbying to push their inputs into the global Platform for Action.

An additional 10,000 women from the Asia Pacific region have trooped to Huairou to attend the NGO Forum, which began last week.

The process of regional consultations began in Manila in November 1993 at the Asia Pacific NGO Symposium, the very first major gathering of NGOs. What the UN Economic and Social Commission for Asia and the Pacific (ESCAP) planned as a meeting of 30 experts ballooned into more than 800 participants who insisted on being heard.

The Manila Declaration was the basis from which NGOs conducted their own nationwide sectoral consultations, listing priority issues.

In June 1994, NGO women set forth for Jakarta, determined to lobby the government delegates at the UN Second Ministerial Meeting for Women in Development. Due to their persistent demands, NGOs were allowed for the first time to sit in as observers and were given limited participation.

The Jakarta Declaration covered ten critical issues of concern: poverty, education, violence against women, effects of armed or other kinds of conflict on women, economic empowerment, political empowerment, mechanisms to promote the advancement of women, women's human rights, media, and environment.

However, the NGO Working Group pointed out some "unheeded concerns". Some of these included the health needs of adolescent girls and older women, food security for rural women, the debt crisis, nuclear testing in the Asia Pacific region, and the labour rights of migrant workers.

The issues of women's health and the girl child were later added to the Global Platform for Action now being debated at the Fourth World Conference on Women.

The Jakarta Platform had been thrashed out in subregional meetings of the Asia Pacific NGO Working Group coordinated by Sumalee Chartikavanij of Thailand and Salamo Fulival of Tonga. An NGO position paper was presented at the final preparatory meeting in New York last March.

The different sub-regions of the Asia Pacific region have a myriad of concerns. Southeast Asia focuses on women in newly industrialising countries. There has been much discussion of industrialisation, environment, sex tourism, trafficking in women, migration, and other issues.

East Asia's central theme is the impact of rapid economic growth on women. Countries here have addressed issues on decision-making, poverty, education and culture, violence against women and human rights.

The four issues of the Pacific are indigenous peoples' rights, decolonisation, a nuclear-free Pacific and militarism.

South Asia's key concerns include development models that are alternatives to those designed by the IMF and World Bank, violence, political empowerment, the politics of identity and ideology and the cultural differences of special groups like indigenous and minority women.

The thread that binds the concerns of the region, as Sen so clearly explained, is "a development model or paradigm that places a higher priority on economic growth rather than human lives." Women only know too well the resulting debt, food, fuel, water and livelihood crises that their families have to bear.

Sen said, "The three crucial aspects of the agenda facing us are to continue to challenge the negative forces unleashed by globalisation across the world. We need to work to transform our governments and our states so that they become more accountable to us and continue to build the institutions of civil society. And we must build on what we have gained from all the UN conferences up to this point."

The women in the Asia Pacific region envision an alternative model that "engenders structures, processes and forms of governance that would empower women and men to work together as equal partners towards equality, democracy, sustainable development and peace," according to an NGO document called 'Voices from Asia and the Pacific.'

Now is the most auspicious time for women to assert themselves. As Sen pointed out, women have the capacity to organise. The real challenge for the women of the Asia Pacific and the other regions is to be heard.

As Nobel Peace Laureate Aung San Suu Kyi of Burma said in her message to the NGO Forum, "In societies where men are truly confident of their own worth women are not merely 'tolerated,' they are valued. Their opinions are listened to with respect, and they are given their rightful place in shaping the society in which they live."

Olivia H. Tripon
(Beijing Watch, September 6, 1995)

THE OECD/DAC-WID INITIATIVE

A Positive Experience

The women's section at the Ministry of Foreign Affairs in the Netherlands, were also the Chair of the OECD/DAC-WID group. I got information about the initaitive from the Netherlands, and passed it on to the Embassy and the donor community in Delhi. DANIDA's staff person said she had got a letter from the head office, saying that they would be the focal point for this area. She also suggested separate coordinators in India, Bangladesh, and Pakistan. Many donors chipped in and there was never any kind of competition between us.

The initiative started early in 1993 as a long lead time for organising was needed. The work was different in the different countries. In India, the British Council opened up their library and stored the Beijing documentation. We made leaflets, informed people, and put in expert advice to the group.

I feel very positive about the OECD/DAC-WID initiative. The process went very well, and we got a lot of NGOs and activists on a common platform all over the country. For Beijing the agenda was clear, which is why we could start the planning and process early, and influence the policy papers. It was timely, there was a vision, and the staff at the CU were very cooperative. When they didn't know something they would ask for guidance—everybody was involved.

When you get donor funding, it is usually with strings attached. But not so in this case. Whosoever got selected by the CU to go to Beijing did so by a very strict criteria. There were other donors who chipped in, and between 160-180 went to Beijing with donor funding, not knowing which donor funding and whom they had to report to. I feel this process was very transparent, and you will surprised at the number of individuals who went to Beijing not caring which donor agency gave the money.

Post Beijing, there was a lull. Everybody said okay, it is done now. But of course it had just started! India had signed the Platform for Action, and we had to have a plan to go forward. One of the things which has emerged from the process is of course NAWO (National Alliance of Women's Organisations). The UN system under the guidance of UNIFEM played a leading role, which I think is good. The donor community is not so active any more. You may ask how much they are involved in the post-Beijing process. We are trying to influence the 9th Five Year Plan, and that is also a post-Beijing activity.

As outcome of Beijing in the region has been the DAC-WID meeting organised in Madras for the South Asian region. Since then there have been a number of regional conferences in which critical areas have been focused on. In India it is political participation training, *panchayat* training, violence against women, and women in the peace process.

It's a big achievement, but I think there needs to be a mechanism for seeing that whatever is in the Platform for Action—the critical areas, the recommendations must be carried out—to ensure that we not have to speak of the same things again just before the next Conference India is doing something at each level—centre, state, region, etc.

There was a regional follow up and there is now an evaluation of the donor funding in certain countries—amongst others India—to see if it reached people, reached women.

Riet Turksma
(As told to Anita Anand)

An Amazing Feat

A huge amount of time was spent on Beijing, going to meetings. The IFCB (Inter-Agency Facilitation Committee for Beijing) was made up of about 12-15 donors, was highly participatory with tremendous enthusiasm. The group came together to coordinate, despite the fact that they had different goals, operating styles, yet agreement on a value system. The IFCB was a facilitating body and NGOs led in determining the agenda.

I thought it was a most unusual experience, to have development agencies working together, and it was successful. It is important to reflect why it worked, because it did. There was a grounding which was participation in Beijing. The initiative worked because we were facilitators not leaders, so as such it was not donor driven. This is very important. There was a joint value system, and it was not an exclusive process. It was so unusual, I am not sure we will see this again.

The experience was much better than we expected. There were moments of frustration and problems. NGOs, like donors, have differences, but of greater importance was making Beijing meaningful. It was not just another UN meeting with the same old UN people. There was a sentiment to do things differently—to include people from small NGOs, people from the North East of India, non-English speakers, and to have different thematic areas. The IFCB saw all this as an opportunity—to promote wider communication on women's issues.

There were times in the Beijing process where I felt frustrated. But I had expected this, and had to get through it. The fact that 12-14 donors came together and made it work is still amazing. We actually got people on planes! We learned a lot and should have had a process of documentation that recorded it all, as institutional memory is lost. I can't remember the details.

After the conference, the follow up work of the CU (Coordination Unit) has been taken over by NAWO. I think we could have done a better job in follow up in terms of policy issues—economic reforms, violence against women, and other issues that could have been worked into a real mobilising strategy. Why has this not happened? The coordinating groups would have to have in place an organisation. NGO advisory committees tried, but it has be a set of people in place, full time, otherwise it can't be done.

The Ford Foundation as an agency is concerned about follow-up, but only if women's movements and NGOs feel it is a concern and want to take it forward. The agenda of Beijing and the work towards it has reinforced our programming, and the recommendations do tally with our concerns. But, I don't see a body working on mobilising people behind the recommendations and going out and doing it. The energy behind getting the follow-up done is dissipated.

As for initiatives for follow-up, a consortium of NGOs or NGO whose focus is policy reform will be the core of this work. People are caught up in their day to day work and their areas. Activists work not on policy, but where the action is, not on documents from Beijing, but issues of poor women in India. Policy needs to be linked to concerns of poor women. There is room for both, but there is nobody that is linked to the groups.

The Indian government responded well. The IFCB concentrated on NGOs, but also linked and influenced the government. But there was a lot of dialogue given the government and NGOs work independently of each other. In India the NGO force is strong. Sophisticated groups are not hostile to the government and work hand in hand with government. There is a precedence here, almost 15 years of working out relationships.

In summary it was a remarkable conference, in terms of a movement towards working together. Post Beijing people went back to what they were doing. Ford Foundation, as an institution, supports coalition building, in different areas such as self help groups. There needs to be a vision, and I am not sure where the vision is.

Jane Rosser
(As told to Anita Anand)

Pacific:

Springing to Life With Activity

Bernadette Rounds Ganilau

The Fourth World Conference on Women held a very special significance for the Pacific region. For the first time in the last two decades, Pacific women participated actively not just in an international conference but also in the many events held over the months leading up to it.

In fact, since 1975 the UN women's conferences and parallel NGO fora had never involved Pacific governments or Pacific NGOs at any decision-making level. The issues and input from this region were usually included in the broader canvas of 'Asia and Pacific', with Asia usually taking the lead.

Beijing was, therefore, a significant first for the region. But it did not start out that way. While the rest of the world began to prepare for the "next international women's meeting" way back after Nairobi in 1975, the Pacific did not start their preparatory activities until late 1993- early 1994.

In 1993, the UNIFEM Pacific office initiated an ad hoc working group to coordinate the preparations of NGOs and governments for the Fourth World Conference on Women and Forum '95.

This working group consisted of UNIFEM, the South Pacific Commission (a regional inter-governmental organisation) 'Pacific Women's Resource Bureau (SPC/PWRB), the Pacific Regional YWCA, the Fiji National Council of Women (FNCW), Fiji YWCA, and some media personnel. Concerted and collective efforts of various organisations led to a series of activities such as:

- Preparation and participation of NGOs at the Asia/Pacific NGO Symposium
- Production of the Pacific Women NGO Programme of Action
- Production of the Pacific Women NGO Gender and Sustainable Development Report
- Inclusion of the issues of concern to NGOs in the Pacific Platform for Action
- Preparation of NGOs and government focal points for the Asia and Pacific Ministerial Meeting on Women and Development in Jakarta
- Coordination of Pacific participation in Jakarta.

The Working Group felt that the issues of denuclearisation, decolonisation/self-determination, militarisation and biodiversity that had been raised at a recently ended meeting for the UN's SIDS in Barbados, would be the major debates to be carried further and taken on to Beijing.

The Pacific NGOs, however, still felt the need to formalise a coordinating committee which they did in Jakarta during ESCAP's Second Ministerial meeting in June 1994 when the Fiji National Council of Women, the UNIFEM Pacific Office and the Pacific YWCA were appointed as the Pacific NGO Coordinating Committee (PNGOCG). These three organisations had the capacity and the relevant structures to facilitate the proposed Pacific programmes. The fact that NGOs needed to have a separate forum was voiced strongly and the PNGOCG was then given the following tasks to implement:

- conduct regional preparatory workshops and assist national workshops where necessary
- prepare NGO participants and conduct an analysis of the draft Plan of Action at the

Commission on the Status of Women meeting in March 1994 to ensure that Pacific concerns are reflected
- produce relevant proposed amendments for distribution to NGOs as a tool for lobbying governments, etc.
- disseminate information regionally and internationally on activities related to Beijing
- coordinate three Pacific issue-based workshops at Forum '95
- work closely with the SPC on all preparations
- fundraise for all of the above activities
- produce narrative and financial reports for all activities.

The Pacific suddenly sprang to life with activity! Follow up and preparatory workshops were in full swing and media reports were sent down the line to national station Radio Fiji and Pacnews for regional dissemination. Issues that had so far been usually relegated to women's programmes, now found their way into mainstream news programmes.

The region was fortunate in having active women leaders like Salamo Fulival of the Pacific YWCA and Dr. Laufitu Taylor of UNIFEM Pacific. They were able to encourage Pacific women and influence fundraising organisations to support many of the preparatory activities both nationally and regionally. The region was even more fortunate, when in 1994, Salamo Fulival was selected to sit on the Facilitating Committee—the international organising arm of Beijing's NGO Forum—and was also elected as co-chair of the Asia Pacific Region's Working Group.

The mandate set down by Pacific NGO's in Jakarta for the PNGOCG started to show results with a hectic progression of activities. For instance, the PNGOCG undertook the development of a regional workplan and monthly Peacesat satellite conferences were conducted recording the activities of NGO's and their needs. In addition, Pacific radio programmes and a bimonthly newsletter called S'Pacifically Speaking were produced, keeping the region abreast with news from New York and China as well our own progress and development. A 'Gender Awareness and Training for Trainers' workshop was held followed by another on 'Negotiating and Lobbying Technique Skills'—which saw government as well as non- governmental members participating.

Preparations also got underway for Pacific issue-based workshops to be held in Beijing on subjects such as militarism, nuclearisation and decolonisation/self determination, etc. Moreover, NGO representatives started getting ready for the CSW meeting in New York in March '95 and to lobby for the inclusion of Pacific issues in the Global Plan of Action. Regional meetings also had PNGOCG reports on their agenda.

The world had never seen as big a contingent of Pacific islands women as they did in Huairou. Although they numbered under 400, their presence in the Asia Pacific Friendship Tent and the Grassroots Tent was felt throughout the compound with their singing and dancing. They could be seen communicating the Pacific's message in the thousands of panels and workshops that were held during the 10-day event.

With France resuming its nuclear testing in the Pacific during the Conference, the women took a united stand and used the Forum in Huairou and the parallel UN Conference to highlight nuclearisation in the Pacific. Speakers like Hilda Lini of Vanuatu and Amelia Rokotuivuna of Fiji spoke out strongly against colonisation and nuclearisation, as well as the economic impact on women's development. Kanaky New Caledonia's Susana Ounei Small's stand on sovereignty and self-determination was very visible. Apart from these presentations the Pacific took part in the 'Once and

Future Pavillion' coordinated by Ruth Lechte, the Beneath Paradise presentation and in Breathing Feminism in Media workshops. The Pacific Media Desk was active sending stories twice daily down the line to Pacnews, Radio Australia's "Pacific Beat" programme, Radio Fiji and NBC in Papua New Guinea.

While the Pacific women were active out in the field, Salamo Fulival was behind closed doors with the Facilitating Committee, negotiating with the China Organising Committee (COC) on the many problems that international NGOs were experiencing such as the intense security, inadequate transport, insufficient meeting spaces, the tremendous language barrier and so forth, and encouraging them on those facilities that were well provided.

While the world was exposed to the Pacific, the Pacific women themselves experienced a sharing of ideas with many women from countries that they had only read about in books. Language barriers were secondary when interchanges were made between Kiribati and Kashmir, Tuvalu and Thailand, the Marshalls and Mongolia, from Nauru to Nepal—women of the world weaving their web of friendship and solidarity that extended beyond cultural, religious, political, economic, social and geographic back-grounds.

The visit to the Asia Pacific Friendship Tent by Secretary General Gertrude Mongella, NGO Forum Convenor Supatra Masdit, the First Ladies of some of the African States, Her Majesty the Queen of Tonga Halaevalu Mara'aho, head of her country's government delegation and Queen Fabiola of Belgium, were some of the highlights of the NGO Forum experienced by women of the Pacific.

Sixteen governments from the Pacific including New Zealand and Australia, attended the Beijing Conference. Three countries, American Samoa, Commonwealth of the Northern Mariana Islands and Guam came as associate members of the regional commissions and were represented by observers. From the island member nations, there were at least 300 representatives, the biggest contingent coming from Papua New Guinea.

While meetings of the Main Committee were held, Working Groups and Contact Groups were formed to continue working on the text of the documents. The G-77 Group to which Pacific belonged, was active at most sessions and was responsible for ensuring that the issues of the Pacific, particularly in relation to the environment, were included. Pacific NGOs had already lobbied their governments in the lead up to Beijing, on the issues of denuclearisation, decolonisation and the right to self-determination, demilitarisation and the rights of the indigenous people, so that these could be prioritised as the region's major concerns.

The Pacific scored a first at the Conference when Solomon Islands YWCA member, Sophie Chottu, delivered the World YWCA statement of commitment during Youth Day Celebrations in Beijing. The theme of her presentation was "Youth—Partners in Equality, Development and Peace."

There was a definite uniqueness about the Pacific representation at the UN Conference in Beijing. The Pacific island government representatives walked into the meeting knowing full well that they had the support of their NGOs who had worked in consultation with them in the entire process leading up to Beijing. The NGOs, in turn, were satisfied that their issues would be taken into the meeting and fought for strongly by their official representatives. This two-way consultation was the modus operandi of governments and NGOs in most Pacific nations.

But the Pacific women never felt that they were in isolation. The region's NGOs sensed a commonality with women throughout the world regarding many issues like violence against women, education, reproductive rights, women at decision-making levels, etc but left it to some of the other regions to address these concerns strongly. They strategised and prioritised their own Pacific issues in the Pacific Platform for Action that was accepted by Pacific governments at the SPC's Ministerial Meeting in Noumea in May 1994. Convincing Pacific governments to incorporate NGO concerns in their respective briefs was then done during national and regional preparatory stages as well as in New York.

In the larger picture, an Asia Pacific NGO strategy lobbying group was set up prior to Beijing with the responsibility of collating the region's input. The group was split in Beijing according to the areas of concern and each sub-group worked with the specific Asia Pacific NGO representative in the government delegation who was dealing with particular issues.

The outcome was quite successful as the NGOs were able to utilise the extent of expertise from both regions. For instance, on the issues of structural adjustment programmes and violence against women, the sub-group consisted of NGOs from Malaysia, India and the Philippines, and the NGOs in government delegations who ensured that the input was incorporated were from Malaysia and the Philippines. Similarly, the sub-group on environment, in particular the nuclear issue, biodiversity/intellectual property rights, transboundary movements, were from Fiji and PNG. The NGO in the Tongan delegation ensured incorporation.

One of the many positive outcomes of the joint Pacific effort was the section on assistance to the colonies. This was an historical event in that in all the earlier UN conferences, the Pacifichad tried to put this language into the documents but had failed.

Commitments were made by the various Pacific governments. What was of great significance was that that government delegations included senior level ministers. At home, this representation was taken as a conformation of the commitment of governments at the highest level to the advancement of women. And governments are beginning to act on these commitments as well. For instance,the government of Tonga recently reduced its military budget and placed this allocation in education programmes.

After intense awareness raising on the Platform for Action by NGOs (and in some cases government departments) in the media and at public meetings, women's groups are consistently lobbying their local representatives and monitoring their situation for progress. As well-known Pacific activist, Amelia Rokotuivuna,says, after a long wait, "the historic moment for our struggles has arrived. Social conditions are now ready for us to act."

South East Asia:

Hong Kong: Sharing the Fate of the State

Cecilia Young Dong-ling

Caught in the changing of sovereignties from Britain to China which was scheduled for 1 July 1997, the pre-Conference period became a time of questionable identity for many of Hong Kong's people. This was also true of Hong Kong's women delegates who headed for the NGO Forum and the Fourth World Conference on Women, hosted by a country that was soon to resume its sovereignty over them.

Two major coalitions were formed by women's groups in Hong Kong. The one to which my organisation belonged, comprised 14 women's groups that had a long history of involvement with women's rights in Hong Kong. The other coalition, spearheaded by a newly formed women's organisation that had close ties with the government in Beijing, had a far greater number of organisations under its umbrella. This coalition was (and still is) very well connected with the establishment and was at that time also extremely well-informed about the preparation for the Conference by the All China Women's Federation.

The Hong Kong British Colonial Government had never developed either a women's policy or a unit to deal with women issues. Therefore, no mechanism was in place to carry out a full consultation process with NGOs prior to the Beijing Conference. The government had never heeded to calls by women's groups for better consultation or for local promotion of the imminent Conference. Government gave no impetus to any awareness building programmes about the Conference and the official Hong Kong Report was hastily compiled and submerged into the United Kingdom's country report.

During the Conference, on two occasions (and after much coercion on our part), Hong Kong's NGO delegates were invited to a briefing and debriefing session held for British NGOs by their government. I happened to be one of the two Hong Kong NGO representatives to attend a final debriefing session for British NGOs by their official delegate to the UN Conference. Never had my colleague and I felt such humiliation in Hong Kong being treated as a non-entity. We were ignored and totally dismissed by the British officer appointed to carry out the debriefing at a time we were still living in a British Dependent Territory, with the British Crown and its icon ubiquituously present on the money we spent, on the walls of buildings and tax returns. The same treatment was reported by women who attended the briefing meeting at the start of the NGO Forum.

Officially, as women we were a non-entity in Hong Kong, for the government in Hong Kong uses the family as a basic social unit.

Although both Britain and China are signatories to CEDAW, it did not extended to the Colony. And then we were a non-entity at the Beijing Conference, not because we were women but because we were from Hong Kong. Hong Kong and its women shared the same fate.

Yet, Beijing was an experience for all of us. Hong Kong has a very homogeneous Southern Chinese ethnic background. Our visions were markedly broadened at Huairou by delegates from different countries and by activists of differing ages. More importantly, the exposure to strong articulation in defining women's rights vis a vis issues such as abortion, homosexuality and human rights, was something we would not have missed for anything. So were the colourful diversities that existed at the Beijing Conference that allowed us to 'look at the world through women's eyes', as suggested by the theme developed for the NGO Forum.

However, at times the diversity also became a frustration for some of us. One of the reasons was that most workshops were carried out in English without translation. Secondly, was the lack of true dialogue between the diverse groups at numerous workshops. Although poignant stories by women from different countries laid the groundwork for an emotional identification of 'sisterhood', there seemed to be a lack of a deeper approach to cross-national and cross-cultural dialogue. Perhaps our obsession with our own country's problems, reveals that we still have a long way to go in achieving women's rights within our own national boundries.

In 1995, we were still at the stage of being considered lucky to be allocated time, space and funds for an NGO Forum of this scale.

Is the celebration, then, simply because we could come together and look forward to a better future? We hope that by the next meeting, we will be able to seek a more active dialogue in NGO workshops that can straddle beyond national and cultural boundaries, in a venue that is closer to the UN Conference.

The Beijing Conference was a catalyst in the sense that the Hong Kong Colonial Government hastily established the Equal Opportunity Commission on Sex and Disability, although with limited terms of reference and basically to address matters on employment. Three consultation papers were circulated, one on equality for women and men, a second on family responsibility and a third on discrimination against sexual orientation. However, the extension of CEDAW to Hong Kong was never mentioned again after the Conference. New conservative women's group sprung up to address women issues along the structures of the UN Plan of Action.

Will the change of sovereignty be positive or negative towards the continued efforts to improve the status of Hong Kong's women ? Both the British and the Chinese promised to keep Hong Kong prosperous and stable for the next 50 years. But 'prosperity' and 'stability' mean different things to different people. For women in this region, it means reduced unemployment and reduced demand for coercing women into the sex industry. It also means a phasing out of outmoded Confucian patriarchal practices.

Much of this will have to be pursued and achieved by women themselves. One of the most important things we learnt as observers during the Beijing Conference, was that in order to be heard we need to become very good negotiators. Certainly, the Hong Kong NGO delegates lacked lobbyists who could have helped us to translate our needs that were voiced in Huairou.

Inspired in Huairou, by the creativity found in performing arts groups—street-theatre, songs and dances — we have now learnt to use that media if and when we are oppressed and if and when our voices are muted by tyranny.

At the time of writing, our future is still unknown. But Beijing showed us a number of survival skills and also the power of effective information dissemination through the electronic network. We hope that women in the rest of the region and the world will hear our voices and we, theirs.

Thailand: The Grassroots Surface

Shashi Ranjan Pandey and Darunee Tantiwiramanond

The NGO Forum site at Huairou was a complex of school buildings, auditoria and a huge, tentlike pavilion. Inside this pavilion were housed other, smaller tents for different groups of women—African, Arab, Asian, Catholic, lesbian, and others. Dressed in their traditional, colourful clothes — kimonos, kangas, batiks, chadors—they visited each other, exchanged information and talked animatedly.

The Chinese police was omnipresent. Sometimes even Nature made her presence felt as torrential rains transformed the Forum site into a maze of muddy lanes! But the women were undeterred. Their activities and discussions went on. They marched, talked and sang their hearts out. One night, 500 women marched in a silent, candle-lit procession for human rights. Another night, 300 of them went to a downtown disco, cutting through all language barriers. Dancing, after all, was a symbol of unity, celebration and liberation.

Over the past two decades, women's NGOs

have often operated within the constrained environments of their governments, or of fundamentalist religious groups. Yet, through the UN, they have worked towards setting up their agendas and creating a space for themselves. For NGO groups, the Beijing Conference was about identity and voice; about power and representation. The distance between the first women's conference at Mexico in 1975 and the fourth at Beijing in 1995 cannot be measured in the number of years but in the progress women made in their consciousness and organisation. Beijing was a culmination of the past 20 years of concerted efforts by women's NGOs. It was a symbol of their rising participation in international dialogue.

Despite the odds, women's NGOs have been able to achieve success in the international setting, largely for two reasons. One, their ability to use the opportunities provided by international organisations and conferences, and find allies in various bureaucracies. And two, by mobilising their own resources in terms of leadership, finance, friendship and perseverance.

Women's NGOs, run by and for women, have often taken up issues that other NGOs will shun or hesitate to deal with. They have pioneered valuable work on issues like violence against women, women's legal and human rights, prostitution and women's reproductive health; they have frequently highlighted some anti-women attitudes implicit in various population and structural adjustment programmes; they have publicised the dearth of women in politics, and have focussed on widespread violent practices like genital mutilation, dowry deaths, rapes and trafficking in women. Due to their own growing awareness and leadership, and with support from international and women's group (including some UN agencies) many women's NGOs have been able to carry these issues to a global level.

This process of agenda-setting has gone through three broad phases:

1. From the early 1970s to the early 1980s was the issues' recognition phase, when women drew international attention to what was being ignored and what was being violated.

2. From the mid-1980s to the early 1990s was the policy emphasis phase, when women's national and international organisations together with individuals and donor agencies attempted to develop policy proposals.

3. The 1990s was the political mobilisation phase, when NGOs actively lobbied and pressurised the UN during its various World Summits to put women's issues on the agenda.

In addition to the success of getting the women's agenda recognised at the global platform, the exercise of preparing for and participating in the Beijing Conference too had a profound (though sometimes unrecognised) impact in raising women's awareness and increasing national mobilisation. In Thailand, several women's organisations were already actively attempting to increase political participation, or were promoting the economic activities of rural women. The most dramatic development was the coming together of rural women into an umbrella of grassroots organisations. This organisation—coordinated by a well-known women's group called 'Foundation of Friends of Women' — was formed specifically for the Beijing Conference, and has been operating since. It has gone through three distinct phases of pre-, during-, and post- Beijing events.

In 1993 at the Asian NGO Preparatory Meeting at Manila for the Beijing Conference, many participants recognised that women who were most adversely affected by development were missing in the meetings. The development establishment often sees women's problems through the lens of academics, middle-class NGOs, or funding agencies. That view may not correspond with the reality of the problems and needs of less privileged women. Several funding agencies, therefore, encouraged city-based NGOs to involve grassroots women in their work and to prepare them and bring them to Beijing. The purpose was to provide grassroots women with a chance to voice their agenda. They would also be able to bring back and share the information and experiences from this global gathering with their own communities.

Grassroots women are the majority of women who live on the margins of the society. They carry the heavier burden of maintaining economic growth, and are often deprived of any benefits of national economic development programmes. They are largely poor, disempowered women in urban and rural areas who have little access to information about their own basic human rights or about raising their voices in public.

In Thailand, discussion of women's issues in general in the process towards Beijing was compounded by language barriers. Thai is the national language but English is the medium of international gatherings. Most available literature was in English — a language understood only by a minority of highly educated women. Therefore, the purpose and progress of the preparatory process for the Beijing Conference was initially limited to only a small circle of privileged, English-speaking women. The Thai public knew very little about the Beijing Conference, as the Thai media gave it scant coverage. It was not possible to have serious discussions on Thai women's issues without inputs from less privileged, grassroots women. The input of grassroots women was essential, but grassroots women were scattered in different sections—agriculture, manufacturing, commercial sex services, local governing system and slums. In addition, these women were often the victims of violence.

It was at a pre-Beijing workshop in November 1994, organised by The Foundation of Friends of Women, with financial support from CIDA and the Ford Foundation, that the first seminar was held on 'Thai Women in the Next Decade: The Forum of Thai Grassroots Women Toward the Global Meeting on Women at Beijing'. Following guidelines set at the Manila meeting and looking at Thai reality, six topics were selected for discussion: violence against women; environment and natural resource use; women workers in agriculture and manufacturing sectors; health and STD/AIDS; migrant workers; and political participation. Over 200 women participated in this meeting. For the first time, grassroots women—with their traditional sarongs—outnumbered the conventionally dominant group of middle class NGOs, academics and funders.

They discussed the "dissemination of information" or "briefings" by the expert group about the problems in the selected six areas, and about the context of the Beijing Conference. This information served as a framework for the smaller group discussions in which grassroots women gave their inputs. In all these information-sharing exercises the contrast between the middle-class and the grassroots women was clear in a strange way: while the grassroots women could understand what the "resource women" talked about in the Bangkok-Thai language, most of the "resource women" who spoke fluent English, could not fully understand what the grassroots women said in a variety of regional dialects.

One woman concluded: "The government deceived us and made us poorer". Another reported the adverse effects of the government's policy of encouraging cash crops for export (in her case it was cassava). She summed up her point: *"Mun maa, paa mod"* ("The cassava comes; the forest disappears"). According to the description of grassroots women, the destruction came in three kinds of geographies: of forest and plane fields (by the cash crops), of mountains (in the form of dams), and of the sea (by the prawn farms). Chain reaction from this environmental destruction might expand into unreliable rain cycles. Many cultivators depend on annual seasonal rainfalls and if the rainfall fails, their production can be disturbed.

One *langon* (a local fruit) grower in the north complained that she invested in growing langon trees (which usually take 5-6 years before they can be harvested), only to see her orchard killed by a prolonged drought. Another woman farmer described how the rain did not arrive on time when she started the rice seedlings, but when she was about to harvest the rice, rain fell for 20 days causing floods and destroying all her rice.

The government's recent policy to "decentralise industry" (that is to take it to rural areas with little regulation) also came under attack by women. One of them said, "We have been using water from our wells for drinking. But since the cement factory began operating in our area, our water has cement residue." Another woman spoke of a brick factory which has turned their vegetable garden into a wasteland.

The north has had an ancient tradition of water management using small dams (locally called *muang faai*) that effectively distributed water and controlled floods. But now, rapid deforestation has made it impossible for this indigenous system to prevent floods. And increasing industrialisation diverts the small waterways and consolidates them into large tanks to feed the factories. More and more, small farms are being marginalised from water usage. At the end of two days of information sharing and listening to each other, the grassroots participants called for stopping this kind of maldevelopment since "the more development there is, the poorer we are." They stressed the need to allow indigenous knowledge and initiatives to rejuvenate before they are totally eliminated.

This initial workshop was organised to identify grassroots women leaders, listen to their problems and outline their agenda. After concentrating on several topics and following a long discussion, a grassroots women's group was formed with a goal to deepen its understanding, and to participate actively in the upcoming Beijing Conference. Finally, 20 grassroots women were selected to participate at the Beijing Conference. Other women's organisations, such as the Foundation of Women, also had grassroots women with them taking the total of grassroots Thai women at Beijing to 40.

It was the first time ever that these women sat in an aircraft or walked on foreign soil. It was also their first time to experience collectively the common difficulties of language, food, living conditions, and a direct exposure to global women's issues. Some had difficulties even in rudimentary things such as handling the faucets in hotel bathrooms. Although they were accompanied by five "resource" women acting as translators, many chose to explore the new environment themselves. They had learned some basic phrases, such as "Where is the toilet?" but there were times when they were left alone to compose their sentences asking for a glass of water, or telling a Chinese officer that they were delegates who had lost their way. In overcoming these mundane obstacles, many not only gained confidence in their abilities but also accrued a sense of solidarity with other grassroots women they were meeting for the first time. As one young delegate recalled, "Before, I saw only my problem. Now I realise others face similar problems, and often their problems are larger".

Since they could not speak English, they used many innovative ways to communicate and establish relations with other women. The first method was singing together. The second was distributing and sharing Thai sweets, which soon became very popular items at the Forum. The third was tying white cotton threads around other women's wrists as a symbol of unity, solidarity and friendship. The fourth method was to participate in marches. When the police tried to stop the march, they used their traditional Thai way of going around the police and carrying on. While they watched other women talking in different panels and dancing in cultural shows, they also noticed that a lot of litter was being thrown around. When they started picking this up, many other women joined them, appreciating their concern and initiative regarding waste removal.

The arrangements at the Beijing NGO Forum were not smooth. Most participants were critical of Chinese mismanagement and the ever-present security guards, often feeling harassed and frustrated by the inadequate arrangements. Thai women were an exception. Despite all the difficulties, before leaving China they organised a "Thank-you march" to express their gratitude to the Chinese government and people for organising and hosting the Conference. Naturally, the Chinese media loved it and were happy to cover this event (one of the few events that made it to Chinese TV!).

Another way the Thai women communicated was by narrating their life stories and feelings either at the panel/forum, or by giving TV and radio interviews to people from Latin America and Japan. Four stories were particularly touching. One woman described how her lungs became severely affected by working in textile factories and how she organised a workers' group to safeguard the health of other factory workers. Many factories in Thailand are run by Japanese agencies and the Japanese media took special interest in the first-hand narration of the affected woman. Another story was of a woman who successfully ran a savings programme in a Bangkok slum. A third woman trained youth leadership in the villages, and a fourth woman was involved in environmental protest and rejuvenation programmes.

At the Beijing Conference, Thai grassroots women showed that although their language might not be English, they could still understand the feelings and concerns of women from other parts of the world, just as they could creatively make themselves understood by others.

To evaluate what these women gained from the Beijing experience, the Foundation of Friends of Women organised a follow-up workshop in Bangkok in November 1995. The grassroots women participants came together again to review their experiences and to discuss what to do next. All of them saw the changes in their lives. They understood the interconnection of issues better. One young woman talked about her dramatic personal life experience: her husband abandoned her because she went to Beijing. One of her neighbours had insinuated to her husband that his wife was going to meet another man instead of going to a "women's meeting". Before leaving for Beijing, this woman used to serve as a volunteer in her village for a women's NGO trying to stop trafficking of women in the north. She said the Beijing experience had strengthened her faith in herself and she was sure that she was doing the right thing, but her husband was not intelligent enough to understand. She vowed to continue her work in spite of the fact that her funded project might come to an end and her husband had already left her!

The energy and enthusiasm this group acquired at Beijing was usefully transmitted to villagers, neighbours and other Thai grassroots women. The group members became more determined. "We learned the strategies of fighting from other women...the methods and the issues." Participants in the workshops discussed their experiences and their determination. They eventually formed an umbrella group, calling themselves 'The Forum of Thai Grassroots Women' (*wae thi ying raak yaa*). They hesitated to use the term "council" (*sapha*), "federation" (*saha phan*) or "union" (*saha phap*), not because such terms had a "radical" tone, but because they felt 'that the leaders of these types of organisations abuse their power even though they may come from the working class.

The grassroots women had many problems related to land, water, forests and employment. They wanted to address these issues immediately to find proper strategies for support and mobilisation. But March 8 was approaching and certain organisers had planned to celebrate Women's Day and had invited these women. UNIFEM was the main force encouraging all major women's organisations in Thailand to celebrate this day at the UN building. The coming together of all these women had both a positive and a negative aspect. The negative side was that the newly emerging 'Grassroots Forum' was eclipsed by the gathering of socialite women, highly vocal and visible progressive NGOs, and academics. Nevertheless, it was the first time that grassroots women stood up at such a prestigious gathering and asked questions to prominent women leaders. They showed that their existence and their concerns could no longer be discounted.

The years 1996 and 1997 were times of intense activities. Rural, grassroots women visited factory workers in Bangkok and joined in the protests and demands of the 'Assembly of the Poor' for land rights. One grassroots woman was invited to a workers' meeting in Hong Kong. By coming together and articulating their issues, grassroots Thai women have begun to recognise their voices. Many of them are gaining new confidence, new knowledge and new friendships. Combining their grassroots base of local participants and forging coalitions with other Thai women, they have begin to organise and increase in number. Women's issues are no longer limited to those defined by privileged women alone; grassroots women are adding fresh knowledge and understanding to the emerging women studies programmes of Thai Universities. All this could happen mainly because of the persistence of international funding agencies and Thai women's organisations, and because of the fervour generated by the Beijing Conference. How long will this resource continue to be available to groups like grassroots women? And how can grassroots women become self-reliant and more effective ? These are questions being asked by grassroots women and those concerned with the sustainability of such efforts. The challenge now is in finding the right answers.

5

Women's Human Rights
A Global Referendum

Charlotte Bunch, Mallika Dutt, and Susana Fried

One of the more striking aspects of the Women's Conference in Beijing was the way in which it focused world attention on the human rights of women.

Women's human rights permeated debates at both the official UN Intergovernmental Fourth World Conference on Women as well as the parallel NGO Forum held 40 miles away in Huairou. The concern was evident in the speeches given by many heads of delegations, including Hillary Rodham Clinton's adoption of the theme "women's rights are human rights"; in the vehement opposition on the part of some governments to what they called the "creation of new rights" in the Platform for Action; in the many workshops and demonstrations at the NGO Forum and in the efforts of the Chinese security to contain that event.

This global focus on women's human rights was accompanied by an insistence that all issues are women's issues and that women's equality, development and peace cannot be discussed in isolation from the global economic, political and cultural forces rapidly reshaping the world.

Thus, as a 'post-Cold War' conference, major divisions that had marked earlier women's conferences (such as divisions between Northern and Southern women over what were crucial women's issues, or over Israel and Palestine), were replaced by political differences over issues like the global economy or the role of religion. And these debates crossed geographical boundaries.

The challenge for women's movements in Beijing was to forge a coherent approach to the Conference that would both, accommodate a range of diverse views and provide enough unity to face down those who sought to utilise the event as a way to counter feminism and the growing influence of women in global debates. The idea that this Conference was about defending and promoting the human rights of women provided just such a cohesive umbrella for many.

That women succeeded not only in holding the line on gains from previous world conferences but also in advancing on some issues, creating new networks and strategies in the process, is a testament to the fortitude of women. It is also a sign of hope for the future. That we succeeded is almost a miracle. For we did so in the face of well-financed opposition from major religious forces; indifference and lack of adequate funding on the part of the UN; a host country uncomfortable with non-governmental organisations; frequent competition among NGOs; and some governments that were either antagonistic or were seeking to co-opt women.

But this miracle did not come out of nowhere. In the ten years between the Third World Conference on Women in Nairobi in 1985 and Beijing in 1995, the global women's movement had become a force to contend with. At the Nairobi Conference, women from third world countries demonstrated that they were creating vibrant, indigenous feminist movements, offering new perspectives on many issues which also provided the basis for solid global networks to develop. This networking forcefully emerged in the cross-cultural alliances formed to influence recent UN world conferences.

For instance, at the Rio Earth Summit in 1992, women won acknowledgment of their critical role in sustaining the environment. At the World Conference on Human Rights in Vienna in 1993, women gained recognition of women's rights as human rights and of violence against women as a human rights issue. At the International Conference on Population and Development (ICPD) in Cairo in 1994, women confronted abusive population policies and lobbied for a Declaration that recognised the centrality of women's empowerment in population and development policy. And at the World Summit on Social Development in Copenhagen in 1995, women forced governments to acknowledge the devastating impact of economic policies on women and to commit to involve them in efforts to eradicate poverty.

Participation in these international arenas enabled women from diverse regions to define common agendas and formulate coordinated strategies for lobbying governments. Corresponding dialogue at the NGO fora intersected with lobbying strategies and allowed women to air differences, to elaborate new ideas and to deepen links with one another. Women also strengthened their networks through electronic mail, newsletters, telephones, faxes, meetings and other events—all of which have been used to expand alliances, negotiate differences, mobilise coordinated actions and confront governments and international institutions.

The connections made among women from 1985 to 1995 were reflected in women's actions even before they arrived in Beijing. For over two years women organised at the local, national, regional and international levels to influence this Conference. In unprecedented numbers, they participated in regional preparatory meetings, held numerous NGO events and formed coalitions to give voice to diverse concerns.

At the two UN international preparatory meetings held in New York, caucuses formed on topics ranging from human rights to peace and economic justice, as well as around constituencies like lesbians and older women. Many of these included networks with experience at previous world conferences. They converged in the Linkage Caucus — a sort of caucus of caucuses—which sought to develop agreed upon NGO proposals for the Platform for Action.

At the Beijing Conference, women's determination to do their work was reflected in the dialogue and networking that took place in Huairou despite logistical problems created by rain, the Forum's disorganisation, harassment by various government agents and the overwhelming size of the event. The story that too often did not make it to the press was how, despite these difficult conditions, women succeeded in holding their programmes, learning from each other and building their movements.

The Forum included a plethora of some 3,000 events that served to educate, involve, sober and inspire at many levels. Women's rights as human rights was a palpable presence throughout. Banners and posters demanding recognition of women's human rights were visible at every turn and the programme listed hundreds of workshops related to the topic.

Panels encompassed the human rights dimension of everything from structural adjustment to education, health, sexuality and violence against women. Migrant women highlighted human rights violations by countries of the North; comfort women demanded increased accountability from the Japanese government for World War II human rights abuses; lesbians insisted on recognition of the human right to control one's sexuality; and women from East Timor, Tibet, Rwanda and the former Yugoslavia utilised human rights concepts to describe violations of women in conflict situations. Sessions also addressed international legal instruments and UN agencies and mechanisms, examining their utility in advancing women's human rights.

Among the multitude of issues discussed, certain themes resonated across regions. The prevention of violence against women in all its forms was clearly of great urgency, as was advancing women's health and reproductive rights. Other priorities included reversing the negative impact of international economic policies, countering the rise of religious and secular conservatism and giving women a greater voice in policy making.

The global dialogue about violence against women ranged from discussions of private acts of incest and domestic abuse, to state violence in conflict situations and military prostitution.

Women's determination to end all forms of violence was reflected in the transformation of this issue from Nairobi to Beijing. Ten years ago governments had only begun to acknowledge domestic violence and rape as social problems in the Forward Looking Strategies. By the 1993 World Conference on Human Rights, women had organised a global campaign and tribunal that politically positioned violence against women in its many forms squarely on the international human rights agenda.

Tribunals, panels, workshops and demonstrations held at the Forum revealed the enormous burden violence places on women's lives and how different constituencies like immigrants and refugees, or ethnic, racial and religious minorities, indigenous, lesbian, disabled or older women experience specific forms of violence.

Thus, over the years, women have moved from making this issue visible to demanding accountability for it from governments and the UN. As Pierre San, Secretary General of Amnesty International and one of the Judges at the Global Tribunal organised by the Center for Women's Global Leadership in Huairou put it, "What we want from governments is not simply to give their assent to the need to protect and promote women's human rights in yet another piece of paper. If it is to achieve anything, the Beijing Conference must be a genuine catalyst for action and the swift delivery of real protection."

The pressure that women's organising in this area has put on governments was evident when it emerged as a priority at all the regional preparatory meetings. In the Beijing Platform, the eradication of violence against women was one of the least controversial strategic objectives and governments acknowledged that it was a state responsibility which called for more action.

A Worldwide Campaign to End Violence Against Women was launched by UNIFEM with several NGOs and a number of governments making concrete commitments to work on this issue. Many agreed to meet with NGOs when they returned home to develop national plans of action against gender-based violence.

The impact on women of the globalisation of the world economy was another central concern at the Forum. Women from North America and Western Europe discussed economic restructuring with its cutbacks in social services and health care, in ways that echoed the devastation of structural adjustment policies described by women from countries of the South. The new voices— of women from Eastern Europe and the former Soviet Union — which emerged at this Conference also reported their negative experiences in the transition to market economies.

In sharp contrast to the Nairobi Conference in 1985 where this issue divided more on North-South lines, in Beijing, women from all

Keep the Church in Church, Not In Politics

As the Catholic Church continues to obstruct negotiations in Beijing over issues relating to women's sexuality and reproductive rights, a growing number of women are calling for an end to the church's status within the United Nations.

Members of the American-based organisation,, Catholics for Free Choice (CFFC), are circulating a petition urging the UN to revoke the Roman Catholic Church's status as a Non-Member State Permanent Observer.

More than 7,000 people, including many Catholic women and nuns, had signed the petition as of last week.

"The time has come for the UN to bite the bullet and acknowledge that the Holy See is not a state, but a nongovernmental religious organisation," said Frances Kissling, CFFC President.

"Many women here are really outraged by the Vatican, the kinds of positions taken on women's issues and the way the church uses its authority to pressure governments to toe the line," she said.

But for Vatican authorities like Rev James Morrow, a member of the Vatican's delegation, the Church has divine authorisation to lead global affairs.

"The fullness of divine revelation has been entrusted to the Catholic Church, which has the authority to ensure that right and just laws are formulated and enforced," said Morrow.

But according to Kissling, the Vatican was able to get involved with the UN because it produced its own postal stamps and was therefore a member of the Universal Postal Union, which was invited to attend UN sessions on an ad hoc basis.

Vatican representatives began to attend meetings of the General Assembly, the World Health Organisation and UNESCO.In 1956, the Holy See was elected a member of the UN Economic and Social Council and became a full member of the International Atomic Energy Agency.

Kissling said that by getting involved in public policy, the Church is trying to compensate for its lack of moral authority. The vast majority of Catholics, she said, do use birth control and have abortions, despite Church prohibitions against both.

"If it cannot control from the pulpit, it would use public policy to advance an intensely conservative agenda," she said.

CFFC which began circulating the petition during the NGO Forum in Huairou, said it would continue to collect signatures for the petition after the Beijing Conference. They will present the petition to the UN General Assembly in October when Pope John Paul II is expected to speak.

During the New York Preparatory Committee, Kissling said, Vatican officials tried to have members of CFFC evicted, claiming they were not free to use the name "Catholic" since they did not abide by the Pope's rulings.

The petition being circulated states in part, "the Pope and his Church is simply immoral and wrong, and will continue to cripple national and international programs to bring humanity's population growth under control."

It has the support of many women from all parts of the world.

Katini Nzau-Ombaka, of Kenya's National Council of NGOs, said the Church's undue influence "is of great concern to the African continent."

"We have a sizable Catholic following and the Vatican has used that position to propagate its views on reproductive rights," Nzau-Ombaka said. "This is why we have to get the UN to revoke their status."

Arguing that the Holy See was entitled to have its ideas heard, Mary Okumu from Senegal said that pressure should be put on Muslim fundamentalists who have been stonewalling the negotiations on equal inheritance and the girl child.

Not every Catholic, however, renounces the political authority of the Vatican. Sister Therese Egita from Uganda feels it is vital for the Holy See to maintain its influence in the UN. "It speaks for the entire Catholic community," Egita said.

Avian Joseph
(Beijing Watch, September 1, 1995)

regions saw international economic and trade policies as placing increasing burdens on them. Still, women from the South tended to understand economic issues as inter-connected to other problems like violence against women, while Northern women more often approached these as separate issues.

Despite broad consensus among many NGOs and documentation of how economic globalisation has harmed women, governments were not willing to address this issue substantially. The Beijing Platform does acknowledge the negative impact of structural adjustment policies and calls for recognition that women's unwaged work constitutes a large percentage of national economies. But no effort was made to address the causes of these problems and governments remain engaged in practices that perpetuate them.

Another issue that was echoed by women from all over the world was the danger posed by the backlash against feminism and the growing power of secular and religious conservatism. Discussion of how to counter these forces politically was interwoven with intense conversation about culture, religion, ethnicity and nationality in women's lives. While there was much resistance to the ideologies of religious fundamentalists and the secular right, passionate debates took place about whether women should organise within religious frameworks or from an entirely secular space.

Such questions of identity politics formed a sub-text throughout the Forum. Many wanted to affirm their distinct identities around race, ethnicity, nationality, religion, age, sexual orientation, disabilities, etc. and to identify areas where their perspectives or problems were often ignored. Some of the tents based on region and diverse identities became lively arenas serving this purpose.

Of particular note was the mobilisation of disabled women who faced extraordinarily difficult conditions at the Forum and utilised these to educate women about the issue. Nevertheless, many did not want to be isolated in a group based only on identity and sought to bring identity-based perspectives into other issues. The struggle to recognise differences while also finding areas of commonality, was a recurring theme throughout the Forum, as it is in women's movements locally.

Women from regions torn by ethnic or religious warfare discussed their responsibilities in the conflicts and often sought to go beyond nationalistic divisions. For example, feminists from countries of the former Yugoslavia who met frequently, ate, sang and protested together, then formed a network to continue contact across national divisions while acknowledging that war often makes this difficult. The Women in Black vigil held at the Forum spoke loudly, with its large numbers of diverse women (often from countries at war with each other) gathered together in silence to protest male warfare and domination around the world. Again, the transformation of the movement from Nairobi to Beijing was evident.

In Nairobi, conflicts between women often degenerated into screaming matches. In Beijing, many women negotiated painful divisions with respect—if not agreement — which underscored the urgent need for more women to be in positions of power if the world is to move toward peace.

Sessions at the Forum dealt with many other topics, such as political participation, health and reproductive rights, literacy and women's studies, media and communications, future technologies, etc. Many of these included human rights questions, such as what conditions are necessary for women to be able to fully exercise their human rights and how to establish government accountability in a time of growing privatisation. Overall, there was a recognition that women must address all aspects of life, not just woman-specific topics, as some argued in previous UN women's conferences.

Indeed, many sought to transform the global debates of our day, building on women's organising at the Rio, Vienna, Cairo and Copenhagen World Conferences. In part, this requires that women both enter mainstream debates, such as those represented by the government conference, as well as challenge their premises. Many who attended the governmental conference in Beijing, which began midway through the NGO Forum, sought to bring the spirit of the challenging discussions and the strength of women's presence in Huairou to that arena.

The governmental conference in Beijing was mandated to produce a concensus Platform for Action that would implement the goals set forth in 1985 in the Nairobi Forward Looking Strategies and advance the Conference themes of Equality, Development and Peace. Over 4,000 NGO delegates who were accredited to that Conference lobbied to get our issues and perspectives reflected there. Human rights language permeated both the Beijing Declaration and the Platform for Action agreed to by all 181 States present.

The Women's Human Rights Caucus was a collaboration of NGOs who lobbied governmental delegates around human rights issues throughout the negotiations on the Platform for Action. The Caucus grew out of the success of the Global Campaign for Women's Human Rights at the 1993 World Conference on Human Right in Vienna, and built on both the global and regional alliances developed with subsequent caucuses in Cairo and Copenhagen, as well as during the two-year preparatory process for Beijing. Moreover, a number of governmental delegations included feminists and women involved in both health and human rights, networking over the past few years, promoting these concepts from the inside.

The distance from the NGO Forum in Huairou made it difficult for many women who wanted to lobby during the first week, to get to the government Conference. Nevertheless, caucus efforts were strengthened by the high visibility of women's human rights activities at the NGO Forum and especially by activities that brought the spirit of the Forum to Beijing. One of these was the delivery to the UN High Commissioner for Human Rights, of over one million signatures to a worldwide petition demanding that the UN act urgently to promote and protect women's human rights.

The combined effect of all these activities formed a groundswell of support for making the entire Platform for Action a comprehensive document about the human rights of women, including women's rights to education, food, health and freedom from violence, as well as rights to the exercise of citizenship in all its manifestations. Previous UN women's conferences were seen as being primarily about women and development or women's rights, rather than about human rights. This expansion of what is generally considered to be a "human rights issue" and its usage to frame a wider set of women's concerns, reflects the extensive organising done over the past several years.

In this sense, Beijing saw the mainstreaming of women's human rights. Previously, women had to make the case that our issues are a legitimate part of the international human rights agenda. In Huairou and Beijing, this legitimacy was assumed. The incorporation of human rights language into their work by governments and women's organisations from all regions indicates more than a rhetorical gesture. It signals a shift in analysis that moves beyond single-issue politics and identity-based organising, and enhances our capacity to build global alliances based on collective political goals and a common agenda. Moreover, since human rights has legitimacy

> ### Guys and (Inflatable Plastic) Dolls
>
> "OK, who's got the dolls?" asked a woman waiting for a workshop called, 'The Role of Inflatable Lifesize Plastic Dolls and Dildos in Improving Health'.
>
> The organisers did not show up, but that did not inhibit the debate on how plastic dolls and dildos could solve global problems and reduce women's burdens. The workshop was one of the smaller and frankly unapologetic events held at the NGO Forum in Huairou.
>
> "I disagree that it's a joke," said American health writer Rebecca Chalker, who stepped forward to lead the discussion. "Do people think it's a joke?"
>
> Chalker said plastic dolls might prevent the spread of sexually transmitted diseases. They could also shrink demand for prostitutes and stop trafficking in women.
>
> "This is a massive problem for women," said Chalker. "Is the demand for a female or is it just for sexual release?"
>
> Meanwhile, men and women slunk into the circle of wooden school desks and asked discreetly whether this was the doll workshop.
>
> "I really fail to see how dolls can solve world problems," said Julia Suryakusuma from Indonesia. "It can only satisfy a small group."
>
> But Chalker persisted. Plastic or rubber dolls could be made life-like and penetrable. They could be mechanical and made-to-order. Men could go to the store, choose a doll and pick a background tape of a woman's voice to accompany intercourse.
>
> "Maybe this is a technological phenomenon that is needed," said Chalker. But others had doubts. "Will it encourage men to think of women as objects," asked one. And a British woman said, "It's not very exciting to have power over a rubber doll."
>
> *Jennifer Griffin*
> (Beijing Watch, September 11, 1995)

among many governments, the appeal to human rights agreements and international norms can fortify women's organising.

Overall, the Platform for Action asserted the universal and holistic nature of the human rights of women. Specific language and commitments that human rights advocates gained in Beijing include: the reaffirmation and extension of commitments to promote and protect women's human rights, including the right to be free from violence; the right to sexual and reproductive health free from discrimination or coercion; access to information about sexual and reproductive health care; equal rights to inheritance for women and girls (although not the "right to equal inheritance"); and the obligation of governments to pursue and punish as war crimes, rape and sexual violence against women and girls in situations of armed conflict.

Universal government ratification of the Convention for the Elimination of All Forms of Discrimination Against Women (CEDAW) and limiting reservations to it were urged, along with consideration of an optional protocol to strengthen its implementation. In this process, commitments to women from previous conferences were maintained and even expanded in cases of the following:

The protection of human rights activists; the acknowledgement that systematic rape during armed conflict is a war crime and in some cases a crime against humanity; the recognition of the rights of women to control their sexual and reproductive health;

that parental rights must be qualified to ensure they respect privacy and access to information by adolescents and children; and the importance of systemwide integration of women's human rights throughout the UN.

However, clear gaps remain. This was most evident in the lack of strong interaction between development and human rights discourses. As the sub-group on women's economic rights noted, the human rights sections of the Platform for Action largely reflect a concern for women's individual rights rather than the collective, systemic or development rights associated with women's economic concerns, particularly around globalisation, economic restructuring and structural adjustment. Similarly, there is not adequate discussion of the relationship between human rights and peace and militarism.

Even within the standard rubric of human rights, there were some disturbing losses. For instance, there was no explicit reference to sexual rights or sexual orientation; there was the replacement of explicit references to race and ethnicity with "demographic factors" in some sections; there was inadequate inclusion of internally displaced women as in need of international protection; there was the use of "indigenous people" rather than "peoples"; and there was weak language about the various forms of "family".

Some major controversies of the Conference illustrate both what women gained and limitations of the Platform for Action. For example, in the contested area of sexual rights, many thought it could not be won and the phrase *per se* was rejected. However, these boundaries were expanded in the health section of the document which states in Paragraph 97 that "the human rights of women include their right to have control over and decide freely and responsibly on matters related to their sexuality, including sexual and reproductive health, free of coercion, discrimination and violence."

Similarly, explicit support for the rights of lesbians and the term "sexual orientation" were excluded from the document in final late-night negotiations. Nevertheless, the door was opened with this first open discussion of the issue in the UN, which also exposed the virulence of homophobia among those who manipulate it to oppose women's human rights generally. At least some governments in each region supported the issue, and a number of them stated that their interpretation of the prohibition of discrimination on the basis of "other status" in several human rights documents applies to lesbians and gays.

Another major debate centered on the term "universal" and the use of religion and culture to limit women's human rights. Women sought to maintain the Vienna World Conference on Human Rights' recognition that women's human rights are universal, inalienable, indivisible and interdependent. The Vatican, its supporter States and some Islamic governments attempted to limit the extent of universal application of women's human rights. However, they used this debate to claim that there is a feminist imperialism that reflects disrespect for religion and culture, an over-zealous individualism and an effort to impose Western values which destroy the family and local communities.

This isn't a new debate, but more thought must go into how to argue for universality of rights without implying homogenisation, especially around religion and culture, aspects of which can also be positive for some women.

Of course, each movement forward for women was met with resistance. For instance, 19 States entered reservations to text that was not in conformity with Islamic law — particularly references to reproductive health and rights, inheritance, sexuality and abortion. The Holy See put forward their

> **Muslim Women Say No to Religious Extremism**
>
> Shouting "No to Fundamentalism," nearly 100 NGO women marched through the streets of Huairou carrying placards with graphic pictures of decapitated men killed by Algerian Islamists.
>
> The women from Iran, Algeria and Afghanistan wore red executioner's hoods to cover their faces and held a hand-painted banner reading, "Condemn Sexual Apartheid and Anti-Woman Barbarism in Islamic Countries."
>
> The group later held a press conference which was disrupted by Iranian women and men affiliated with the Islamic government in Iran. A woman who was filming the press conference on behalf of the group was threatened by an Iranian man in the midst of the proceedings.
>
> "This is very dangerous for us to be speaking here," said Algerian women's rights activist Zazi Zadou. "This is not Islam. This is the manipulation of Islam by political groups."
>
> *(Beijing Watch, September 7, 1995)*

interpretation of much of the Platform for Action, especially the health and human rights sections, as expressing "exaggerated individualism". The extensive reservations on religious and cultural grounds reflect on-going debates about the human rights of women which could not have been resolved in Beijing, but which did lay out the contours of future collaborations and confrontations.

In the critical area of implementation and resources, the promises of the Platform for Action were not backed up with adequate commitments from either governments or the UN. While the document includes strong language about gender integration and coordination within the UN, these are rarely assigned to specific agencies or actors, and there is little clarity about who is responsible for which institutional tasks. The idea of making this a conference of commitments was proposed by Australia and promoted by many NGOs but did not get widespread government acceptance. Nevertheless, NGOs kept track of commitments referred to in government speeches and these can form the basis for demanding accountability from governments.

Throughout the Platform for Action, paragraphs call for re-evaluation of all policies by using gender analysis which might ultimately lead to a fundamentally different way of constructing programmes, and certainly provide guidance for action. Paragraph 297 notes that States should, as soon as possible, develop strategies to implement the Platform for Action. Member States should be reminded of through the next stage of translating the document into concrete strategies and ensuring that its promises are carried forward.

How much the Platform for Action advances women's human rights ultimately depends on how much women are able to use it to further their efforts to influence policy and action at all levels, from the local to the global. For now, it provides us with a global affirmation that the rights of women are human rights and that they are in urgent need of world attention.

6

UN Secretariat
The Gatekeepers of Ideas

John Mathiason

During the Beijing Conference—as during its preparations—the staff of the United Nations Secretariat were seen but hardly ever heard. They were omnipresent but could have passed off as passive observers. If officials did speak during negotiations, it was merely to provide information or answer questions on procedure.

Of course, some UN officials like Gertrude Mongella, Secretary-General of the Conference, or Ismat Kittani, representative of the UN Secretary-General, as well as heads of specialised agencies and UN programmes, were more audible as they made their statements at the Plenary. But what about the remaining 250 staff members of the UN Secretariat. And what exactly was their role there?

For the 3,000 government delegates, Beijing was the culmination of a process. They would read the main conference documents, like the 1995 Review and Appraisal of the Implementation of the Nairobi Forward-Looking Strategies for the Advancement of Women to the year 2000, or the 1994 World Survey on the Role of Women in Development, or The World's Women 1995: Trends and Statistics, to see the factual basis for the draft Platform for Action. They would study the draft Platform with its many bracketed texts. They would go to meetings where the discussions followed UN procedures, enforced by a chair supported by a committee secretary. Their work would be summarised in a press release and the results of their deliberations would be reflected in drafts carefully taken down from the discussion and translated into the six official languages of the Organisation.

All this work was done by the invisible staff members of the UN Secretariat. And if the work was not noticed, the Secretariat would have done its job.

That job was to make it relatively easy for Member States to make complex agreements that would satisfy 189 different countries in the relatively short span of 10 working days. If they failed to do so, part of the failure would have been due to the Secretariat. If they succeeded, the Secretariat, silently, shared in the success.

For 50 years prior to Beijing, there has been a unit in the UN Secretariat supporting government negotiations to establish global norms about the advancement of women. It provided the institutional memory of agreements, facts and the basis for agreement. It could defend against backsliding by stating the simple words "this has already been agreed...." Not always visible at receptions and infrequently seen in public, the international civil servants who supported the Conference, assured (within the limits of what governments could agree) its success.

Who are these civil servants? The UN is several things, as can be seen from its Charter. It is governments who, under the model of national sovereignty, rule the Organisation. It is the peoples of those countries who are members, including their NGOs. And, from articles 95-102, it is the international civil service. If there has been one innovation of the 20th century in public administration, it is the creation of that civil service. Today, the UN staff has some 15,000 people from almost all of the 189 member states of the UN, who are beholden in practice to none of those States. It is a staff whose operative norm is to reflect "the highest standard of competence, integrity and efficiency".

Recruited from virtually every profession, the international civil service constitutes a triumph of multinationalism. Without losing their national identity, each official becomes part of a culture that transcends nationality. Most of the civil servants, according to their own reporting, joined the Organisation because of its ideals. Their identity is based on the norms set out in international agreements like the Charter, the Universal Declaration of Human Rights and other normative statements of States.

The civil service is arranged into organisational units with specific functions. One of these, in 1995, was the Division for the Advancement of Women (DAW), which had been named ex officio Secretariat of the Conference. With a total establishment of 19 professional posts out of the 10,000 in the Secretariat, augmented for the Conference by an additional 14 posts, the Secretariat was a small part of the whole.

It could trace its origins to the earliest days of the UN when, in 1946, the first chairperson of the new Commission on the Status of Women asked that "a United Nations Office of Women's Affairs in the framework of the Secretariat, run by a highly competent woman be established to be the planning centre for the work and clearing house for information about the status of women and women's activities. It would give women all over the world a feeling of satisfaction to have a special office at the Headquarters of the United Nations".

Over the next 49 years, the staff members of DAW, under various names and headed by only 10 different persons, provided the basis for intergovernmental discussion. It was their task to judge how far it was possible to push the consensus, how to structure agendas so that realistic issues could be discussed, to prepare the reports containing information that was the starting point of discussions, to provide information to non-governmental organisations.

Transferred to Vienna in 1979, DAW underwent an almost complete changeover in personnel. It helped organise the UN women's conference in Nairobi in 1985 and was designated as the Secretariat for the Fourth World Conference on Women in Beijing. It was moved back to New York in 1993, on the eve of the Conference. This time most of the staff moved with the Division.

Under Mrs. Mongella's general supervision, the staff consisted of a core of international career civil servants from the USA, Germany, Austria, Tanzania, the Dominican Republic, Nicaragua, the Russian Federation, the Philippines, Haiti, UK, Canada and Poland. The temporary staff came from Thailand, Jordan, the Gambia, Tanzania, Bangladesh, Nigeria, the Russian Federation, Spain, Kenya, China, Jamaica, Egypt, Argentina, Sweden and Austria. Almost all were women. All were committed. They were lawyers, economists, sociologists, political scientists, demographers, journalists, administrators and secretaries. They included staff who worked for the UN for almost 30 years and others who had just joined the organisation. Despite their varied backgrounds they worked comfortably together in teams.

What did they do? A few examples can show their work.

One of the main steps forward at Beijing was to recognise that for women to enjoy their right to equal participation in power and decision-making, they would have to be involved in decision-making in sufficient numbers to make a difference. The Platform for Action in paragraph 192 calls for action by governments, national bodies, the private sector, political parties, trade unions, employers' organisations, research and academic institutions, subregional and regional bodies and non-governmental and international organisations to take positive action to build a critical mass of women leaders, executives and managers in strategic decision-making positions.

In terms of targets, this critical mass was set by the Economic and Social Council at 30 percent. The introduction of the concept of critical mass and the setting of the target level was a result of work by DAW.

Women's equal right to vote and hold public office has been recognised since the beginning of the UN. The first international human rights treaty on women's equal rights dealt with political rights of women (1952). However, the gap between right and reality continued to be very wide. By the time of the Nairobi Conference, there had been only six women who had been elected heads of State or governmen in human history since World War II. The proportion of women in parliaments was extremely low. Thid, despite the fact that women made up over half of the electorates in all countries where voting took place. An important policy question in advancement of women was why this disparity persisted.

In some countries, the question was addressed by simply appointing a number of women to decision-making positions as a matter of quotas. In Eastern Europe, for example, parliaments were supposed to be representative of the population and a certain number of seats were set aside for women, a practice which gave that region the highest average proportions of women in parliament in the world. However, women were virtually absent in the governmental and political party circles where real decisions were taken. Moreover, in most countries, resistance was faced by any attempts at achieving equality by simply appinting women to positions of power as a matter of quota.

In examining the question, the UN could draw on research which showed that a major reason for women not being elected to public office was that they were not presented as candidates. One reason that they were not put up as candidates was that the largely male political party leaders argued that women could not win elections, or at least didn't make any difference in election outcomes. The reason given for this belief was that women themselves did not vote for women, because sex made no difference in political decision-making.

Whenever someone would say that women in power had different approaches than men, particularly on issues of peace and security, the response would be "Hah! Look at Indira Gandhi, Golda Meir and Margaret Thatcher!" The three women heads of government who had led their countries into war.

Confronted with these issues, DAW decided to address the question of participation in terms of "critical mass". (The concept itself derives from nuclear physics and refers to the quantity of plutonium that needs to be brought together to produce a nuclear explosion.)

A number of scholars had begun to speak of the need to reach a "critical mass" of women in decision-making groups. In the mid-1970s, an American feminist scholar did a study of the incidence of women in business, looking for sex-based differences. She reviewed studies of the behaviour of minorities in task-oriented groups to find out the level of participation that was necessary for the minority members to function effectively as a group to press their interests. The scholar estimated that when the proportion of minority members reached about 30 percent, they were able to influence decision-making by pressing their own interests. At levels lower than that, effectiveness required the minority members to act more like those of the majority and, failing that, they would be ineffective dissenters.

In the 1980s, these findings were picked up by a Danish feminist political scientist, Drude Dahlerup, who argued that the critical mass phenomenon could apply to politics as well. In some countries in Scandinavia, critical mass levels were being approached as some levels of government and it was possible to see whether this made a difference. The concept of critical mass, however, circulated only in feminist scholarly circles. It was not part of the debate at either national or international level in terms of public policy. It fell to the UN Secretariat to bring the information into the policy debate.

The Commission on the Status of Women decided to take up the issue of women and decision-making as a priority theme at its session in 1990. To prepare for it, DAW decided to organise an expert group meeting. The Division prepared a paper reviewing what was known about factors that restricted women's access to decision-making. The staff member responsible for the expert group meeting was Dorota Gierycz, a political scientist from Poland who had been on DAW's staff since 1981. She had read Dahlerup's studies and brought them to my attention. We decided to include in DAW's paper the finding that a critical mass of at least 30 percent was necessary for women to make an impact on decision-making bodies.

The experts, who were a mix of European and North American academic specialists as well as political leaders from the developing countries (including Gertrude Mongella, then a cabinet minister in Tanzania), took the finding about critical mass and included it in their recommendations. The Division duly reported this and also included it in the report reviewing progress in implementing the Nairobi Strategies. That document was one of the bases for the recommendations and conclusions adopted by the Commission on the Status of Women in 1990 when it carried out its first review and appraisal of the Nairobi Strategies. Once the recommendations were endorsed by the Economic and Social Council in the summer of 1990, they became an agreed international norm.

The Secretariat continued to publicise the finding. Dorota Gierycz made a presentation on women and decision-making to the meeting of the International Political Science Association at its convention in Buenos Aires, including the norm of a critical mass. In the UN's statistical publications on advancement of women, the norm of 30 percent was used as an indicator of progress, including The World's Women: Trends and Statistics and its 1995 update.

Over the next few years, women's advocates could refer to the finding in lobbying their own governments to take special measures to increase the proportion of women in decision-making. In several countries, political parties set the norm of 30 percent women into their rules. In several others, constitutional amendments were adopted to give effect to the minimum target.

During negotiations on the section in the Platform for Action on women in power and decision-making, it was argued by some governments that targets and quotas were not acceptable, or realistic. The Secretariat representatives could help break the impasse by pointing out that the standard had already been set and that a number of countries had met it.

Another issue that had impacted women was that of structural adjustments. The relationship between structural adjustment policies that characterised the 1980s and early 1990s and advancement of women, had been a highly contentious North-South issue.

Developing countries had been affected by adjustment policies that had slowed economic growth and reduced social programmes. A major study by UNICEF entitled 'The Invisible Adjustment' had pointed out that at the household level, it was women who had borne the brunt of coping with reductions in social services and increase in the cost of living that ensued. The notion that women and children were being hurt by structural adjustment policies was used to embarrass developed countries and international financial institutions, appealing to a notion that women and children were particularly vulnerable.

The Commission on the Status of Women had decided, also for 1990, to consider the global economic crisis as its development priority theme. DAW decided to organise an expert group meeting in 1988 on the subject.

The Division prepared for the meeting by undertaking its own review of the literature. The staff member assigned was Marion Barthelemy, a young French economist who had joined the Secretariat by way of the national competitive examination. She quickly noticed that the short-term impact on women, noted in 'The Invisible Adjustment' was due to the immediate stabilisation programmes, where shock treatment was given to ensure currency stability including elimination of food subsidies. This meant that women, as managers of household consumption, would have to find means of coping within reduced real income. The longer term effects of structural adjustment programmes, she found, were less clear. One of the presumed effects of structural adjustment was a reduction in government expenditures and it was assumed that this might impact differentially on women. Using newly-available statistics from the UN Women's Indicators and Statistics Database, as well as statistics collected by the United Nations Educational, Scientific and Cultural Organization (UNESCO), Ms. Barthelemy was able to show that in terms of education, there was no immediate effect of structural adjustment on educational expenditure, but that trends of improvement in girls' relative access to education stopped.

DAW also began to question whether the focus on women as victims of structural adjustment was the most appropriate, either normatively or in terms of facts. The Division had begun to see women in the economy as an asset rather than a liability. It raised these issues in its paper to the expert group meeting. The expert group meeting concluded that while structural adjustment had impacted on women, attention to gender factors could help mitigate the overall negative effects. It began to see that the most important adjustment strategies should involve investment in women, particularly in terms of the growth areas of the economy.

The conclusions of the expert group meeting were incorporated in a major economic study prepared by DAW, The World Survey on the Role of Women in Development which was issued in 1989. That document stated:

"Women, however, remain a major force for change. Modification in policies, both to reflect the global norm of equality between men and women, and to enable women to exercise the potential that they have, can have significant effects on the economy. On the one hand, this means ensuring that short— and medium—term policies do not have a negative impact on women, but rather are consistent with long-term objectives of equality. On the other hand, it means seeing long-term structural transformation as a means of accommodating women's increasing economic role for the betterment of society as a whole.

"It also means seeing policies in an integrated way, in which changes in one aspect of women's life can have reinforcing and multiplying positive effects on other aspects. Development for women means development for society. Achieving this means identifying critical points in the economic process where intervention by policies and programmes can have the greatest impact. It means a sharpening of focus on the basic obstacles to women's full participation and on the policies that can address them directly.

This theme was adopted in the recommendations arising from the 1990 review and appraisal of the Nairobi Strategies, which emphasised the need for positive actions:

- An economic environment of growth with equitable distribution, both at the national level and in the international economic system, is essential, as is the recognition of women's full participation. The feminisation of poverty reflects the underlying structural problems faced by women in the midst of economic change. Prevailing economic policies at the national and international levels have frequently failed to take into account potential negative effects on women or women's potential contribution and have accordingly not succeeded.
- In order to help revitalise economic growth, international economic and social cooperation, together with sound economic policies, should be pursued. Structural adjustment and other economic reform measures should be designed and implemented so as to promote the full participation of women in the development process, while avoiding the negative economic and social effects. They should be accompanied by policies giving women equal access to credit, productive inputs, markets and decision-making and this should be incorporated fully into national economic policy and planning.

Once agreed, this became part of the agreed language. As Beijing approached, other organisations began to take up the issue of women in credit, something that had been raised in the 1988 expert group meeting. With new UN statistics available, DAW began to explore some of the long-term consequences for women of the global economic transformation.

Two young economists on the Division staff, Semia Guermas de Tapia from Nicaragua and Marina Ploutakhina from the Russian Federation, analysed changes in women's participation in the labour force over a 20 year period. They noticed that women's participation relative to men was rising, especially in growth sectors. This foreshadowed a major gender shift in employment and entrepreneurship that was also being noticed by the International Labour Organization. Their findings were incorporated in the 1994 World Survey on the Role of Women in Development. The focus was on specific government policies that could take women's potential into account. Its sections on the global economy, women and employment and women in economic decision-making provided a broad panorama that showed both the negative and positive aspects of structural adjustment.

During 1994, DAW organised an expert group meeting on women in economic decision-making that explored the implications of small-scale credit on women as entrepreneurs.

Much of the language of Sections IV A and IV F of the Platform for Action, dealing with women in the economy and women and poverty benefited from DAW's analysis.

There are many other examples of how work done by the Division had an impact on the Platform for Action. DAW was playing a role that international secretariats should play in the development of global norms. It tried to identify those trends that were backed by facts but were acceptable to governments. It tried to write up this information in a politically-neutral way and mobilise support for the underlying ideas. To do so, staff members had to maintain contacts with a highly varied group of people: academic professionals, officials of other UN agencies, members of NGOs, delegates of meetings. They had to have a sense of the direction that ideas were taking. They were not innovators, but they were gatekeepers of ideas.

A good gatekeeper is someone who can recognise what is important and to do that she must also be committed to the issue. The Division staff, women and men alike, but predominately female, worked out of a strong commitment to advancement of women. For them, the issues were not abstractions. Most had suffered discrimination at some point in their lives. Many had themselves faced the double burden of work and family responsibility. With their variety of national and professional backgrounds they were, in some ways, a cross-section of the world's women.

This meant that in the internal meetings and brainstorming sessions before Secretariat drafts were prepared, heated discussions took place. Many of these mirrored the kinds of debates that would have taken place at the intergovernmental level. By finding common ground within the Secretariat, documents could be produced that made it easier for governments to find common ground.

The Division for the Advancement of Women with its colleagues in the Secretariat was a real—if not always visible—part of the process of elaborating the Platform for Action. That this was not noticed means that the Secretariat was doing its job properly. And doing their job properly, and affecting the outcome of history, is the main reward of the women and men who were the human faces of the United Nations at Beijing.

SECTION
FOUR

What the Media said, and didn't say

1
Introduction
Anita Anand

The earlier section included views, analysis and description of the ten-day conference in Beijing. It highlighted the work behind the scenes, what it meant to those who got to Beijing, the organisers, and how it transformed thousands of them.

But what of those that did not get to Beijing? How do they view the conference? What are their sources of information (other than accounts from those who went to Beijing)? Where do they get their images from? The media. Television and radio, newspapers and magazines brought Beijing home to millions of viewers, listeners and readers. What did the media say?

Georgina Ashworth in her contribution in the last section, points out that no two people experienced Beijing the same way. The media also had its own style of interpreting and reporting on Beijing. But there were some alarming (and refreshing) facts and trends that are noteworthy.

To get a picture of what the media said, we asked professionals with a background in media research and analysis to make a contribution. Margaret Gallagher, Paris based researcher and commentator on women and media was at the conference, and agreed to write a piece on the research she was doing.

From the United States we were put in touch with two researchers, Lauren Danner and Susan Walsh, who had presented a paper on their monitoring of the *New York Times* and *Washington Post*, looking at 'backlash' bias in reporting on the Beijing conference.

Beijing-based Huang Qing, deputy editor of the English-language *China Daily,* who served as the editor-in-chief of the daily WORLD WOMEN during the conference published in English and Chinese, was requested to make a contribution from her point of view.

Gallagher's contribution features her research of the UK based English dailies *The Times* and *Guardian,* the Jamaican Daily *Gleaner,* The Malaysian *New Straits Times,* the *Australian Age*, and the Senagelese French-language dailies *La Soleil, Sud Quotidien* and *Sud Hebdo.*

The Times coverage as a whole, Gallagher says, captures many of the inadequacies of a particular strand in mainstream press reporting of the Beijing Conference, especially in the industrialised world. She uses the example of the obsessive focus on Chinese politics (China was referred to in 27 of the 40 Times headlines) putting a harsh spotlight on topics such as China's one-child policy or female infanticide, rarely linking them to China's wider social and economic decision-making, or these phenomena in other parts of the world.

Gallagher contrasts this with the relatively enlightened coverage by the *Guardian* which pointed out "the complex issues raised by the conference should not have been reduced to a struggle between our `free speech' and their 'secret police'...." And she points out that in describing some of the problems faced by participants in Huairou "not as a Chinese plot but a simple muddle", the paper demonstrated an unusual open-mindedness.

One of the reasons for differences of approach of the two British dailies is the profiles of key journalists. The *Times* relied on male foreign correspondents based in the Asian region and the *Guardian* sent two women journalists with a substantial background and experience in reporting on women.

There were 3,200 journalists and media representatives in Beijing (of which non-Chinese men were 33 percent), compared to 1,400 in Nairobi in 1985 (of which 17 percent were non-Kenyan male).

In terms of quantity of material generated, there was a dramatic difference, says Gallagher. The *New York Times* published 30 stories on the women's conference in Mexico City, 20 on Copenhagen, 26 on Nairobi, and 78 on Beijing.

The *Australian Age* published 11 stories on the women's conference in Mexico City, 18 on Copenhagen, 22 on Nairobi, and 85 on Beijing.

The *New Straits Times* of Malaysia published 109 stories on Beijing, and less than 15 on the previous conferences. And, geographical factors do play a role in coverage.

But the *Daily Gleaner* in Jamaica published 60 stories on Beijing compared to 31 on Mexico City (closer to it geographically). *Le Soleil* of Senegal carried 47 on Beijing, compared to 13 on Nairobi (in its region).

In terms of content, Gallagher points out that the Southern dailies covered Beijing in a different way to the Northern media. For example, 57 percent of the stories in *Le Soleil* and 44 percent in *Sud Quotidien* centred on substantive issues of concern to women, compared with only 11 percent in the British *Times*. Issues such as female headed households, contraception rights, violence against women, impact of structural adjustment on women, and the question of adequate financing for the Platform for Action were addressed.

Gallagher says that a citizen of Senegal or Jamaica who travelled to Australia or the United Kingdom during the Beijing Conference might have wondered which was the 'real' Beijing Conference. Was it an 'organisational shambles', and a 'UN jamboree', as reported in the British *Times,* or was it 'an irreversible leap forward in women's long march' as reported in *Le Soleil*?

Lauren Danner and Susan Walsh in their contribution of how the US media covered Beijing, do so with the premise that coverage of women's issues in mainstream US media is representative of a more insidious trend in media (and American society generally) that perpetuates a dominance which devalues and debases women. This trend – backlash – is the basis for their research.

They suggest that the US media was the normal channel for most American readers to know and learn about the Beijing Conference. And, this would influence their perception of the event and women, generally. US reporters, say Danner and Walsh, are trained to report news that is timely, impacts people, has human interest elements, is unusual or different, happens close to home and shows drama or conflict.

The researchers chose the *New York Times* and the *Washington Post's* coverage of the Conference during August and September 1995, collected and analysed it. The *New York Times* was chosen as it is a national newspaper, and acknowledged to set standards for national and international news for smaller newspapers in the US. Any backlash thus appearing in the *New York Times* would appear in hundreds of newspapers that reprinted its stories.

The *Washington Post* was chosen as it is the major daily of Washington DC, the centre of policy making and foreign relations. The two papers represent a cross-section of elite US newspaper coverage of the Conference.

Of the 60 stories analysed, barely one-fourth dealt with issues and agenda items at the Conference. The authors say that there was substantial evidence of backlash in the two dailies and that the US newspaper coverage of the Conference did not allow an opportunity to appreciate the commonalities shared by the world's women, nor the uniqueness of their differences.

The observations and conclusions of Gallagher, Danner and Walsh find a resonance in the contribution of Huang Qing. She says it was an enormous challenge to have the Conference in China, and there was immense expectation by the Government and the Chinese people.

But the challenges included not only some Chinese men viewing the event as a "women's thing", but the increase in global prejudice against China.

Like other media professionals who were in Beijing not because they had to, but wanted to, Quing says that she and her Chinese colleagues had a twin challenge – media bias against China's hosting of the Conference, and drawing the attention of the world to issues that women cared about.

Many of Quing's colleagues felt that the Western media came to Beijing not so much to cover the Conference but to look for conflicts between nations. She, like Danner and Walsh, wonders if much of the Western reportage was biased because the Conference and its theme did not have much news value for these journalists, or was it because of the very conflict-oriented definition of news?

John Mathiason's "Gatekeepers of Ideas" in the last section refers to the study of the American feminist scholar whose study in the mid-1970s pointed out that when the proportion of minorities reached about 30 percent, they were able to influence decision-making by pressing their own interests. At levels lower than that, effectiveness required the minority members to act more like those of the majority, and failing that, they would be ineffective dissenters.

Of the 3,200 media representatives in Beijing, 33 percent were non-Chinese male. This could explain why the coverage in mainstream press was the way it was.

Danner and Walsh point out that the number of women journalists in the US are up from 20 percent in 1960 to 40 in 1984 (and perhaps more since then). Yet, women's empowered activities remain overlooked and underplayed by mainstream print media. They suggest that this debunks the notion that any gains in women's employment within media organisations would result in increased coverage of women and issues in which they have a stake.

But this may not be true if the women were in decision-making positions, which clearly they are not – at least not in the *New York Times* and *Washington Post*.

The western media's obsession with issues of China's human rights and dismissal of the issues at the Conference may also be linked to their lack of experience in countries where there is no free press and where foreign correspondents' brief is essentially politics and economics (and where they are myopic to women's existence). All three contributions in the section suggest this.

The lack of women in decision-making positions in media (print and electronic) is an area of concern in the Beijing Plan of Action. And unless the crucial 30 percent is reached, we may well see another generation of women as ineffective dissenters in media, and the coverage of women trivialised and relegated to the beauty, lifestyle and home pages. Or, in a minority, they would become more like the majority (the men), which is what is happening.

2
Which Was The Real Beijing Conference?

Margaret Gallagher

"Feminists Hail UN China Meeting as Key to Next Century"
— The Times (London) 16 September, 1995

After a month of almost unremittingly negative coverage surrounding the UN's Fourth World Conference on Women, *The Times* had finally found something positive to report. Against all odds, or so it must have seemed to anyone scanning the paper's earlier headlines, the Conference had emerged triumphant from the "security circus" (5 September) and the "chaos" (7 September) — not to mention the "emotions" stirred up by "flirting lesbians" (6 September) and the "Papal-EU rights feud" (9 September). The Beijing Platform for Action — all brackets removed — had been adopted by consensus. Here, indeed, was a potential "key to the next century".

But readers of *The Times* could be forgiven if they failed to grasp its importance for women and men around the globe or, indeed, the importance of the entire process of which the Beijing Conference was a part. The headline's reference to "feminists" (the only such headline reference throughout the paper's Beijing coverage) was innocent. It made a particular statement, limiting the Conference's significance to a specific group and disassociating it from mainstream concerns.

In a substantive valedictory speech on the final day of the Conference, the Norwegian Prime Minister, Gro Harlem Brundtland, declared: "The views expressed here — and the news which escaped from here — will irrevocably shape world opinion. The story of Beijing cannot be untold."

However, the story of Beijing was told in many different ways. For example, *The Times* might have chosen to report the Brundtland speech delivered by one of the world's longest-serving, democratically-elected leaders, an international figure of well-nigh impeccable political credentials. Instead, the paper chose to lead its closing report on the intergovernmental Conference and non-governmental Forum with statements from "two veteran feminist firebrands" — the Americans Bella Abzug and Betty Friedan — who were said to be "optimistic that the conferences would have a lasting effect on China".

Conference delegates, including Abzug and Friedan themselves, might have been perplexed by this particular slant on what the Conference had achieved. But of course, *The Times* reporter had merely set up the notion that the Conference might benefit Chinese women so as to knock it down (it was "difficult to see what Chinese women had gained from the two events") and in a round-about way, to remind readers of the Chinese government's record on free speech (it had moved the NGO Forum to Huairou because it feared "the virus of free discussion") and human rights (it had stamped out any sign of demonstrations "since the Tiananmen Square massacre").

This particular report and, indeed, *The Times* coverage as a whole, encapsulates many

Communication Without Limits

When NGOs tried to fax their home or office from Huairou's Business Center, many were less than thrilled with the price. A one-page fax to Eastern Europe cost 94 yuan.

It's not surprising then, that the computer-filled room provided by the Association for Progressive Communication (APC) was packed with women eagerly waiting their turn to e-mail.

Helping women here touch base with distant colleagues fits in well with the larger mission of APC, said Sally Burch, a spokesperson for the network. The group began a women's networking support programme three years ago.

"We realised that electronic networking has become bigger and bigger in the world, but women were behind in using this new technology," explained Burch.

"The ability to work with e-mail gives women more access to information and communication. This is very important to any kind of joint initiative especially on an international level as international communication is very expensive."

At an NGO Forum workshop sponsored by the Dutch agency NOVIB, experts stressed the importance of using modern communication technology like e-mail to build global links within the women's movement.

If women "don't create our own solidarity networks, if we don't identify our own common realities, if we don't undertake joint actions, we are going to end up being completely ineffectual in a global process that is advancing and is obviously not controlled by women from a gender perspective," said Irene Leon, Ecuadorean director of the Women's Section of the Latin American Information Agency.

Forty APC members from 24 countries arrived in China on August 25 to set up and maintain two email networks for the NGO Forum in Huairou and the UN Conference in Beijing.

Five Eastern European members of the team said they are enjoying the opportunity to work with women from other countries. In addition to the conference languages they help send e-mail messages in Romanian, Ukrainian, Russian and Czech.

Jitka Klinkerova and Monika Satavova are members of Prague Mothers, an environmental NGO, and also work for the Econect environmental network.

"Econect will be a member of APC soon and that is why I am excited to meet and work here with women from APC and especially from Eastern Europe," said Klinkerova.

She helps APC network users if they need it; many people here are using software they have never seen before. But she doesn't think that there will be many people from the Czech Republic or other Eastern European countries among her clients. Communication technology is not so well known in these countries and especially not by women.

"There were a lot of problems facing Internet users in Romania because of the communist regime," said Marina Magdalena Girju, 24, a computer systems engineer who works in an academic network of university centres and researchers all around Romania.

"I feel it's useful to work here to assist in overcoming barriers in communication," she said.

She and other members of the APC team encouraged women to learn skills useful for them when they return to their home countries.

The focus of APC's global computer communications network programs has been mainly on promoting health and environmental sustainability, peace, women's rights, development, education, and social justice via electronic networking.

APC is also providing users with continuous information from the NGO Forum and WFW Conference. Three women in London review all information coming out of Beijing, select the most relevant and channel it to users, along with the lists of available documents.

In many countries, women's organisations and media are disseminating information from the computer networks to the local media, women's groups and officials to give them a women's perspective on the events.

Oksana Kuts
(*Beijing Watch*, September 12, 1995)

of the inadequacies of a particular strand in mainstream press reporting of the Beijing Conference, especially in the industrialised world. For example, the obsessive focus on Chinese politics (China itself was referred to in 27 of the 40 Times headlines) put a harsh spotlight on topics such as China's one-child policy or female infanticide, but very rarely linked these to wider issues of economic and political decision-making, or of systematic discrimination against women worldwide. The suspense over Hillary Rodham Clinton's participation also transfixed sections of the western press, helping to push other substantive stories off the agenda.

The Times was fairly typical. Starting with "Harry and Hillary: The tale of two American visitors to China" (25 August) and ending with "Peking takes last swipe at First Lady" (8 September), the paper devoted five news reports, two editorials and a page one photograph to that matter. Of course, the fact that this was a women's conference was in itself a source of ridicule and trivialisation for some. Publications like *The Spectator*, a British weekly, followed this tack remorselessly, announcing the "First blast of a Peking trumpet against the monstrous regiment of feminists" (2 September) and denouncing, "Feminism the final form of western imperialism" (9 September).

Fortunately, not all coverage was so blinkered. Indeed, the cynicism and prejudice displayed by certain sections of the media was the target of criticism from journalists themselves. For instance, in an editorial entitled "Beijing's week: It was not just about Hillary" (11 September) another British daily, *The Guardian*, pointed out that "the complex issues raised by the conference should not have been reduced to a struggle between our 'free speech' and their 'secret police'." In describing some of the problems experienced by participants in Huairou "not as a Chinese plot but a simple muddle", the paper demonstrated an unusual open-mindedness.

By asserting that "it is right to acknowledge that since the revolution Chinese women have advanced on a scale well ahead of many other developing countries", *The Guardian*, adopted an almost heretical stance vis a vis that of most other British media, whose determination to show that "China cares nothing for its women" (*The Times*, 25 August), or to expose "China's secret war against women" (*Sunday Times*, 3 September) seemed less an expression of concern for Chinese women than a means of firing yet another political broadside. Other stories in these same papers, for instance, "Daunting China dolls' (*The Times*, 2 September), "Mother of all conferences" (*Sunday Times*, 10 September), amply illustrated the hollowness of their professed outrage at the situation of women in China, and, indeed, their fundamental lack of sympathy for the goal of the Beijing Conference.

Compared with that of other British media, coverage in *The Guardian* was more even-handed, more focused on substantive issues and less centered on accounts of conflict. The paper did not shy away from issues of free speech ("Free Speech Curbed at Forum", 30 August), security ("Police scuffles cloud opening", 4 September) or human rights ("Amnesty International Hails Debut in China", 1 September). But throughout almost all of the reporting, the central focus was clearly on women. Starting with its pre-Conference analysis of the UNDP 1995 Human Development Report ("Count the cost of women's work", 18 August) to its final round-up on the likely impact of the Conference ("Been there, done what?", 18 September), reports ranged over a spectrum of issues. Women's employment rights, rape as an instrument of war, the environment, women's rights in Tibet, women's status in Islam: these topics were dealt with in some detail by *The Guardian*.

If the list seems short it nevertheless compares well with coverage in other British media. In *The Times*, for instance, the only substantive issue taken up was that of women in Tibet. The remaining coverage focused entirely on questions of security, policing, human rights in China and the unfolding events at the Conference. At least one of the reasons for the difference in approach of these major British dailies can be found in the profiles of key journalists on each paper. For its reports, *The Times* relied on two male journalists from its foreign staff — one permanently based in Hong Kong, the other in Beijing. *The Guardian* sent two female journalists specially to cover the Conference who, between them, had considerable experience in reporting on development, women's issues and social affairs. Inevitably, the perspective of these women and the background knowledge they brought with them, was utterly different from that of *The Times* reporters whose slant was essentially the political one typical of foreign correspondents. This raises a broader question about the extent and nature of press coverage of the Fourth World Conference on Women.

Over 3,200 journalists and media representatives were present in Beijing, compared with just 1,400 at the 1985 UN Conference on Women in Nairobi. Yet it is legitimate to ask — as Irene Santiago, Executive Director of the NGO Forum, did at the opening press conference in Huairou — why the world's media turned up in such strength. Sitting behind me at the press conference were two white, male journalists who muttered their replies almost in unison: "My editor told me to: human rights in China".

To this anecdote can be added a statistical fact: about 33% of the accredited non-Chinese media representatives at the Beijing Conference were male. By contrast, men accounted for only 17% of the non-Kenyan media accredited to the 1985 Nairobi Conference. But many of the men reporting from Beijing and Huairou were there neither by choice nor because of any knowledge of the Conference issues. Particularly in the case of major western media, they were there because they happened to be based in Hong Kong or in Beijing itself — generally working as China-watchers or South East Asia correspondents. It is reasonable to speculate that the particular slant of these political and foreign affairs journalists may have resulted in fewer issue-based stories than would have been produced by journalists more firmly grounded in the subject matter.

In terms of mere quantity, the amount of coverage generated by the Beijing Conference was quite dramatic when compared with the three earlier UN women's conferences in Mexico City, 1975, Copenhagen, 1980 and Nairobi, 1985. For example, during the two-month period surrounding each of the conferences, The *New York Times* (USA) published 30 stories on Mexico City, 20 on Copenhagen, 26 on Nairobi, but 78 on Beijing. *The Age* (Australia) published 11 stories on Mexico City, 18 on Copenhagen, 22 on Nairobi, and 85 on Beijing. There was a particularly striking increase in coverage in *The New Straits Times* (Malaysia), which published 109 stories on the Beijing Conference, compared with less than 15 on each of the earlier conferences. Of course, geographical proximity to the Conference location is a factor in the amount of coverage likely to appear in specific national media. Media in countries within the region can be expected to carry a larger number of stories than media elsewhere. But in the case of Beijing, there appeared to be almost universal media interest. For example *The Daily Gleaner* (Jamaica) published 60 stories on the Beijing Conference, compared with only 31 on the Mexico City; *Le Soleil* (Senegal) carried 47 stories on Beijing, compared with only 13 on Nairobi.

Papers like these covered the Beijing Conference in quite a different way from many of the western media. Relatively few stories

Pushing Mickey Mouse Media to Make Way for Women

"*M*um's the Word as the Big Yak-Yak Begins," announced the Sydney Morning Herald of Australia, as the World Conference for International Women's Year got underway in Mexico City in 1975.

Twenty years later, despite the criticism - much of it justified - which has surrounded media coverage of the Fourth World Conference on Women, it is difficult to imagine any news organisation publicly indulging in such outright sexism and ridicule.

The over 3000-strong media contingent that has descended on Beijing is just one indication that the women's agenda is now taken more seriously. Some of those who have come are certainly locked into blinkered - and lazy - journalistic routines that focus only on personalities, conflicts and hostilities.

But the vast majority are not. And with two satellite channels - CNN and WETV - broadcasting 30 minutes of news and analyses each day from the Conference, substantive issues of concern to women the world over are reaching audiences around the globe. Twenty years ago, this would have been inconceivable.

Much has changed over the past two decades. The world communication scene has dramatically transformed, offering women new opportunities - but also presenting immense new challenges. The revolution in information technology has indeed increased communication possibilities for some. But most people are not part of the "global village" - a metaphor which is compellingly simple, but profoundly misleading. In fact, the global communication system perpetuates many inequalities.

In 1992 the sales revenue of the top 20 media companies - all located in the USA, Japan and Western Europe - amounted to US $102 billion. That is US $20 billion more than the combined GNP of the 45 least developed countries.

The recently announced US $19 billion merger deal between Walt Disney Corporation and Capital Cities/ABC is equivalent to the extra amount UNICEF estimates would be needed to meet worldwide needs in basic health nutrition and primary education.

In a world where Mickey Mouse and Donald Duck are seen as a better financial investment than fundamental human needs, Neil Postman's apocalyptic assertion that we would finish by "Amusing Ourselves to Death" seems dangerously close to becoming real.

The increasing homogenisation and commodification of culture that goes hand in hand with this market-driven communication system is in total conflict with women's pursuit of diversity and balance in media content.

A quick zap through the television channels available in many Beijing hotels serves up a depressingly familiar crop of female stereotypes: the harried housewife in search of the perfect detergent, the docile nymph waiting for her man to call, the smoldering siren of male fantasy. Twenty years ago, in this part of the world, that too would have been inconceivable.

Curiously enough, at the first three UN women's conferences, discussions about the women and media relationship were muted.

Perhaps, for the developing world, the media did not merit the urgent attention demanded by issues such as health, literacy and poverty.

Perhaps, for the industrialised countries, the hysteria provoked by ill-fated attempts in the 1980s to promote the concept of a New World Information and Communication Order made the communication media a no-go area.

As we approach the millennium, the crucial part played by the media in determining modern cultural practices can no longer be ignored. Vibrant women's media associations in every world region have lobbied tirelessly to ensure that the Draft Platform of Action addresses the media comprehensively. And they have succeeded.

The 32 actions proposed in the Draft Platform do provide the basis for a coherent approach to the problems. And the problems are pressing. For until communication structures demonstrate more diversity and balance, it will be impossible to claim that the media and their messages are genuinely democratic.

Margaret Gallagher
(Beijing Watch, September 13, 1995)

focused on conflict or politics. For example, 57 percent of items in *Le Soleil* and 44 percent in *Sud Quotidien*, another Senegalese daily, centred on substantive issues of concern to women — compared with only 11 percent in the British *Times*. Issues such as female-headed households, contraception rights, violence against women, sexual rights, the impact on women of structural adjustment policies, the role of NGOs and the question of adequate financing for the implementation of the Platform of Action were main topics in articles in *Le Soleil*. Among the sub-topics covered by the paper were: women in trade union, the issue of female circumcision and the link between women's status and economic development. Although both Senegalese dailies covered the Clinton speech — *Le Soleil* ("Hillary Clinton in the Limelight", 6 September: author's translation) with rather less warmth than *Sud Hebdo* ("Hillary Clinton: A speech without concession", 6 September; author's translation) — this was not a centrepiece in the coverage of either.

Both papers tackled the issue of intrusive policing (for example, reporting the case of two Senegalese journalists whose room was searched by security staff; attempts to close the Forum newspaper and to break up demonstrations), but without dwelling on it. The Senegalese press treated the unseasonal, heavy rain with humour: at Huairou, it was reported, the price of an umbrella had doubled in an hour; women in *chadors* had been searching — without success—for black raincoats. But for some western media the weather became just another stick with which to beat the Chinese organisers. *The Times*, reporting on the Clinton speech at the NGO Forum, noted that "the Chinese police....shut half the audience out in a downpour" ("China guys the dolls", 7 September). A *Reuters* report describing the " rivers of mud" at the Forum Site, and an Associated Press picture of participants stepping on the bricks to cross flooded ground, were among the most widely used agency material.

A citizen of Senegal or Jamaica who travelled to Australia or the United Kingdom during the Fourth World Conference on Women might well have wondered which was the 'real' Beijing Conference. Was it an "organisational shambles" at a "UN· Jamboree" where there had been a "roughing up of delegates" (*The Times*: quotes from three separate 7 September reports)? Or was it "an irreversible leap forward in women's long march" (*Le Soleil*, 2 October, author's translation)?

The world's press in the North and in the South gave very different answers.

[Acknowledgement: Based on a 12-country study-in-progress of media coverage of the four UN conferences on women (1975-95), funded by UNIFEM and UNICEF.]

3

'Radical Feminists' and 'Bickering Women'
Backlash in U.S. Media Coverage of Beijing

Lauren Danner and Susan Walsh

Substantial research exists indicating an extreme lack of US media news coverage of women newsmakers and/or issues which affect women on both international and national levels. When stories about women's issues or women leaders do appear, they are most often relegated to lesser, inside pages, such as lifestyle sections. Further marginalisation occurs as a result of mainstream Western news writers' apparent inability to recognise the "multiple identities" of news sources or subjects who are both female and members of an ethnic group.

The news media surreptitiously shape a dominant world view. But despite an increase in the number of female journalists (up 20 to 40 percent from 1960 to 1984), reports on empowered women's activities remain essentially overlooked and underplayed by the mainstream US print media. This debunks the notion that any gains in women's employment within media organisations would result in increased coverage of women and issues which affect them.

The ways that international women's conferences (such as the UN's Decade for Women conferences held in 1975, 1980 and 1985) have historically been covered in US newspapers is illustrative of this phenomenon and is of particular interest in this study. Such gatherings typically address substantive issues of development, human rights and women's rights and roles within the context of economic, political and social change. However, the majority of mainstream news coverage has tended to focus on conflict among women participants and the disorganisation of meetings.

It is a premise of this research that how women's issues are covered in mainstream US media is representative of a more insidious trend in media (and American society generally) that perpetuates a hegemony that devalues and debases women. This trend—backlash—is the basis for the conceptual and theoretical underpinnings of this study, which examines US newspaper coverage of the UN's Fourth World Conference on Women to see whether themes and indicators of Backlash are present.

In 1991, Susan Faludi's book, *Backlash: The Undeclared War Against American Women*, "startled [many women] into the awareness of their precarious position in most areas of modern life everywhere in the world". Faludi's detailed investigation of American political, economic and social institutions reveals a covert movement in mainstream America to "remind women to embrace traditional roles or suffer the consequences".

Of particular significance was the role that mainstream Western news media play in escalating this backlash sentiment. Perhaps most compelling was Faludi's ability to identify the complicity of the media in shaping a form of oppression which attempted to discredit and disable feminism through forms of communication intended to "undermine

Setting the Airwaves on Fire

It was supposed to be broadcast out of a soundproof glass booth at the NGO Forum. But the FIRE-place — Feminist International Radio Endeavor — has been burning up the airwaves from day one, despite its unsuccessful attempt to secure a noise-free environment from Forum organisers.

The setback was no deterrent for FIRE-place coordinator Maria Suarez, who once broadcast from the back of a horse to emphasise the need for forest preservation in her native Costa Rica.

Suarez, along with Katarina Alfossi and Nancy Vargas, form the core of FIRE which was conceived in 1985 following the Nairobi World Women's Conference. Six years later, FIRE went on the air and has been burning brightly ever since.

FIRE broadcasts via shortwave radio every day from Costa Rica for two hours in Spanish and English. For the duration of the NGO Forum the transmission has been expanded to four hours daily, broadcasting live from within a partitioned area in the Alternative Media Center.

For the first two days of the Forum, a telephone transmission line on the proposed site could not be arranged; Suarez acted quickly and set up her remote equipment in a hotel room, conducting the entire first day's broadcast over a hotel phone.

"This is like having the whole world right here at the FIRE-place," Suarez gushed, still enthusiastic and energetic after seven gruelling days.

It's not the first time FIRE has taken its show on the road. FIRE has given voice to thousands at several regional and world conferences, including the Social Summit in Copenhagen in March and the Population Conference last year in Cairo.

Programme producers, hosts and engineers from 17 countries are participating in putting together the FIRE-place's daily programmes at the Forum, with countless others lined up hoping for a spot on the air. For most, FIRE is their best bet to get their voices and concerns heard internationally.

Suarez and her faithful contingent are dedicated to highlighting the views and activities of grassroots organisations, and FIRE often finds itself in the middle of the action.

Last year when Suarez heard there was a plan to turn some rare forestland near FIRE's Costa Rican offices into a landfill, she felt compelled to take action.

"I decided to bring the sounds of the forest and its caretakers to the listeners," Suarez said. She mounted a horse, armed with a walkie talkie and a microphone, the weapons of her war against environmental degradation. As she rode through the forest she described the flora and fauna that would be destroyed and talked to residents, broadcasting all the while.

Suarez received both local and international attention for her effort. City officials later had a change of heart and decided against the landfill.

At the NGO Forum, FIRE-place hosts and producers have put hundreds of conferees on the air. Many had never been behind a microphone, and for several the trip to China was the first time they had ever left their communities.

"I am so happy to be here and telling the stories of my people," said Durga Sob of Nepal. Sob founded the Feminist Dalit Organisation in her rural region; "dalit" is a Hindu concept meaning untouchable, a circumstance of birth and an illegal but persistent practice of class discrimination in its most extreme form.

"There are many NGOs in Nepal, but no one wants to work with the dalits," Sob said. "My parents could not attend school, but they made sure I went to school so that I could improve my life. I don't know how they got me into the school."

The FIRE-place also features taped excerpts from speeches and workshops going on at the Forum. But the heart of its programming is the live interviews, some completely spontaneous.

> Suarez acknowledges that most shortwave listeners are men. Not surprisingly, she views this fact as a golden opportunity.
>
> "I finally asked one of our male listeners why he liked the programming," Suarez related. "He said, 'Because on the air you and your guests say a lot of the same things my wife and her friends are always saying, but with FIRE if I don't like it I can turn it off.' That's when I realised our programmes are a way to get through to men without being a threat to them."
>
> The FIRE-place broadcasts take place between 12-noon and 4 p.m. local time on A.M. shortwave band frequencies 6.200, 7.385 and 15.050.
>
> **Linda Neuman**
> (Beijing Watch, September 9, 1995)

women's confidence and obstruct further efforts toward equality".

The presence or absence of backlash themes in US media coverage of the Beijing Conference is the chief concern of this study. In an attempt to gauge the degree to which backlash might exist in coverage of women and women's issues, a qualitative analysis was conducted of coverage by two major mainstream US newspapers—the *New York Times* and the *Washington Post*.

A number of factors influence media coverage of any event; not least among those is the agenda of the event. The Beijing Conference had a number of objectives. Among them were: reviewing and appraising women's advances (since the Nairobi Forward-Looking Strategies); mobilising women and men at policy-making and grassroots levels to promote those strategies; adopting a Declaration and Platform for Action that would address key areas of concern to the advancement of women and suggesting ways in which governments, NGOs, the private sector and community groups could incorporate the suggestions made; and determining what concerns needed priority action between 1996 and 2001.

While success of the implementation of recommendations based on the Beijing Declaration remains to be seen, it is reasonable to assume that at least some US media coverage of the Conference would include issues raised in the agenda. For, as a number of studies have shown, the US mass media "are the major source of international events in far places. The way in which the mass media...construct and interpret events, what they focus on and what they omit, helps construct a public opinion".

It is reasonable to suggest, then, that US media were the only channel through which most US readers got information about the Beijing Conference. It also follows that this information was likely to have influenced their perceptions of the event and perhaps, of women generally.

This coverage, like all media coverage, was not unaffected by outside influences. Apart from the Conference agenda, a number of factors may have influenced coverage, including constraints on international news coverage, journalistic newsgathering routines and values, and context.

It has been noted that US media, constrained by tight budgets, foreign censorship and crisis-oriented reporting, have increasingly turned to pre-planned international events to fill foreign news holes. How that news is defined is a product of journalistic values.

US reporters are trained to report news that is timely, impacts people, has human interest elements, is unusual or different, happens close to home and shows drama or conflict. It has been argued that news exhibits four biases: it focuses people instead of problems; emphasises crises over continuity; is fragmented and hard to understand as a "big picture"; and relies on officials as information sources. Such biases conform well to a predilection for covering international events.

Most communication scholars agree that media construct portrayals which are different from reality, and one of the reasons for these constructions lies in the nature of the media themselves. One of them notes: "Those involved in making, reporting and editing news... have an incentive to shape it so as to attract audiences and, sometimes, to encourage particular interpretations through its content and form."

This is especially true in the strongly competitive US media which have powerful commercial imperatives to attract audiences almost exclusively for advertisers. Characteristics of the media influence how information is presented and outside pressures often influence the context in which news is covered.

In the case of China, US relations upto and during the Conference might be best described as warily cordial. The past two decades have seen both burgeoning economic relations with China (which instituted an open-door trade policy in the early 1980s) as well as tensions over human rights abuses and pro-democracy movements, culminating with the Tiananmen Square massacre in 1989. The visit of Taiwan's president to the US in mid-1995 drew disapproval from the Chinese government, which arrested Chinese dissident Harry Wu and jailed him until just before the Beijing Conference opened.

For foreign correspondents in China, the situation is strained. Reporters live in one of four government-run compounds, phone calls and mail are monitored and official clearance is needed to leave Beijing. American media available in China, such as *Newsweek* magazine, are regularly censored and both Chinese and other journalists are vulnerable to expulsion, imprisonment and other restrictions.

The fact that foreign correspondents in China are so closely watched is indicative of the Chinese government's attitude toward any outside press coverage. While reporters covering the UN Conference were not subjected to restrictions as severe as those placed on permanent foreign correspondents, they did operate under many limitations, including visa delays and content restrictions.

This study uses qualitative analysis to examine US media coverage of the Beijing Conference for Backlash themes. *New York Times* and *Washington Post* coverage of the Conference during August and September 1995 was collected and analysed. Only bylined stories written by reporters who worked for either of these newspapers were included in the analysis.

The *New York Times* was chosen because it is a national newspaper that is acknowledged to set the national and international news agenda for smaller newspapers in the United States. Any Backlash themes that appeared in its coverage of the Conference, therefore, are likely to have reappeared in hundreds of newspapers that reprinted its stories. The *Washington Post* was chosen because it is the major daily newspaper in Washington D.C, the national centre for international policy-making and foreign relations. As such, its Conference coverage was considered to be substantial in amount, and also likely to be picked up by smaller newspapers. The two newspapers represent a cross-section of elite US newspaper coverage of the Conference.

Altogether 31 articles ran in the *New York Times* between August 18 and September 26, 1995; 29 stories ran in the *Washington Post* between August 16 and September 21, 1995. Articles were considered to be about the Conference if they were about a topic directly related to the topic of the Conference events (i.e., they explicitly mentioned the Conference), or if they referred to the Conference at least once, but referred to it indirectly in that the story most probably would not have been published had the Conference not taken place. Each article was examined for words, phrases, themes or topics that may have indicated Backlash.

Seven themes were identified as indicative of Backlash and operationalised as follows:

1. **Conflict:** women protesting, angry women, women competing with each other.

2. **Stereotypes:** of women as unfeminine, as having "no sense of style" or as having "let themselves go."

3. **Marital/family status:** emphasis on traditional roles, motherhood as desirable over a career.

4. **Feminism fallout:** women portrayed as suffering from feminist gains; women without relationships or children whose "biological clocks" are ticking ever more loudly.

5. Stories ostensibly about women, but which fail to cite women as sources, experts or examples.

6. **Superwomen:** women suffering under pressure of managing career and family.

7. **Stories which appear to ask:** "They have equality; what more do these women want?"

Stories were considered to exhibit backlash themes if coverage could not be substantially linked to the Conference and if it appeared to be included for no reason other than to portray women in a particular way. For example, thousands of women participated in protests at the Conference, but if coverage of the protests was clearly linked to the issues raised at the Conference, it was not considered Backlash. If, however, the protest was covered simply as women protesting and no reason for the demonstration was given, the story was considered to exhibit the conflict theme.

Of the *Washington Post's* 29 stories and the *New York Times'* 31 stories that explicitly mentioned the Conference, only five *Washington Post* stories and 11 *New York Times* stories (that is, barely one quarter of all stories) focused specifically on substantive Conference issues. Reporter gender was also noted: in the *Washington Post*, seven stories were written by women and 19 by men (the gender of three authors could not be determined from the bylines); in the *New York Times*, five stories were written by women and 26 by men.

Below, we discuss findings within six of the backlash themes. We do not devote a section to the superwomen theme, primarily because no substantial evidence of it surfaced in the analysis of either newspaper. However, there may be symbolism in its absence: a hegemonic shift has occurred with regard to the ideology that surrounds "women's work" as a result of the economic realities of contemporary Western society. The debate in the US over whether women should work either in or outside the home has become irrelevant because the state of the economy often mandates two-income households. Moreover, the majority of women at the Beijing conference were not likely to be confronted with the "superwoman" dichotomy of family vs. career; women who are faced with more overwhelming issues, such as oppression and violence, are unlikely to be subjects of that particular brand of media backlash.

Symbols of conflict were ubiquitous in both newspapers' stories about the Conference. References in nearly every article produced the following list of words and phrases, which characterised women as conflicting with each other, or with Beijing officials: complained/complain/complaints, battles, clashes, chafed/chafe, refused outright, shouted down, spat, commotion, jostle, defiance, angry, agitating, fighting, demanded, resist, tensions, dispute, haggled, disagree/disagreement, differences, demeaned, threat/threaten/threatened, meddling, disrupted, outrage, boil, brazenly pushy, unruly, exasperated, frustrated, divided, confrontation, controversies, intrusion, debate, hostility/overt hostility, fiasco, pandemonium.

US First Lady Hillary Rodham Clinton was said to have "made a thirty mile road trip to

Lights, Camera, Conference

As over 3,000 journalists covering the Beijing Conference comb the halls for news, women here are keeping a close watch on how the media makes them look.

For the first time at a major UN conference on women, media is one of the critical areas of concern in the Platform for Action.

"We must begin to think of ourselves as consumers of news and we must begin to demand news about women," says Lisa Veneklasen, a member of the NGO media caucus.

Some 3,200 journalists are covering the Beijing Conference, according to the UN Department of Public Information. CNN, which has helped create the global village, has a 30-member team, one of the largest ever to cover a UN conference.

"Ordinary women and the amazing capacity they have for organising, forming caucuses and getting women's issues to the stage where it is at now, don't make headline news," says Veneklasen. "It seems easier for media to focus on the big names. It takes the innovative journalist to get behind the scenes and turn what has never been an international story, into one."

Gertrude Mongella, Secretary-General of the Fourth World Conference, has challenged the media to put women's issues on the international agenda and to hold governments accountable on policies and programmes for women.

But who checks media, women activists ask?

"At first, media tried to make this a story about China instead of about women and their conference," says Jane Benbow of the media caucus. "Many press stories expressed disappointment with the special Plenary speech by Hillary (Rodham) Clinton, because she did not specifically mention China. But we (women) were thrilled with her speech, because she talked about our issues."

Journalists, however, argue that "bad" stories get the most play around the world, overshadowing the other reports they send back home which focus on the issues.

Arit Kahuma, an editor with the New Vision newspaper in Uganda, says her newspaper picks up breaking news from the major wire agencies. Her job is to provide features that offer an insight into the issues.

"If you want to focus on the bad news, you only write bad news," says Kahuma. "I've decided to focus on the issues rather than the rain, the mud and the problems."

WE-TV, a global network which made its debut in Beijing, is also trying to balance the coverage provided by the major networks. The goal of WE-TV is to bring issue-based programmes produced in developing countries to audiences in the industrialised world.

Their coverage of the Beijing meeting is being broadcast in 31 countries.

"We try to stay focused on the issues," says Sylvia Spring, a producer with WE-TV. "Although there has been strong pressure on us (already) to do news, this is not our mandate."

Media researcher Margaret Gallagher says that at the beginning of the Conference, the major media did focus primarily on demonstrations, criticisms of Chinese officials and other controversies surrounding the Conference venue. But in the past week there was movement towards covering poverty, violence against women, and other critical Conference issues.

"Not all journalists came here to focus on China, and US-China relations," Gallagher says, adding that she has seen a big difference in the way women and men are covering the Conference.

"The big political news conferences are packed with the guys. The press conferences on issues called by agencies like UNICEF, UNESCO and UNIFEM are attended more by women, and they are the ones asking the substantive questions."

Pat Made
(Beijing Watch, September 11, 1995)

[Huairou] to address a boisterous crowd of women from around the world..." (*Washington Post*, 7 September 1995); the town itself was described as the site of a training centre "before the commotion of the women's meeting" (*Washington Post*, 16 August 1995).

"Prominent democratic activists for women's rights" were in conflict with "Republican [male] House members" who, it was reported, were trying unsuccessfully to deny funding for US delegates to travel to China (*Washington Post*, 16 August 1995). And, according to five female, Republican House members, "The 'Platform for Action' to be debated in Beijing is at odds with the basic beliefs and morals of the vast majority of Americans" (*New York Times*, 26 August 1995).

Moreover, the occasional story that suggested commonality and agreement was framed tentatively, as exemplified by this quote: "Despite differences, many women here argued that there are threads that bind women together and join the world's women in some directions as they struggle for equal rights" (*Washington Post*, 17 September 1995).

A *New York Times* article noted, "The Conference ground to its conclusion with far less rancor than anyone had expected" (15 September 1995). Taken at their denotative level, these terms might contribute to an understanding of the manifest meaning of the content; namely, differences of opinion which might exist among conference participants relative to the organisation and planning. However, the steady diet of terms such as "boisterous"and "commotion" transforms the content to a connotative level that depicts women doing men's work (decision-making) in a state of disorganisation and disarray. Clearly, the latent meaning to consider involves women's failed attempts to conduct events outside their element. The underlying structure of "keeping women in their place" is evident in these meanings.

Female conferees were described as "radical feminists" and were often portrayed as unfeminine, irrelevant, undignified and trivial. A *New York Times* article about delegate Bella Abzug, former US Congresswoman and current NGO director, began with quotes from former president George Bush who said he felt "sorry for the Chinese, having Bella Abzug running around in China. Bella Abzug is one who has always represented the extremes of the women's movement" , and presidential contender Bob Dole who said he "could not imagine why anyone would want to attend a conference co-chaired by Bella Abzug" which served to frame the article as a profile of an insignificant yet annoying feminist (12 September 1995).

An article about Chinese police harassing conferees described a Canadian woman as "really scared"(*New York Times*, 4 September 1995); another described women who could not get into Hillary Rodham Clinton's speech as "generous" because they held umbrellas over soaked Chinese security officers (*New York Times*, 7 September 1995). Still another reported that "for many of Beijing-based Chinese, the Conference is a curiosity or a nuisance" (*Washington Post*, 30 August 1995). Similarly, another story reported that "the [Chinese] government didn't take the women groups seriously, assuming that their meeting would be dominated by shopping and polite conversation" (*Washington Post*, 11 September 1995).

The Conference itself was referred to by the *Washington Post* as having a "carnival like atmosphere" (30 August 1995). The *New York Times* wrote that the Vatican called the Conference agenda the "work of Western feminists" (25 August 1995). US Health and Human Services Secretary Donna Shalala was reported to have "...pushed through like a fullback going for short yardage on fourth down before gaining entry" into the building where Hillary Rodham Clinton was speaking (*Washington Post*, 7 September 1995).

A headline in the *Washington Post* read "Chinese Get Word: Shun Naked Women" (30

August 1995). The story's first three paragraphs told of Beijing police officers and hotel clerks who were warned to "toss a white sheet or coat on top of naked women". It went on to describe how taxi drivers were cautioned to avoid picking up naked women; workers in Huairou (site of the NGO forum) were told to wear bug spray because "flies might transmit AIDS carried by lesbian attendees". The article described a "bedraggled group" of women arriving from Poland on a "Peace Train" and recounted "sharp criticism" of the Chinese government. The remainder of the article focussed on the disputes between Beijing officials and Conference organisers.

Chinese police "pointed to the ground as if trying to bring a dog to heel" in their efforts to stop marchers (*New York Times*, 5 September 1995). An article comparing feminism around the world was headlined 'The Second Sex in the Third World,' and noted that "Western-style feminists have become increasingly irrelevant" (10 September 1995). Women in the North, it continued, "bicker over history and theory" instead of focusing on "pragmatic goals". The same article referred to African women as "always good storytellers" in an anecdote about computers crashing at another meeting.

Social and political climate in Beijing notwithstanding, in emphasising these details over more substantive issues, the reporters diminished the significance of the Conference by failing to provide necessary details regarding the groups in attendance, and the context within which these events occurred.

Faludi (1991) identified a macro-level Backlash theme that centred around the notion that the Second Wave women's movement caused the ultimate ruin of the family structure. Thus, attention was given to references regarding women's marital and/or family status, and to traditional feminine roles or role-related behaviours. Several articles referred to "women's work" in their headlines: 'Women's Work, Women's Worth' (*New York Times*, 18 August 1995); 'Women's Work is Never Done' (*Washington Post*, 24 August 1995) and 'Women's Work: New Options - Debating Focus of Conference, Traditionalists Want Motherhood Stressed' (*Washington Post*, 27 August 1995). The last headline points to an increasingly common Backlash theme surrounding the dichotomous nature of motherhood: one can be a feminist or a traditional mother, but not both.

Indeed, the Vatican's chief conference delegate, Harvard law professor Mary Ann Glendson "did not fit easily into stereotypes" (*New York Times*, 29 August, 1995) and descriptions of her included: "an articulate, respected legal scholar", "married with three children", "the perfect weapon," (*New York Times*, 25 and 29 August, 1995). And, no doubt to the Vatican's delight, she "rejects much of the feminist movement as.... old-line sidelined [and] marginal to the concerns of most women" (29 August 1995). In one article, she was quoted as saying that "real equality involves an affirmation of motherhood and family life" (25 August 1995). In a related story, the *Washington Post* focussed on the Vatican's criticism of the Conference Platform: "The underlying tension is between those women who want to honor the role of the family, uncritical support for abortion and an angry anthropology" (5 September 1995).

Several articles included references to" families," and "family values". Then-presidential candidate, Phil Gramm, called the Conference an "Unsanctioned festival of anti-American sentiment" (*New York Times*, 25 August 1995). President Clinton and Hillary Rodham Clinton were described as defending the Conference as not a radical, anti-family event; instead, they said it is "an attempt to improve the lot of women worldwide" (*New York Times*, 27 August 1995). However, the article went on to note that Bill Clinton needs women's vote if he is to win re-election, casting the Clinton's comments in a highly political light.

Groups in opposition to the inclusion of abortion and birth control in the Platform were described as "conservative". Here, the symbolism of dichotomous thinking is represented: if a participant does not belong to a conservative group, she/he must be a liberal. Moreover, given contemporary society's negative connotation of the term "liberal", the audience is offered the opportunity to presume that a particular ideology will naturally accompany the classification.

Several stories portrayed women as "casualties" of the women's movement — as oddities and misfits whose deviation from the feminine norm was caused by feminism. One such story, which purported to discuss the logistics of the NGO Forum, reported: "The [NGO Forum] is expected to attract groups that include feminists, lesbians, prostitutes and Hawaiian nationalists. There is even a 'peace train' of women en route here from Helsinki" (*Washington Post*, 16 August 1995). The article goes on to quote a "worried Western diplomat—who for the record is a skeptical male—as saying, "This is like a big locomotive heading in our direction".

Trivialisation of the women's movement by those who work in print media is well-documented. One of the more striking examples of this appeared in an article by William F. Powers titled 'The China Syndrome' (*Washington Post*, 29 August 1995). At first glance, the story appears to be about the Conference and the "trouble [women had] agreeing on the definition of "gender". However, by the third paragraph, Powers shifts to a critique of women's magazines and in particular, an article written by feminist activist Andrea Dworkin, whom he describes as "one of those fabulously foaming feminists still knocking around from the 1970's [who]...hates the Bill of Rights because it was written by the founding Fathers... a phrase which makes her 'physically ill' ". The overt hostility toward feminism apparent in this article serves as a disturbing reminder of the prevailing misogynist tendencies of Western culture.

The headline reads 'Women Face 'Global Glass Ceiling' UN Says' (*Washington Post*, 18 August 1995) and the Conference is mentioned once, in the second paragraph. However, the article which addresses the lack of opportunities available for women's progress or empowerment, fails to cite even one woman as source or expert. Instead, several men from both the private and public sectors of various countries are featured discussing the economic plight of the world's women. Similarly a *New York Times* article titled 'Star at Conference: Banker who Lends to the Poor' (14 September 1995) focussed on a Bangladeshi man who loans money to poor women. While this practice is certainly praiseworthy, the reporter could have focused on any of a number of women-run organisations that do the same thing. Another article, headlined 'Women's Conference Opens with Fanfare' (*Washington Post*, 5 September 1995) devotes two inches of a 32-inch story to the opening ceremony. Not surprisingly, the remainder of the report focuses on conflicts and disputes over the platform, and protests against the Chinese government. A *New York Times* article about the problems that the NGO Forum attendees were having with Chinese security, devoted two paragraphs to quotes from a Conference spokeswoman; the rest of the article was filled with the pronouncements of two (male) Chinese government officials and the (male) head of Amnesty International, a human rights organisation (30 August 1995).

A sense of this Backlash theme surfaced in a Washington Post story which appeared at the end of the conference (17 September 1995). The report stated that, "In drawing up a declaration and program for action here, women lobbyists women lawyers and (mostly) women politicians traded proposals, bargained over paragraphs and programs and talked about how the dense, 150-page docu-

Media Focuses on the Wrong Issues

"How many of you all are pissed?" asked Loretta Ross, a vociferous American with flowing beaded hair swathed in a bright hand-printed cloth jumpsuit. Everyone at the revival-style workshop in Huairou last week raised their hands.

As journalists and commentators continue tracking changes in prosecutor Marcia Clark's hairstyle and wardrobe, NGO delegates attacked media coverage of the O.J. Simpson double murder trial.

"We wanted to show what the men pay attention to while the women die," said Ross, who chairs Sister Love, a US-based AIDS awareness group. "All we're hearing about is poor O.J. And I'm a little pissed."

A woman from Belgium stopped by the packed, rowdy tent to learn the latest news from the American football hero's trial in Los Angeles. She was given a quick update from the audience, which included women from countries as far-flung as Ireland, New Zealand and the United States.

"We sometimes stay up until 2 or 3 in the morning watching it on CNN," said a South African woman wearing a t-shirt that read, "There's no excuse for abuse."

The workshop, 'O.J, Simpson: Black Women Speak on Black Men, Violence and Interracial Relationships,' was organised by Sister Love.

In the straw poll conducted in the first minutes of the workshop, Simpson did not fare well.

"How many of you think he's guilty?" asked Ross. Nine out of 10 women raised their hands. "Do you think he'll be let off," Ross continued. The hands stayed up.

News of Simpson's arrest last year rocked his fans in the United States and captured headlines around the world.

"When I first heard about it, I cried," said Dorothy Meade of Bridge Street Rites of Passage Program, a New York-based group. "I cried from the point of view of a black man having risen so high and then having fallen so low."

Ross criticised black men for asking black women to put race before gender and stand by Simpson regardless of whether he killed his ex-wife Nicole Brown Simpson and her friend Ronald Goldman last June.

"You can't let race blind you," said Ross. "I'm not in the struggle for the right of men to kill women."

But audience member Rene Dubose said reporters writing about the black community's response to the trial were assuming black viewers could not differentiate between real and circumstantial evidence or DNA findings and police conspiracy.

"We are not voodoo people," said Dubose, a representative of the Washington D.C.-based National Council for Women. "We can see the evidence."

Audience members also agreed that if Brown Simpson had been black, the trial would not receive as much publicity. They listed recent scandals in which black women had been the victims of violence or sexual exploitation, but they said their voices had not been heard in the press.

The women attending the outdoor workshop said they are angry that reporters and analysts focus on the racial elements of the trial and not domestic violence.

"If you can beat your wife, you can kill her," said Ross.

Jennifer Griffin
(Beijing Watch)

ment could be used for action back home. If that document seemed sometimes long-winded and uninformed, it also reflected a women's movement that has become more diverse and worldwide". In this rather equivocal commentary on both the purpose and usefulness of the Platform, the writer implies that for all the good it did, the simple fact is that this conference may have created more problems than it succeeded in addressing.

In a similar, conference follow-up article, a New York Times reporter noted, "If some delegates felt a certain satisfaction just in having woven a multi-layered consensus among delegates from 189 states ranging from Libya to the Vatican to the United States, others were mindful that talking about rights is easier than actually achieving them... And previous women's conference are well-known for issuing proclamations that lead to breathtakingly few concrete results. Has anything changed?" (17 September 1995)

We have presented substantial evidence that six themes of backlash were present in New York Times and Washington Post coverage of the United Nations Fourth World Conference on Women. We realise, though that our evidence is based on an examination of coverage in toto and that to a normal reader, such themes might not be as apparent. This realisation speaks of one of the most insidious aspects of backlash; namely, that its presence is so ingrained in media content and coverage that if it is not actively being sought it is likely to be missed. In fact, that is perhaps the most disturbing aspect of the newspaper coverage analysed for this research, and it is manifested dramatically in the topics covered in articles. Of the 60 stories analysed, barely one-fourth dealt with issues and agenda items raised at the conference. This lack of coverage of substantive conference issues implies a kind of meta-Backlash; i.e. if the media do not cover the conference, they do not have to acknowledge the existence of these issues and they maintain the hegemony of the dominant ideology. The dominant ideology of Backlash became invisible because it was translated into common sense; it became natural and nonpolitical: What is happening to women has little to do with political events or social pressures—women's conflict is not with society or culture, but with itself. We believe that this study shows how Western print media contributed to the hegemonic process by being critical of women for being women, rather than for their political ideologies or the legitimate debate on issues.

This also points to a contribution this research might make: it is a step away from examining representations and a step toward understanding the meanings inherent in media messages. Ironically, newspaper editors' reactions to a recent Media Watch study indicate that while scholarship may be looking beyond studies of representation, media organisations continue to assign little credibility to either the substance or the meanings of such studies.

We share the views of our colleagues who, for various reasons have called for methodological shifts in gender and/ or feminist media scholarship that look beyond the media's representation of women and issues that affect them. However, we also acknowledge the danger in eliminating a key component of feminist research., which for all of its shortcomings has made an enormous contribution to our understanding of the role of gender in society.

The assumption that media messages are inherently polysemic, and that audiences may resist particular meanings, presents a useful alternative to analysing content. We are, however, resistant toward embracing, "feminist reconstructions" of media analysis. Indeed, we consider worthwhile any scholarship which contributes to our knowledge of what it means to be female or male subjects of language and symbols which define or construct the culture in which we live.

Finally, to the extent that media, as purveyors of language and symbols, exist to inform, the US newspaper coverage of the Beijing conference did not allow an opportunity to appreciate the commonalities shared by the world's women, nor the uniqueness of their differences. As other scholars have observed, conceptualising difference has to happen through the sharing of experiential diversity. In the case of the Beijing conference, by essentially ignoring the many varied manifestations of ideological and institutional practices in the lives of the world's women, US newspapers — and more importantly, their women readers — missed that opportunity.

[Excerpted from a study first presented at the 1996 Convention of the Association for Education and Journalism and Mass Communication, International Communication Division. Full paper, with references, avilable with authors, care of : School of Journalism and Communication, 1275 University of Oregon, Eugene, Oregon, 97403-1275 USA. The authors thank Leslie Steeves for her invaluable guidance on this research.]

4

Covering the Conference
The Chinese Perspective

Huang Qing

The Fourth World Conference on Women promised to be a controversial event before it was even inaugurated. But controversy aside, it turned out to be a memorable experience, if not a milestone, for women in general and China in particular.

As a Chinese woman journalist, I was personally involved in the preparations and hosting of the event. When the country was awarded this opportunity, I and many of my compatriots (mostly women) committed ourselves from day one, to one of the largest endeavours China had ever undertaken.

The government viewed the event as China's great opportunity to showcase its organisational capability to the world and demonstrate the country's willingness to share responsibility in international affairs. In 1992 the State Council set up the China Organising Committee for the Conference. It consisted of 37 members from 30 government agencies and NGOs, including 12 women ministers and vice-ministers and four representatives of NGOs. The message was amply clear: the Conference had to be a success.

But that was easier said than done. The next three years leading up to the Conference turned out to be a tough uphill struggle on two fronts. On the home front, despite the fact that the event had been widely publicised, people (mostly men) tended to look upon it as nothing more than a 'female talk fest' and therefore, not to be taken seriously.

Indifference was evident everywhere—in the workplace, at home and during social occasions. I remember the time one of my male colleagues wrote a commentary in which he stated that the Conference would have great significance for all the world's women. I had to rewrite it stating clearly that the Conference was not just for women but was one that would be of great significance for all the people in the world — men included. Women activists throughout China took time off from their huge task of logistical preparations and campaigned to drive home the message that this was a worthwhile effort in which everyone should participate.

The other struggle, of course, was on the global front. On the one hand, tens of thousands of Chinese women were going all out to prepare assiduously for the Conference and the NGO Forum—events which they hoped would go a long way to advance women's status and seek further commitments from governments and world organisations. On the other hand, however, prejudice against China was building up.

Western media was shifting the focus to all but the issues and concerns of the Beijing Conference, misleading the international community and creating public opinion not very conducive to the success of the Conference.

A case in point was the media coverage given to the new NGO Forum site. It was only expected that the change of the Forum site would be reported. But to highlight it for six months running and make it the predomi-

On the Air and Making Waves

It is early morning as Bernadette Rounds Ganilau settles in behind the console at Radio Fiji in Suva. She snaps on her headset, adjusts her microphone, and welcomes listeners to another edition of "The A.M. Show."

Within minutes, a roaring, no-holds-barred debate is beamed out on the airwaves across the Pacific to listeners scattered on Fiji's more than 300 separate islands.

One women calls in to complain about her family's response after a neighbour raped her. Another woman weeps as she says that her father-in-law — a respected village elder — has molested her two daughters for several years. A father whose son has contracted HIV/AIDS grieves openly.

Welcome to talk-back radio, Fiji-style.

In a traditional society where even uttering the word "sex" is taboo, Ganilau's chatty, six-days a week English-language show is a revolution. Each morning, she leads a frank, provocative, roundtable discussion on sex, domestic violence, homosexuality, AIDS and other topics once considered too private for public airing.

None of the country's other five radio stations-which broadcast in English, Hindustani, and Fijian have anything like it.

"On our formal Fijian network, we can't even say these words because our listeners are elders, traditional leaders," Ganilau says. "But on my programme, anything goes."

Ganilau, 42 was born in Fiji, but moved to New Zealand with her family for primary school. After completing college in Australia, Ganilau travelled the world.

"I tried to find myself," she says. But always, she says, her heart was in the Pacific.

Eventually, she returned to Fiji. But her experiences abroad gave her an attitude "markedly different from others in Fiji."

You can say that again.

Before Ganilau took over the breakfast show, it was a sleepy women's programme focusing on polite topics deemed appropriate for "the ladies." Ganilau changed all that.

"We talk about everything," she says. "I have to talk to the young and old, the sentimental and the radical, the passive and the active. I do believe in getting angry about some issues — and if people want to be angry, that's fine."

Ganilau also opened up the floor for anyone — woman or man — who has an opinion to express.

"I don't believe there are just women's issues," she says. "They are issues that affect everyone and everyone should have a say."

All the talking generates more than just hot air. By bringing issues like rape and domestic violence out into the open, the programme has helped set the agenda for Fiji's women's movement.

Ganilau also invites guests from Fiji's Women's Ministry, the Women's Crises Centre, and the Legal Literacy Centre to discuss complex issues and brainstorm with the public.

"We can't just talk about problems," she says. "We have to analyse the situation and come up with solutions. It has to be a community effort and that's what talk-back radio is all about."

Radio is a popular medium in Fiji. Although literacy rates jumped from 61.6 per cent in 1980 to 87 percent in 1993, many Fijians still prefer broadcast over newspapers, especially on the outer Islands where the literacy rate is lower then the national average.

"Fiji has many problems," Ganilau says. "But if we get change on one issue - like opening up discussions on pap smears or even incest - then I will have done my job."

Julie Beun-Chown

nant topic in media coverage of the Women's Conference was certainly in aberration.

As journalists, my colleagues and I saw a real need to address these twin problems: media bias against China's hosting of the Conference, as well as drawing world attention to women's issues. We agreed that the best we could do was to bring out publications that addressed these problems, to disseminate information and to rectify unfair distortions of the Conference. At least we hoped we could succeed.

In March 1994 we started with a very small venture—a leaf-size, four page monthly called NGO Forum '95 — and we ended with a tabloid-size, eight-page daily newspaper for the duration of the Beijing Conference and the NGO Forum.

We decided to call the daily *World Women* not only in order to have an international appeal but also to reflect the essence of a world conference on women. We decided that the daily should be in colour as we believed that the meeting would be of many shades and hues. We also felt that we should begin publication prior to the NGO Forum and continue through the Conference and that since the gathering was of a parallel structure, space should be give to both the Conference and the Forum.

Our team of 38 (15 men, mostly photographers, and women reporting, editing and making up the pages) set up a newsroom on the third floor of the *China Daily* building and a small bureau office in Huairou as well. We took up the challenge with confidence but did not quite expect the event to be on a collision course with prejudice and provocation.

First, was the very negative projection of the NGO Forum by Western media. Then, it was the Tibetan issue. The publicity stunts by some Western women who controlled Tibetans-in-exile outraged not only our reporters but also Tibetans from Tibet. Tibetan women were denied the right to speak at the Western women-sponsored Forum sessions and the right to talk to their fellow Tibetans-in-exile. Every time they approached their sisters, some Western women would interfere and lead away those in exile.

One of our reporters asked one such Western "escort" if she had any real life experience in Tibet and advised her to listen and talk to those who lived in Tibet for 50 years or more.

The purpose of these people to exploit the power of the dramatic media image was apparent and it was not difficult to find TV cameras following close by.

Certainly, we covered the episode and voiced our opinion in *World Women*. Of course, it was a different view from that of the Western media. In the light of the Conference theme of 'Equality, Development and Peace', we advocated that we should first try to understand each other. If we were not prepared to talk, then predictably, a bare-knuckle showdown would follow but in the ultimate analysis, would women benefit from this?

The next point of conflict came with Mrs Hillary Clinton's speech at the Conference. She said: "It is indefensible that many women in NGOs who wished to participate in this Conference have not been able to attend, or have been prohibited from fully taking part...." *UPI* chose to interpret her statement in this manner: "Although 36,000 registered to attend the Forum, only 19,000 made it to Huairou, with women supporting independence for Tibet and greater international stature for Taiwan among those turned down."

The message that readers got from *UPI*'s report was that China turned down the remaining aspiring women participants. I do not know whether this was, indeed, what Mrs Clinton implied or whether it was *UPI*'s own comment. But I did learn from a US newspaper that a New York-based fund which wanted to send "the largest delegation of

American women" to the Conference, with a total target of 500 people, managed to send a delegation of only 200. As a result the Conference remained a dream for many grassroots women. If what the US paper said was true, then 300 women had been "turned down" because there was no funding. Women and women's cause evidently need financial support.

We heard so many stories at the Conference and the Forum of women struggling just to stay alive. Since many women were not able to make it to Beijing because of money, why did the wire service turn a blind eye to the fact? Instead of addressing the aid issue that many participants discussed at the Forum, the wire services turned Mrs Clinton's speech into a diplomatic issue at best; American domestic politics at worst. The more important Conference agenda was sidelined.

Many of my Chinese colleagues had the feeling that the Western media came to Beijing not so much to cover the Conference but, in fact, to look for conflicts between nations. Was much of their reportage shaded because the Conference and its theme did not appear to have any news value for these journalists, or was it because of the very conflict-oriented definition of news today?

These are only some of the questions we all need to ask ourselves.

We did cover Mrs Clinton's Huairou visits for *World Women* but we did not give space to her speech at the Conference. Allen H. Neuharth, founder of *USA Today*, asked us why, when he visited us during the Conference. I responded by asking, "Why didn't *CNN* or *USA Today* report Madam Chen Muhua's opening address? She is the chairperson not only of the Chinese delegation, but also of the Conference."

Of course, we also had our moments of success and jubilation. We finally did 19 issues of which three issues had 16 pages. We gave space to 112 countries and regions and over 1,000 people in our paper. We also came to the indisputable conclusion that if women wanted a change, they had to first change the media.

And to this end, I am glad to see that after the Conference, the Chinese media no longer portrays the Beijing Conference as a mere 'female talk fest'; it has been reported as a social discourse on gender and gender equality.

As Luo Xiaolu, a woman activist who coordinated media efforts under the Publicity and Mobilisation Committee of the China Organising Committee recently put it, "The Conference has definitely made a change".

SECTION
FIVE

Into the Millennium

SECTION FIVE

Into the Millenium

1
Introduction

Anita Anand

Despite what mainstream media in the North and South would have people believe about the Beijing Conference, the people who attended felt it was a great achievement.

We asked three women who have been key players in the women and development movement to share their views about what came out of Beijing, and where things would go from here.

Bella S. Abzug, a great woman, thinker, speaker and mobiliser of many causes, active in the world conferences on women, writes candidly (as only Bella can) about her experiences and insights.

Charlotte Bunch is a feminist thinker and writer who has given a major impetus to the women's human rights movement. She has tremendous insight into cross-cultural collective processes and has been able to take the issues of female sexual slavery and violence against women across national boundaries, in all regions.

Noeleen Heyzer is well known in academic and research circles for her writings on women and development. As the first Executive Director of UNIFEM from the South, she has worked hard to make the agency relevant to the notion of Beijing.

Abzug says that by the time the women's movement went to Beijing, they had a tremendous and unprecedented influence. It was the largest UN conference of the century. The agreements reached came out of a process of consensus of official representatives of 189 countries and 30,000 NGO representatives. When the press asked Abzug what it all meant she said, "It's a contract with the world's women. It is not legally binding, but it is politically binding and must be honoured."

A veteran of conferences, Abzug knew adopting policy statements in the UN may come easy, but implementing them is tough, especially when it involves money, resources, and participation of women in policy-making.

At the US national level since Beijing, says Abzug, the formation of the InterAgency Council on Women—an official mechanism through which agencies of the US government are asked to spell out how they are implementing the Beijing commitments—is a major achievement.

With the NGOs, a Contract With Women of the USA was formed, to develop national plans based on the Beijing Plan of Action. Other countries including Nigeria, Brazil and Costa Rica have developed contracts and campaigns, says Abzug, encouraged by WEDO and their national groups and networks.

Abzug describes the advocacy and lobbying that WEDO, the organisation she heads, undertook during Beijing and other UN conferences. WEDO sees the women's caucus methodology as a democratic political vehicle for consensus-building and open discussion, recognising different viewpoints, emphases and independent action, where they exist.

This process, says Abzug, started when she observed that the preparatory documents for the Earth Summit being planned for the Rio 1992 conference had only a random mention of women. In 1991, WEDO organised the First World Women's Conference for a Healthy Planet in Miami, Florida. 1,500 women from 83 countries attended, developed their Action Agenda 21, and lobbied to have it incorporated into the official conference agenda and document. This success led to the women's caucus continuing through all the conferences till and after Beijing.

For Abzug, the Beijing Conference and the follow-up work has been the "most significant and thrilling personal experience" she has had. Abzug has not done this alone, and gives credit to the world's women that have inspired her and been her allies.

From her personal and professional experiences Abzug feels that women will change the nature of power rather than power changing the nature of women. She says women don't want to be mainstreamed into a polluted stream; they want to change the stream, make it fresh, clean, and one that will flow in new directions. For Abzug, the 21st century will be the century of women.

Charlotte Bunch writes that women did not expect a lot of concrete action at Beijing—certainly not those that knew something about UN conferences! She also points out that if and when governments affirm the rights of women, then getting this in action is another organising job (spoken like an organiser!)

Bunch feels that it is crucial for governments to come together periodically to share what they doing and for the women's movement to engage with them. For the NGOs, the fact that it was a UN event mobilised women to gather to share strategies and see that the movement is alive. This too, says Bunch, should happen at least every ten years, because a new generation of women needs an opportunity to have that kind of experience.

Being the largest conference in history, Beijing had to have an impact. Earlier, the crowds the Earth Summit drew gave the impression that people really cared about the environment. But the numbers in Beijing showed that women are just as major a concern in the world.

Bunch highlights the economy, women's health and political participation as being a focus of attention in the near future. 1998 will be the 50th anniversary of the World Declaration of Human Rights and the fifth anniversary of the World Conference on Human Rights. It will be a good time to raise the issues of the human rights of women and an opportunity—says Bunch—to focus on the positive measures taken that will lead to the enjoyment of women's human rights.

Noeleen Heyzer situates her analysis of Beijing within the context of the marketplace, the changes in the economy, globalisation, the end of the Cold War—and how these developments related to the issues that would take women and men into the 21st century.

For Heyzer, a major realisation of this period was that this discussion could not be had without a gender perspective, as processes affect women and men differently. In terms of size and agenda it showed clearly that the issues were not only of Western feminists, as it was said all along. It was an international concern.

Heyzer points out that of major significance was the level of mobilisation that took place at the country and village level in preparation for Beijing. She sees the commitment to addressing the feminisation of poverty, the revitalisation of CEDAW and action for the implementation of the Plan of Action, as major achievements.

She further elaborates the goals of UNIFEM—women's economic capacity, engendering governance and leadership, peace building and conflict resolution, and women's human rights and CEDAW.

All three women—Bella Abzug, Charlotte Bunch and Noeleen Heyzer—are actively working in institutions that have been at the negotiating table, both in and out of the UN. Their skills are multiple and their analyses far reaching.

They are women who have come from and shaped the women's movement, and made a major contribution to bridging the gap between women's organisations, networks, women's movements and development concerns, between women in the North and South, and women in and outside the establishment.

Post Beijing many learnings have taken place. As all three of them say, the time has come to convert language adopted to action. And this means ensuring that governments that have signed on the dotted line carry out their promise, and take the Plan of Action seriously. The NGO and women's movements must engage with their governments to ensure this happens.

2
A Contract With the World's Women
Bella S. Abzug

They used to give us a day—it was called International Women's Day. Then in 1975, the UN declared it to be International Women's Year. That year they gave us a year. Then the UN declared 1975-1985 to be the Decade of Women. I said at the time: "Who knows, if we behave they may let us into the whole thing!"

But we haven't behaved, and that's why we're making progress.

In the past 25 years, the women's movement has expanded enormously, reaching many places where it hasn't been before. It has become a truly global movement, with arms that reach out to women everywhere, legs that carry us to the places where decisions are made and brains that provide a new world vision for women and men, girls and boys.

The movement grew exponentially during the Decade of Women—three international women's conferences—first in 1975 in Mexico City, in Copenhagen in 1980, and in Nairobi in 1985. These conferences revealed to us the potential of the international women's movement in maximising advocacy efforts worldwide to empower women and create constituencies that would overcome the male-dominated United Nations and the governments women seek to influence.

Since that decade, in which networks and international contacts multiplied, women have been working together on key issues that affect women worldwide—the issues of economic survival, the global economy, empowerment, poverty, affordable health care, human rights, workplace rights, educational equity, reproductive and sexual rights, struggles against violence, protecting a healthy environment, and an end to wars and militarism. Our efforts continued through subsequent UN conferences in Rio de Janeiro, Vienna, Cairo, Small Islands, Copenhagen and Habitat II.

In September 1995, we came to the UN's Fourth World Conference on Women in Beijing and the NGO Forum in Huairou, steeped in the issues we had been working on for so many years. We had a tremendous and unprecedented amount of influence. It was the largest UN conference the world has ever seen. The agreements developed there came about through a consensus of official representatives from 189 countries and some 30,000 non-government individuals, mostly women. When the press came to me afterwards and asked what it all meant, I told them, "It's a contract—a contract with the world's women. It is not legally binding but it is politically binding and it must be honoured."

The specific recommendations in the Platform for Action adopted at the Beijing Conference constitute the strongest consensus statement on women's equality, empowerment and justice ever produced by the world's governments. In addition, we labeled this a "conference of commitments". Having been through many conferences and many agendas, I knew that we may get the words, but not necessarily the follow-up music. A lot of policy statements are adopted at the UN, but implementing them is a very tough thing to do, especially if they involve money, resources and participation of women in policy-making. So we wanted governments to agree in advance to make Beijing a conference of commitments. And we were very successful.

In the US alone, significant commitments have been made. The President set up an InterAgency Council on Women, an official mechanism through which agencies of the US government are asked to spell out how they are carrying out some eight to ten commitments. The Council's plans included holding a nationwide teleconference (via satellite) linked to some 450 women's meetings, large and small, across the country on September 28, 1996. The InterAgency Council reported on its post-Beijing activities to implement the Platform for Action and is at present soliciting inputs from women on what they want included in a strengthened and official National Action Agenda.

Something I personally fought for very hard was that national governments should develop their own national plans of action based on the Beijing Platform for Action, and that they do this in consultation with NGOs by the end of 1996. As a follow-up, WEDO, the international network that I co-founded with women activists from every region, developed a Contract With Women of the USA, patterned on the Beijing Platform but adapted to US needs. Women in other countries, including Nigeria, Costa Rica and Brazil, have also developed contracts and campaigns.

The Contract With Women of the USA has already been endorsed by about 600 national and community-based organisations, representing millions of women, as well as by members of the US Senate and House of Representatives. We are collaborating with the Center for Women Policy Studies in Washington, D.C., as they urge state legislators to enter into contracts with their constituents. More than 300 legislators from all 50 states have signed on to the contract. Making everyone more concerned with issues that their own government endorsed is vital to raising the status of women and girls. Many other governments have taken similar actions. WEDO's one-year progress report* on implementation of the Beijing Platform documents some of the many actions taken by governments to live up to their promises.

The Beijing Conference was so effective because women had direct input into the Platform in a much more meaningful way than in the past. And that is largely because WEDO developed a methodology to organise women's caucuses to advocate for change throughout the UN conference process. It was based largely on my experience as a member of the US Congress for six years, during which we were able to transform the language and substance of proposed laws by offering specific amended language and mobilising constituencies to advocate progressive policies and programmes.

At WEDO, we envision the women's caucus methodology as a democratic political vehicle for consensus-building and open discussion, recognising different viewpoints, emphases and independent actions where they exist. It encourages the broadest possible participation by grassroots women and the many new women's networks that have been organised since the 1985 women's conference in Nairobi. It provides NGOs participating in UN conference preparatory committees and regional meetings with a daily meeting place at which they can exchange information, jointly analyse and discuss the official documents, define areas of agreement and disagreement on issues, strategies and tactics, and then go out to lobby their government representatives. Its overall goal is to strengthen and broaden women's advocacy roles in helping to ensure that the official UN conference documents positively reflect the scope and diversity of the needs, perspectives and recommendations of women from every region of the world.

The women's caucus is open to all NGOs as well as to UN delegates who may wish to participate. The chairperson position is rotated to assure that all regions are included in leadership roles. The agenda, which usually includes briefings, updates, discussion of strategies and substantive issues, is responsive to the participants' special concerns. Any caucus statements or actions are taken by consensus, without in any way limiting the rights of participants to take independent actions.

This process began when I first read documents concerning the Rio Earth Summit. I noticed there were only a few random mentions of women and knew that we had a real problem. So WEDO organised the First World Women's Conference for a Healthy Planet in Miami, Florida, in November 1991. It drew 1,500 women from 83 countries, and we developed our own Women's Action Agenda 21. We used this agenda to do line-by-line analyses of the draft of the official UN government document for the Rio Earth Summit and amended it to include greater emphasis on women and issues women care about. We lobbied official UN delegates at the four official preparatory meetings before Rio. By the time of the UN conference, we had won 120 provisions affecting women, plus a whole chapter on women.

The women's caucus and advocacy methodology was not only successful at the 1991-92 UNCED process but was the key to getting literally hundreds of women's recommendations incorporated into the official UN Conference on Environment and Development (UNCED). Agenda 21 was approved at the Rio Earth Summit. It proved to be so effective and popular that we followed up by organising caucuses at the Commission on Sustainable Development meetings and other international conferences, including preparatory meetings for the 1994 International Conference on Population and Development (ICPD), the 1995 Social Summit, Small Islands Developing States Conference, the 1995 Fourth World Conference on Women and, most recently, the Habitat II conference.

We created a sense of movement and advocacy for change. At each international conference, major women's caucuses were held, sometimes involving several thousand people. We work on the document; we set up task forces; and we lobby the governments and the secretariat to support our amendments. This has proved to be an especially effective means of policy intervention.

The Beijing Conference and the follow-up work we have been doing is one of the most significant and thrilling personal experiences that I have ever had. I have received tremendous strength and inspiration from working with women from developing countries—women who despite overwhelming odds are having victories in their fight to overcome discrimination and win decent lives for themselves and their families.

There are many inspiring stories of the ways in which women have "brought Beijing home". One of the women in our network from Cameroon developed a major campaign called "Mothers for Mayor". This led to the doubling of the number of women elected to local public office from 400 to 800 as a result of being inspired by the power, strength and collective wisdom of women at the Beijing Conference and the NGO Forum. In Brazil, one of our steering committee members, Thais Corral, was instrumental in getting the government to sign protocols in six cities committing them to implement the Beijing recommendations, including more women in government. Her mother, Alba Corral, campaigned for and won a seat in the city council in her home town of Macae in northern Rio de Janeiro state in the 1996 elections.

In Kenya, another WEDO steering committee member, the great Wangari Maathai, founder of the Green Belt Movement, has facilitated monthly forums on issues of environmental awareness, government corruption, erosion of cultural values and the political and economic implications of actions by multinational corporations. She is conducting a major struggle for democracy under an oppressive government and she does this at great risk to her personal safety. She has been jailed several times and viciously beaten by the police but she refuses to be intimidated. She is one of the most courageous and principled women I know.

Much of this courage and dedication comes from knowing that women are not alone in fighting any of these battles in their countries and communities. Networking with women everywhere is one of WEDO's greatest strengths. As a global activist, advocacy and information organisation based in New York near UN headquarters, it connects with over 20,000 groups and individuals around the world. In many ways, WEDO is a network of other networks and national organisations. It has also steadily developed strong collaborative relationships with many significant international networks and organisations as well as regional groups.

For example, WEDO works with and is part of the Vrajbhumi network of women environmental organisations in Latin America and the Caribbean which was started in July 1994, with the Brazilian Network for the Defense of Humankind (REDEH) and with (CEDEA). WEDO also organised an environment and development collaborative "web" for Beijing comprising 100 NGOs and networks around the world. WEDO now aims to build an effective monitoring and advocacy network to be watchdogs for Beijing and all six "engendered" UN conference agendas.

WEDO collaborates with many other networks, including Parliamentarians for Global Action, Development Alternatives for Women in a New Era (DAWN), Alternatives- Women in Development (Alt-WID), Network Women in Development Europe (WIDE), Global Alliance for Economic Alternatives, International Association of Feminist Economists, Third World Network, International Women's Tribune Center, ISIS, Women Living Under Muslim Laws, Sisterhood is Global, Social Watch, Earth Summit Watch, International Women's Rights Action Watch (IWRAW), Women's Eyes on the World Bank Campaign and 50 Years is Enough, National Coalition for Health and Environmental Justice, The Center for Education, Development and Population Activities (CEDPA), International Women's Health Coalition and the Center for Global Women's Leadership, the Center for Women Policy Studies and Interaction.

When women come together and see the accomplishments of others they gain further strength. While we look for security in our lives and countries, security starts from within. We each have our own inner strength and commitments. When we bring this to international conferences, whether in Beijing or Cairo, and see how women are using their own special strengths to change the world, it creates a tremendous sense of self-empowerment.

Women have been participating by the thousands in post- Beijing meetings all over the world, strategising how to concretise and implement programmes from the Platform for Action. I believe there will be increased and wider participation of women as we move into the 21st century. We are going to see a more dramatic representation of women in the parliaments of the world, which now have a shameful average of 11 per cent representation of women (though there are some inspiring exceptions in the Scandinavian countries and more recently in South Africa). I foresee an enormous step forward—women in leadership in all sectors in more countries—economic, political and governmental. As a result of some proposals that came out of Beijing, women are also more likely to be at peace negotiating tables.

Women succeeded in maintaining their gains from previous conferences at Habitat II, the last conference of the series. Habitat II also brought together new players such as builders, architects and housing ministers, many of whom didn't have an international background, which meant that many of the issues had to be rethought. There was also a serious organisation of the right wing at this conference, led by some Arab states and Vatican representatives, who looked on this conference—the last in a series—as their last chance to reverse positive results from prior conferences.

But women stood firm. The Super Coalition, which consisted of the Women's Caucus run by WEDO, GROOTS, Habitat International Coalition/Women in Shelter Network and the International Council of Women, demanded that such issues as reproductive rights, sexual rights, family planning, definition of family and environmental issues already agreed upon in previous conferences, be reaffirmed. And we succeeded.

Looking back on this series of UN conferences, I see many positive gains and some trade-offs. A clear gain is that the global women's movement has grown and has come to play a robust and visible role in influencing policy and actions, internationally and nationally, though UN international conferences and monitoring the implementation of the results of these conferences. More important, the conferences have politically strengthened the women's movement while reinforcing its diversity, dynamism and futuristic outlook. Bringing new challenges, ideas and visions to diplomatic interchange has made a significant difference to the process of policy-making at the UN as well as to the policies themselves. The conferences have also had the additional impact of bringing pressure on individual governments, as well as on NGO constituencies.

As for trade-offs, we have had to make the intellectual leap from being not only protesters but partners, which can be a risky move for NGOs who have gained their strength and credibility from maintaining a critical and usually adversarial distance from policy-makers. But I don't think that as women's activists we have compromised our independence as we seek to influence policy-making from the inside. We continue to challenge as we engage and we have achieved respect for our expertise, experience and ability. Even where NGOs have become official participants in their national delegations, earlier fears of co-optation have not significantly materialised. On the contrary, the presence of so many NGO representatives in delegations has had many positive results in bringing education, information and a political voice with which to pressure these delegations.

I think women will change the nature of power rather than power changing the nature of women. Women don't want to be mainstreamed into a polluted stream; we want to change the stream—we want to make it fresh; we want to make it clean; we want to make it flow in new directions. Women are not committed to the policies and mistakes of the past because those in power didn't let us craft them. In all cultures, women were raised differently and are more likely to resolve conflict through peaceful means.

I think women have a much greater sense of independence. Most of us don't represent multinational corporations and other big special-interest groups. If you analyse the pasts of most women who run for office, you find they usually came into politics because they were moved by an issue. For example, in the United States, Democratic and Republican women vote together a lot more than Democratic and Republican men. US polls show, for instance, that even women who are themselves not affected by economic discrimination still object to efforts being made to sacrifice poor women, children and elderly people to decrease the taxes of the rich. I believe women will not accept these policies as their own, but will seek to change them.

In fact, the recent re-election of President Clinton was based on the "gender gap", the winning margin of support provided by women voters. In significantly large numbers, more women than men voted for Bill Clinton, the Democratic candidate, over Robert Dole, the Republican candidate, believing that Clinton represented the hope of more compassionate government. Media surveys of voters after they had voted showed that women supported President Clinton over Dole by 54 per cent to 38 per cent, and backed Democrats over Republicans in House contests by 59 per cent to 41 per cent.

Women cross boundaries on many important issues, like war and peace, economic justice, social development, the environment and consumption, human rights, health and reproductive rights. I have always said the 21st century should be the women's century. But we will be different. We will work together with men and I hope we will prove to them that economic exploitation, violence, greed and war are the wrong recipe for a secure and healthy planet.

(*Beyond Promises: Governments in Motion One Year After the Beijing Women's Conference*, a follow-up report published by WEDO in September 1996, can be ordered by making a $5 check or money order payable to WEDO, 355 Lexington Avenue, New York, NY 10017, USA.)

3
What We Know We Have To Do

Charlotte Bunch

Different women expected different things from the Fourth World Conference on Women in Beijing. In general, most women who went to the conference were just hoping that it would affirm in some broad and general sense women's rights—or women's human rights—and counter a lot of the backlash against women that's going on in the world today, as well as the various forms of fundamentalism that are threatening to women. Most women did not expect a lot of concrete action—certainly not women who know anything about the UN and world conferences. But most of us did expect a reaffirmation of the rights of women from which we could then organise and say: 'Look, the world community believes this, the governments and the UN affirmed this as a counter to some of the attitude that women shouldn't have these rights.' That is what women could realistically expect from the conference.

Perhaps some women did not have realistic expectations and since they did not really know what it was all about they thought governments meant everything that they said. My view is that you get the governments to say they affirm these principles and make some commitments, and then if you want them to do anything that's another organising job that comes later. But at least you have a document to say they should do these things.

The conference realised most of our expectations rather well. The Beijing Platform is in general a pretty good document. It has a lot of limitations, but it does reaffirm the human rights of women and it does so in a fairly broad spectrum of areas — from the right to education, to economic rights to freedom from violence, health rights, etc. The weakest part, probably, is the economic section, because that's what governments are most unwilling to react on since it involves the question of the global economy, which many governments realise they do not have control over (or if they do, the do not want to exercise it). But even in the area of the economy or issues of poverty, governments certainly reaffirmed the principle that they should in some way be engaged in dealing with poverty—a principle that is especially important at a time when right wing forces are saying the market can regulate everything and privatisation can take care of everything.

In a broad sense, the most significant factor from the Conference was that so many people came, in spite of all the obstacles on the path to getting there. So many people cared about these issues. In that sense, there was a strong statement that women and their role in society is a very central and vibrant question in the world today. In the course of the Conference it was evident through the NGO Forum that there was a strong affirmation that women's organising is alive, vibrant and ongoing, and that women are a force to contend with, even if we are not as powerful as we would like.

In the conference document, the section on violence against women is very good and very strong. We have a huge amount of work to do to get that implemented, but if it were taken seriously as a platform for work on violence it's excellent. The sections on education and the girl child too are good in terms of what women and girls need and their rights. The issue of education has been on the agenda from the beginning but this is the first time a conference actually phrased issues of education in human rights language.

The issue of violence too came up in the Nairobi Conference, but not nearly as strongly as in Beijing. It makes it a stronger statement (in human rights language) and lifts it from something that ought to be to something that governments have an obligation to do. In some cases it means there's the theoretical possibility of women taking legal action towards the realisation of some of these things because they are enshrined in various international human rights documents. In the case of social and economic rights, that is fairly complicated to do. But at least it provides a strong sense of obligation for governments in these areas.

Having said this, I'd like to add that it is crucial for governments to come together at periodic points and say something about what they are doing in these. This would force them to have to think about the issues and even if they do not do as much as we want, it gives us an opportunity to engage with them about what their obligations are.

The Beijing Conference has provided a point of reference. Although the event seemed so exhausting that many of us felt 'Oh my god, never again!' some people, including myself, have already begun to feel that we do need to think about putting consistent pressure and that there will be another conference in the future to keep that momentum going.

On the non-governmental side, it was one of those rare moments when the fact that it was a UN event, enabled women to get together resources to gather internationally and get the impetus of meeting with each other, sharing strategies and seeing that the movement is alive. That too should happen at least every ten years because a new generation of women needs to experience that every time it happens. Some of us were in Nairobi, some in Copenhagen, some even in Mexico City, but each generation needs an opportunity to have that kind of experience.

In spite of all the problems that arose out of the conference being in China, that the fact it was in China put it on the radar screen. Even though at the time we fought all the time with the Western media that it was about women and not about China, because they were so focused on China at least in the beginning, at least they went there, and once there at least some of them got interested in the issues as well. Obviously some women reporters were interested all along but I think it would have been harder to get media attention if the conference had been somewhere else. Does that make it worth the hassles we had? No, but it was at least a positive byproduct of being in China.

Secondly, was the size. This was the largest world conference in history. That had to have an impact. Just the number of people interested and the amount of grassroots response evoked, countered at least to some degree the feeling that these issues were passe and no one cared anymore. People thought the Rio Earth Summit was mammoth. But this was even bigger. There's a perception that the environmental movement is a major global concern in the world, but Beijing showed that the issue of women is just as major a concern in the world.

I am always reluctant to prioritise what are the most important issues and say that certain issues need more focus. I think every woman and man works on the issues that come to them in their life as the ones they care about the most. However, there are certain issues on which it is harder to get action on and one of them, I feel is to get progress on the issues of the economy — the economic situation of women both in terms of discrimination between men and women, but also in terms of women and men who are in poverty. So it is not exclusive to women. It is probably the toughest issue to get action on and it's certainly the area in which a lot of thought and work needs to be done on what can we do.

Equally important are issues of women's health, of women's sexuality, and violence against women. Often the movement you get around such issues about which women feel intimately and immediately, provides an impetus for getting them into the policy arena — which is probably necessary for any action or change on the economic issues.

Therefore, when I say the economic issues are the toughest, it does not mean I think everyone should stop working on other things. It means that we need to think through why it is so hard, and how we can approach it more efficiently in order to get somewhere.

The third issue is of political participation and of ensuring that women get a voice in what happens in all of the above, since they are all clearly interconnected. If you get women into politics then they can begin to address the policy questions in the other areas. So the priority would seem to be to continue to follow-up on all of these questions; all the areas of the Platform for Action. Our goals etched out in the Platform are so far away from where life is today that we need a lot of thinking, when we talk about implementation and national plans of action.

In 1998, when the Commission on the Status of Women will be reviewing the sections of the Platform that deal with the human rights of women, it will be the fifth anniversary of the Human Rights Conference in Vienna and the 50th anniversary of the World Declaration on Human Rights. Next year, therefore, will be another occasion to focus once more on women's human rights. Not only will we focus on the violations of human rights, but also on the positive measures taken that will lead to the enjoyment of women's human rights.

We can record positive things that have happened and show by example what governments could be doing if women's human rights were to become a reality. We need to find all kinds of strategies that make this concrete for people; we need to know about things that we can achieve at the state or local level anywhere. Ultimately, we need to realise that this is not just a wonderful abstraction, and feel that wouldn't it be nice if the world was like that—we need to know that we can actually do something to move in the direction of achieving all the issues of the Beijing Platform for Action.

(As told to Gretchen Sidhu)

4
Seizing the Opportunity
Noeleen Heyzer

The Fourth World Conference on Women was one part of a continuum of UN conferences that emerged in the 1990s — a series that brought focus on social priorities. This series occurred at the end of the Cold War; it happened also at the time when there was re-focusing and re-emphasis on going to the market as a way of developing the economy. People began talking about economic globalisation, structural adjustment programmes, trade agendas and so on. But with this kind of focus on the economy it was necessary to draw attention to issues such as what kind of economic growth and what kind of development we needed, keeping in mind some of the critical issues that will face humankind as we go into the 21st century.

These issues were identified in that continuum of conferences, beginning from the environment, to human rights, to issues of poverty, social integration, employment, the issue on the advancement of women, habitat and so on. What emerged out of most of these conferences was a recognition that you cannot talk about social priorities and sustainable human development without addressing the life chances of half the population—that is, women. Also, that it was really necessary to develop a gender perspective on all these issues because these processes affect men and women differently. Therefore, what came into focus was the whole issue of mainstreaming gender perspective in development so that the goal of gender equality would become a desired goal.

In terms of the sheer size of the Beijing Conference, it was a show of strength. It showed that there are people who take the issues seriously. It also showed that concern for the issues being debated had spread—that it was not a few Western feminists pushing their own agenda, as it was believed at one stage. In fact, it was not an agenda of Western society; it was an international concern.

Women wanted to be recognised as a global force for change. Not just for themselves, but also in terms of a kind of development which they want and which will benefit humankind. And it wasn't just women either. If you attended the plenary of the UN conference you found at least 40 percent men involved in it. So the whole issue of gender equality was brought to the fore.

In this manner too, Beijing was different from the other women's conferences. This is why in Beijing one of the things that really emerged clearly was that gender equality and the responsibility for achieving it does not belong to only women. Although women have been the ones pushing it, it is extremely important to have more men concerned with the kind of development that they bring about, from a gender perspective. It was evident that there were sufficient men who came on board—and that visibility was important, because they were very senior men.

Three World Conferences had taken place before this one but in many ways, this one was taken more seriously than any of the earlier ones. Therefore, preparations too were more serious. Basically, people wanted more commitment and there were many women who were very concerned with making it a process whereby these issues could be put onto the agenda of development.

They also wanted to make sure that in the preparatory processes, more people were involved—not only those in the women's movement. It was an opportunity to build partnerships and to forge common grounds. It was also an opportunity to rethink development. In fact, for many people it was not just a World Conference on Women but it was the first time that women really built a World Conference on 'development'. It was truly a women's conference on the shape of the world and what needed to be done to make it better.

One of the most significant things about this Conference was that during the preparatory stages, mechanisms were put in place at village and national levels. Earlier conferences did not reach that kind of mobilisation, and their action plans were more consultative. This time around, more people were involved in the preparation. If you think about the 50,000 who went to Beijing you could almost triple that number for the preparatory process. What was being generated was political will, visibility of issues, commitment, mechanisms and processes. People hoped that there would be resources — additional resources — in financial terms. However, that never quite happened. So there were achievements and there were also some disappointments.

But the achievements were significant. It is worth focusing on the kind of commitments that came out of Beijing and the fact that it was a time of reflection on what had been achieved (in terms of a closing of the gender gap over the last 20 years, in education, basic needs and so on). Among the number of major commitments that emerged from the Beijing Conference was the one to close the remaining gender gaps in various areas of development.

Another commitment was to address the feminisation of poverty, especially now when the possibilities of new forms of poverty can emerge side by side with new wealth. The third area of commitment was around eliminating all forms of violence against women. One of the most vital achievements was that the systematic rape of women in war-torn countries be seen as a war crime.

The revitalisation of the women's Convention was a fourth commitment. For the last two decades, CEDAW was not very well known. Now the legal framework within which some of this work needs to take place at the country level can be routed in the Convention. What was of major concern here was that the reservations that governments have in ratifying the Convention be removed. Women were extremely concerned with these reservations. Therefore, the work around the removal of reservations and the optional protocol is an important one.

Yet another commitment was that of action—of ensuring that implementation is constantly being talked about. The focus is now on commitment to action and therefore, thinking of the kind of mechanisms and resources that need to be put in place to make that shift to action.

As Director, UNIFEM, I have personally focused UNIFEM on three areas of work, because we cannot concentrate on everything and we do want to bring about significant results and impact. Of our three areas, one talks about the building of women's economic capacity, especially in the context of the new trade agenda and the global economy. This is very closely tied to the question of how to eradicate feminised poverty. We have taken the stand that it is not complicated — that basically, the global economy is with us. It creates winners and losers and we need to look for opportunities in which women producers can benefit from new, emerging markets. For this, we need to look at the kind of barriers that prevent women from participating. We need to look at how women can come together — how community producers, for instance, can come together—to become a transnational force.

One example at UNIFEM is the shea butter producers. We were able to identify that in Europe a new market was emerging for shea butter nuts because cocoa butter was being substituted with shea butter. So with that information, and because we were also working with shea butter nut collectors in West Africa, we mediated and intervened so the local shea butter nut collectors formed a transnational network to supply the new, emerging markets in the bulk that was required.

However, we also simultaneously trained the women in managing this network as a business, so that by the time the multinationals came in to use piece rate workers, they would have to first negotiate with these women as producers and as an established business. The village women grabbed the opportunity, improved their income and benefitted from this new opening.

The second area of work is in engendering of governance and leadership. Here we are looking at two areas. The first deals with the market; the second deals with the state. But states differ. There are those states that are relatively strong with stable state mechanisms, in which case the work is to identify the priorities that government has from the Beijing Platform and to convert those priorities into policies and programmes, and into their national budgets as well. This can work when you have a stable government and an active civil society.

At the other end of the spectrum are the breakdown states, as in many of the war-torn countries. We can't play the same role here in creating gender sensitive policies. But what we can do is to get involved with peace-building and conflict-resolution. So through the issue of governance, we get women involved in this peace-building and conflict-resolution; in shifting out of crisis into a development mode. In many of the transitional situations this actually means developing leadership to rebuild civil societies and civil institutions. And we have to get women more involved in this. Many of the states have shifted from a military situation—or a breakdown situation—into a relatively stable state, but most of the institutions have broken down. That's where the governance and the leadership part comes in.

We have also trained new parliamentarians to read budgets so that they can tell when there is a commitment to the Beijing Platform. We also train people to do gender impact analyses and to build community leadership. We train people to run for election, but also to have commitment from male and female politicians to the Beijing agenda. The whole exercise is not merely to put women in positions of power but to make sure there is a commitment to a particular agenda.

And our third area of work is on women's human rights and CEDAW.

In general, we need to activate our civil society as well, to make sure there is accountability and to bring in the private sector, which so far has been totally left out of this kind of process. There is a huge question mark about what kind of private sector. What we want is to hold market and state accountable; to have an ethics of doing business, to have social accountability. We can see how our private sector has benefitted from all these social investments. We are just starting to move in that direction. I think there is interest because of the consumer power of women and increasingly people will support this, even for their own self interest because there are many movements that are interested in having businesses that are ecologically and socially sound. And let us not forget that increasingly, the power of the consumer will make these businesses more profitable than others.

Our goal over the next few years, therefore, is to not lose enthusiasm. It is far too easy to merely go from one conference to another. I think the UN system too is committing itself to conference follow-up and all of us need to make sure that this actually happens.

[As told to Gretchen Sidhu]

5 Authors' Profile

Anita Anand is Director, Women's Feature Service, New Delhi, India. She started her career as a volunteer in rural development 28 years ago. She has worked in public policy issues in Washington DC, and over a time became more involved in media's role in development coverage, and eventually her involvement with the Women's Feature Service.

Anita has written numerous articles on development topics for books, magazines, journals and mainstream media in the North and South. She has extensive experience with media and development—print, television, film, video, radio and non-formal methods of communication.

In WFS Anita has raised funds and directed WFS projects worth $3.5 million on gender, population, and sustainable development. This included journalists workshops, media awareness campaigns, coverage in print and electronic media, advocacy and lobbying.

Anne S. Walker, Executive Director, International Women's Tribune Centre (IWTC) is an Australian feminist activist, educationist, artist and writer.

Anne lived and worked in Fiji from 1962 to 1972, working with a local group of women to start the programmes of the Fiji YWCA. In 1976, she came to New York to support a fledgling women's project (later known as IWTC) that had developed out of the IWY meetings in Mexico City 1975. Working collaboratively with women worldwide, IWTC now undertakes a programme of technical assistance and training, collaborative projects, skill-sharing, and the collecting, producing and disseminating of information on a wide range of women and development issues.

Asha Ramesh is an activist and was part of the support team of the Coordination Unit (CU) which facilitated Indian grassroots women's participation in the Fourth World Conference in Beijing in 1995.

At present, Asha is working on Women in Panchayati Raj.

Ramesh helped organise two important conferences - The Conference of Commitment, which was a major Pre-Bejing interface between Government delegates/Ministry of Human Resource Development & grassroots groups proceeding to Beijing. The other was the National Federation of Dalit Women Conference.

Bella S. Abzug one of the twentieth century's best known and respected public figures, died while this book was in process. Turned down by Harvard Law School, which did not then admit women, she graduated from Columbia Law School in the US.

In 1970 at the age of 50, Bella ran for US Congress with the now famous slogan: "This woman's place is in the House - House of Representatives". She went on to win the general election and the national spotlight.

One of only nine women in the then 435

member House of Representatives, Bella was the first woman to run for (and win) on a women's rights and peace platform. She championed the Equal Rights Amendment, wrote the first law banning discrimination against women seeking credit, introduced legislation calling for comprehensive childcare, Social Security for home makers, and abortion rights.

For the UN Decade of Women, Bella was Congressional adviser to the US delegation at the 1975 UN conference in Mexico City; a leading observer and speaker at the UN women's conference in Copenhagen; and a key NGO leader at the women's conference in Nairobi.

At Beijing, Bella led the Women's Linkage Caucus at the Conference. She was the recipient of the first Bradford Morse Award for Women in Development and numerous other honors which include the Association of Women in Development award for service to the field of women in development, the U.S. Committee for UNIFEM's 1996 Award of Excellence.

Bernadette Rounds Ganilau is a Fiji based radio journalist who specialises in gender and development issues. She has been associated with various media organisation, has been an activist, author and organiser in the women's and civil rights movements.

Cecilia Young Dong-ling has been active in the women's movement in Hong Kong for ever 15 years. Among other things, she was Chair of the Hong Kong Council of women and a Founding Member of AWARE, Hong Kong and the Hong Kong Federation of Women. Her interest include local government policies and actions on women and the empowerment of women.

Charlotte Bunch, Founder and Executive Director of the Center for Women's Global Leadership at Douglas College, Rutgers, the State University of New Jersey, has been an activist, author and organiser in the women's and civil rights movements for three decades. Before her work at the Global Center, Bunch was Founding Director of the Public Resource Center, a tenured fellow at the Institute for Policy Studies,and a founder of D.C. Women's Liberation and Quest: *A Feminist Quarterly.*

Darunee Tantiramanond is a Thai activist and feminist who is based at the Asian Institute of Technology (ATI) in Bangkok, Thailand.

Fatima Sbaity-Kassem is Chief of the Women and Development Unit at ESCWA since 1993, and the regional coordinator and focal point in the UN on women's issues and gender equality in ESCWA countries. She was responsible for preparations at the regional level for the 1995 Beijing Conference.

She joined the UN in 1970 where she served in Beirut, Amman, and Baghdad, working as an economist and publishing in international trade and regional cooperation until 1990.

Georgina Ashworth is a writer who likes to see what she writes about come into effect, and thus has been a vigorous feminist advocate in the international arena, especially making space for others. Her most recent text is *Equal Rule? Women, Men, Democracy and Governance.*

Georgina formed CHANGE in 1979 to publish country reports written by women from their own country. CHANGE has gone on to lead the movement for women's human rights and to pioneer " gender mainstreaming" in international debt and trade, as well as national economies.

Her latest books are *Passionate Politics: Feminist Theory in Action and Demanding Accountability; The Global Campaign; and Vienna Tribunal for Women's Human Rights.*

Gouri Salvi is a freelance journalist with a special interest in gender and development issues. She has worked for over 20 years with various magazines in India and as an editor with the Women's Feature Service in New Delhi. She has recently compiled and edited a book on the Indian Cooperative Union.

Haifa Abu Ghazaleh was one of the Coordinators of the NGO Forum from West Asia.

Helvi Sipila was president of the National Association of Women Lawyers 1954-56 and of the International Federation of women Lawyers. In 1972 she was appointed Assistant Secretary-General of the United Nations. Sipila has been Finland's member on the UN Commission on the Status of Women, 1960-67 and Secretary General for the First UN World Conference on the Advancement of women, 1975. In 1981, Sipila founded UNIFEM, Finland and chaired it 1981-87.

Huang Qing is Deputy Editor of *China Daily*. During the Beijing conference, she was editor of the daily *WORLD WOMEN* published in English and Chinese.

John R. Mathiason was a member of the United Nations Secretariat for over twenty-five years. During the last ten of these he served as Deputy Director of the Division for the Advancement of Women, where he was responsible for managing substantive preparations for the Beijing Conference and support to the negotiation process. He is currently an Adjunct Professor of Public Administration at the Wagner Graduate School of Public Service of New York University, teaching international public management.

Lauren Danner is a doctoral candidate at the University of Oregon School of Journalism and Communication. Her dissertation research investigates how media reflect changing public perceptions of the environment in the Pacific Northwest. Her research on Norway's national image was recently published in *Global Spotlights in Lillehammer: How the World Viewed Norway During the 1994 Winter Olympics.*

Mallica Vajrathon, is Managing Editor of *Women of Asia Magazine* and a Thai political and social scientist. She has worked for the UN for the last 32 years in many parts of the world. Her international assignment included the preparation of all four United Nations World Conferences on Women - Mexico in 1976, Copenhagen in 1980, Nairobi in 1985, and Beijing in 1995.

As Principle Adviser of the Secretary General of the FWCW in Beijing in 1995, she was actively involved with the two years of preparation for the regional conferences in Indonesia, Austria, Jordan, Argentina & Senegal.

As senior United Nations officer of the Conference Secretariat she participated in all discussions leading up to the drafting of the regional and the world Platform for Action adopted at all regional conferences and at the end of the World Conference in Beijing in September 1995.

Mallika Dutt, formerly Associate Director of the Center for Women's Global Leadership, has been a lawyer-activist in the women's movement for over a decade. She is a founding member of Sakhi for South Asian Women in New York City, and has served on the Boards of several foundations, women's groups and human rights organisations. Mallika is currently Programme Officer for Rights and Social Justice at the Ford Foundation in India.

Manjula Padmanabhan: Manjula Padmanabhan, responsible for the graphics for "Beijing" is a Delhi based writer. Multi-talented, Padmanabhan is a writer, cartoonist, illustrator, designer, painter — all with the eye of a social observer.

She won the first prize in the Onassis International Cultural Competition in the "Theatrical Plays" category for her play "Harvest".

Padmanabhan contributes a daily comic strip called Suki and a fortnightly column, in the newspaper Pioneer.

Margaret Gallagher is a Paris-based media consultant who specialises in gender issues. She has carried out projects for the United Nations and several of its agencies. In 1986 she established the European Commission's Steering Committee for Equal Opportunities in Broadcasting. Since 1990 she has worked on the biennial European television prize and conference, the Prix Niki, which aims to improve the portrayal of women in the media.

Njoki Wainaina is the Chairperson of the African Women's Development and Communication Network (FEMNET) which hosted the Secretariat of African Regional Steering Committee. She is a consultant on gender and development, trainer programme adviser and an activist for gender equality and women's empowerment. She is a Kenyan sociologist specialising in gender issues and based in Malawi.

Noeleen Heyzer has been the Director of the United Nations Development Fund for Women (UNIFEM) since October 1994.

Noeleen has been responsible for the identification, formulation and implementation of action programmes, advocacy and policy-centred research involving more than 20 countries in the Asia-Pacific region. The outcome from the research has had a direct impact on policy planning and programme implementation for women in the region.

She is an author of repute on development and women's issues. Some of her publications include *Missing Women: Development Planning in Asia and the Pacific, International Migration and Women; A Commitment to the World's Women: Perspective on Development for Beijing and Beyond.*

S. K. Guha is senior consultant with UNIFEM in New Delhi. During the Beijing conference he was Joint Secretary in the Department of Women and Child Development and very active in the preparations.

Sara Longwe is a women's rights activist and gender consultant based in Lusaka. During the Beijing Conference she served as the African representative on the global NGO lobby team, EQUIPO. Currently, she is the Chairperson of the African Women's Development and Communication Network (FEMNET), which was the regional focal point for the Beijing NGO Forum 1995.

Shashi Ranjan Pandey is a development specialist. He has been associated with several NGOs in India and Thailand, and has also lived and worked with over 30 rural voluntary groups. Shashi has been a guest lecturer in several courses at the University of Wisconsin and at various campuses in US. He is currently on the faculty of the University of Wisconsin.

Soon Young Yoon is an activist/ anthropologist and one of the organisers of the NGO Forum on Women. She is currently a research associate of the Graduate Centre at the City University of New York and columnist for the Earth Times Newspaper.

Suneeta Dhar is currently with the (Technical Cooperation, Federal Republic of Germany. GTZ) in New Delhi. She was the Coordinator of the Coordination Unit in India during the Beijing process and preceded this with considerable experience in grassroots organising

Susana T Fried is the Program Director for Policy Advocacy at the Center for Women's Global Leadership. She coordinates the Center's women's human rights advocacy at the United Nations, including a recent "Women's Human Rights Advocacy Training" at the 1997 session of the Commission on Human Rights in Geneva, and directs the Center's international mobilisation activities. She has worked and written on a variety of issues including sexual rights, lesbian and gay rights, feminist leadership, economic justice and community organisation.

Susan Walsh is an Assistant Professor of Communication at Southern Oregon's School of Journalism and Communication, she is writing her dissertation on coverage of international women's conferences in American women's magazines.

Beijing Watch contributors and technicians

Ajoa Yeboah-Afari
Akhila Sivadas
Amparo Claro
Amy Louise Kazmin
Angela Castellanos
Angela Mackay
Anita Anand
Anuradha Mukherjee
Avian Joseph
Carol Bellamy
Charlotte Bunch
Charis Varnum
Christine Feeny
Colleen Lowe Morna
Drusilla Menaker
Fiona Lloyd
Garima Khandelwal
Gita Sen
Gretchen Sidhu
Isis Campos
Jan Paschal
Jennifer Griffin
Joan Dunlop
Judith Sudilovsky
Jumana Al-Tamimi
Juliana Omale
Julie Beun - Chown
Leslie George

Leila Deeb
Linda Neuman
Liudmyla Kohkanets
Mahesh Uppal
Margaret Gallagher
Mona Eltahawy
Natacha Henry
Nora Ogamolo
Oksana Kuts
Olivia H Tripon
Pat Made
Patralekha Chatterjee
Peggy Antrobus
Rajeev Jhanji
Rebecea Foster
Rosemary Auma Okello
Samme Chittum
S.K. Venkatraman
Susan Njanji-Matetakufa
Sujata Madhok
Talli Nauman
Taposhi Roy Chowdhury
Thais Aguilar
Valeria Zapesochny
Victoria Ebin
Vinay Aditya
Zaida Rojas
Zarina Geloo
Zoraida Portillo

Index

A

abortion 29, 39, 68, 69, 125, 126, 146, 147, 152, 153, 161, 178, 188, 192, 222, 223, 252

abuse 29, 49, 50, 52, 71, 73, 80, 81, 91, 133, 161, 184, 186, 187, 218, 224

activist 24, 51, 70, 99, 158, 177, 193, 223, 230, 240, 251, 252, 253, 254, 255

activists 65, 66, 70, 71, 83, 97, 102, 104, 107, 113, 131, 161, 172, 173, 178, 191, 220, 221, 227, 238, 241

adolescents 49, 111, 126, 192

Advancement of Women 3, 5, 6, 7, 8, 9, 11, 13, 15, 18, 19, 20, 31, 32, 33, 35, 86, 87, 88, 89, 90, 92, 93, 94, 100, 122, 125, 131, 148, 156, 157, 170, 177, 195, 196, 197, 198, 201, 217, 247, 253

Africa 71, 78, 93, 103, 119, 144, 145, 148, 149, 152, 155, 156, 157, 241, 249

African 39, 40, 53, 99, 118, 119, 120, 133, 146, 148, 149, 150, 151, 152, 153, 154, 155, 176, 179, 188, 222, 224, 254

agenda 13, 25, 27, 85, 88, 100, 101, 102, 104, 129, 132, 138, 139, 141, 146, 149, 150, 153, 156, 159, 166, 167, 169, 171, 172, 173, 175, 180, 181, 182, 187, 188, 190, 206, 211, 213, 217, 218, 220, 221, 225, 228, 230, 234, 238, 239, 244, 247, 248, 249

agendas 88, 119, 138, 139, 180, 186, 196, 238, 240, 247

agricultural techniques 75

All China Women's Federation 178

American media 69, 218

Amman 93, 103, 120, 156, 157, 162, 163, 252

Anita Anand 23, 112, 117, 168, 172, 173, 205, 233, 251, 257

Anne S. Walker 97

APC 25, 101, 210

Arab region 93, 120

Argentina 42, 43, 92, 97, 103, 140, 145, 196, 253

Armed Conflict 8, 29, 30, 51, 53, 91, 93, 95, 103, 162, 163, 191

Asha Ramesh 168, 251

Asia and Pacific 92, 103, 121, 170, 171, 174, 254

Association for Progressive Communications 25, 101

Australia 3, 121, 133, 176, 193, 206, 212, 213, 214, 228

Australian 205, 206, 251

Austria 3, 86, 88, 92, 196, 253

Avian Joseph 188, 257

B

Backlash 69, 189, 205, 206, 207, 215, 217, 218, 219, 221, 222, 223, 225, 243

Bangladesh 57, 78, 92, 170, 172, 196

Bangladeshi 223

banking 57

Beijing Declaration 17, 19, 23, 27, 161, 190, 217

Beijing Watch 112, 117, 123, 125, 127, 129, 132, 134, 135, 141, 147, 153, 158, 162, 163, 171, 188, 191, 193, 210, 213, 217, 220, 224

Belgium 88, 176, 224
Bella Abzug 25, 100, 209, 221, 233, 235, 237
Benazir Bhutto 124
Boutros Boutros Ghali 87
Brazil 62, 78, 100, 233, 238, 239
Buchy Rao 77

C

Cambodia 62, 63, 64
Cambodian 62, 63
Canada 15, 45, 46, 62, 83, 88, 142, 144, 196
Caribbean 73, 92, 103, 118, 137, 138, 139, 140, 141, 144, 240
Carol Bellamy 123, 257
Catholics for Free Choice 188
Cecilia Young Dong-ling 121, 177, 252
CEDAW 5, 10, 12, 14, 89, 96, 151, 162, 178, 179, 191, 234, 248, 249
CEDEA 240
CEFEMINA 49
Central American 24, 49, 138
CEPLA 118, 138
CHANGE 119, 145, 147, 252
Charlotte Bunch 121, 185, 233, 234, 235, 243, 252, 257
Charter of the United Nations 3, 7, 15, 17
Chernobyl disaster 47, 142
child labour 33, 81, 82, 83
child workers 82, 83
children 7, 8, 11, 12, 17, 23, 24, 28, 29, 37, 38, 39, 40, 41, 42, 43, 46, 47, 48, 49, 50, 51, 53, 54, 55, 56, 57, 58, 63, 65, 67, 68, 73, 75, 76, 78, 80, 81, 82, 83, 95, 109, 123, 124, 126, 127, 128, 132, 133, 134, 192, 199, 219, 222, 242
Chile 92
China 13, 27, 86, 88, 91, 103, 104, 108, 129, 130, 133, 134, 145, 147, 151, 170, 175, 176, 177, 178, 183, 196, 205, 207, 209, 210, 211, 212, 214, 216, 218, 220, 221, 223, 227, 229, 230, 244, 253
Chinese Organising Committee 25, 87, 130

church 36, 68, 69, 118, 127, 129, 138, 139, 188
civil rights 69, 252
civil war 53, 54, 152
CNN 134, 213, 220, 224, 230
COC 26, 104, 130, 176
Colleen Lowe Morna 153, 257
Columbia 70, 78, 251
Commission on the Status of Women 3, 5, 6, 86, 122, 143, 150, 175, 196, 198, 199, 245, 253
Conference of NGO's 104
CONGO 26, 104, 108, 111
Coordination Unit 120, 165, 166, 168, 169, 173, 251, 255
Costa Rica 24, 49, 50, 216, 233, 238
Critical Areas of Concern 23, 26, 27, 35, 37, 39, 41, 43, 45, 47, 49, 51, 53, 55, 57, 59, 61, 63, 65, 67, 69, 71, 73, 75, 77, 79, 81, 83, 86, 94, 110, 152, 159, 220
CSW 3, 4, 7, 11, 13, 14, 23, 86, 87, 88, 89, 90, 91, 94, 95, 110, 111, 122, 150, 175
Czech Republic 210

D

DAC/WID 144
Dakar 93, 103, 119, 149, 150, 151, 152
DANIDA 172
Danner 205, 206, 207, 215, 253
Darunee Tantiwiramanond 120, 179
DAW 87, 92, 122, 196, 197, 198, 199, 200
DAWN 25, 99, 170, 240
Debby Tomecek 24, 38
Decade for Women 3, 8, 9, 10, 11, 25, 98, 142, 143, 149, 215
Decade of Women 99, 237, 252
Decision-Making 59, 60, 62
decision-making 18, 30, 31, 32, 85, 88, 90, 92, 93, 98, 104, 109, 140, 157, 163, 168, 171, 174, 176, 196, 197, 198, 200, 205, 207, 211, 221
democracy 18, 30, 39, 59, 61, 62, 63, 140, 141, 145, 155, 171, 218, 240, 252

Denmark 3, 25, 82, 83, 88, 96, 144
Department of Public Information 15, 33, 86, 220
developing countries 5, 6, 7, 9, 20, 27, 77, 78, 87, 112, 119, 123, 124, 144, 145, 148, 198, 199, 211, 220, 239
development 3, 5, 7, 8, 10, 11, 12, 13, 14, 17, 18, 19, 20, 23, 25, 27, 28, 30, 31, 32, 33, 40, 42, 51, 54, 57, 65, 66, 71, 72, 73, 75, 76, 77, 78, 82, 83, 86, 87, 88, 89, 90, 92, 93, 94, 95, 96, 98, 99, 100, 101, 102, 103, 109, 110, 112, 119, 120, 121, 123, 124, 125, 126, 133, 140, 141, 144, 145, 146, 148, 151, 155, 156, 159, 160, 161, 163, 165, 167, 169, 170, 171, 173, 174, 175, 176, 180, 181, 182, 185, 186, 190, 192, 195, 199, 200, 210, 211, 212, 214, 215, 229, 233, 234, 235, 239, 240, 242, 247, 248, 249, 251, 252, 253, 254
Development Alternatives of Women in a New Era 170
discrimination 3, 4, 5, 6, 7, 8, 9, 10, 12, 13, 14, 17, 19, 27, 28, 29, 30, 31, 32, 33, 39, 43, 88, 89, 90, 95, 131, 132, 135, 140, 148, 151, 152, 154, 179, 191, 192, 201, 211, 216, 239, 242, 245, 252
displaced women 122, 192
domestic violence 24, 49, 50, 51, 72, 73, 110, 112, 187, 224, 228
Dominican Republic 10, 108, 118, 137, 140, 196
Dong-ling 121, 177, 252
donors 88, 119, 121, 144, 155, 168, 169, 172, 173
Dutt 121, 185

E

Earth Summit 100, 101, 186, 234, 239, 240, 244
ECA 93, 152
ECE 93, 142, 143, 148
ECLA 118, 138
ECLAT 92
Economic and Social Commission for Western Asia 120, 156
Economic Commission for Europe 92, 93
Economic Commission for Western Asia 93
ECOSOC 3, 4, 5, 7, 8, 11, 13, 85, 86, 90, 95, 99, 101, 104
education 7, 9, 12, 13, 19, 27, 28, 30, 31, 33, 39, 40, 41, 42, 47, 49, 51, 53, 54, 59, 60, 63, 69, 73, 75, 76, 80, 81, 90, 91, 92, 93, 95, 96, 110, 112, 131, 134, 135, 140, 146, 157, 158, 161, 163, 168, 170, 171, 176, 177, 186, 190, 199, 210, 213, 226, 240, 241, 243, 244, 248
educational 5, 10, 12, 13, 28, 35, 62, 73, 112, 146, 161, 199, 237
educationist 39, 251
Egypt 91, 127, 156, 158, 160, 161, 196
Egyptian 158
elderly 36, 46, 49, 53, 242
emancipation 71, 72
employment 5, 9, 12, 14, 19, 30, 36, 37, 41, 42, 53, 56, 83, 90, 93, 121, 142, 146, 148, 179, 184, 200, 207, 211, 215, 247
empowerment 14, 17, 18, 19, 23, 24, 27, 57, 58, 93, 94, 110, 112, 118, 120, 123, 125, 152, 167, 168, 170, 171, 186, 223, 237, 240, 252, 254
End of the Decade of Women World Conference 99
environment 13, 15, 17, 23, 25, 32, 45, 47, 53, 75, 76, 77, 78, 80, 92, 93, 100, 101, 113, 133, 142, 146, 157, 165, 170, 176, 177, 181, 182, 186, 200, 211, 216, 234, 237, 239, 240, 242, 247, 253
environmental 18, 20, 23, 27, 32, 45, 46, 47, 76, 77, 100, 102, 110, 182, 183, 210, 216, 240, 241, 244
environments 180
equality 3, 7, 8, 11, 14, 17, 18, 19, 23, 27, 28, 29, 32, 45, 66, 71, 90, 92, 93, 94, 95, 98, 105, 128, 140, 145, 146, 150, 151, 152, 154, 157, 161, 162, 163, 171, 176, 179, 185, 190, 197, 199, 217, 219, 222, 229, 230, 237, 247, 252, 254

Equality, Development and Peace 3, 8, 11, 17, 94, 98, 151, 176, 190
Equipo 26, 104, 111, 118, 137, 254
equity 14, 92, 93, 95, 146, 237
ESCAP 92, 165, 170
ESCWA 93, 120, 156, 157, 159, 160, 252
Ethiopia 60, 61, 62
Europe 92, 93, 97, 103, 119, 142, 143, 144, 145, 146, 147, 148, 187, 197, 210, 213, 240, 249
Europe and North America 92, 93, 103
European Commission 119, 145, 160
European Commissioner 147
European Community 24, 36, 63, 83
European Union 142, 143, 144, 147, 148

F

Facilitation Initiative 144
Faludi 215, 222
families 13, 18, 24, 32, 37, 40, 41, 42, 52, 53, 54, 57, 58, 66, 67, 78, 81, 83, 124, 126, 127, 140, 161, 162, 171, 222, 239
family 6, 7, 9, 10, 14, 18, 26, 30, 32, 33, 37, 38, 40, 41, 42, 43, 49, 50, 52, 54, 55, 56, 58, 59, 63, 65, 66, 67, 68, 71, 75, 76, 78, 80, 81, 90, 91, 92, 93, 95, 110, 111, 112, 122, 124, 125, 126, 127, 129, 133, 140, 146, 152, 158, 159, 160, 161, 178, 179, 192, 201, 219, 222, 228, 241
family planning 55, 56, 63, 93, 95, 129, 241
farming 61, 75, 80
Fatima Kassem 120, 156
Female breadwinners 37
feminism 50, 119, 128, 132, 142, 176, 185, 189, 211, 215, 219, 222, 223
feminist 27, 43, 49, 50, 69, 70, 120, 128, 131, 134, 137, 141, 142, 143, 144, 155, 156, 166, 185, 189, 190, 192, 197, 198, 207, 209, 211, 215, 216, 219, 221, 222, 223, 225, 233, 234, 240, 247, 251, 252, 253, 255

FEMNET 119, 149, 150, 152, 254
Fiji 121, 174, 175, 176, 177, 228, 251, 252
Fijian 228
Finland 8, 88, 253
Ford Foundation 88, 173, 181, 254
Forward 11, 14, 18, 25, 86, 89, 100, 120, 124, 151, 154, 156, 187, 190, 195, 217
France 3, 62, 64, 88, 121, 144, 147, 175
Frances Kissling 69, 188
free market economy 37, 38
Fujimori 129
fundamentalism 68, 69, 134, 153, 193, 243
fundamentalist 26, 69, 70, 102, 111, 112, 118, 124, 126, 127, 138, 146, 153, 158, 180, 188, 189
fundamentalist movements 26, 111
funders 108, 181
funding 10, 20, 46, 63, 113, 119, 120, 124, 143, 145, 154, 164, 172, 181, 184, 185, 221, 230

G

Gambia 196
Ganilau 174, 228, 252
gender 37, 38, 39, 43, 44, 59, 60, 66, 72, 73, 74, 77, 88, 90, 92, 93, 95, 110, 111, 118, 125, 127, 129, 138, 140, 145, 146, 147, 150, 152, 153, 154, 155, 156, 160, 165, 171, 174, 175, 187, 193, 199, 200, 251, 252, 253, 254
gender equality 93, 95, 140, 145, 150, 152, 154
gender perspective 92, 110, 140, 160
General Assembly 3, 4, 5, 6, 7, 8, 9, 10, 12, 14, 15, 24, 85, 86, 87, 89, 90, 98, 188
Georgina Ashworth 119, 142
Germany 88, 196
Gertrude Mongella 86, 87, 91, 124, 129, 176, 195, 198
girl child 17, 19, 93, 94, 110, 132, 152, 156, 170, 188, 244
girl workers 82

girls 5, 11, 12, 19, 28, 29, 32, 33, 39, 40, 68, 76, 80, 81, 82, 91, 95, 96, 111, 132, 134, 135, 150, 152, 158, 161, 170, 191, 199, 237, 238, 244
Global Campaign for Women's Human Rights 190
Global Forum 77, 101
globalisation 145, 171, 187, 189, 192, 234, 247
Gouri Salvi 167, 169, 253
government 4, 5, 6, 8, 13, 14, 15, 17, 18, 19, 20, 25, 27, 28, 30, 31, 32, 33, 35, 36, 37, 38, 39, 40, 41, 42, 45, 46, 47, 51, 52, 53, 54, 56, 57, 59, 60, 61, 62, 63, 65, 66, 75, 82, 83, 85, 86, 87, 88, 89, 90, 93, 97, 98, 99, 100, 101, 102, 103, 104, 105, 107, 108, 109, 110, 111, 113, 117, 118, 120, 121, 124, 128, 129, 130, 138, 139, 141, 142, 143, 144, 145, 148, 150, 151, 152, 153, 154, 155, 156, 157, 158, 159, 160, 161, 162, 163, 164, 165, 166, 167, 168, 169, 170, 171, 173, 174, 175, 176, 177, 178, 179, 180, 181, 182, 183, 185, 186, 187, 188, 189, 190, 191, 192, 193, 195, 197, 198, 199, 200, 201, 207, 209, 217, 218, 220, 221, 222, 223, 227, 233, 234, 235, 237, 238, 239, 240, 241, 242, 243, 244, 245, 248, 249, 251, 252
Grace Franklin 24, 36
Grace Virtue 23, 74
grassroots women 75, 121, 146, 157, 166, 168, 169, 181, 182, 183, 184, 230, 238, 251
Gretchen Peters 64
Gretchen Sidhu 245, 250, 257
GROOTS 146, 241

H

Hadera Tesfay 62
Haifa Abu Ghazaleh 120, 160, 161, 253
health 5, 13, 18, 19, 23, 28, 29, 32, 33, 36, 45, 46, 47, 48, 51, 53, 56, 57, 59, 65, 66, 75, 76, 77, 78, 80, 82, 90, 91, 92, 93, 95, 96, 102, 110, 111, 121, 125, 131, 133, 139, 140, 148, 152, 153, 157, 161, 163, 165, 168, 170, 180, 181, 183, 186, 187, 188, 189, 190, 191, 192, 193, 210, 213, 221, 234, 240, 242, 243, 245
health care 19, 27, 29, 45, 46, 60, 62, 63, 91, 135, 146, 187, 191, 237
Healthy 25, 48, 100, 113, 234, 237, 239, 242
Helvi Sipila 8, 253
Hillary Clinton 124, 134, 214
Hoda Badran 161
Holy See 110, 126, 188, 192
Hong Kong 121, 177, 178, 179, 184, 212, 252
Huang Qing 205, 207, 227, 253
human rights 3, 4, 5, 6, 7, 13, 14, 15, 17, 18, 19, 23, 25, 27, 29, 31, 51, 61, 62, 63, 65, 67, 68, 69, 70, 88, 90, 91, 92, 93, 95, 96, 101, 102, 109, 110, 111, 113, 121, 133, 140, 145, 151, 153, 154, 155, 158, 161, 165, 170, 171, 178, 179, 180, 181, 185, 186, 187, 189, 190, 191, 192, 193, 196, 197, 207, 209, 211, 212, 215, 218, 223, 233, 234, 237, 242, 243, 244, 245, 247, 249, 252, 253, 254, 255
Human Rights Conference 109, 245

I

ICPD 102, 109, 110, 126, 164, 186, 239
IFCB 168, 173
including New Zealand 121, 176
India 40, 41, 65, 75, 81, 82, 83, 87, 96, 120, 121, 164, 165, 166, 167, 168, 169, 170, 172, 173, 177, 251, 253, 254, 255
Indian 40, 41, 56, 69, 70, 75, 76, 82, 83, 118, 164, 166, 173, 251, 253
indigenous women 109, 113, 119, 139
Indonesia 91, 92, 103, 191, 253
inequities 98, 103
Ingvar Carlsson 128
International Conference on Population and Develop 14, 95, 102, 109, 126, 186, 239

International Women's Tribune 25, 98, 240, 251
International Women's Year 7, 8, 24, 85, 97, 213, 237
Irene Santiago 108, 212
Isabel Sanchez 24, 50
Isabella Matambanadzo 72
Israel 67, 185
Italy 88, 89
Ivanka Corti 89
Ivy Morna 153
IWTC 25, 26, 98, 99, 103, 104, 251
IWY Tribune 25, 97, 98

J

Jakarta Declaration 92, 170
Jamaica 9, 23, 72, 73, 196, 206, 212, 214
Jane Rosser 173
Japan 11, 15, 88, 134, 158, 170, 183, 213
Jennifer Griffin 134, 191, 224, 257
Jill Vardy 46
John Mathiason 122, 195
Jordan 93, 103, 120, 156, 157, 159, 160, 162, 163, 196, 253
journalist 57, 67, 71, 86, 92, 132, 133, 134, 196, 206, 207, 211, 212, 214, 215, 218, 220, 224, 227, 229, 230, 251, 252, 253

K

Kenya 25, 39, 40, 92, 97, 99, 119, 196, 240
Kissling 69, 188

L

Latin America 92, 103, 118, 137, 138, 139, 140, 141, 144, 183, 240
Latin American 50, 118, 139, 140, 141, 210
law 5, 6, 7, 8, 10, 11, 14, 19, 25, 28, 29, 31, 32, 33, 38, 41, 49, 50, 51, 56, 65, 78, 89, 90, 99, 125, 127, 143, 147, 153, 154, 158, 160, 161, 167, 188, 192, 222, 228, 238, 240, 251, 252
League of Arab States 93, 157, 159

Leila Deeb 158, 162, 163, 257
lesbian 109, 111, 113, 117, 179, 186, 187, 192, 209, 222, 223, 255
Leticia Ramos 112
liberalisation 165
liberation 51, 71, 119, 142, 179, 252
Liechtenstein 88
Linkage Caucus 103, 104, 186, 252
lobbying 24, 25, 26, 97, 99, 100, 102, 104, 107, 109, 110, 111, 118, 135, 137, 139, 143, 157, 167, 170, 175, 177, 186, 198, 233, 251

M

Malaysia 121, 177, 206, 212
Mallica Vajrathon 23, 85, 117, 253
Mallika Dutt 121, 185, 253
Malta 88
Manila Declaration 170
Margaret Gallagher 205, 209, 213, 220, 254, 257
marginalisation of women 62
Marsha Talcin 70
mass media 32, 138, 217
media 15, 23, 25, 31, 32, 47, 53, 69, 71, 72, 73, 74, 85, 86, 87, 89, 92, 94, 97, 104, 110, 118, 120, 125, 126, 129, 133, 134, 137, 138, 157, 158, 163, 168, 170, 174, 175, 176, 177, 179, 181, 183, 189, 203, 205, 206, 207, 210, 211, 212, 213, 214, 215, 216, 217, 218, 219, 220, 221, 223, 224, 225, 226, 227, 229, 230, 233, 242, 244, 251, 252, 253, 254
Melissa Butcher 52
member of 62, 75, 92, 140, 153, 158, 163, 188, 210, 220, 238, 252, 253, 254
Millie Phiri 153
Mona Eltahawy 162, 257
motherhood 40, 95, 124, 129, 147, 219, 222
mothers 24, 36, 37, 38, 39, 40, 41, 46, 47, 75, 76, 124, 210, 239
Muslim women 69, 70, 158, 193

N

NAFTA 83
Nairobi Conference 27, 88, 112, 142, 144, 153, 164, 185, 187, 197, 212, 244
Nairobi Forward Looking Strategies 120, 151, 154, 156, 190
Nairobi Strategies 86, 88, 90, 92, 95, 154, 198, 200
Natacha Henry 147, 257
National Commission for Women 66
National Report on the Status of Women 23, 73
Neena Bhandari 66
Neimat Bilal 54
Netherlands 88, 91, 144, 172
New York Times 205, 206, 207, 212, 217, 218, 219, 221, 222, 223, 225
Newspaper 255
newspaper 63, 71, 98, 206, 207, 214, 215, 218, 219, 220, 225, 226, 229, 254
newspaper stories 71
newspapers 23, 49, 67, 72, 125, 133, 205, 206, 215, 217, 218, 226, 228
NGO Forum 9, 11, 24, 26, 86, 89, 97, 98, 99, 101, 102, 103, 104, 107, 108, 109, 111, 117, 119, 120, 124, 132, 134, 135, 137, 143, 148, 149, 150, 151, 152, 153, 157, 161, 165, 170, 171, 175, 176, 177, 178, 179, 183, 185, 188, 190, 191, 209, 210, 212, 214, 216, 222, 223, 227, 229, 237, 239, 243, 253, 254, 255
NGOs 8, 24, 25, 26, 32, 83, 86, 88, 89, 91, 92, 93, 95, 97, 99, 100, 101, 103, 104, 107, 108, 109, 110, 111, 112, 113, 118, 119, 120, 121, 125, 128, 129, 130, 137, 138, 141, 143, 144, 145, 146, 147, 148, 151, 152, 155, 156, 157, 160, 161, 162, 163, 164, 165, 168, 170, 172, 173, 174, 175, 176, 177, 178, 179, 180, 181, 184, 185, 187, 188, 189, 190, 193, 195, 200, 210, 214, 216, 217, 227, 229, 233, 234, 238, 239, 240, 241, 254
Nigeria 134, 158, 196, 233, 238

Nitin Desai 87
Nitin Jugran Bahuguna 83
Njoki Wainaina 119, 148, 152, 254
Noeleen Heyzer 124, 233, 234, 235, 247, 254
North America 92, 93, 97, 103, 146, 187
North Atlantic Free Trade Agreement 83
Norway 88, 147, 253

O

OECD/DAC 144, 172
OECD/DAC-WID 172
Oksana Kuts 23, 48, 210, 257
Olivia H. Tripon 112, 171

P

Pacific 92, 103, 118, 121, 170, 171, 174, 175, 176, 177, 228, 253, 254
Pakistan 11, 15, 69, 158, 172
Pat Made 132, 134, 220, 257
Patralekha Chatterjee 79, 257
patriarchy 128, 155
peace 3, 7, 8, 10, 11, 13, 17, 18, 19, 23, 27, 28, 29, 30, 52, 53, 54, 62, 63, 64, 70, 90, 91, 92, 93, 94, 95, 98, 99, 101, 103, 110, 134, 140, 144, 151, 157, 160, 162, 163, 171, 172, 176, 185, 186, 189, 190, 192, 197, 210, 222, 223, 234, 241, 242, 249, 252
People's Republic of China 86
Peru 77, 80, 81, 129
Philippines 11, 55, 91, 112, 121, 177, 196
Platform For Action 90, 112
Platform for Action 17, 18, 19, 20, 23, 24, 27, 29, 31, 33, 85, 86, 89, 90, 91, 92, 93, 94, 95, 96, 103, 104, 107, 108, 109, 110, 111, 119, 121, 122, 123, 124, 126, 128, 129, 130, 132, 139, 141, 143, 145, 146, 148, 150, 151, 152, 154, 155, 157, 159, 160, 161, 163, 164, 169, 170, 172, 174, 177, 185, 186, 190, 191, 192, 193, 195, 197, 198, 200, 201, 206, 209, 217, 220, 237, 238, 240, 245, 253

PNGOCG 174, 175
political participation 107, 168, 172, 180, 181, 189, 234, 245
population 7, 11, 14, 15, 18, 23, 25, 32, 39, 41, 46, 51, 55, 56, 77, 86, 88, 95, 102, 109, 113, 117, 126, 131, 140, 147, 153, 161, 180, 186, 188, 197, 216, 239, 240, 247, 251
populations 161
portrayal of women 32, 74, 92, 125, 254
poverty 14, 17, 18, 19, 20, 24, 27, 28, 35, 36, 37, 45, 53, 56, 75, 77, 83, 90, 91, 92, 93, 96, 110, 140, 142, 146, 152, 157, 160, 163, 165, 170, 171, 186, 200, 213, 220, 234, 237, 243, 245, 247, 248
Preeti Singh 68
preparatory process 24, 36, 89, 91, 119, 149, 150, 164, 166, 181, 190, 248
PrepCom 94, 95, 102, 103, 104, 109, 110, 130, 137
PrepComs 24, 85, 92, 101, 103
print media 207, 215, 223, 225
prostitution 4, 12, 40, 41, 42, 180, 187

R

Rachel Sarah 60
radio 15, 61, 73, 86, 121, 125, 175, 176, 183, 205, 216, 228, 251, 252
rape 29, 30, 49, 50, 65, 66, 70, 71, 72, 73, 91, 126, 148, 165, 180, 187, 191, 211, 228, 248
Red Cross 54
REDEH 240
Regional Focal Points 26, 108, 144
religion 3, 5, 18, 19, 31, 52, 63, 69, 70, 95, 107, 158, 161, 185, 189, 192
reproductive health 19, 29, 45, 91, 93, 95, 96, 110, 152, 165, 180, 191, 192
reproductive rights 95, 102, 112, 121, 140, 146, 147, 161, 176, 187, 188, 189, 241, 242
Rockefeller Foundation 88
Rosemary Omale 153

S

S.K. Guha 120
Salamo Fulival 170, 175, 176
Samme Chittum 147, 257
Scotland 24, 35, 36
Second Asian and Pacific Ministerial Conference on 92
Secretariat 3, 11, 12, 13, 26, 40, 87, 88, 91, 92, 93, 94, 95, 96, 108, 118, 122, 132, 138, 142, 144, 145, 148, 149, 150, 166, 195, 196, 198, 199, 200, 201, 239, 253, 254
Secretary-General 5, 8, 9, 11, 12, 13, 15, 26, 33, 86, 87, 88, 89, 91, 94, 96, 195, 220, 253
sexist 72, 131, 145, 151
sexual assault 71
sexual harassment 29, 73, 147
sexuality 95, 126, 186, 187, 188, 192, 245
sexworkers 41
Shahani 11, 112
Sharmila Banerjee 42
Shashi Ranjan Pandey 120, 179, 254
Sistren 73
Sixth Regional Conference on the Integration of Women into Economic and Social Development of Latin America and the Caribbean 92
Slovakia 24, 37
Social Development Summit 109
Soon Young-Yoon 255
South Asia 144, 164, 166, 167
Southeast Asia 120, 121, 170
Spain 88, 92
Sri Lanka 51, 56
Status of Women 3, 4, 5, 6, 7, 11, 13, 17, 23, 26, 55, 73, 196, 238, 245
Status of women 9
stereotyping 39
strategising 98, 99, 100, 105, 121, 166, 240
structural adjustment 27, 39, 94, 103, 110, 121, 140, 152, 165, 177, 180, 186, 187, 189, 192, 198, 199, 200, 206, 214, 247

structural adjustment programmes 27, 39, 140, 152, 177, 180, 199, 247
Sudan 53, 54, 69, 153, 161
Sumalee Chartikavanij 170
Suneeta Dhar 120, 167, 255
Supatra Masdit 108, 176
Susan Faludi 215
Susan Walsh 205, 206, 215, 255
Susana Fried 121, 185
Sweden 88, 128, 144, 147, 196

T

Tanzania 15, 77, 87, 148, 196, 198
Teen Mothers 39
Thailand 12, 120, 170, 176, 179, 180, 181, 183, 184, 196, 252, 254
Third World 35, 78, 99, 119, 151, 154, 156, 185, 222, 240
trafficking 29, 170, 180, 183, 191
Trust Fund 88
Trust Fund for Conference Preparations 88
Turkey 147, 158

U

UK 24, 35, 36, 77, 88, 119, 143, 144, 145, 196, 205
Ukraine 23, 46, 47
UN 15, 24, 25, 26, 29, 31, 63, 69, 85, 86, 87, 88, 89, 90, 91, 92, 95, 96, 97, 98, 99, 100, 101, 102, 103, 104, 107, 108, 109, 110, 111, 112, 113, 117, 118, 119, 122, 123, 125, 126, 127, 128, 129, 130, 132, 133, 134, 137, 138, 142, 143, 144, 145, 148, 149, 150, 151, 153, 154, 157, 159, 160, 162, 163, 164, 165, 167, 170, 171, 172, 173, 174, 175, 176, 177, 178, 179, 180, 184, 185, 186, 187, 188, 190, 192, 193, 195, 196, 197, 198, 199, 200, 206, 209, 210, 212, 213, 214, 218, 220, 223, 233, 234, 235, 237, 238, 239, 240, 241, 243, 244, 247, 250, 252, 253
UN Secretary General 104
UNCED 25, 100, 104, 109, 133, 164, 239

UNDP 54, 123, 148, 167, 211
UNFPA 55, 56, 88
UNICEF 15, 88, 123, 199, 213, 214, 220
Unicef 54, 112
UNIFEM 10, 14, 88, 101, 120, 124, 156, 160, 162, 172, 174, 175, 184, 187, 214, 220, 233, 234, 248, 249, 253, 254
United Kingdom 11, 12, 15, 35, 77, 206, 214
United Nations 3, 4, 5, 6, 7, 8, 9, 10, 11, 12, 13, 14, 15, 17, 20, 23, 27, 31, 33, 54, 55, 68, 85, 98, 124, 133, 140, 141, 163, 188, 195, 196, 199, 201, 225, 237, 253, 254, 255
United Nations Fund for Population Activities 55
United Nations High 12, 54
United Press International 133
United Republic of Tanzania 15, 87
United States 3, 15, 83, 132, 133, 151, 205, 218, 224, 225, 242
UPI 133, 229
USA 15, 33, 68, 69, 88, 91, 96, 144, 196, 212, 213, 226, 230, 233, 238, 242

V

Valeria Belloro 44
Vatican 69, 124, 138, 152, 153, 188, 192, 221, 225, 241
Vienna Conference 101, 102
Vijita Fernando 58
violence 12, 13, 14, 17, 19, 24, 27, 29, 33, 45, 49, 50, 51, 52, 66, 68, 69, 70, 72, 73, 90, 91, 92, 93, 102, 103, 110, 112, 121, 133, 140, 161, 163, 165, 168, 170, 171, 172, 173, 176, 177, 180, 181, 186, 187, 189, 190, 191, 192, 206, 214, 219, 220, 224, 228, 233, 237, 242, 243, 244, 245, 248
violence against women 12, 13, 14, 17, 19, 24, 27, 29, 45, 50, 51, 68, 72, 73, 90, 91, 93, 102, 110, 121, 161, 168, 170, 171, 172, 173, 176, 177, 180, 181, 186, 187, 189, 191, 206, 214, 220, 233, 244, 245, 248

Virginia Vargas 118, 137, 141

W

Wangari Maathai 240
war 8, 29, 30, 51, 53, 54, 62, 68, 70, 71, 91, 93, 110, 112, 142, 148, 152, 162, 186, 189, 191, 197, 211, 215, 216, 234, 242, 247, 248, 249
Washington Post 205, 206, 207, 217, 218, 219, 221, 222, 223, 225
WEDO 25, 100, 101, 233, 234, 238, 239, 240, 241, 242
West Asia 103, 120, 121, 156, 160, 253
WFS 23, 35, 37, 39, 41, 43, 45, 47, 49, 51, 53, 55, 57, 59, 61, 63, 65, 67, 69, 71, 73, 75, 77, 79, 81, 83, 117, 123, 251
WIDE 119, 145, 240
women activists 24, 65, 66, 70, 97, 104, 107, 220, 227, 238
Women and Development 72, 92, 156, 160, 163, 174, 252
Women in Development Europe 119, 145, 240
women in parliament 152, 154, 167, 197
women in public life 60, 88, 93
women in public office 59, 60
women of colour 113
women scientists 43
Women's Affairs Office 60, 62
women's caucus 25, 101, 102, 103, 108, 109, 145, 152, 233, 234, 238, 239, 241
women's concerns 77, 78, 90, 93, 159, 190
women's economic rights 30, 192
women's empowerment 18, 27, 110, 112, 118, 120, 123, 186, 254
women's health 28, 29, 36, 45, 46, 91, 93, 102, 110, 121, 153, 163, 170, 187, 234, 240, 245

women's human rights 31, 69, 90, 92, 93, 101, 102, 121, 153, 170, 185, 186, 187, 190, 191, 192, 193, 233, 234, 243, 245, 249, 252, 253, 255
women's issues 4, 8, 59, 61, 100, 101, 110, 138, 157, 159, 173, 180, 181, 182, 184, 185, 188, 206, 212, 215, 217, 220, 228, 229, 252, 254
Women's Linkage Caucus 103, 104, 252
women's movement 25, 26, 99, 100, 107, 108, 109, 111, 113, 118, 119, 120, 124, 137, 138, 139, 141, 142, 143, 145, 148, 155, 156, 165, 166, 167, 169, 170, 173, 185, 189, 210, 221, 222, 223, 225, 228, 233, 234, 235, 237, 241, 248, 252, 253
women's organisations 27, 62, 72, 75, 101, 118, 141, 142, 165, 166, 167, 172, 180, 182, 184, 190, 210
women's rights 5, 6, 18, 49, 63, 66, 69, 89, 90, 107, 110, 111, 140, 141, 151, 153, 155, 161, 177, 178, 185, 186, 190, 193, 210, 211, 215, 221, 240, 243, 252, 254
women's work 78, 211, 219, 222
World Conference on Human Rights 88, 95, 101, 102, 186, 187, 234
World Social Summit 117
WORLD WOMEN 205, 253
World Women 229, 230

Y

Yolanda Sotelo-Fuertes 56
youth 17, 93, 109, 117, 125, 126, 131, 132, 133, 134, 135, 157, 176, 183

Z

Zoraida Portillo 81, 257